RELATIONS OF GOLKONDA
WITH IRAN

Relations of Golkonda with Iran

Diplomacy, Ideas, and Commerce
1518–1687

Foreword by

MUZAFFAR ALAM

M.Z.A. Shakeb

With an Introduction by the Editor

SUBAH DAYAL

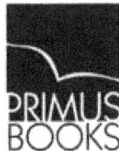

PRIMUS
BOOKS

PRIMUS BOOKS

An imprint of Ratna Sagar P. Ltd.
Virat Bhavan
Mukherjee Nagar Commercial Complex
Delhi 110 009

Offices at CHENNAI LUCKNOW
AGRA AHMEDABAD BENGALURU COIMBATORE DEHRADUN
GUWAHATI HYDERABAD JAIPUR JALANDHAR KANPUR KOCHI
KOLKATA MADURAI MUMBAI PATNA RANCHI VARANASI

First published 2017

ISBN: 978-93-84082-91-8 (hardback)
ISBN: 978-93-84092-42-9 (POD)
ISBN: 978-93-84092-43-6 (e-book)

Published by Primus Books

Laser typeset by Shine Graphics
Amar Colony, East Gokalpur, Delhi 110 094

Printed and bound in India by Replika Press Pvt. Ltd.

To

My grandchildren

ITRAT

TAHA

MAHAMID

KHADIJA

TAWSIN

MAHAD

ISTIFA

FATIMA

‘ALI

NUHA

and those who are yet to arrive

Contents

Maps

Foreword

IT IS A DISTINCT pleasure and privilege for me to write a foreword to this work by my old friend, a senior and a highly respected scholar, Dr Ziauddin Shakeb. Dr Shakeb is known to many of us as a connoisseur of diverse aspects of Indo-Islamic culture, ranging from archives and texts to paintings and treatises, which come not only from the Deccan but also from other parts of India. In this work, which was first completed as his Ph.D. thesis in 1976, he has brought together the discussions on a variety of relevant issues concerning Deccan-Iran relations in the sixteenth and seventeenth centuries, before the eventual Mughal conquest of the Deccan in 1687 under Aurangzeb 'Alamgir. At the time that he did the bulk of this research, there was virtually nothing available on the subject beyond a handful of dispersed articles. Whatever had been written was on diplomatic relations and largely focused on Mughal India (for example, the work of Abdul Rahim). In Aligarh Muslim University, Dr M. Raza Naqvi had written a dissertation on political and diplomatic relations between the Mughals and Iran, especially focusing on their border disputes at Qandahar. Dr Shakeb has widened his concerns beyond diplomatic and political relations to some aspects of the commercial dealings, but above all to religious interaction. He has discussed these with a reasonable level of detail, based on his intimate knowledge of manuscript collections and archives. Indeed, it may be said that Dr Shakeb has read almost all the relevant Persian texts that are available on the matter.

By the time Dr Shakeb had completed his dissertation, the important work of Dr Riazul Islam, *Indo-Persian Relations*, had appeared in 1970. In another work, Dr Islam also compiled a large number of relevant documents on Indo-Persian diplomacy with a comprehensive introduction. Subsequently, on the religious side, Sayyid Athar Abbas Rizvi's bulky work, *A Socio-Intellectual History of the Isna Ashari Shi'is in India*, also appeared in two volumes in 1986, and raised some relevant issues on religious history. But, in many ways, the work of Dr Shakeb has not yet been surpassed. For example, he has showed how in the seventeenth century, as Iran moved towards a strong form of orthodox Shi'ism, Shi'i *mujtahids* came to the Deccan where they were welcomed in the courts. However, despite this, Deccani Islam remained quite distinct in many respects from that of Safavid Iran. The often uncompromising dealings the Safavids had with many of the other communities, whether

Muslims or non-Muslims, did not take place here. We are aware that Shi'ism and the state came to be so closely identified in Safavid Iran that, as the well-known scholar, Kathryn Babayan, has shown, its influence continued till the time of Imam Khomeini and the Iranian Revolution of 1979. On the other hand, as Dr Shakeb shows, that while the Deccani sultans may often have been Shi'ite, the Golkonda Sultanate accommodated many sects of Islam, including some heterodox groups.

Of course, the nature of the changes in Safavid Iran must also be studied in a nuanced way, as a number of scholars such as Andrew Newman now insist. But the contrast with the Deccan is nevertheless marked. Dr Shakeb has also shown that in terms of rituals. Sunnis and Hindus participated in festivals such as Muharram without losing their social footing. Muhammad Rabi, the Iranian author of the travel narrative from the 1680s, *Safina-i Sulaimani*, also openly shows his disapproval and dismay at what he perceives as these differences between Iran and the Deccan. But Dr Shakeb does more than assert a static comparison. He also shows the gradual evolution and change in matters as the nature of relations with the Mughals altered after Shah Jahan imposed the treaty in the 1630s. There is no doubt that the religious policy of the Golkonda sultans would require further study. The publication of this work should inspire future research and writing on these themes.

We should all be grateful therefore to Subah Dayal, a young scholar from UCLA, who has retrieved this work, edited it, and brought it to light with an intelligent introduction and summary description. It is heartening to note that the transmission of knowledge and scholarly skills continues in this way from generation to generation, not only in the university but also away from it.

Chicago   MUZAFFAR ALAM

Acknowledgements

I N THE COURSE of this study, the seniors with whom I discussed my ideas and from whom I benefitted greatly were P.M. Joshi, H.K. Sherwani, Pagdi Setu Madho Rao, B.P. Saksena, S. Nurul Hasan, S. Mohibbul Hasan and A.R. Kulkarni. After moving to London, I also shared my interests with Riazul Islam and late Tapan Raychaudhuri, both at Oxford.

My grateful thanks to V.K. Bawa for his encouragement, Mir Najmuddin Ali Khan for his unfailing assistance and Najma Siddiqua for procuring many important sources. I cannot avoid remembering the late Vijay Bharat, who typed the original dissertation on a manual typewriter and the late Sadiq Husain, cartographer at the Survey of India, who assisted in translating my ideas into the two maps of Golkonda and Iran.

I must also thank Muzaffar Alam, Leonard Lewisohn and Fasih Ul-Islam for going through the draft of this book and making useful suggestions. Lastly, if it weren't for the wilful and obstinate Subah Dayal, this book would have never seen the light of day. I thank Farhat and my children for their love and support.

M.Z.A. SHAKEB

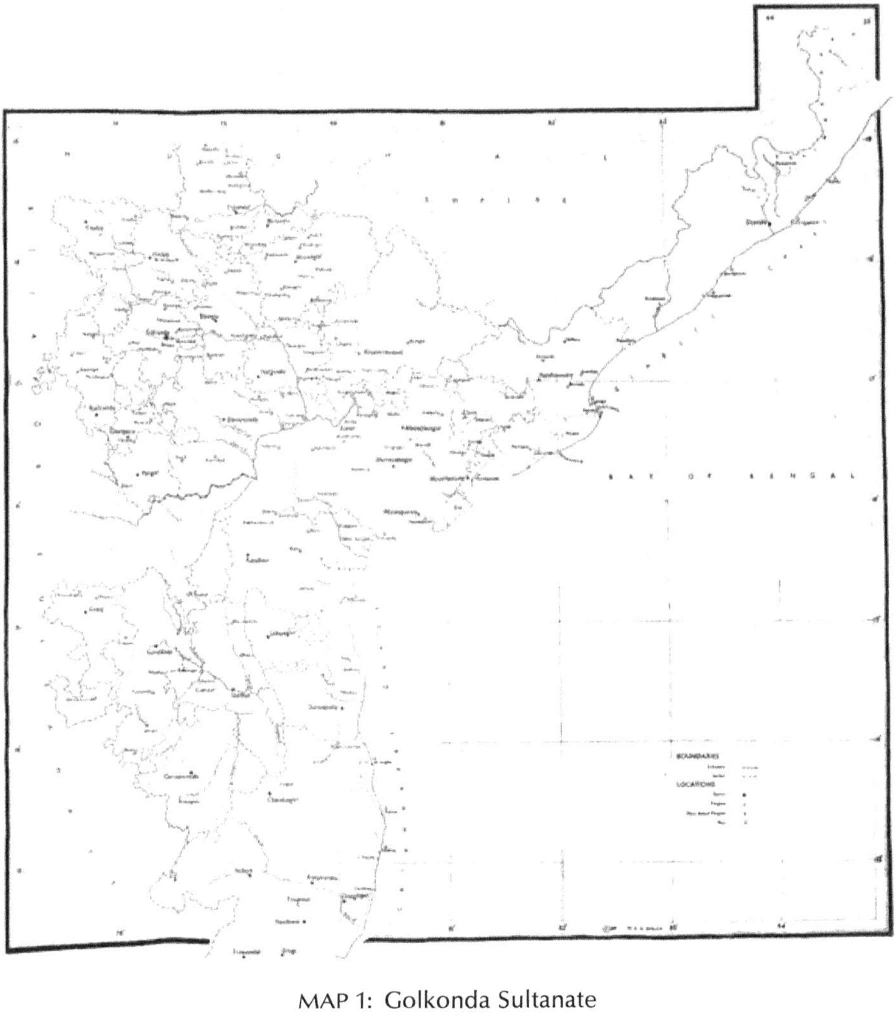

MAP 1: Golkonda Sultanate

MAP 2: Safavid Iran

Editor's Introduction

THE PRESENT WORK originally took the form of a doctoral thesis entitled 'Relations of Golkonda with Iran, 1518–1687' submitted by Mohammed Ziauddin Ahmed Shakeb to the Department of History at Deccan College, Poona, in 1976. When I first encountered his dissertation in 2011, it was apparent to me that the author had been well ahead of his times. Reading his enquiry into the political, cultural and institutional connections across three kindred polities in the Islamic world—Safavid Iran, Mughal Hindustan and the Golkonda Sultanate—reaffirmed much that is widely accepted today about the early modern period: the use of multilingual archives, the shared lineages of Eurasian polities and the circulation of people, goods and ideas across spaces in this period. Nearly forty years ago, the author presented a viewpoint on these ties from the perspective of a Deccan kingdom and its unique historical conditions, fulfilling an important gap in our understanding of regions and empires in this period.

The three fields of Safavid, Mughal and Deccan studies have been completely transformed since the 1970s with the appearance of a fresh body of work penned by a new generation of scholars. While Safavid and Mughal studies have made significant strides in recent decades, Deccan studies still remain relatively neglected, despite its abundant archival sources and manuscript treasures, to which Shakeb's work provides the most potent leads. It is for this reason that we urgently felt the need to revise his dissertation for publication, preserving much its original style and content while pointing to new directions of further research.

Since the horizons of his dissertation are a reflection of the author's training and eclectic interests, it will be helpful here to provide a brief biography of him to better understand the significance of this work and situate Shakeb's career and studies in the wider context of the historiography of the medieval and early modern Deccan, especially within the body of work that was being done across the world during the 1960s and 1970s.

ABOUT THE AUTHOR

It is a humbling, if not intimidating, task to introduce Dr Shakeb, whose interests and expertise transcend so many disciplinary, linguistic and geographic boundaries. He has

also filled many different roles through the years as a historian, linguist, geographer, archivist, literary critic, and above all—as a teacher. For the past five years during which I have had the honour and privilege of studying with him, my lessons have ranged from memorizing and reciting Dakani Urdu poetry to mapping the architectural and geographic layout of Golkonda and Bijapur, to deciphering and dating Indo-Persian administrative documents, and absorbing historiography through Dr Shakeb's vivid memories of his generation of Deccan scholars who did pioneering work in Hyderabad and Poona in the 1960s and 1970s.

According to official records, the author was born on 21 October 1933 and grew up in Hyderabad and Aurangabad.[1] After completing his Bachelor of Arts in Political Science with minors in English and Economics at Osmania University, he headed to Aligarh Muslim University in 1956. There, he completed a Master's degree along with postgraduate diplomas in Foreign Affairs and French. At Aligarh, he was taught by renowned personalities such as Mohammad Habib and S. Nurul Hasan. After completing his degree, he worked in different capacities as a broadcaster, village developer and translator. In 1962, he was appointed as an archivist at the State Archives of Andhra Pradesh (formerly known as the Central Record Office) in Hyderabad.

His tenure as an archivist fell in a period of transition that occurred under the directorship of the State Archives by Hadi Bilgrami and Vasant Kumar Bawa. In 1914, a huge body of Mughal archival documents had been discovered in the Arak fort near Aurangabad, Maharashtra, by Ghulam Yazdani, the importance of which was well understood by both directors. During the first half of the twentieth century, these administrative materials were gathered and put under the purview of a separate department of the Nizam's state in Hyderabad.[2] In the post-Independence period, a new generation of scholar-administrators, with a deep interest in the preservation and processing of historical materials, set out to build institutions that would organize and sift through these sources. It was during this period that Shakeb acquired his skills in deciphering and decoding a variety of Arabic and Persian calligraphic styles, such as *shikastah*, and identifying the countless categories, genres, and forms of archival documents—skills which he largely acquired from the last generation of the traditional *jagirdari* staff of the Nizam's state, who were on the verge of retirement when he joined the State Archives.

At the instance and encouragement of Hadi Bilgrami, he then began the task of examining and restoring the documents from Shah Jahan's reign. At an extra allowance of Rs.2 per month, working day and night, he completed the first catalogue in 1972, which was published in 1977 as *Mughal Archives: A Descriptive Catalogue of the documents pertaining to the reign of Shah Jahan (1628–1658), Vol. 1, Durbar papers and a miscellany of singular documents.* Prior to this catalogue and his dissertation, Shakeb had also published *Jāmiʿ al-ʿatiyāt,* a compendium on late Mughal administration, which provides a typology of land grants, Arabic notation (*siyāq*), bookkeeping, calendars and systems of weights and measures. This reference work still remains an essential read for any student seeking to learn how to read administrative documents in Indo-Persian.[3] It was in the context of processing and systematizing the Mughal chancellery that Shakeb was one of the earliest to use the term 'early modern' (*ibtedāyī 'ahd-i jadīd*) for the period from 1500 to 1700 in his Urdu writings.[4]

Along with examining and cataloguing these Mughal records, he simultaneously worked on his own dissertation for which he enrolled at Deccan College, Poona, in 1969, at the encouragement of his supervisor P.M. Joshi. This was a particularly vibrant period for history and literary studies in Hyderabad, Poona, and numerous other cities in the Deccan. In the field of Urdu literary studies, Muhiuddin Qadri Zor, who was also one of Shakeb's teachers, had founded the Idara-i Adabiyat-i Urdu in 1951.[5] In Andhra Pradesh, the government approved a research fellowship scheme at par with the University Grants Commission, wherein ten doctoral candidates were selected to process a body of materials at the State Archives.[6] Shakeb supervised and helped these aspiring young scholars.[7]

This was also the time when the first generation of foreign scholars like John F. Richards, Richard M. Eaton, Karen I. Leonard and Joseph J. Brennig arrived in Hyderabad, all of whom interacted closely with Shakeb. He held palaeography classes and seminars at the archives, where researchers gained the skills to read these new sources and discuss their work with others in the field. One should also mention many other scholars who, during this period and in later years, passed through Hyderabad, including Annemarie Schimmel, Carl Ernst, David Matthews, Stuart Cary Welch, Robert Elgood, Wayne E. Begley and William Dalrymple, all of whom have acknowledged Shakeb's assistance and guidance through their writings.

It will be useful here to briefly survey the genealogy of Deccan historians from the pre-Independence period to the time when Shakeb began his dissertation. One of the earliest scholars who worked on the medieval period was Shamsullah Qadri (d.1953), who knew both European and Indian languages, and began to incorporate newly found sources in his work. Although Qadri's insights often surpass all those who came after him, his work has not been paid due attention in Deccan historiography as he wrote entirely in Urdu. He was the editor of a magazine called *Tārīkh* and the publisher of his own books.[8] His work laid a foundation for the field that later became known as 'Deccan Studies', which had just begun to flourish when Shakeb started working in Hyderabad in the 1960s. Another early historian of the Deccan and teacher of the author was Abdul Majeed Siddiqui, who first published his *Tārīkh-i Golkonda* in Urdu in 1939 and later translated into English in 1964 as *History of Golcunda*. The year 1974 saw the publication of Haroon Khan Sherwani's monumental *History of the*

Qutb Shahi Dynasty.[9] Although the main focus of these seminal works was political history, these historians were deeply aware of the range of sources that could be used to write the cultural, religious, social, and economic histories of the medieval Deccan.[10] Shakeb studied with this pioneering generation of Deccan historians, who were philologically meticulous yet broad-minded in the breadth of their enquiries.

While employed at the archives, Shakeb engaged a new generation of young scholars to process a huge body of materials that was put under the purview of the State Archives of Andhra Pradesh. Under the State Archives' Research Scholars programmes these students incorporated administrative materials, literature in Islamic Studies such as commentaries and didactic treatises, while others edited Persian and Urdu manuscripts. Some of the work accomplished by this team of scholars still remains unpublished and has not received the attention it deserves, largely due to the presumption that still prevails that Deccan historiography stopped after Sherwani. The variety of sources and themes tapped into by Shakeb's students—who included the likes of Najma Siddiqua, Najmuddin Ali Khan, Najmunissa Begam and many others—was not limited by ideological affinities or affiliation to a particular 'school' of history-writing, but was part of the larger project of processing selected bodies of materials acquired by the archives.[11]

Shakeb's commitment to the preservation and study of archival materials is a trait rarely found in historians. Several collections and manuscripts were processed under his supervision at the State Archives while the author was writing his dissertation. In 1978, noted Deccan historian, Pagdi Setu Madhavrao, had read and made suggestions for the publication of this dissertation, but due to a variety of reasons, both personal and professional, this did not happen. Shakeb continued to work at the State Archives until 1980, when, at the invitation of the School of Oriental and African Studies (SOAS), University of London, he migrated to London. He taught at SOAS, North London University and Middlesex University for some years and simultaneously began to work as a consultant for Christie's in their department of Islamic Art. While in London, he continued to be involved in the cataloguing of Persian materials in the British Library,[12] and the development of Urdu pedagogical materials for students and universities in the UK. Shakeb's professional activities have never been limited to his work for governmental archives, universities, museums or auction houses, as his love for Persian and Dakani Urdu literature has drawn him into organizing many conferences and commemorations of major poets and writers such as Bedil, Ghalib, Dagh, Amir Minai, Iqbal and Zor. His publications include many catalogues of Mughal archival documents as well as a large number of articles in Indo-Persian studies and Urdu literature.[13]

However, certainly the most important work that Shakeb has authored is the present book, the arguments and structure of which is outlined.

To properly situate *Relations of Golkonda with Iran: 1518–1687* in the constellation of contemporary Safavid, Mughal and Deccan studies, the final section of my introduction will conclude with a review of significant works that have touched upon similar themes of diplomacy, religion and trade between these three regions in the sixteenth and seventeenth centuries.

THE STRUCTURE OF THE PRESENT STUDY

The first chapter of this study aims at introducing the dynasties of the Qutb Shahis and the Safavids, and tracks the evolution of the geographies of the two polities and the demographic and linguistic profile of state and society in these two regions. It locates a regional, non-imperial polity in the wider context of the early modern world where people, knowledge, and commodities circulated over great distances. In most studies, a regional sultanate is usually seen as a receiver of influences from larger imperial states. Shakeb, however, was one of the earliest to raise the possibility of reversing the direction of this movement. For instance, in the opening chapter of this book, he points to Ibrahim Qutb Shah's donations to the holy shrine at Mashhad in Iran in 1562, indicative of Golkonda's investments in imperial domains.[14]

The second chapter chronologically surveys the circulation of diplomats, ambassadors and spies between Golkonda, Safavid Iran and Mughal India. It draws on Persian court chronicles, diplomatic correspondence, administrative documents and intelligencers' reports from all three polities, piecing together several intriguing diplomatic episodes that unfolded during the course of the sixteenth and seventeenth centuries. All three polities were relatively new in the early sixteenth century, and the question of their sovereignty was closely linked to obtaining acknowledgement and recognition by their neighbours, whether friend or foe, in other parts of the world. While the Mughals and Safavids operated in this triangular nexus alongside their diplomatic relations with other polities such as the Ottomans and the Shaybanid Uzbeks, for a regional sultanate like Golkonda, the interface with these two larger empires formed a critical component of its foreign policy. In addition to well-known Mughal, Safavid and Deccan chronicles such as Abul-Fazl's *Ā'īn-i Akbarī*, Iskander Beg Munshi's *Tārīkh-i 'Ālam Ārā-i-'Abbāsī* and the anonymous *Tārīkh-i Sultān Muhammad Qutb Shāh*, several new sources are introduced in this chapter, including the unpublished correspondence of Sultan 'Abdullah Qutb Shah (d.1672) of Golkonda called *Munsha'āt-i-dabīr-ul-mulk* and *Munsha'āt-i-munshī-ul-mulk*, authored by the Royal Epistolarian, Haji 'Abdu'l-'Ali Talqani, and his son, 'Abdu'l-'Azim Talqani, respectively. The author accessed these letters from the private collection of the late Nawab Inayat Jang, while writing his dissertation.[15] Another important source in this chapter is *Makātib-i-Zamānah-i-Salātīn-i-Safaviyah*, which contains the correspondence of the Safavids with the Mughals, the Ottomans, the Uzbeks of Transoxiana and the Deccan sultans. This collection was compiled by 'Abdu'l Husain bin Adham during the reign of Shah Safi Safavi (d.1642).[16]

The second chapter, divided into two sections, evaluates the ties of religion and the exchange of ideas between Safavid Iran and Golkonda. The author begins by emphasizing the unity between religion and politics in these polities.[17] In Safavid Iran, a Shi'i state evolved out of a Sufi order that gradually assumed political power. In Golkonda, under very different circumstances, institutions similar in form and structure were produced by the migration of religious missionaries and administrators from Central Asia. The frequent exchange of people created a unique context for an exchange of ideas about statecraft, religious education and medical knowledge. Noting that the Qutb Shahs were not the first to adhere to Shi'ism in the Deccan, the author begins with the earliest preceptors of Shi'i thought such as Mir Fazlullah Inju (d.1394) in the Bahmani period and later Shah Tahir Husaini (d.1549), who arrived in the Deccan from Iran in the early sixteenth century and served in the Ahmadnagar Sultanate.[18] The ties of these notables with Iran can be gleaned from chronicles as well as from a vast body of literature in Islamic sciences that travelled along with them to the Deccan.

In the second half of the chapter, the author traces a longer genealogy of ethics and philosophy in Golkonda back to its origins in Hellenistic thought, beginning with *Akhlāq-i-Nāsirī* of Nasiruddin Tusi (d.1274), which had already arrived in the Deccan long before the foundation of the Safavids.[19] During the sixteenth and seventeenth centuries, works on ethics and natural philosophy began to bear marks of Shi'ite ideology. The presence of several codices of treatises authored by major Shi'i philosophers and theologians such as Mulla Sadra (d.1640) and Baqir Majlisi (d.1698) in the library of the Qutb Shahs is an obvious indicator of these intellectual connections. We also find numerous works from schools of Islamic philosophy such as the writings of the founder of the Akhbari Shi'ite school of jurisprudence, Muhammad Amin Astarabadi (d.1640).[20] Shakeb emphasizes that the reception of these ideas was not necessarily an indication of Shi'i ascendancy in Golkonda, but one aspect of a complex and diverse religious and courtly milieu, which had been shaped by the lasting presence and influence of Sufis, Sunnis and various non-Muslim sects in the Deccan.

The third chapter lays the foundation for the study of the full impact of intellectual exchange between Safavid Iran and Golkonda, thus initiating a separate line of enquiry. Here, Shakeb's analysis of the impact of Shi'i religious missionaries in the Deccan as well as the reception of different schools of Islamic philosophy, moves beyond Persian court chronicles, and closely analyses the ambit of treatises in Islamic sciences found in the library of the Qutb Shahs of Golkonda and the 'Adil Shahs of Bijapur.

The fourth chapter assesses the role of Golkonda in the trading world of the Indian Ocean, specifically in the context of its commercial contacts with Safavid Iran.[21] Drawing on secondary literature, published European sources and travel accounts, it constructs a profile of one important trading zone with two anchors—one in Iran and the other in Golkonda. It supplements the data available in these sources with Persian treatises on weights and measures such as *Risālah-i Miqdāriyah* authored by Mir Mu'min Astarabadi (d.1624) who exhaustively researched classical authorities and sought to create a standardized system of measurement.[22] A well-known Iranian migrant-administrator during the reigns of Golkonda sultans, Muhammad Quli Qutb Shah (r.1580–1611) and Muhammad Qutb Shah (r.1612–26), Mir Mu'min's fields of expertise were not limited to religion and politics, but also spanned the discipline of mathematics and architecture.[23] Technical literature in Persian, authored by such courtly elites, has rarely been integrated into economic histories of the Deccan, which have tended to rely on the abundant and well-preserved records of the European trading companies. This chapter underlines the fact that Golkonda served as a transit point for Iranian, Indian and European merchants where goods and currency were exchanged and traded further to South-East Asia. The author argues that while the roles and resources of different mercantile communities varied, their participation in this trading world was fairly competitive. The conclusion briefly summarizes the main arguments of each chapter, emphasizing the continuously evolving relationship between regional polities and empires in this period.

This book also includes two maps and appendices. The map of Golkonda is especially fascinating as it provides details of all the medieval *parganas* (administrative divisions) with their boundaries. It is supplemented with information from an important Persian manuscript called 'Village by Village' (*Dih ba dih*) from the period of Mughal Emperor Aurangzeb currently in the State Archives of Andhra Pradesh.[24] Although the boundaries of the Deccan sultanates were not fixed and fluctuated continuously in this period, this map shows the Golkonda Sultanate at its greatest territorial extent during the mid-seventeenth century.[25] All the maps drawn by the author were based on manuscripts and archival documents that mention names of places, districts and travel routes. The appendices also include a valuable evaluation of the Persian, Arabic and Urdu sources used in this study, along with their descriptions. The original dissertation included facsimiles of all the documents used in this study. In the book, we have only been able to reproduce a handful of these in one of the appendices.

All the various documents and letters that were scattered in many institutions and private collections have been culled together and arranged chronologically by Shakeb. Although most of the diplomatic documents examined were undated and indicated neither the name of the addressee nor the writer, in most cases Shakeb was able to ascertain these details with the help of internal evidence and study them in the light of other contemporary sources. In this way, the names of bearers, the parties in the correspondence and the estimated dates of the letters were determined. All dates have been given according to the Muslim and Christian calendars.

RECENT STUDIES ON THE DECCAN, MUGHAL INDIA AND SAFAVID IRAN

The closely linked fields of Deccan, Mughal and Safavid studies have witnessed a great deal of transformation and elaboration since the 1970s. Below I have attempted a brief survey of the most relevant works in all three fields, focusing on political, cultural and economic relations between Golkonda, Safavid Iran, and Mughal India. Since, as stated above, the author evaluates relations between these empires from the vantage point of the Golkonda Sultanate, this study obviously makes no claim to encompass all of the complex and vast interfaces of political, economic and cultural relations that have been analysed over recent decades by scholars of Safavid Iran.

Shakeb's story is told from a Deccani standpoint, with the singular aim of gauging the ambitions of a regional sultanate locked into complicated alliances and rivalries with larger empires. The author's central argument emphasizes that although symbolically linked as Shi'i states, the Deccan sultanates were not simply passive receptacles of the vagaries of Safavid politics and ideology. The unique socio-cultural heterogeneity of state and society in Golkonda and historical circumstances continually produced changes in this relationship. However, while several different aspects of the Mughals and Safavids have received a great deal of scholarly attention, *Relations of Golkonda with Iran, 1518–1687* still remains the first study that synthesizes the specific triangular nexus of relations between these two empires and Golkonda.

Within the field of South Asia, the theme of diplomacy was first covered by Riazul Islam's *Indo-Persian Relations* (1970),[26] which marked the first attempt to study relations between the Mughal Empire and Iran. Muzaffar Alam and Sanjay Subrahmanyam, in their recent evaluation of Mughal historiography, pointing to Islam's work, have suggested the need for more studies of diplomatic ties between regional Indian states and larger empires.[27] With a similar template of diplomatic history as that of Islam, in the first chapter of this book, Shakeb draws on diplomatic correspondence, court chronicles and princely memoirs to track the exchange of ambassadors and diplomats between these three polities.

In the field of Safavid studies, the diplomatic world of Iran has recently received attention through the publication of an edited volume, *Iran and the World in the Safavid Age*,[28] which takes an important and innovative approach to existing historiography. We may safely suggest that from the perspective of the Safavid court, the alliance with Golkonda was just one of many complicated diplomatic relations that Iran had with the world at large. Historians of the Deccan cannot, therefore, easily overemphasize the significance of Safavid Iran's symbolic, intermittent (and quite calculated) support of the Deccan sultanates against the Mughals.

The most important contributions to Safavid studies have been devoted to the subject of the complex foundations of the early Safavids and second, to the evolution of Twelver Shi'ism and Muslim philosophy in this period. John Woods's early work on the Aq Quyunlu has shown that the Safavids were the culmination of conflict and interaction between two defining geographic-political systems in Central Asia—the nomadic-military elite (Turkic-Mongol) and urban settled elite of eastern Anatolia and Iran (Tajiks).[29] The pre-Islamic, messianic and gnostic roots of the spiritual and religious milieu of Imami Shi'ism in Safavid Iran has been a subject of enquiry as has been the study of the changes that took place as the dynasty consolidated political power from the late sixteenth century onwards.[30] Well-known Safavid chronicles, used in this book, such as Iskander Beg Munshi's *Tārīkh-i 'Ālam Ārā-i-'Abbāsī*, have now been closely studied for their language and form, revealing the techniques, methods and conventions of history writing under different Safavid rulers.[31] Broader surveys of the Safavid period, consolidating key questions in historiography, have appeared since the 1980s.[32]

The body of work on different schools of Islamic philosophy, especially within the Persian tradition, is much too rich and vibrant to review here.[33] Some debates directly raise questions on the migration to and circulation of Shi'i religious knowledge to Golkonda from Iran.[34] In the third chapter of this book, we can follow the eastward migration, towards the Deccan, of the ideas and descendants of the much debated Arab Shi'i scholars such as Husain bin 'Abd al-Samad al-'Amili who migrated from Jabal 'Amil (present-day Lebanon) and helped in the consolidation of the Safavid state.[35] Husain's son-in-law, Muhammad b. 'Ali b. Khatun also known as Ibn Khatun, who served as *peshwā* (prime minister) under Golkonda Sultan 'Abdullah Qutb Shah, probably died in a shipwreck near Mocha in 1649,[36] and was perhaps, the ghost author of the well-known Golkonda chronicle *Hadiqat-us-Salātīn*.[37] These prominent Shi'i scholars from Safavid Iran undoubtedly would have encountered a very different social and religious milieu in Golkonda. Although limited to a selected reading circle, the treatises brought from Iran and authored by these Shi'i learned elites are strewn about libraries in Hyderabad and deserve further attention from students of Islamic studies.

A study of religious knowledge and education in the Deccan would however, as the author of this book shows, first need to account for the diversity of courtly elites in Golkonda, who comprised Sunnis, Sufis, as well as non-Muslims. In his article, 'The Role of the Sufis in the Changing

Society of the Deccan: 1500–1750', Shakeb first discussed the competition among learned religious elites, especially between Sufis and Shi'is.[38] Unlike the neighbouring kingdom of Bijapur, where Sunnis intermittently came to power, Golkonda saw a continuous series of Shi'ite rulers.[39] This however did not mean nor translate into a uniform, courtly and religious environment. The reception of certain genres of religious literature would need to be measured against the multilingual and multi-religious context of the Deccan.

A recent study of religious education in late Safavid Iran has discussed how certain types of religious knowledge were produced and transmitted at the *Madrasā-i Sultānī*. The preoccupations of Shi'i scholars such as Mir Muhammad Baqir Khatunabadi (d.1715) and the *Shaikh al-Islām* of Qum, Mullah Muhammad Tahir Qummi (d.1689), their opposition to Sufis and their critiques of Sunni *tafsīr* and *hadīth* were directly related to the internal demands of Safavid politics and society.[40] Such polemics and the curriculum of Shi'i higher learning were also sent to Golkonda, but the function of these treatises, nearly all in manuscript form, is less clear in this new and unique landscape. Ibn Khatun's polemical writings such as *Kitāb al-Imāmah*,[41] execrations against the first three caliphs, follow certain conventions of Shi'i scholarly texts in this period. Further research on these traditions may reveal what was replicated from earlier commentators and what shifts, if any, took place in the ideas of these Shi'i learned elites after their migration to the Deccan.

The economic relations between Iran and Golkonda, which is the third theme of this book, needs to be examined in the context of the body of work done on economic histories of the Coromandel Coast as well as of the Persian Gulf.[42] While Shakeb was writing his dissertation in the 1970s, one of his close interlocutors was Joseph J. Brennig from the University of Wisconsin-Madison, who visited the State Archives of Andhra Pradesh in the early 1970s to conduct research on his dissertation on the textile trade in northern Coromandel.[43] Taking a cue from conversations with Brennig who was working on Dutch sources, Shakeb drew on existing data from a diversity of secondary sources, such as European travel accounts and Persian treatises, to isolate the zone between Iran and Golkonda, and thus evaluate one incremental unit of the Indian Ocean trading world.

The fourth chapter underlines that capital, goods and merchants from Iran often first came to Golkonda and then moved further east towards South-East Asia. Since the composition of Shakeb's work, the specific role of Iranians abroad and their dispersal in various parts of the Indian Ocean has been evaluated further.[44] A multi-sited and multilingual study could potentially confirm Golkonda's connection with polities in South-East Asia, as has been observed in Jean Aubin and Sanjay Subrahmanyam's discussions of Iranians in the court of Narai in the Kingdom of Ayutthaya—modern-day Thailand—in the second half of the seventeenth century.[45] Shakeb's use of Persian technical treatises in this chapter suggests an alternative to histories of European expansion in Asia by incorporating new types of non-European sources in studies of economic connections between regions within the Indian Ocean.

CONCLUSION

As stated in the beginning, we have attempted to preserve the ethos of the original dissertation and writing style of the author. The arguments of each chapter at times remain implicit, leaving the reader to draw conclusions from the evidence presented. This approach stems partially from Shakeb's cautious approach and discomfort with over-theorizing, and preference to let the sources ask and answer our questions.

The long list of manuscripts in Persian, Arabic and Urdu in the bibliography at the end of this book constitutes a rich archive that deserves to be revisited and carefully researched by future scholars. South Asian historians have, in more recent years, tended to focus excessively on the colonial period, greatly underestimating the treasures of materials we still have left on the pre-colonial epoch that deserve urgent care and attention. The use of multilingual archives, as Shakeb's work shows, inevitably builds political, economic and cultural connections across different regions, themes that have been well-articulated by scholars since the 1990s, of what we now identify not as the medieval but the early modern world.[46]

The severe decline and dire current state of repositories, archives and libraries in the Deccan is a matter beyond this introduction. Needless to say, the work of those who founded these institutions and pioneered the preservation of historical materials needs to be incorporated in the historiography of the Deccan. We owe much to Shakeb's generation of scholars, who have an encyclopaedic knowledge of these sources and a formidable memory of the past. But his was also a generation that prefers a more classical method to train younger scholars, not through writing and the publication of its ideas, but through the transmission of knowledge orally from teacher to student, which may explain why it took nearly forty years for his dissertation to appear in print!

Los Angeles Subah Dayal

NOTES

1. But his family records say 1931. His publications have appeared under several different combinations of his name—M.Z.A. Shakeb, Ziauddin A. Shakeb and Mohammed Ziauddin Ahmed.

2. For the background on the transition and centralization of the *Daftar-i Diwānī* from the Nizam's period to the constitution of the State Archives in the post-Independence period, see *Archival Organization and Records Management in the State of Andhra Pradesh*, vol. I, State Archives, Hyderabad: Government of Andhra Pradesh, 1980.

3. Ziauddin Shakeb and Hasanuddin Ahmed, *Jāmi'ul'Atiyāt*, Hyderabad: Villa Academy, 1974.

4. Ziauddin Ahmed Shakeb, 'Muqaddimah' and 'Introduction' to *Jami' ul- 'atīyāt*, p. alif, p. 7. Interestingly, given the context of the 1970s, Shakeb oscillated between the usage of medieval or early modern *'qarūn-iwastāyāibtedāyī 'ahd-ijadīd'*.

5. A very large body of historiography in Urdu on the Deccan sultanates and numerous editions of Dakani Urdu manuscripts were produced under Zor's supervision in this period. See *Dāktar Sayyid Muhīuddīn Qādri Zor: Hayāt, shaksiyataurkārnāme*, ed. Sulaiman Athar Javed, Muhammad Manzur Ahmed, Sayyid Rafi'uddin Qadri, Delhi: Educational Publishing House, 2005.

6. *Archival Organization and Records Management,* p. xxxvi.

7. The list of his students in the disciplines of history, Urdu and Persian literature over the last forty years is quite long. To name just a few who worked closely with the author—Muhammad Suleman Siddiqui, author of *The Bahmani Sufis*, New Delhi: South Asia Books, 1990; Najma Siddiqua, who recently published her dissertation from 1976, *Persian Language and Literature in Golconda*, New Delhi: Adam Publishers, 2011; Najmuddin Ali Khan, 'The Islamic Educational System in the Deccan during the Bahmani Period from 1347–1500', Unpublished dissertation, Osmania University, Hyderabad, 1977; Zaib Hyder, *Dar ul-Insha: The Nizam's Personal Secretariat 1762–1803*, Hyderabad: Discovery Publishers, 2002.

8. The collection of Shamsullah Qadri was deposited in the *Idara-i Adabiyat-i Urdu*, but has not yet received any attention. See Special Volume of *Sab Ras* on Shamsullah Qadri, *Idara-i Adabiyat-i Urdu*, Hyderabad, June 2011.

9. Muzaffar Alam and Sanjay Subrahmanyam, 'Introduction', in *Writing the Mughal World: Studies on Culture and Politics*, New York: Columbia University Press, 2011, pp. 19–21; P.M. Joshi, 'H.K. Sherwani: Evolution of a Historian', in *Studies in the Foreign Relations of India (From the Earliest Times to 1947): Professor H.K. Sherwani Felicitation Volume*, ed. P.M. Joshi et al., Hyderabad: State Archives, Government of Andhra Pradesh, 1975, pp. 1–17.

10. P.M. Joshi and H.K. Sherwani, eds., *History of Medieval Deccan (1294–1724)*, vols. I–II, Hyderabad: Government of Andhra Pradesh, 1974.

11. Alam and Subrahmanyam have alerted us to different moments even in the careers of Aligarh historians, who did not always adhere to the political precepts they were later identified with. See their discussion on Muhammad Habib in Alam and Subrahmanyam, *Writing the Mughal World*, pp. 14–15.

12. M.Z.A. Shakeb, *A Descriptive Catalogue of the Batala Collection of Mughal Documents, AD 1527–1757,* London: British Library, 1990; *A Descriptive Catalogue of Miscellaneous Persian Mughal Documents from Akbar to Bahadur Shah II*, London: India Office Library and Records, British Library, 1982; *A Descriptive*

Catalogue of Persian Letters from Arcot and Baroda, London: India Office Library and Records, British Library, 1982.

13. A full list of his publications can be found in the bibliography.

14. See Chapter 1, p. 23, fn. 34.

15. See Appendix (i): Evaluation of Sources.

16. *Makātīb-i-Zamānah-i-Salātīn-i-Safaviyah* is currently in the Government Oriental Manuscripts Library and Research Institute in Hyderabad, Andhra Pradesh. The contents of this manuscript are nearly the same as *Nuskha-i-Jāmi'–i-Murāsalātulul Albāb* in the British Library (MS. Add 7688; also Or. 3482). A critical edition of this manuscript was compiled and transcribed as a dissertation by one of Shakeb's students, Najmunissa Begam in 1978, but till today remains unpublished. Najmunissa Begam, 'A Critical Edition of Makātīb-i Shāh 'Abbās Safavī', Unpublished dissertation, Osmania University, 1978. See Appendix (i): Evaluation of Sources.

17. The author had presented and written a piece on this subject soon after the completion of his dissertation, M.Z.A. Shakeb, *Religion and Politics in Golconda: A Chapter in Religion and Politics in South India*, Hyderabad: The Institute of Asian Studies, 1978.

18. For a similar discussion see Colin Paul Mitchell, 'Sister Shi'a States: Safavid Iran and the Deccan in the 16th Century', *Deccan Studies*, vol. 2, no. 2, 2004, pp. 44–72. A brief discussion of Shah Tahir's descendants is also in Roy Fischel, 'Society, Space, and the State in the Deccan Sultanates, 1565–1636', Pro Quest Digital Dissertations, University of Chicago, 2012, pp. 215–18. Also see, Farhad Daftary, 'Shah Tahir b. Radi al-Din Hu-sayni', in *The Biographical Encyclopaedia of Islamic Philosophy*, ed. Oliver Leaman, London: Continuum International, 2006, pp. 209–11.

19. The influence of Tusi on Mughal political ideology has been evaluated in Muzaffar Alam, 'Akhlaqi Norms and Mughal Governance', in *The Making of Indo-Persian Culture: Indian and French Studies*, ed. Muzaffar Alam, Françoise Nalini Delvoye and Marc Gaborieau, Delhi: Manohar Publications, 2000, pp. 67–95.

20. Muhammad Amin bin Muhammad Sharif Astarabadi, *Dānish Nāmah-i-Shāhī*, MS. no. 54, Aqaid, SJM & L. For an evaluation of the context of Muhammad Amin Astarabadi's writings, see Andrew J. Newman, 'The Nature of the Akhbārī/Uṣūlī Dispute in Late Safawid Iran. Part 1: 'Abdallāh al-Samāhijī's 'Munyat al-Mumārisīn', *Bulletin of the School of Oriental and African Studies*, vol. 55, no. 1, 1992, pp. 22–51.

21. A version of this chapter was published as 'Aspects of Golconda-Iran Commercial Contacts', *Islamic Culture*, vol. 69, no. 2, 1995, pp. 1–39.

22. *Risālah-i Miqdāriyah*, Ms. no. 127, Tibb, SJM & L. Also see Appendix (i): Evaluation of Sources.

23. Syed Mohiuddin Qadri Zor, *Hayāt-i Mir Mu'min*, Hyderabad: Idara-i Adabiyat-i Urdu, 1941.

24. *Dih ba Dih*, Ms. no. 372, State Archives, Government of Andhra Pradesh.

25. Ziauddin A. Shakeb, 'The Map of the Sultanate of Golconda', *Islamic Culture*, vol. 76, no. 2, 2002, pp. 1–10.

26. Riazul Islam, *Indo-Persian Relations: A Study of the Political and Diplomatic Relations between the Mughul Empire and Iran*, Tehran: Iran Cultural Foundation, 1970. Islam too included a chapter, albeit brief, on cultural connections between these states entitled 'Literature, Arts and Culture' in this early work. Numerous other diplomatic studies have since appeared such as Naimur Rahman Farooqi's *Mughal–Ottoman Relations: A Study of Political and Diplomatic Relations between Mughal India and the Ottoman Empire, 1556–1748*, Delhi, 1989; M. Siraj Anwar, *Mughals in the Deccan*, New Delhi: B.R. Publishing, 2007.

27. Alam and Subrahmanyam, *Writing the Mughal World*, pp. 23–4.

28. Willem Floor and Edmund Herzig, eds., *Iran and the World in the Safavid Age*, London: I.B. Tauris, 2012.

29. John E. Woods, *The Aqquyunlu: Clan, Confederation, Empire*, 2nd edn., Salt Lake City: University of Utah Press, 1999.

30. Kathryn Babayan, *Mystics, Monarchs, and Messiahs: Cultural Landscapes of Early Modern Iran*, Cambridge, Massachusetts: Center for Middle Eastern Studies of Harvard University, 2002; Sa'id Arjomand, *The Shadow of God and the Hidden Imam: Religion, Political Organization and Societal Change in Shi'ite Iran from the Beginning to 1890*, Chicago: University of Chicago Press, 1984.

31. Sholeh A. Quinn, *Historical Writing during the Reign of Shah 'Abbas: Ideology, Imitation and Legitimacy in Safavid Chronicles*, Salt Lake City: University of Utah Press, 2000.

32. Roger Savory, *Iran under the Safavids*, Cambridge: Cambridge University Press, 1980; Andrew J. Newman, *Safavid Iran: Rebirth of a Persian Empire*, London: I.B. Tauris, 2006.

33. Seyyed Hossein Nasr, *Islamic Philosophy from Its Origin to the Present: Philosophy in the Land of Prophecy*, New York: State University of New York Press, 2006; Majid Fakhry, *A History of Islamic Philosophy*, New York: Columbia University Press, 2003. Also see idem, 'The School of Ispahan', in *A History of Muslim Philosophy*, edited and introduced by M.M. Sharif, Delhi: Low Price Publications, 1961, pp. 904–31.

34. Devin J. Stewart, 'Notes on the Migration of 'Āmilī Scholars to Safavid Iran', *Journal of Near Eastern Studies*, vol. 55, no. 2, 1996, p. 100; Andrew J. Newmàn, 'The Myth of the Clerical Migration to Safavid Iran: Arab Shi'ite Opposition to Ali al-Karakī and Safawid Shi'ism', *Welt der Islams*, vol. 33, 1993, pp. 66–112.

35. Devin J. Stewart, 'An Episode in the 'Amili Migration to Safavid Iran: Husayn b. 'Abd al-Samadal-' Amili's Travel Account', *Iranian Studies*, vol. 39, no. 4, 2006, p. 486.

36. See Chapter 3 of this book, fn. 64.

37. Mirza Nizamuddin Ahmed, *Hadīqat-us-Salātīn*, Syed 'Ali Asghar Biligramid, Hyderabad: Islamic Publications Society, 1961; Siddiqua, *Persian Language and Literature in Golconda*, pp. 130–1.

38. M.Z.A. Shakeb, 'The Role of the Sufis in the Changing Society of the Deccan, 1500–1750', in *The Heritage of Sufism Vol. III: Late Classical Persianate Sufism (1501–1750)*, ed. Leonard Lewisohn and David Morgan, London: Oxford Publications, 2000, pp. 361–75.

39. Richard M. Eaton, *The Sufis of Bijapur 1300–1700: Social Roles of Sufis in Medieval India*, Princeton: Princeton University Press, 1978; D.C. Bredi, 'Shi'ism Political Valence in Medieval Deccani Kingdoms', in *Islam and Indian Regions,* ed. A.L. Dallapicola and S.Z. Lallemant, vol. 1, Stuttgart: Franz Steiner Verlag, 1994.

40. Maryam Moazzen, 'Shi'ite Higher Learning and the Role of the Madrasa-i Sultānī in Late Safavid Iran', Pro Quest Digital Dissertations, University of Toronto, 2011, pp. 19–20.

41. Ibn Khatun, *Kitāb al-Imāmāh*, MS. no. 10, Manaqib, SJM & L.

42. S. Arasaratnam, *Merchants, Companies, and Commerce on the Coromandel Coast, 1650–1740,* Delhi: Oxford University Press, 1986; Sanjay Subrahmanyam, *The Political Economy of Commerce: Southern India, 1500–1650*, Cambridge: Cambridge University Press, 1990. For Safavid Iran see, Rudi Matthee, *The Politics of Trade in Safavid Iran: Silk for Silver, 1600–1730,* Cambridge: Cambridge University Press, 1999; Willem M. Floor, *The Economy of Safavid Persia*, Wiesbaden: Reichert, 2000.

43. Joseph J. Brennig, 'The Textile Trade of Seventeenth Century Northern Coromandel: A Study of a Pre-Modern Asian Export Industry', University of Wisconsin, Madison, 1975; idem, 'Textile producers and production in late seventeenth century Coromandel', *The Indian Economic and Social History Review*, vol. 23, no. 4, 1986, pp. 333–55; idem, 'Chief Merchants and European Enclaves of 17th Century Coromandel', *Modern Asian Studies*, vol. 11, no. 3, 1977, pp. 321–46.

44. Sanjay Subrahmanyam, 'Iranians Abroad: Intra-Asian Elite Migration and Early Modern State Formation', *Journal of Asian Studies,* vol. 51, no. 2, 1992, pp. 340–62.

45. Ibid., pp. 348–50. Also see Jean Aubin, 'Les Persans au Siam sous le règne de Narai (1656–1688)', *Mare Luso-Indicum*, vol. 4, 1980, pp. 95–126.

46. John F. Richards, 'Early Modern India and World History', *Journal of World History*, vol. 8, no. 2, 1997; Sanjay Subrahmanyam, 'Connected Histories: Notes towards a Reconfiguration of Early Modern Eurasia', *Modern Asian Studies*, vol. 31, no. 3, 1997, pp. 735–62.

Abbreviations

A.A.A.	*Tārīkh-i ʿĀlam-i Ārā-i ʿAbbāsī*: Munshi, Iskander Beg
ʿAmal	*ʿAmal-i-Sālih*: Kamboh, Muhammad Salih
Ausāf	*Ausāf-ul-Amsār*: Mustaufi, Muhammad Mufid
Barbosa	*The Book of Duarte Barbosa*, ed. Longworth, James
Bedyabinod	*Supplementary catalogue of the coins in the Indian Museum*: Bedyabinod, B.B.
Bilgirami	*Landmarks of the Deccan*: Bilgirami, S.A.A.
B.N.	*Babur Nāmah*: tr. A. Beveridge
Bowrey	*A Geographical Account of Countries Round the Bay of Bengal*: Bowrey, Thomas
Browne	*Literary History of Persia*: Browne, E.G.
Burhān	*Burhān-i-Maʾāsir*: Taba Taba, Sayyid ʿAli
Careri	*Indian Travels of Thevenot and Careri*, ed. Surendranath Sen
C.H.I.	*The Cambridge History of Iran*, vol. I, ed. Fisher, W.B.
Census A.P.	Census of India Atlas Volume of Andhra Pradesh, 1961
Census Madras	Census of India Atlas Volume of Madras, 1961
Census (M)	Report of the Census of Madras Presidency, 1871
Contarini	*Travels to Tana and Persia*: Josafa Barbaro Contarini Ambrogio
Dabistān	Zulfiqar bin Azar Sasani
Dānish	*Dānish Nāmah-i-Shāhī* (Ms.): Amin, Muhammad bin Muhammad Sharif
Danvers	*The Portuguese in India* (2 vols.): Danvers, F. Charles
Devare	*A Short History of Persian Literature*: Devare, T.N.
Dih ba dih	*Dih ba Dih* (Ms.): Anonymous
Dilkasha	*Tārīkh-i-Dilkasha*: Bhimsen
E.F.I.	*English Factories in India*: Foster, William (13 vols.)
Elchi	*Tārīkh-i-Qutbī* or *Tārīkh-i-Elchī-Nizām Shah*: Khurshah bin Qubadul Husaini

Elliot	*The Coins of Southern India*: Elliot, Walter
E.R.B.I.	*Early Records of British India*: Talboys, Wheeler James
Ethe	*Catalogue of Persian manuscripts in the library of India Office*
Far. Sh.	*Farmānhā-i Shāhān-i-Hind-Wa-Deccan*: Anonymous
Firishtah	*Gulshan-i-Ibrahimī*: Firishtah, Abu'l Qasim
Fryer	*East India and Persia*: Fryer, John
F.S.D.S.	*Farmans and Sanads of the Deccan Sultans*: Yusuf Husayn Khan
Habib	*Agrarian System of the Mughals*: Habib, Irfan
H.S.	*Habib-us-Siyār*: Khwand Amir, Ghiyasuddin
Hadāiq	*Hadāiq-us-Salātīn*: 'Ali bin Taifur Bistami
Hadīqat	*Hadīqat-us-Salātīn*: Nizamuddin Shirazi
Hamilton	East India: Hamilton, Alexander
H.Y.	*Haqq-ul-Yaqīn*: Majlisi, Muhammad Baqir
Herbert	*Dodmore Cotton Mission*: Herbert
H.M.P.	*A History of Muslim Philosophy* (2 vols): Sharif, M.M.
Hitti	*A History of Arabs*: Hitti, Philip K.
Hobson Jobson	*A glossary of Anglo-Indian colloquial words and phrases*: Yule and Burnell
Hodivala	*Historical studies in Mughal Numismatic*: Hodivala
Hunter	*A history of British India*: Hunter, William Wilson
Ikhtiyarāt	*Ikhtiyarāt-i-Qutb Shāhī*
Imāmah	*Kitāb-ul-Imāmah*: Ibn Khatun
I.N.	*Iqbāl Nāmah-i-Jahāngīrī*
Iran Atlas	*Historical Atlas of Iran*
I.T.W.	*Inshā'-i-Tāhir Wahīd*
Joshi (Coins)	Coins Current in the Kingdom of Golconda (Article): Joshi, P.M.
Joshi (Textile)	Textile Industry and Trade in the Kingdom of Golconda (Article): Joshi, P.M.
Kashf	*Kashf-ul-Hijab wal Astār* (Ms.): I'jaz Husayn
K.K.	*Muntakhab-ul-Lubāb*: Khafi Khan
Khirqah	*Khirqah-i-'Ulamā* (Ms.): Ibn Imad Ruzbihan Isfahani
K.M.M.	*Kitāb-ul-Masālik Wal Mamālik*: Ibn Khurdad bih
Kulliyāt	*Kulliyāt-i-Muhammad Quli Qutb Shah*

Lambton	*Landlord and Peasant in Persia*: Lambton, Ann K.S.
Legacy	Legacy of Islam: Arnold, T.W.
L.R.E.I.C.	*Letter received by the East India Company*: Danvers
Mackenzie	*Manual Krishna District*: Mackenzie
Majālis	*Majālis-ul-Mu'minīn*: Nurullah Shustari
Makātīb (S)	*Makātīb-i-Shāhān-i-Safavi-wa-Shāhān-i-Hind-wa-Rum Naghayrah (Ms)*: Anonymous
Makātīb (Z)	*Makātīb-i-Zamanah-i-Salātīn-i-Safaviyah* (Ms.): 'Abdul Husain Bin Adham
Malcolm	*History of Persia*: Malcolm, John
Manucci	*Storia Do Mogor* (1653–1708): Manucci Niccolao Tr. Irvine, William
Master	*The Dairies of Streynsham Master*, ed. Temple, R.C.
Ma'sumiyah	*Risālah-i-Ma'sumiyah*: 'Ali bin Taifur
Matla'	*Matla' us Sa'dain* (Ms.): Kamaluddin Samarqandi 'Abdul Razzaq
M.D.H.	*Medieval Deccan History*: Sherwani and Joshi
Minorsky	'The Qara-Qoyunlu And The Qutb-Shahs' (Article)
Miqdāriyah	*Risālah-i-Miqdāriyah* (MS.): Mir Muhammad Mu'min
Mīzān	*Mizān-ut-tabā'i Qutb Shāhī*: Muhammad, Taqiuddin
Moreland	*From Akbar to Aurangzeb*: Moreland, W.H.
Mufid	*Jāmi'-i-Mufīdī*: Mustaufi, Muhammad Mufid
Muir	The Caliphate: its rise, decline and fall: Muir, William
Muntakhab (B)	*Muntakhab-ut-Tawārīkh*: Badayuni, 'Abdul Qadir
Nujūm	*Nujūm u'ssam*: Mirza Muhammad 'Ali
Nafāyis	*Nafāyis ul funūn fi 'arā'is ul 'uyūn* (Ms.): Muhammad b. Mahmud Amoli
Naqshah	*Naqshah-i-Irān*: Abdu'r Razzaq Khan Muhandis and E. Girard
Nasrabadi	*Tazkirah*: Nasrabadi, Tahir
Pope	*Survey of Persian Art*: Pope, A.U.
P.N.	*Pādshah Nāmah*: Lahori, 'Abdul Hamid
Prasad	*History of Jahangir*: Prasad, Beni
Purchas	*Purchas His Pilgrimage*
K.	*The Koran*
Qazvini	*Pādshah Nāmah*: Muhammad Amin Qazvini Ms. No. 85, S.A.A.P.

Rao	*Religion in Andhra*: Rao, B.S.L. Hanumantha
Rauzat	*Rauzat us Safā'*: Mir Khwand
Raychaudhuri	*Jan Company in Coromandel*: Raychaudhuri, Tapan
Relations	*Relations of Golconda*: Moreland, W.H.
R.I.	*Indo-Persian Relations*: Riazul Islam
Risālah Ghaib-wa-Zuhūr	*Risālah dar bāb-i-Subūt-i-ghaib wa-Zuhūr-i-hazrat sāhib-us zamān*: Mir Muhammad Baqir Majlisi
R.N.R.	*Corporate Life in Medieval Andhra Desa*: Rao R. Narasimha
Ross	*Persian Art*: Ross, E. Denison
Ruq'āt	*Ruq'āt-i 'Ālamgīrī*: Aurangzeb
Saksena	*History of Shah Jahan of Delhi*: Saksena, Banarasi Prasad
Sanai	*Sanai Irān ba'd az Islām*: Hasan, Zaki Muhammad
Sarwar	*History of Shah Isma'il Safavi*: Ghulam Sarwar
Schouten	*Voyage aux Indes Orientales, 1658–1665*: Schouten, Wouter
Scott	*An Atlas of the Southern Part of India*: Scott, Major F.J.
S.D.A.R.	*Selected documents of Aurangzeb*: Yusuf Husayn Khan
S.D.S.J.R.	*Selected documents of Shah Jahan's reign*: Yusuf Husayn Khan
Shajar	*Shajar-i-Dānish* (Ms.): Gilani Nizamuddin Hakim ul Mulk
Shakeb	*Jāmi' ul 'Atiyāt*: Ahmed, Shakeb Ziauddin
Qadri (I)	*Imadiyah*: Qadri, Shamsullah
Qadri (M)	*Muarrikhīn-i-Hind*: Qadri, Shamsullah
Sherwani (B)	*Bahmanis of the Deccan*: Sherwani, H.K.
Sherwani (Q)	*History of Qutb Shahi Dynasty*: Sherwani, H.K.
Shuzūr	*Shuzūr ul 'Iqyān*: Abu al-A'la al-Ma'arri; Mustafaa Sultani Makhzumi
Silsilah	*Silsilāt-un-nasab-i-Safawiyah*: Husain Ibn Abdal Zahidi
Sirāt	*Sirāt-ul-mustaqīm wa dīn-i-qawīm* (Ms.): Anonymous
S.I.T.	*Sources of Indian Traditions*: ed. Bary W. Theodore
S.W.D.	*Selected Waqai of the Deccan*: Yusuf Husayn Khan
Sykes	*A History of Persia*: Sykes, Percy

Tabsirah	*Tabsirat-ul-'Awām* (Ms.): Alam ul-Huda Sayyid Murtaza
Taftazani	*A Commentary on the creed of Islam*: Taftazani
Talqani	*Munsha'āt-i-dabīr-ul-mulk*: 'Abdul 'Ali, Talqani
Talqani (A)	*Maktubāt-i-Sultān Abu'l Hasan*: Talqani Haji 'Abdul 'Azim
Tavernier	*Travels in India*: Tavernier
Terpstra	*De vestiging van de Nederlanders aan dekust van koromandel*: Terpstra, H.
Thevenot	*Indian Travels of Thevenot and Careri*, Sen Surendranath
T.M.	*Tazkirat-ul-Mūlūk*: tr. Minorsky
T.Q.S.	*Tārīkh-i-Muhammad Qutb Shāh* (Ms.): Anonymous
Tuhfah	*Tuhfah-i-Shāhī Atiyah-i-Ilāhī* (Ms.): Badakshi, Zainuddin 'Ali
Tuzuk	*Tuzuk-i-Jahāngīrī*: Jahangir
Usūl	*Usūl-i-Khamsah-i-Imāmiyah* (Ms.): Anonymous
Wali	*Qutb Shahi Coins in Andhra*
Wali 'Abdul	Andhra Pradesh Government Museum: Wali, 'Abdul
Wilson	*The Persian Gulf*: Wilson, Arnold T.
Wilson, H.H.	*A Glossary of Indian Judicial and Revenue terms*: Wilson, H.H.
Zafrah	*Tārīkh-i-Zafrah*: Ahqar, Girdhari Lal
Zamīmah	*Zamīmah-i-Tārīkh-i-Qutb Shāhī* (MS.): Anonymous
Z.N.	*Zafar Nāmah*: Yazdi, Sharfuddin 'Ali
Zonis	*Political Elite of Iran*: Zonis, Marvin
Zor	*Hayāt-i Mir Mu'min*: Zor, Mohiuddin Qadri.

INSTITUTIONS

B.M.	British Museum
Bod.	Bodleian Library Oxford
B.S.O.A.S.	Bulletin of the School of Oriental and African Studies
H.A.K.C.	Husain Ali Khan Collection, S.A.A.P.
H.Y.C.	Husain-al-Yafa-i Collection, S.A.A.P.
I.A.U.	Idara-i-Adabiyat-i-Urdu, Hyderabad, A.P.

K.H.C.	Khusro Husaini Collection, S.A.A.P.
S.A.A.P.	State Archives Andhra Pradesh
S.A.C.	Sajjad Ali Collection, S.A.A.P.
OMLRI	Oriental Manuscripts Library and Research Institute
SJM & L	Salar Jung Museum and Library, Hyderabad

1

Introduction: Two Dynasties

THIS CHAPTER INTRODUCES the Qutb Shahi and Safavid dynasties, and the geographic and socio-cultural characteristics of the two polities relevant to our study. It presents brief biographies of the rulers of each dynasty and the major political events that marked their reigns. It also discusses the territorial and oceanic expanse of the two regions. It shows that the political geography of the two states fluctuated according to political rivalries and confrontations in different time periods. Ports, overland and maritime trade routes facilitated commerce and the exchange of emissaries and travellers between Safavid Iran and the Deccan sultanates. Lastly, this chapter lays out some of the ethnic and linguistic features of Golkonda and Iran. Populations of both regions were diverse at the level of the court as well as society. A discussion of the physical and demographic context of the two polities serves as a foundation for the diplomatic, intellectual and commercial ties discussed in the subsequent chapters of this book.

THE QUTB SHAHS

Five different sultanates came into being in the Deccan after the break-up of the Bahmani kingdom towards the end of the fifteenth century and the beginning of the sixteenth century. Golkonda was one of these sultanates. Sultan Quli, a member of the Black Sheep (Qara Quyunlu) tribe, founded the Qutb Shahi dynasty.[1] During Bahmani rule, a number of foreigners from Iran and other parts of Central Asia migrated to the Deccan, which was, for them, a land of opportunities. Some of these migrants rose to high positions and Sultan Quli became the governor (*tarafdār*) of Tilangana.[2]

Sultan Quli Qutb Shah

Sultan Quli entered the service of Mahmud Shah Bahmani during a time when a conflict between such newcomers (*āfāqīs*) and the native elite (Deccanis) became a decisive factor in the power politics of the Deccan. The Bahmani

Sultanate was disintegrating under the pressure of this conflict. Select nobles manoeuvred to break away from the sultanate and assumed autonomy within a jurisdiction under their control. Sultan Quli was no less ambitious and aspired for such autonomy for his domains.[3]

Sultan Quli Qutb Shah was a disciple of Shah Na'yimuddin Ni'matullah of Yazd.[4] However, by the close of the fifteenth century, Sufi households of Iran were assuming a Shi'ite character, and Sultan Quli Qutb Shah embraced the Shi'ite faith as well.[5] Sultan Quli was a good administrator and military expert. By 921/1515, he had captured Venuconda, Bellamconda, Nagarjunaconda and a few other forts from Vijayanagar. He then annexed Vijayawada, and had to resist the invasions of the Rayas of Vijayanagar and the Gajapatis to recapture Warangal, Kammammet, Devarconda and Nalgonda.[6]

He first strengthened the fort of Golkonda and then advanced to restore the territories he had lost.[7] He defeated Achyuta Deva Raya (d.1542) and annexed Pangal, Ghanapura, Koilconda to his sultanate. The reign of Sultan Quli Qutb Shah spanned twenty-six years and was marked by several notable conquests. His sultanate stretched over many parts of the Telugu-speaking region.[8] He was assassinated by Mir Mahmud Hamadani on 2nd Jumada II 950/2 September 1543. It is alleged that Mir Mahmud Hamadani was instigated by Sultan Quli's son, Yar Quli Jamshid.[9]

Yar Quli Jamshid and Subhan Quli Qutb Shah

Yar Quli Jamshid succeeded Sultan Quli in Jumada II 950/September 1543. His younger brother Ibrahim Quli fled to Vijayanagar. Jamshid neither cared for recognition nor was he recognized by any of the new sultans of the Deccan except Burhan Shah I of the Nizam Shahi kingdom. Jamshid died of cancer on 3rd Muharram 957/22 January 1550 after ailing for over two years. His reign, especially in the context of international connections, was the least eventful. There is no evidence of his coming into contact with his contemporary, Shah Tahmasp Safavi.[10] He was immediately succeeded by his son, Subhan Quli, but the latter was overthrown within a few months by the partisans of his uncle, Ibrahim Qutb Shah.[11]

Ibrahim Quli Qutb Shah

Ibrahim Qutb Shah was the youngest of Sultan Quli's sons and was barely fourteen years old at the time of his father's death. Fearing for his life at the hands of his brother Jamshid, he fled to Vijayanagar where he was warmly received. He stayed there as the guest of Rama Raj for over seven years. During the reign of Subhan Quli, the court politics in Golkonda took a turn in favour of Ibrahim Quli. Two nobles in particular, Mustafa Khan Ardestani and Jagdev Rao, were his strong supporters, and enabled him to occupy the Qutb Shahi throne on 12th Rajab 957/27 July 1550.

Having lived for a considerable period at Vijayanagar, Ibrahim Qutb Shah had a better understanding of the Deccan's affairs than his predecessors. He pursued a policy of peace and non-alignment for a decade before getting involved in the politics of the Deccan. He joined an alliance with the other Deccan sultanates against Vijayanagar in the Battle of Banihatti, which took place on 28th Jumada II 972/23 January 1565.[12] Although Vijayanagar was not completely annihilated, it was seriously weakened. During Ibrahim Quli Qutb Shah's time, Akbar had consolidated Mughal power in India. This led the Deccan sultans to reorientate their foreign policy. Ibrahim Quli sent his representatives both to the Mughal and Safavid courts. During his reign, the capital of Golkonda developed into a cosmopolitan city and the presence of Iranian elites increased considerably in the Deccan. The distinctive character of Golkonda also took its shape at this time. Ibrahim Quli died on 21st Rabi II 988/5 June 1580 after ruling for thirty-one years.[13]

Muhammad Quli Qutb Shah

Muhammad Quli was the third son of Ibrahim Qutb Shah and about fourteen years old at the time of his accession. He was not trained in the art of conducting state affairs and was more interested in art and culture. Mir Muhammad Mu'min Astarabadi, who was appointed *peshwā* of the sultanate, virtually looked after the administration and Muhammad Amin Shahrastani held the post of *Mir Jumla* (Prime Minister).

There were a series of minor skirmishes on the frontiers and revolts by certain chieftains within the sultanate, most of which were checked through the effective military strategies of *Mir Jumla*. Though Vijayanagar ceased to be a threat, the Deccan was subjected to Mughal invasions from the north. Following the failure of the allied Deccan sultanates to save Ahmednagar in the Battle of Sonepat in 1005/1600, Golkonda and Bijapur were now directly exposed to the advancing forces of Hindustan but they survived either by resisting the Mughal army or by negotiating terms of concessions and tribute. In such circumstances, Mir Muhammad Mu'min played a major role in creating harmony among the various factions within Golkonda as well as maintaining a balance of power in foreign policy.

The reign of Muhammad Quli Qutb Shah is considered to have been the zenith of the Qutb Shahi dynasty. During this period, the city of Hyderabad was founded in which both Deccani and Iranian culture flourished.

Muhammad Quli Qutb Shah died on 17th Zilqada 1020/11 January 1612 at the age of forty-seven, after a reign of thirty-two years.[14]

Muhammad Qutb Shah

Sultan Muhammad Quli Qutb Shah had only one daughter, Hayat Bakshi
Begam. His nephew and son-in-law, Prince Muhammad, succeeded him and
ruled as Sultan Muhammad Qutb Shah. Sultan Muhammad had received
his training as a prince from Mir Muhammad Mu'min who continued as
peshwā till his death on 2nd Jumada I 1034/31 January, 1625. The reign
of Sultan Muhammad Qutb Shah was a period of peace and prosperity. He
did not face as much pressure from the Mughals whom he had placated
by paying *peshkash* or tribute. He had supported Prince Khurram when the
latter revolted against Jahangir. Being a scholar himself, Muhammad Qutb
Shah encouraged the influx of Iranian intellectuals on a very large scale. He
also patronized Shi'i scholarship in Golkonda. He died on 13th Jumada I
1035/31 January 1626 after ruling for fourteen years.[15]

'Abdullah Qutb Shah

'Abdullah Qutb Shah ascended the throne on 14th Jumada I 1035/1
February 1626 at the age of about twelve. His mother, Hayat Bakshi Begam,
controlled the affairs of state as the queen dowager. Many administrative
changes occurred during the first two years of his reign. On 9th Ramazan
1038/22 April 1629, Shaikh Muhammad Ibn Khatun was appointed as
peshwā of the sultanate.[16] During the reign of Shah Jahan, Mughal pressure
had increased on Golkonda and Bijapur. The new *peshwā*, therefore, played
a very significant role in negotiating peace with the Mughals.

In Zilhijja 1045/May 1636, 'Abdullah Qutb Shah had to pledge his
allegiance to the Mughals through a Deed of Submission (*inqīyād nāmah*)
which rendered Golkonda weak and open to Mughal interference. The
same year Mir Muhammad Sa'id Ardestani was appointed as *sar-i-daftar*
of the important *sarkārs* (districts) of Masulipatnam, Nizampatam and
Mustafanagar.[17] Muhammad Sa'id soon rose to the position of *havālādār*
or keeper of Masulipatam[18] and then *sar-khayl* (Revenue Administrator)[19]
in the year 1052/1642. Consequent to the death of Shaikh Ibn Khatun in
1058/1648, he was appointed *Mir Jumla* and became the most powerful
official in the sultanate. Mir Muhammad Sa'id Ardestani was an able
administrator, an expert military leader and an influential trader. He made
a remarkable contribution by expanding and strengthening the sultanate.
He conquered the provinces (*atrāf*) of eastern Karnatak up to Jingi and
annexed them to Golkonda. He exploited diamond mines on a large scale
and promoted overseas trade. Although the sultanate prospered and became
strong under him, the sultan himself was intimidated by the presence of
such a dominating personality. This led to a misunderstanding and strained
relations between the two. In the year 1066/1655, Mir Muhammad Sa'id,

reacting to court politics, crossed over to the Mughals and was favoured with a *mansab* of 5,000 *zāt* and 5,000 *sawār* by Shah Jahan.[20]

The defection of *Mir Jumla* was followed by Mughal invasion and plunder of Hyderabad, which weakened the sultanate in many ways. Prince Aurangzeb, who had built up an enormous military force in the Deccan, put both Golkonda and Bijapur under immense pressure. However, he was suddenly diverted by the news of his father's illness on Jumada 1068/ February 1658, left Aurangabad for Delhi and became deeply embroiled in the contest for his father's succession. Because of this diversion, 'Abdullah Qutb Shah enjoyed a peaceful respite from the hitherto remorseless threat, and the final years of his reign were almost undisturbed. He died on 3rd Muharram 1083/April 1672.[21]

Abul Hasan

'Abdullah Qutb Shah was succeeded by his third son-in-law, Abul Hasan on Muharram 1083/April 1672. The news of this succession was sent to Aurangzeb for his approval, which he granted with a set of conditions. Abul Hasan had to submit his allegiance to the Mughals and rule over Golkonda as their appointee. Further, the assignment of the sultanate to Abul Hasan was contingent upon his loyalty and he was warned not to enter into an alliance with Shivaji.[22]

Abul Hasan was not trained in statecraft, and failed to bring about a balance among the different elements of his nobility. Two of his prime ministers Mir Jumla Muhammad Ibrahim Khalilullah and Sayyid Muzaffar crossed over to Aurangzeb. Ultimately, he appointed the two brothers, Akkanna and Madanna, as *Mir Jumla* and *peshkar* (accountant) respectively. He also entered into an alliance with Shivaji, an action that angered the Mughal emperor. Above all he attempted to secure military aid from Safavid Iran against the Mughals. Aurangzeb took decisive action, annexed Golkonda and took Abul Hasan prisoner on 24th Zilqada 1098/21 September 1687.[23]

THE SAFAVIDS

Shah Isma'il I

Shah Isma'il, the founder of the Safavid dynasty, was a descendant of Shaikh Safiu'ddin Ishaq (d.735/1334), a Sufi saint of Ardabil, who is said to have traced his lineage to the Seventh Imam, Musa Kazim.

He began his campaigns when he was only thirteen years of age. Seven Turkmen tribes who were called 'lovers of the king' (*shāh-seven*), supported Shah Isma'il. They included the Shamlu, Ustajlu, Ramulu, Takulu, Zul Qadr,

Afshar and Qajar clans, collectively known as the Qizilbash.[24] As he advanced towards Tarum, Khalkhal, Baku and Shamakhi, he was able to increase his forces at every stage until they numbered about 16,000 men by the end of 906/1500. He fought with Sherwan Shah near Gulistan and decisively routed him. Following this victory, various *amīrs* such as Muhammad Zakariyah, the Aq Quyunlu Prime Minister, and others submitted their allegiance to him. In 907/1501 he defeated Aq Quyunlu chief, Alvand Mirza, at Nakhchivan and brought the entire province of Azerbaijan under his sway. The same year, the young Isma'il Mirza was crowned at Tabriz as the sovereign and was called Shah Isma'il. His name together with the names of the Twelve Imams was included in the *khutbah* (sermon) and coins were struck in his name.[25]

Shah Isma'il rose to remarkable power and within twenty years he had brought all of northern and western Iran under his rule. His dynamic career owed its success to a strong movement, which he organized and is frequently referred to, in this study, as the Safavid Movement. The power of this movement was rooted in three major elements. First, its military forces were known as the Qizilbash or Red Heads, who wore red caps as a mark of their identity.[26] They were fanatic soldiers who fought for their cause and constituted the core of the Safavid army. Second, the movement had a distinct religious and political character. Shah Isma'il was an ardent advocate of the Shi'ite faith and declared that it must be accepted by all in his domains.[27] This aspect played a governing role in the formulation of Safavid Iran's foreign policy not only during his reign, but also throughout this dynasty. It was perhaps Shah Isma'il's achievements and the spectacular success of this movement which resulted in serious responses from the Ottomans, the Uzbeks and the other Sunni political entities.

With strong Qizilbash support, Shah Isma'il captured Dayar-i-Bakr, Ahlat Bitlis, Arjish and finally Baghdad in 914/1508. He was challenged and insulted by the Uzbek Chief Shaybani Khan, with whom he fought a decisive battle at Tahirabad near Marv. Shaybani Khan was defeated and killed on 24th Rajab 916/1 December 1510.[28] It may be mentioned here that Babur's sister was among the captives of Marv; however, she was treated with respect by the Safavid monarch and sent to Babur. This gesture led to the establishment of good relations between Babur and Shah Isma'il. Subsequently in 918/1512, with the help of a large Persian army, Babur conquered Samarqand.[29]

In Rajab 920/September 1514, Shah Isma'il was drawn into a battle with Sultan Selim I at Chaldiran, a plain to the east of Lake Urmia. In this battle, Shah Isma'il lost Kurdistan, Dayar-i-Bakr and Georgia.[30] Shah Isma'il died at Ardabil on 19th Rajab 930/23 May 1524 and was succeeded by his son Shah Tahmasp who was only ten years old.

Shah Tahmasp

Tahmasp was the eldest son of Shah Isma'il and was guided by the Qizilbash chiefs during his early reign. Yet he faced many challenges from them and took drastic measures against them later. Still, his most pressing concerns were the Uzbeks and Ottomans. His generals defeated the Uzbeks near Turbat-i-Shaikh Jam in 934/1527, however, the Uzbeks took over Herat again in 937/1530 and it remained under their control for eighteen months.

In 940/1534 Ottoman Sultan, Suleiman I, invaded Safavid Iran, and Shah Tahmasp mounted a defence with great difficulty. Four years later, Suleiman I advanced again and took possession of Baghdad and Tabriz, and most of the rulers of Sherwan and Gilan submitted their allegiance to him.

One of the major events in the reign of Shah Tahmasp, in the context of this study, was Humayun's refuge in Iran. Humayun had fled to Iran after having lost his kingdom in Hindustan. He wrote a letter to Shah Tahmasp before entering his territory in Shawwal 950/December 1543.[31] In response, Shah Tahmasp issued a *farmān* making arrangements for Humayun's reception. He entertained Humayun in a number of ways and ultimately assisted him in re-establishing his suzerainty over Hindustan, but in return Humayun was obliged to accept the Shi'ite faith in a rather peculiar way.[32] In 961/1554 both the Safavids and Ottomans, weary of hostile relations, entered into a peace treaty. The later years of his reign were uneventful except for the frequent skirmishes with the Georgians and the independent rulers of Gilan.[33] Shah Tahmasp died on 15th Safar 984/14 May 1576.

Shah Isma'il II and Muhammad Khudabandah

Shah Tahmasp was immediately succeeded by his fourth son Shah Isma'il II, who had been imprisoned by his father for twenty-five years in the castle of Qahqaha. He ruled for about a year and a half from 24th Safar 984/23 May 1576 to 13th Ramazan 985/24 November 1577, during which period he put to death his brothers and all other possible aspirants to the throne. Out of the eleven sons of Shah Tahmasp about nine had survived him. The first of them was Muhammad Khudabandah who was regarded as unqualified for succession since he was totally blind, but he was ruling Khorasan. Shah Isma'il II first put to death his two brothers, Suleiman[34] and Mustafa, even before his father had been buried at Mashhad and his own coronation had taken place. In the end, he even sent Aqa Quli Khan, chief of the Shamlu tribe, to kill Muhammad Khudabandah and his six-year old son 'Abbas Mirza. Before these instructions could be implemented, Shah Isma'il II died from alcohol and an overdose of opium. Since Muhammad Khudabandah was the only surviving prince, he succeeded Shah Isma'il II.[35]

Khudabandah was a weak ruler. Increasing conflicts between the Qizilbash tribes and their defections as well as the contest for succession between his sons weakened his regime. Externally, the Uzbeks had encroached upon the north-eastern frontiers while the Ottomans controlled lands as far as Tabriz in the west.

Mughal Emperor Akbar had great sympathy for Shah Khudbandah and sought to help him against the rebellious Qizilbash. But Khudabandah abdicated the throne in Zilqada 995/October 1587 in favour of his second son 'Abbas Mirza, who was destined to be the most influential Safavid ruler.[36] He was about seventeen years old at the time of his accession.

Shah 'Abbas I

The young Shah 'Abbas I faced many problems during his early career. The foremost of these was the rivalry between 'Ali Quli Khan Shamlu and Murshid Quli Khan Ustajlu, both from the Qizilbash tribes, over the guardianship of the young prince. Murshid Quli Khan used force to oust 'Ali Quli Khan from this position and assume control as guardian of 'Abbas. However, as soon as 'Abbas was proclaimed as the Shah, he had Murshid Quli Khan killed and seized the reins of power. Qizilbash domination thus came to an end and Shah 'Abbas was free from opposition.[37]

During the reign of Shah Khudabandah, the elder brother of Shah 'Abbas I, Hamza Mirza, forcefully resisted Ottoman invasions. But his death encouraged the Ottoman Turks to invade Iran again. In the year 996/1588 Farhad Pasha, in alliance with the governor of Sherwan, invaded Qara Bagh and captured Ganja. At the same time, the Uzbeks had encroached upon north-eastern Iran. Shah 'Abbas I was in a weak position and so entered into a peace agreement with the Ottomans in 998/1590 losing Tabriz, Sherwan, Georgia, Lorestan and the ports of Caspian.[38]

The Uzbek chief 'Abdullah II promptly seized the opportunity and invaded Iran. By 1002/1593 he had seized and plundered Herat, Mashhad, Nishabur, Sabzevar, Tun, Tabas and many other cities in Khorasan. It was only in 1006/1597 that Shah 'Abbas I was able to drive the Uzbeks away from the territories of Iran. For many years thereafter the Uzbeks could not repeat their annual raids.[39]

One of the important measures taken by Shah 'Abbas I was to reorganize his military forces along European lines. He employed two Englishmen, the Sherley brothers, to train his army which was put under the command of Allah Verdi Beg. He also formed a new elite corps of 'lovers of the king' (*shāh-seven*), which replaced the former Qizilbash.

Fifteen years after his succession, Shah 'Abbas I was strong enough to recover the provinces he had lost. In 1001/1603 he led a campaign against the Ottomans and recaptured Tabriz on 5th Jumada II 1012/1 October 1603.

He then took Irvan and Sherwan. In 1012/1604, Sultan Muhammad III of the Ottoman Empire died and was succeeded by Sultan Ahmad who sent a large force against Iran. The Ottoman army was defeated in the vicinity of Lake Urmia and Shah 'Abbas I was able to recapture Azerbaijan, Kurdistan, Baghdad, Mosul, Dayar-i-Bakr, Karbala and Najaf. Peace was concluded in 1012/1604, and the Ottomans agreed upon the frontiers of Iran with its extended territories.[40]

The reign of Shah 'Abbas I was marked not only by his conquest in the west and north-east but also by major administrative reforms. He encouraged English and European merchants, which augmented commercial activities in the Persian Gulf. He maintained diplomatic relations with many contemporary states of the Indian Ocean.[41] He appointed Sir Robert Sherley as his roving ambassador to European states.[42] His fraternal relations with Emperor Jahangir were remarkable.[43] He exercised influence in protecting the Deccan sultans. It was because of Shah 'Abbas I that Mashhad was declared a place of Shi'ite pilgrimage.[44] He died on 25th Jumada I 1038/10 January 1629 at the age of sixty, after ruling for forty-three years.[45] It was during his reign that Safavid Iran reached the height of its power.

Shah Safi

Shah 'Abbas was succeeded, in accordance with his own will, by his grandson Sam Mirza, who on his accession assumed the name of his father and occupied the throne of Iran as Shah Safi. Shah Safi was so preoccupied with the execution of every possible claimant to the throne that he lost most of the territories conquered by Shah 'Abbas I. During his reign, the Ottoman ruler Murad IV maintained an aggressive policy against Iran, and by 1039/1630 he captured Mosul, Kurdistan and Hamadan. In 1035/1626 Murad led another campaign in north-western Iran and took control of Irvan and Tabriz. In 1048/1638 Murad led a second campaign against Baghdad by way of Mosul and captured it. A peace treaty was concluded according to which Baghdad was surrendered to the Ottomans and Irvan was restored to Safavids.

The Uzbeks continued to be a menace to the solidarity of Safavid Iran. Under the leadership of Imam Quli, they invaded Khorasan and forced the evacuation of Qandahar by the Iranian governor. It was a period when Qandahar was lost by both Iran and Hindustan. Shah Safi died at Kashan on 12th Safar 1052/16 May 1642 and was succeeded by his son Shah 'Abbas II.[46]

Shah 'Abbas II

Shah 'Abbas II was ten years old when he ascended the throne in Safar 1052/ May 1642. Iran had had little trouble on its western frontiers, ever since the peace settlement between the Ottomans and Shah Safi. In the north-east, the Khanate of Uzbeks had been weakened due to internal discord on the one hand, and the Russian aggression, on the other. One Uzbek prince and even one Uzbek Khan Nazir Muhammad sought the protection of Shah 'Abbas. They were treated with unusual generosity and honour. Shah 'Abbas II maintained good diplomatic relations with Hindustan and the Deccan sultanates.[47] In Safar 1059/February 1649 he re-occupied Qandahar so very skillfully that the Mughal Emperor Shah Jahan found it difficult to regain it either by diplomacy or by use of force.[48] In 1074/1664 he successfully repelled a raid by the Russians at Mazandran. The twenty-five years of his reign were generally marked by a period of peace and prosperity. He died at Farhabad (Mazandaran) in Rabi I 1077/1666.

Shah Suleiman

Shah 'Abbas II was succeeded by his eldest son Shah Suleiman in 1077/1668. Although he was twenty years old at the time of his succession, he was not trained in the affairs of the state.[49] He had also been blinded as a prince. He ruled for more than twenty-eight years until 1105/1694, but his reign marked the beginning of Safavid decline.[50]

GEOGRAPHY AND PROVINCIAL ADMINISTRATION

Golkonda

The territories of the Golkonda Sultanate were located along the eastern coast of the southern Indian peninsula between 13° N latitude and 19° N latitude and between 77.4° E longitude and 84.7° E longitude. The territorial limits of the sultanate, at one time or another, extended beyond 20° N latitude and were marginally unstable in the south-west.

The expanse of the sultanate is distinguished by its geographical features such as soil and climate, and anthropological characteristics such as ethnicity and language. The frontiers of Golkonda were more stable in the east, from St. Thomé to Kalinga Ghat near Chilka Lake along the Bay of Bengal. In the north, it ran along the southern banks of Godavari River from Srikakulam to Kaulas. In the west, it shared a common border with the sultanate of Bijapur and stretched over the *sarkārs* of Kaulas and *taraf-i-karnātak* or Arcot. In the south it had a fluctuating border at St. Thomé.

The geographic extent of Golkonda gradually evolved out of the Bahmani Province (*taraf*) of Tilangana. It ultimately grew to its full size by stretching over the entire area of the Telugu-speaking region, marginally covering parts of Tamil, Oriya, Marathi and Kannada-speaking regions, which were often bilingual with Telugu.[51]

The kingdom comprised thirty-seven *sarkārs*, which were further sub-divided into *parganas*. There were altogether 517 *parganas*.[52] A village or *dih* was the basic unit. A larger village or town was called a *qasbah*. The new settlements around big towns and cities were developed as sub-urban localities (*havelī*). Almost all the provinces had more than one stronghold (*qil'ah*).[53]

Iran

Safavid Iran stretched between 37° E and 69.5° E longitude and between 23° N to 44.5° N latitude. The actual territories on its western and eastern borders were unstable and shifted according to political conditions. From the beginning of the Safavid dynasty in 1502 and especially during the reign of Shah 'Abbas I, the political geography of Iran changed drastically. In the north-west, its frontier stretched from the Black Sea to the Caspian Sea almost along the river Terek. In the east, it touched the Caspian Sea up to the river Atrak. It stretched up to Hasarasb and Balkh along the southern banks of the Oxus (present-day Aras). In the south-west, the frontiers of Safavid Iran ran from Kharput to Najaf and then to Bahrain and Oman. The extreme south-eastern border was naturally drawn by the Sea of Oman and Persian Gulf. The western frontier started from the eastern coast of the Black Sea, ran southward to Irvan and Mosul and from there to Arran and Kharput. In the east, the frontier ran from Balkh to Bamian. Southwards, it shared a common frontier with the Mughal provinces of Kabul and Sindh.[54]

The provincial organization of Iran changed frequently. Most of the cities and towns retained ancient names. There were certain regional divisions of the country such as Iraq-i-Arab, Iraq-i-Ajam, Azerbaijan, Khorasan and Sistan, etc., the expanse of which was always elastic and variable.[55] Such divisions developed into an established pattern in Iranian provincial organization and therefore, continued during the times of Safavids as well. The minor divisions were those of towns (*qasbāt*), villages (*qaryāt*), and cities (*shahr*). Larger administrative units equivalent to districts were called *vilāyat*. Most of the villages, towns and cities of a *vilāyat* would have a number of strongholds (*qil'ah*).[56] When the population in towns and forts became too much, new settlements formed around them called the *havelī* of a town or a fort.

Many of the provinces or regional divisions and subdivisions had dependencies (*tawābi'*) attached to them such as those in Irvan, Sherwan and Sistan. Similarly Makran, Daghistan, Rustamdar and Gurgan consisted of a number of dependencies. Such dependencies constituted the foundation of the Safavid Empire and played a decisive role in the general conduct of the state and shaping of its foreign policy.

PORTS AND ROADS

There was heavy maritime traffic between Golkonda and Iran, and, therefore, both the regions had a number of developed harbours. These harbours occupied an important strategic position in the maritime traffic between the eastern and western Indian Ocean. These ports combined with overland trade routes enabled the movements of goods and people.

Ports of Golkonda

The eastern coast of south India, forming the eastern most territories of the sultanate, was traditionally divided into two coastal lines. The northern one known as the Gingili coast, from Ganjam to Rajahmundry, and the Coromandel coast in the south from Masulipatnam down to Nagapatam. Both the Gingili and Coromandel coasts had several harbours. The ports from south to north were Madras,[57] Pulicat,[58] Nizampatam (Petapuli),[59] Masulipatam,[60] Vizagapatam,[61] Bimlipatam (Peddapally),[62] Coringo,[63] Vattara, Pondy, Manichapatam and Kalingapatam.[64] Among these, Masulipatam, Madras, Nizampatam and Vizagapatam were the major ports.

Since Golkonda was on the eastern coast of the Indian subcontinent, the connecting sea routes with Iran were rather circuitous. Ships from Iran had to proceed through the Persian Gulf, the Sea of Oman, then southward around Cape Comorin and north again to reach the ports of Golkonda. The ships moving along these sea routes had to halt along the coasts of Iran, south-western India and around southernmost India. The western and southern ports included the area governed by the 'Adil Shahs (from north to south)—Chaul, Dabhol, Goa, Calicut and Cochin. Turning northward up to the east coast were Negapatam, Porto Novo, Tegnapatam and Fort St. Thomé (Mylapore). On occasions, some travellers had to circle even further south touching Ponte De Galle in Ceylon.[65]

Ports of Iran

In Safavid Iran, there were a score of ports and harbours that cleared ships from Iran to the world and also served as naval stations for the exchange of ships from the Indian Ocean all the way to the Mediterranean Sea. Some of the important shipping stations of Safavid Iran from west to east were Bandar-i-M'ashur[66] (to the north of the present Bandar-i-Shahpur) on the inland sea at the mouth of Euphrates-Tigris delta, Bandar-i-Dilam,[67] Bandar-i-Kharg[68] (or Khark), a small island near the coastal land of Kazerun, Bandar-i-Rig,[69] Bandar-i-Asaluyeh, Bandar-i-Rishahr,[70] Bandar-i-Nakhilu,[71] Bandar-i-Kung,[72] Bandar-i-Abbas[73] (Gombroon), Hormuz[74] and Qishm,[75] all located on the Persian Gulf. Kharg, Hormuz and Qishm were islands near the coast.

Roads and Routes

Civil engineering, capable of constructing roads and highways, had already developed both in Iran and India a couple of centuries before the period of our study. Muhammad bin Tughlaq first constructed a trunk road from Delhi to the Deccan in the first quarter of the eighth century Hijri (fourteenth century). The Mughals and the sultans of the Deccan revived highway construction on a more methodical basis.[76] There were many routes facilitating traffic between Iran and India, e.g. from Kabul in the north to Baluchistan across Registan, Garamsier and down to Makran. This region was mountainous and extremely impassable and discouraged heavy traffic through most of its inlets. There are instances of visitors crossing the border through Registan and Garamsier. The defeated Mughal Emperor Humayun had proceeded to Persia from the same route.[77] The main highway that carried heavy traffic from the Mughal *subah* of Kabul was established during the times of Mughal Emperor Babur. It had become a highly developed route by the time of Aurangzeb. It had the following main stations from Kabul to the Deccan right up to Aurangabad and Ahmednagar:

1. From Kabul to Lahore   300 krohs (miles)
2. From Lahore to Akbarabad   300 krohs
3. From Akbarabad to Burhanpur   300 krohs
4. From Burhanpur to Aurangabad   80 krohs
5. From Aurangabad to Ahmadnagar   40 krohs[78]

This highway was guarded by outposts (*chaukīs*) after every twenty miles (10 krohs) and there were about 102 stations with 14 main stations:

1. Kabul
2. Peshwar
3. Lahore
4. Sehrand (Sar Hind)
5. Shahjahanabad
6. Akbarabad
7. Gwalior
8. Saronj
9. Between Saronj and Ujjain
10. Ujjain
11. Burhanpur
12. Between Burhanpur and Aurangabad
13. Aurangabad
14. Urdu-i-Mu'alla[79] (Daulatabad)

For traffic from the western coast of India, there were two trunk routes:

1. From Surat to Aurangabad and from Aurangabad to Hyderabad via Nanded and Kaulas.
2. From Panjim (Goa) to Hyderabad via Belgaum, Bijapur and Malkhed.[80]

PEOPLE

By the period of this study, due to several reasons, there had been large-scale migrations of people across linguistic and ethnic boundaries. In some cases, the interactions had minor and superficial influences on the social and cultural life of different ethnic communities. In other cases, the interaction was far deeper and more pervasive, so much so that an analysis of the diverse ethnic and linguistic groups that constituted state and society in Golkonda and Iran becomes a complex and difficult task. This section briefly introduces the different socio-linguistic groups in the Qutb Shahi and Safavid courts as well as their roles in the politics of the two regions.

The People of Golkonda

The Native Element

It is common knowledge to reiterate that Golkonda's population consisted of Hindus and Muslims. This broad classification is rather misleading. Both Hindus and Muslims consisted of different sects and groups sometimes hostile to each other. The Muslims were divided by their sectarian religious denominations such as Sunni, Shi'i or Mahdavis, while the Hindus were cross cut by differences of cult and caste. Hindus were broadly divided as Shaivites and Vaishnavites. Apart from them, there were also Vira Shaivite Lingayats and Jains. In addition to these major groups, there were hundreds of indigenous tribes who adhered to different practices, some of which could be traced to cults of Vedic and Dravidian origin.[81] These various castes and sects formed Golkonda society's basic structure and participated in organizations at different levels from village to state.[82]

The Deccanis

Another group of people who became native to the Deccan had arrived from parts of Central Asia and Arabia in different periods of history. Some had migrated from the southern coast of India where they had traded since ancient times. Others came from northern India during the time of the Tughlaqs. These Muslims were Sunnis and Sufi in religious inclination. Many belonged to the Qadiri order (*silsilah*) of Sufis. They were conversant in regional languages and had developed a separate Indo-Persian dialect called Dakani.[83]

Foreigners

Among the foreigners there were people from different regions who had settled down permanently or had been staying in the eastern Deccan for long periods of time. They may be classified into the following groups:

1. The Iranians or *āfāqīs*:
   Most of the nobility was drawn from this group and 80 per cent of the supervisory staff in Golkonda's administration was from Iranian stock.

2. The Turks or Turkmen:
   They were either warriors[84] or slaves.[85]

3. The Abyssinians (*habshīs*):
   Those Abyssinians who had attained the rank of nobility during the times of the Bahmanis maintained their position during the Qutb Shahi dynasty as well. Malik Mansur Khan Habshi was first appointed a *vazīr* and subsequently promoted as *Mir Jumla*.[86] Some of the Abyssinians were warriors (*jangjū*) and were given a place in the seventh rank of the Majlis.[87] The rest were slaves (*ghulām*).[88]

4. Afghans or Pathans:
   They were exclusively warriors or horse-traders.[89]

5. Arabs:
   The term Arab included those who were not Sayyids (*sadāt*). Sayyids were of a highly respected class and were teachers, leaders or nobles of high rank. The Sayyids hailing from Iran were all Shi'i.
   Other Arabs were not necessarily Shi'i. Most of them were warriors. They had their place in the seventh rank of the Qutb Shahi Majlis with the Turks, the Pathans, the Brahmins and others.[90]

6. Iraqis:
   There are not many references to Iraqis; however, the few that exist show that they were persons of high skill and held positions such as builders (*mi'mār*), architects (*tarrahān*), artists (*naqqāsh*), physicians (*hukamā*) and soldier.[91]

7. Armenians:
   They were all Christians and were generally physicians, civil engineers, architects and traders. Considerable numbers seem to have settled in Golkonda.[92]

8. Georgians or Girjis:
   Sometimes they are sub-classified as Caucasians (*qafqāzī*) or Circassians (*chirkas*). The Persian slave poet Kaukabi Girji, who had

come to Golkonda was Circassian.[93] The Georgians were mostly slaves.[94]

9. Tajiks:
    They had the same stature as the Turks.[95]

10. Dutch (*valandez*):
    They had settled on the Coromandel coast, where they had established factories and were carrying on trade. They promoted overseas trade from Golkonda.[96]

11. Danes (*dighmār*):
    The Danes too carried on their business on the coastal parts of the Sultanate and promoted overseas trade from India across the regions of the Indian Ocean.[97]

12. English (*angrez*):
    The English merchants had started their business in Golkondá at the beginning of the seventeenth century and established their factories at St. Thomé.[98]

13. Portuguese (*firangī*):
    The Portuguese had a presence in Golkonda but the sultanate was not included in their maritime empire. Private Portuguese traders had settled on the sultanate's coasts to promote their trade with the regions of the eastern Indian Ocean.[99]

The Indigenous Elite

Apart from various castes and sects discussed above, the Brahmins and then the Reddis constituted an indigenous class, which participated in local administration and affairs of the state. They commanded a two-fold hold in Golkonda.[100] First, they had immediate control over the agrarian system and set themselves up in various functions as village officials—Nayakvaris,[101] Manivars,[102] Deshpande,[103] Kulkarnis,[104] Thalkarnis,[105] Desais,[106] Patils,[107] Dharvis,[108] and others. Above them were small Hindu potentates (*sardārān-i-hunūd*) who maintained a considerable influence in local politics.[109] Second, these elites occupied a place in the Qutb Shahi Majlis and held administrative positions such as that of a State Secretary (*dabīr*)[110] or District Revenue Collector (*majmu'ādār*)[111] or an Assessor (*sharh navīs*).[112] During the last days of the kingdom, the posts of chief minister and finance minister were held by Akkanna and Madanna. There is also evidence of them working as *havāldārs* (keepers), *harkāra* (mailmen) and in other similar positions at low ministerial and executive levels. The fact that the Brahmins who had knowledge of Persian were entitled to receive a large stipend suggests that the indigenous elites were encouraged to join service at the ministerial level of administration.[113] The peasantry, artisans, merchants, artists, bankers, architects and physicians were all predominantly natives.[114]

The leaders of these professions had their connections with the nobility and also had access to the court.

The Nobility

All the *sarkārs* and their subdivisions were farmed out to the nobles of Iranian origin. It is an interesting aspect of Qutb Shahi administration that the agrarian system, which was a continuation of the elaborate system implemented by the Kakatiyas and the Rayas of Vijayanagar, remained basically unchanged. In principle, everything belonged to the sultan who had farmed out various administrative divisions of the sultanate to his nobles of foreign (predominantly Iranian) origin. Such nobles received a part of land revenue from the peasantry through landlords by way of *peshkash*. They maintained law and order in their jurisdiction, occasionally taking harsh measures. They pressurized landlords for the payment of land revenue due from them.[115] The actual ownership of land remained with the indigenous landlord. A close examination of this situation reveals the relations between the native and the foreign sections of population, and what fell under the jurisdiction of each of these groups. The role of the Iranian element in Golkonda's political and diplomatic affairs can be well appreciated through an observation of the structure of the Qutb Shahi Majlis discussed below.

Majlis

The Qutb Shahi Majlis was a bicameral institution, the lower chamber of which was called Majlis-i-Daulat Mahal, which was mostly a private consultative body of the sultan.[116] The upper chamber was the Grand Majlis (variably attributed as supreme or grand) and was the chief assembly of the state. Although Iranians dominated the composition of the Majlis, it is interesting to note that some of those who were naturalized in the Deccan were also appointed as its members. Even ambassadors and visitors of different states were assigned seats in the forefront of the Majlis. A layout of the Majlis during the reign of Sultan 'Abdullah Qutb Shah is briefly outlined below to illustrate the dominance of the Iranian element in the body:

Row 1. About 100 persons who were the choicest of the elite and who were closely associated with the sultan occupied the first row. Such members of the first rank were called the Royal Members (*majlisiyān-i-hūzūr*). All those members were Iranians with a few exceptions.[117]

Row 2. The ambassadors of Iran, Hindustan and of other major states sat in the second row.

Row 3. In the third row stood the members of the Majlis-i-Daulat, largely made up of the descendants of the members of the Grand Majlis.

Row 4. In the fourth row stood the *silahdārs* (armed military officers) and *havāldārs* (keepers and deputies). Most of them were Iranians.

Row 5. In the fifth row stood the *sar-i-naubat* (chief of kettle-drum) and the men of the Royal Retinue. Most of them were Iranians.

Row 6. In the sixth row, places were assigned to the Turk and Abyssinian military officers, the Deccanis and the Brahmins.

Language

As mentioned earlier, Golkonda was a land of Telugu-speaking people. Telugu was a richly developed language with many regional dialects and was the only effective medium of communication in all parts of the sultanate.[118] The Qutb Shahi monarchs like Ibrahim Quli Qutb Shah and Muhammad Quli Qutb Shah were well conversant in Telugu. Telugu literature flourished in Golkonda.[119]

Persian was the language of the court, nobility and administration. The indigenous writing castes, especially Brahmins who learnt Persian, were entitled to receive a stipend.[120] The Qutb Shahi court and the palaces of the sultans and nobles were the rendezvous of Iranian intellectuals, literati, historians and *mujtahids*.

Deccanis spoke and wrote in the Dakani language and devoted their creative talents to this idiom. As a result it developed into a rich literary medium, especially creating a wealth of Sufi literature.[121] While the contribution of Golkonda's elite to the Persian language and literature is certainly large and valuable, their contribution to Dakani was more creative and significant. The synthesis and amalgamation of Golkonda and Iranian thoughts, sentiments, faiths, values, idioms and culture was most apparent in Dakani literary circles.[122]

Additionally, many Europeans who settled on the Coromandel coast spoke a variety of languages. Since they had to deal with the nobility and the court as well as the local people in the course of trade, many of them attempted to learn Persian and sometimes even Telugu. They needed translators and interpreters. In such situations, there was constant need for translation and interpretation by those who were conversant in more than one language (*dubāsh*). There were many persons in Golkonda, both native and foreign, who knew several languages and could serve in this capacity.

Religion

The Qutb Shahi nobility was predominantly Shi'i and wielded great influence over the court. Religious discussions within the Shi'ite point of view were conducted in the court especially from the times of Muhammad

Qutb Shah onwards.[123] Under the influence of these nobles, the Shi'i population was concentrated in urban areas. The Sunni elite were pushed aside and were at times detached from the body politic. Consequently, the Deccanis and the Sunnis turned to the Sufi monasteries (*khānqāhs*), where they received their religious education and, spiritual and social guidance.

The People of Iran

Safavid Iran had a population composed of heterogeneous groups integrated with each other. Since ancient times, Iran and India shared common ethno-linguistic traits due to the migration of various groups such as the Aryans (who had migrated from parts of Turkestan and settled almost all over Iran). In different periods of time, the Greeks, the Mongols, Turkmen and the Arabs ruled over Iran. In addition to the above elements, there were, of course, many tribal communities in Azerbaijan, Kurdistan, Kerman and Khorasan that constituted the bulk of the rural population.

Urban Iran under the Safavids had the following main elements in its population, the proportion of which varied from province to province— the Indo-Aryans, the Arabs and the Turks.

The Indo-Aryans

Agriculturists and pastoralists who spoke Indo-Aryan languages constituted one of the groups of Safavid society. Feudal hierarchies determined the social, economic, and occupational structure and the status of the Iranian peasantry, who were the main source of revenue.[124]

There were many traditional industries in Iran that had been developed by the families of artisans. These goods were traded overland across Central Asia and via sea across the Indian Ocean. Whether it was glass, gold, iron or clay, Persian artisanal products were richly adorned and sought after by merchants and patrons.

The Iranian artisanal communities did not adhere to their professions by caste, as was the case in Golkonda. Rather, different geographic regions produced specific kinds of artisanal products due to the resources available in their immediate environs. These traditional industries paved the way for bazaars all across the region and even stretched overseas. The Indo-Aryan Iranians, the Arabs and the European merchants governed these bazaars.[125]

The Arabs

Since the conquest of Iran by the Arabs in the seventh century and the advent of Islam, the Iranian population and its religious, linguistic and ideological features underwent drastic changes. By this time, different ethnolinguistic groups in Persia were considerably mixed with the Arabs, particularly the nobility. The Sayyids were held as superior because it was believed that their lineage was connected with the Persian royalty on the one hand, and the household of the Prophet on the other. They occupied a distinguished position in society as religious leaders, preceptors, educationists, diplomats and statesmen. They held seats in the Majlis as well. Most of them were scholars and men of letters of high stature who dominated intellectual circles.[126]

The Turkmen

The Turkmen tribal complex is one of the most important aspects of the history of Central Asia. Although tribal orders were governed by an unwritten law, there was constant struggle among them to maintain their power and distinct identities. Tribal relationships of alliance and rivalry followed traditional principles and, more often than not, were marked by hostility. Many of the Turkmen were attracted by the pastures and protective highlands of Iran and had migrated there. They were well accustomed to a life of hardship and served as the backbone of different rival armies. Some Turkmen attained high positions among the Iranian nobility and most of them had their appanages in parts of Azerbaijan. The Aq Quyunlus and the Qara Quyunlus rose to the status of the rulers of Iran challenging and defeating the Jalayirs, the Chaghtais and the Sherwanshahs.

The Turkmen tribes had settled not only in Iran but also in the Ottoman Empire and in the parts of Transoxiana. They were originally orthodox Sunnis, but the clans that were devoted to the Safavid household gradually became orthodox Shi'i, joined the Qizilbash order and grew to dominate it.[127]

The Nobility

The structure of the Safavid nobility was basically the same as the one built up by Shah Isma'il, at least throughout the sixteenth and seventeenth centuries.[128] It matured by the time of Shah 'Abbas I. There were two levels of nobility: one was the order of the state nobility and the other of Crown lands (*khāssah sharīfah*).[129] Even the Crown nobility played an important role in domestic and foreign policies and its members could be deputed as *elchis* (emissaries) to the other polities. No doubt such *elchis* were often the ruler's personal confidants but their role was no less than that of a formal state ambassador.

The Safavid nobility was an elaborate order having many vertical and horizontal relationships. It had nobles, officials and representatives of various clans, poets, literati, physicians and artists in its ranks. It could not be said in definite terms if all such elements had a place in the Safavid Majlis, nevertheless they were conveniently recognized as nobles and the ruling elite of Iranian society.

The grand nobles (*umara-i-'uzzām*) of the reign of Shah 'Abbas I were divided into two broad categories. The first category comprised various clans (*tawāif*) of the Qizilbash order, while the second group, though drawn from the same stock, was honoured with the titles of Khans and Sultans. It constituted the Crown land nobility (*mulāzimān-i-khāssah sharīfah*). The average strength of the first category was about seventy-two and that of the second twenty-one. Such nobles were generally assigned responsibility like that of a governor (*hākim*) of a province or a stronghold. The head of state administration after the Shah was the Prime Minister or *vazīr-i-āzam* who was further assisted by several other *vazīrs*. The next important administrative category was that of the Grand Accountant (*mustaufiān-i-'uzzām*) appointed throughout the state.[130]

Language

Iran is the home of Indo-Aryan, Semitic and Turkic languages as well as other dialects such as Turki, Gilaki, Luri, Bakhtiari, Kurdi, Mazandarani, Baluchi, Turkmani, Armenian, Assyrian, etc., which are still spoken in one part or the other of the country.[131] The Persian language developed as the most advanced and effective medium for all educational, scientific, administrative and political purposes, absorbing a profound influence of Arabic, and at the same time, assimilating influences of other dialects in variable proportions.

The brief and flexible structure of its grammar, its assimilative character and euphony made it equally widespread throughout Hindustan, regions of Transoxiana and the Ottoman territories. Thus it also functioned as a medium of diplomatic exchange. Despite its linguistic and territorial spread, and other merits it was, and still is, the language of the urban population. Keeping in view the rate of urban growth in Iran one may infer that not more than one-fourth of the people of Safavid Iran spoke Persian. Nevertheless in the context of diplomatic and cultural connections, the role of Persian is comparable both in Golkonda and Iran. Except perhaps for Arabic and Turki, other languages had little and indirect effect on other aspects of these relations. Arabic and Turki, which had usurped the educational and administrative jurisdiction of Persian in its homeland, eventually receded to make room for it during the Safavid period.[132]

Religion

Iran, on the eve of the Safavid revolution, was predominantly Sunni, which rapidly changed under the pressures of the ruling elite's predisposition towards the Shi'ite faith. The process of balancing Sunni and Shi'i elements was particularly fraught.[133] Apart from Muslims there were adherents of pre-Islamic religions as well. Among such faiths mention may be made of Zoroastrianism, the adherents of which were variously known as the Parsis, Atishparast, Gabr, or Majus who were all fire-worshippers. They followed an ancient faith, the influence of which was considerably assimilated by Islam in its new Iranian environment.[134] The tribals of Azerbaijan, Kurdistan, Loristan, Baluchistan and Khorasan adhered to different faiths but these are difficult to find in historical sources. Judaism and Christianity too existed in north-western and southern Iran from ancient times.

NOTES

1. For details see Ziauddin Ahmed Shakeb, 'The Black Sheep Tribe from Lake Van to Golconda', *Itihas—Journal of the State Archives Andhra Pradesh*, vol. III, no. 2, 1975, pp. 60–5.
2. *T.Q.S.*, fol. 24(a) to 25(b); Sherwani (Q), p. 9.
3. See Chap. 2, 'The First Phase—Recognition', pp. 29–34.
4. Shakeb, 'The Black Sheep Tribe', pp. 60–5.
5. See Chap. 4, 'Commercial Contacts', pp. 129–62.
6. *T.Q.S.*, fol. 24(a) to 25(a); Sherwani (Q), pp. 20–1.
7. *T.Q.S.*, fol. 26(a); Sherwani (Q), pp. 21–2.
8. These areas included Kaulas, Elgandal, Melangur, Warangal, Ramgir, Khammammet, Rajahmundry, Srikakulam, Kaulas, Medak, Golkonda, Koilconda, Pangal, Devarconda, Nalgonda, Kondavidu and Udayagiri; *T.Q.S.*, fol. 27(a) to 46(a), Sherwani (Q), Chap. I, pp. 1–52.
9. *T.Q.S.*, fol. 49(b) to 50(a); Sherwani (Q), p. 37.
10. For the details of the career of Jamshid see *T.Q.S.*, fol. 50(b) to 59(b); Sherwani, Chap. II, pp. 81–105.
11. *T.Q.S.*, fol. 60(b) to 62(a); Sherwani (Q), p. 99.
12. What was so far known as the Battle of Talikota has been correctly renamed as Battle of Banihatti in Sherwani (Q), p. 137.
13. *T.Q.S.*, fol. 62(a) to 102(b); Sherwani (Q), Chap. III, pp. 119–206.
14. *T.Q.S.*, fol. 102(b) to 136(a); Sherwani (Q), Chap. IV, pp. 257–334.
15. Sherwani (Q), Chap. V, pp. 385–418.
16. *Hadīqat*, p. 78.
17. Ibid., p. 167.
18. Ibid., p. 190.
19. Ibid., p. 231.
20. *'Amal* III, 213, Talqani, Letter no. 70.
21. See *Hadīqat* for his career up to 1053/1643. Also see Sherwani (Q), Chap. VI.
22. See Chap. 2, 'Sinking Sultanate', pp. 54–9.
23. *Zamīmah* from fol. 183(b) provides a vivid account of the reign of Abul Hasan, also see Sherwani (Q), Chap. VII, pp. 559–654.
24. *Ahsan-ul-Tawārīkh* of Hasan Beg Ramulu, pp. 221–2; Browne IV, p. 106; Sykes II, p. 159; Sarwar, p. 35.
25. *H.S.* III Part IV, pp. 28, 32, 34; *A.A.A.*, pp. 20–1; Sarwar, p. 39. For a full account of the early career and rise of Shah Isma'il, see the study of Ghulam Sarwar, *History of Shah Isma'il Safavi*, Aligarh Muslim University, 1939.
26. Browne IV, pp. 68–9, 74, 93, 236; Sykes II, pp. 159, 167, 171.

27. Browne IV, pp. 15–24, 54.
28. Ibid., pp. 64–5; Sykes II, p. 160; Sarwar, p. 60.
29. Ibid., p. 66; Sykes II; R.I., Chap. II and Appendix B; Sarwar, p. 66.
30. Ibid., p. 75; Sykes II, p. 163; Sarwar, p. 78.
31. Aftabchi, p. 54; also see Sukumar Ray, *Humayun in Persia*, Calcutta: Royal Asiatic Society of Bengal, 1948.
32. R.I., Chap. III, pp. 22–47.
33. Browne, pp. 95–6.
34. Here it may be interesting to note that according to Shaikh Abdul 'Ali bin Mahmud Tablaqi, Ibrahim Qutb Shah had endowed the sultanate of Golkonda to the holy shrine of Mashhad. Sultan Suleiman Mirza Safavi was appointed the *vali* of the endowed sultanate with his station at Mashhad by Shah Tahmasp Safavi. This act has not been verified by any official document and may not therefore be taken as politically significant, *Fihrist-i-Kutub Khana-i-Mashhad-i-Muqaddas II*, Fiqh, pp. 273–4, also see Qadri (I), pp. 171–2.
35. Sykes II, p. 170.
36. A.A.A., pp. 100, 171, 272; R.I., 51.
37. For Shah 'Abbas' subjugation of the Qizilbash, see *A.A.A. passim*.
38. A.A.A., p. 273; Browne IV, p. 104; Sykes II, p. 173.
39. Sykes II, p. 174.
40. Ibid.
41. *A.A.A., passim*.
42. Sykes II, p. 176.
43. R.I., p. 68.
44. Sykes II, p. 181.
45. A.A.A., p. 757; Sykes, p. 211.
46. Ibid.
47. For details see Chap. 2, pp. 28–92.
48. R.I., p. 110.
49. Sykes, p. 212.
50. Ibid.
51. The boundaries given here are tentative. For a full discussion on the territorial expanse of Golkonda see map and note in appendix.
52. Ibid.
53. These terms have been well defined by H.H. Wilson in his *A Glossary of Judicial and Revenue Terms* and frequently occur in most of Qutb Shahi documents preserved in the State Archives Andhra Pradesh and in contemporary chronicles. Also see note on the map of Golkonda.
54. *The Historical Atlas of Iran* draws an eastern border that touches Balkh and Kabul but leaves both outside of Safavid domains. One contemporary writer, Muhammad Mufid Mustaufi, however included Balkh within Safavid territories and extended the frontiers even beyond Talqan in the east and Hazarasb in the north-east. Similarly, he includes Lake Van, and Armenia up to Arzanjan in Safavid Iran, see *Ausaf*, fols. 115, 132, 137, 152 and 212; Iran Atlas Pl. 21. See note on the map of Iran in appendix.

55. *Ausāf*, fols. 15, 56, 111, 135; *Mumālik*, fol. 90(b). Also see their expanse in various narrations of *Matla'* and *H.S.*
56. *Ausāf*, fols. 1–13.
57. *Early Records*, pp. 61–84; Fryer, pp. 46–7; Thevenot, p. 142; Scott Atlas, Pl. 9; Master I, p. 241.
58. Thevenot, p. 148; Bowrey, pp. 51–3; Schouten I, p. 489; Hamilton I, p. 369; Scott Atlas, Pl. 9, *Relations*, p. 3.
59. *Hadīqat*, p. 167; Bowrey, pp. 53, 55; Times Atlas, pp. 77–8; *T.Q.S.* (Briggs), p. 112.
60. *T.Q.S.*, fol. 14–70; *Hadīqat*, pp. 71–6; Talqani, pp. 96–7; Master I, pp. 265–97; Bowrey, pp. 60–4; Schouten I, p. 91; Hamilton I, p. 370; Mackenzie, pp. 88–99; Scott Atlas, Pl. 24; *Waqāi'* dated 8th Muharram 1072/24th August 1661; dated 23rd Safar 1072/8th October 1661.
61. Vizagapatam is also known by other names as Inzapatam, Bizipatam, Vasingepatam; Bowrey, p. 123.
62. Bowrey, pp. 123–4; Schouten I, p. 493; Master I, p. 298; Master II, p. 72 fn. 2, pp. 94, 115; Thevenot, p. 148; Scott Atlas, Pl. 26.
63. Bowrey, p. 123.
64. *Hadīqat*, pp. 94, 144, 168, 242; Bowrey, p. 124, fn. 1.
65. Tavernier I, p. 199.
66. *Ausāf*, fol. 240; *Naqshah*; *C.H.I.*, pp. 529–33.
67. Ibid.; Wilson, pp. 5, 72 and map; Iran Atlas, Pl. nos. 9–15, 19–20.
68. Ibid.; Wilson, pp. 51, 179–83 and map; Iran Atlas, Pls. 22–23.
69. Ibid.; Wilson, pp. 41, 140–1 and map; *C.H.I.*, p. 93; Careri, p. 196.
70. Ibid.; Wilson, pp. 72–4 and map; *Naqshah*; Iran Atlas, Pls. 13, 15.
71. Ibid.; Wilson, 140 and map; *Naqshah*.
72. Ibid., fol. 240; *Naqshah*.
73. *Ausāf*, fol. 240; Wilson, pp. 11, 140, 151–2; Bowrey, p. 216; Careri, p. 242; Tavernier, pp. 1–4; *C.H.I.*, pp. 8, 26, 31, 81; Iran Atlas, Pls. 21, 24.
74. *Ausāf*, fol. 242; Wilson, pp. 5, 10, 11, 19, 40–4; *C.H.I.*, pp. 8, 84; Iran Atlas, Pl. 21; *Naqshah*; Careri, pp. 196–9.
75. *Ausāf*, fol. 245; Wilson, pp. 5, 41, 44, 104 and map; *C.H.I.*, p. 299; *Naqshah*; Iran Atlas, Pl. 21; Careri, p. 196.
76. For the roads within Golkonda kingdom, see Sherwani (Q), pp. 493–502 and also Thevenot, pp. 150–1; Tavernier, pp. 115–21. For general facilities on highways and maintenance of roads in Golkonda see Bowrey, pp. 117–18.
77. R.I., p. 26; for details also see Raychaudhuri, pp. 64–5.
78. A *kroh* is approximately equal to two English miles.
79. *Dastūr*, fol. 2.
80. Tavernier, pp. 115–21 and map; *Dastūr*, p. 147 and map.
81. Persian chronicles refer to all classes of indigenous Indians invariably as 'Hindus'. The indigenous epigraphic sources bear ample information on various orders of cult, castes and subcastes of Andhradesa, which was covered by the Qutb Shahi Sultanate. Later during the second half of the nineteenth century, the Census reports of British India also contain broad classifications of Hindu castes and tribes. The basis of information in the following discussion is

mainly *Castes and Tribes of Southern Indian* by Thurston; *The Report on Census of Madras Presidency*, 1871, and *The Castes and Tribes of HEH the Nizam's Dominion* by Syed Siraj-ul-Hasan.

82. For an account of the corporate life in Andhradesa, based on inscriptional sources, see the work of Narasimha Rao, *Corporate Life in Medieval Andhra Desa*, Hyderabad, 1967. Though the book covers a period from AD 1000 to AD 1400, yet the contemporary and later sources attest that the corporate bodies of Andhradesa continued during the Qutb Shahi period; Madras Census, 1871.

83. The issue of the origin of the Dakani language is much disputed. For authoritative discussions on it see Sharma; for the presence of Deccanis in Golkonda see *Hadīqat*, pp. 39, 77, 81, 85, 92, 106, 111–15, 142, 148, 210–11, 258.

84. Ibid., pp. 46, 117, 137, 221.

85. Ibid., pp. 35, 42, 231.

86. Ibid., pp. 21, 33.

87. Ibid., pp. 46, 137.

88. Ibid., pp. 35, 45, 71, 110, 231.

89. Ibid., pp. 77, 85, 106–7.

90. Ibid., pp. 46, 77, 117.

91. Ibid., pp. 21, 26, 191, 201, 216, 221.

92. These facts have been ascertained from epitaphs of an Armenian cemetery located in the southern outskirts of Hyderabad city near Uppuguda Railway Station and adjacent to a place called Chatri Naka. The earliest date inscribed on an epitaph is 1052/1642. A cross is engraved on each epitaph. One grave was excavated by the Director of Archaeology Andhra Pradesh in the presence of the author in June 1972. A community burial of thirteen persons was discovered. There had been about forty-six tombs with large slabs of black stones each with an epitaph in Armenian. See section on Armenian cemetery in *Annual Report of the Department of Archaeology & Museums 1971–1972*, Government of Andhra Pradesh, 1985.

93. R. Shura, fol. 351.

94. *Hadīqat*, pp. 35, 77.

95. Ibid., p. 205.

96. For details, see Chap. 4, 'Commercial Contacts'. Also see 'Introduction' of *Relations*, pp. xxxvii to xlv and 'Schorer's Relation', pp. 51 to 65; Bowrey, pp. 2–3, 47, 54, 64, 88, 98, 105; Terpstra; Schouten; Raychaudhuri.

97. *Hadīqat*, p. 245; *Relations*, Chaps. XXV, XLI, pp. 2, 61, 92; *S.W.D.*, p. 5.

98. For details, see Chap. 4, 'Commercial Contacts'; see Talqani (A), Letter no. 20; *S.W.D.*, p. 17 with plate; *Relations*, Chap. XXIII and pp. 6, 55; Bowrey, p. 93; Fryer I, pp. 124, 132, and II, pp. 115, 243; Wheeler and the records of East India Company; Thevenot, pp. 135–6, 330.

99. *Hadīqat*, p. 225; *Relations*, Chaps. XX–XXV, pp. 3–5; Bowrey, pp. 2, 38, 45; Fryer I, p. 107; Thevenot, p. 135. A Portuguese cemetery was extant in Jahan Numa in Hyderabad until 1975 when it was demolished for extending a church building. Luckily, the tombstones containing inscriptions were saved by tucking them into the walls of the newly extended church at the suggestion

of the present author. The tombstones date mostly from the seventeenth and eighteenth centuries.

100. The role of Brahmins was appreciated and cursed both by the Golkonda elite and European merchants. See *Hadīqat*, pp. 34, 44; Bowrey, pp. 9, 16–17, 25, 36–9, 205; Fryer II, pp. 39, 80, 101; *Relations*, pp. 14–15, 55, 70.

101. A chief of a village, *Hadīqat*, pp. 30, 36, 94; Bowrey, pp. 38–9; *Relations*, pp. 2–3, 11, 79; Fryer II, pp. 36, 42; *F.S.D.S.*, p. 33; *T.Q.S.*, fol. 54(b).

102. *Maniwār*: A revenue accountant of a district. *Hadīqat*, pp. 23, 28, 48, 119, 168; Shakeb, pp. 11, 115–17.

103. *Deshpande*: A revenue accountant of certain number of villages, Wilson, p. 132; Shakeb, pp. 119–21; *F.S.D.S.*, pp. 33, 42; K.H.C., p. 49.

104. *Kulkarnī*: The registrar and accountant of a village who served as a liaison between the state and the cultivator. Wilson, pp. 53, 300; K.H.C., p. 41; *F.S.D.S.*, pp. 40, 42.

105. A landlord or a *zamindār* of a village. *F.S.D.S.*, pp. 36–9; K.H.C., p. 41; *F.S.D.S.*, pp. 40–2; K.H.C., p. 49.

106. The superintendent of a *pargana* and the Principal Revenue Officer of a District. Shakeb, pp. 13, 119; Fryer I, p. 301, II, pp. 4–6, 101; K.H.C., p. 30; *F.S.D.S.*, p. 33; K.H.C., pp. 11, 21, 33–4; *F.S.D.S.*, pp. 36–7, 40, 42.

107. The headman of a village who has the general control and management of the village affairs, Wilson, p. 407; Shakeb, pp. 120, 124; K.H.C., pp. 45, 41.

108. A man who controls the weighing of grain. *Hadīqat*, p. 144; *F.S.D.S.*, p. 40.

109. *T.Q.S.*, fols. 54(b); *Hadīqat*, pp. 94, 110, 119.

110. During the reign of 'Abdullah Qutb Shah I'timad; Rao Brahmin was appointed as *dabīr*.

111. Narayan Rao Brahmin as *majmu'ādār* and Sarv Rao Brahmin as *sharh navīs*. *Hadīqat*, p. 36.

112. For Hindu element in Majlis see *Hadīqat*, p. 46.

113. *Zafrah*, p. 175.

114. For an account of various agricultural and industrial communities of Golkonda see R. Narasimha Rao, *Corporate Life in Medieval Andhra Desa*, Hyderabad, 1967.

115. *Relations*, pp. 11, 32, 55–7, 81.

116. *Hadīqat*, pp. 167, 226. The Majlis of Daulat Mahal were much like the employees of the *khāssah-i sharīfah* of Iran.

117. Ibid., p. 44.

118. For details see P. Chenchiah and Bhujang Rao, *History of Telugu Literature*, Calcutta: The Heritage India Series, 1928.

119. For details see E. Vasumati, *Telugu Literature in Qutb Shahi Period.*

120. *Zafrah*, p. 175.

121. For details about the Deccani dialects see Nasiru'ddin Hashmi, *Dakan Men Urdu*, Lahore, 1952; *Dakhnī (Qadīm Urdu) Ke Chand Tahqīqī Mazāmīn*, Delhi, 1953.

122. Ibid.

123. *Khirqah*, fols. 131(b), pp. 56–7. Also see Chap. 3 'Ties of Religion and the Traffic of Ideas'.
124. For an account of the feudal pressure on Safavid peasantry see Lambton, Chap. V, pp. 105–29.
125. For details see Chap. 4 'Commercial Contacts'.
126. Majlis holds best evidence for this observation.
127. Ibid.; Hasan Beg Rumlu, *Ahsan-ul-Tawārīkh*, pp. 221–2; Sarwar, p. 35; Sykes II, p. 159; Browne IV, p. 106.
128. For the early structure of nobility during the times of Shah Tahmasp, see *A.A.A.*, pp. 104–6.
129. Ibid., pp. 761–3.
130. Ibid., pp. 763–7.
131. Zonis, p. 79.
132. Browne IV, pp. 13–15.
133. See Chap. 3, pp. 93–120.
134. Regarding Zoroastrianism in Iran see Sykes I, pp. 103, 397–98; Sykes II, pp. 12, 14. For the role of Christians it may be remembered that Shah Isma'il and his brothers were provided a secret refuge by Armenian Christians when they were young and the Aq Quyunlu chief, Rustam Mirza, wanted to put them to death, Browne IV, p. 49.

2

Political and Diplomatic Relations

POLITICAL AND DIPLOMATIC relations between two states can never be merely bilateral; neither can they be isolated from and unaffected by the relations they share with their immediate and distant allies and rivals. The political, cultural and economic relations of Golkonda and Iran with their immediate neighbours—the contemporary Deccan sultanates, the Mughals, the Uzbegs of Transoxiana and the Ottomans—had a profound bearing on the conduct of both states. Further a field, relations with the Russians, Dutch, Portuguese, French and English on one hand, and with the Egyptians, Abyssinians, Acehnese, Thai and Chinese on the other, affected the relations of these two polities. These contacts constituted a colossal network of sixteenth- and seventeenth-century diplomatic relations, the foundations of which were deep and intertwined with ethnic, linguistic and economic factors. The influence of these contacts, on the relations of Golkonda with Iran, were mostly indirect, therefore the political aspect of these bilateral relations may be isolated from this colossal complex for the convenience of this study. Yet it cannot be detached from Mughal India.

Safavid Iran and Mughal India would gradually attain the status of empires after their inception, whereas Golkonda, despite its manifold relations with contemporary states, did not rise above the level of a regional polity. But in its struggle for political ascendency, Golkonda developed cordial relations with Iran, which provided it with political and diplomatic support in critical moments. Such bilateral relations, between a regional Indian sultanate and a distant but powerful Safavid Iran, involved the risk of creating disharmony in the relations between the latter and Mughal India. The Mughals, with all justification, assumed a superior role in determining the character and scope of the relations of Golkonda with Iran. Thus the study of the relations, particularly political, between Golkonda and Iran, needs to be observed in the context of Mughal relations with Iran.

This chapter gives a chronological account of these three states from their birth in the early sixteenth century to the end of the seventeenth century when the Mughals

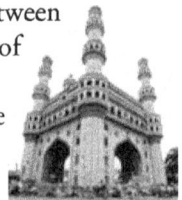

conquered the Golkonda Sultanate, effectively putting an end to trilateral diplomatic relations. The text begins with the earliest moment of contact and exchange between the Bahmani Sultanate in the Deccan and the Timurids in Central Asia. The shared genealogical, linguistic and geographic roots of these polities set the basis for the movement of emissaries, military officials and diplomats across the domains of their political descendants—the Qutb Shahis, the Safavids and the Mughals. The earliest phase involved the problem of mutual recognition. As each new state emerged, it sought the acceptance of pre-existing polities and faced unique challenges in attaining political recognition. In the decades following the foundation and recognition of these three states, there were also times when the evidence of diplomatic contact is nominal or the few available sources do not discuss the arrival and reception of embassies. The trilateral diplomatic relations entered a period of stasis at times, when each of the states dealt with an internal political crisis or were preoccupied with military challenges against other rivals. In the earliest decades of the seventeenth century, there were also instances of a delicate balance of power among the three polities. Over several decades, the reigning monarch's temperament, his ambitions and immediate political conditions determined the purpose of each embassy and had distinct repercussions on each polity. In the latter half of the seventeenth century, epistolary evidence opens a window into the secret correspondence of royal travellers, the volatile political negotiations between heads of state and diplomatic crises that unfolded among all three states. As a result of the constant exchange of emissaries, political expectations and obligations among the Safavids, Mughals and Qutb Shahs accumulated and evolved over the course of the period under study.

Recognition—The First Phase of Relations

From their moment of birth, Golkonda, Safavid Iran and Mughal India faced unique but similar challenges as they sought recognition from pre-existing states. The forms and methods of recognition were variable and each new ruler encountered distinct political conditions within and around his domains.

As stated in the Introduction, Sultan Quli, a descendent of the Qara chiefs and a recent migrant to the Deccan, founded the Qutb Shahi kingdom in Golkonda in a province of the declining Bahmani kingdom.[1] Sultan Quli Qutb Shah and his descendants had to rule over subjects of different ethnicities, religion and language, with the help of an elite that they drew from their homeland in Central Asia. Other Deccan kingdoms also grew on more or less similar foundations, and were often a source of support for each other during periods of political duress.[2] The relations between these sultanates were extremely changeable. At times they were in alliance, at others they were hostile to each other. Nevertheless, Golkonda, Bijapur and to some extent Ahmednagar maintained a uniform policy with respect to their relations with Iran, as all three shared similar challenges and situations vis-à-vis other states beyond their borders.

In contrast, Safavid Iran faced an acute crisis of legitimacy as it emerged after years of political turmoil among Turkic, Mongol and Persian elements. Shah Isma'il revolted in 905/1499, claiming to be a Sayyid with the blood of the last Sassanid Emperor of Persia, Yazdegird III.[3] At the beginning of the sixteenth century, the Safavids were up against their own supporters who were of mixed linguistic and religious descent and also faced powerful rivals at their borders. Mongol and Turkic elements, were either driven to the lands beyond Sayhun or Sirdarya[4] towards India or militarily incapacitated. The Safavid rulers established a state based on religion, emphasizing their descent from 'Ali, the son-in-law of the Prophet.[5] Responses to external threats and changes within the Safavid state would force the migration of different populations from its domains, many of whom moved to the Deccan sultanates. Collaboration with Golkonda and other Deccan kingdoms would be an important step in the internationalization of Safavid political ideology.

While Safavid Iran and the Deccan sultanates were in the initial stages of stabilization, the Chaghtai prince Babur was in quest of a kingdom. After his desperate efforts in Transoxiana and Khorasan, he set out for India. Babur defeated Ibrahim Lodi in Delhi and laid the foundation of the Mughal Empire in 932/1526. A little more than a century earlier, the Chaghtai dynasty's founder, Timur, had reached Delhi and received allegiance from the rulers of north and south India. Firoz Shah Bahmani was quick to submit his allegiance to Timur and encouraged his plan to send one of his sons to rule over India with the promise that the Bahmanis would come forward with military aid. Timur, pleased with the monarch's loyalty, issued a *farmān* (order), assigning Firoz Shah with the title of 'well-wishing son' (*farzand-i-khair khwāh*).[6] However, Timur's descendant, Babur, destined to come to India, encountered a different set of challenges when he founded the Mughal dynasty nearly a hundred years later.

It was particularly difficult for Safavid Iran to secure its dominions and make claims to sovereignty, despite Shah Isma'il's use of his sacred descent for political objectives. His lineage from a dervish family and claims to Sayyid status could not ensure actual political recognition due to several reasons. The Safavid state was unrecognized by its arch-rivals and closest neighbours, the Uzbegs and Ottomans, both of whom were Sunni. Shah Isma'il Safavi had sought to eliminate Turko-Mongol influence in Persia, a move that rendered him ideologically isolated and hostile to the major and minor political entities all around his frontiers. It was this situation that led the Safavids to look far and wide, away from their immediate neighbours, to distant states with similar sentiments and ambitions in order to forge political alliances. The Uzbeg chief Shaybani Khan, a direct descendant of Genghis Khan, was perhaps the first ruler who contemptuously refused to recognize Shah Isma'il as a legitimate monarch. He sent him a lady's veil and a beggar's bowl, advising him to follow his father's profession, namely, the life of a dervish.[7] Although Shah Isma'il eventually defeated Shaybani Khan in the Battle of Marv in 916/1510, his derisive response indicates that Shah Isma'il faced obstacles to gain recognition. Similarly, the Ottoman Caliph Selim I was determined to crush the upstart Safavid dynasty and the heresy it represented. He massacred 40,000 out of a total of 70,000 Shi'is residing in his domains and launched an attack on the western territories of Safavid Iran, leading to the famous Battle of Chaldiran of 920/1514. In this battle, Iran lost Kurdistan and Dayar-i-Bakr. Shah Isma'il regained other parts occupied by Selim I. The motive of this confrontation was to deliver a setback to the Safavids and their ideological movement.[8] The Ottomans refused to recognize the spirit of this movement and continued to oppose it over the next few centuries. In contrast, Mughal recognition of the Safavids was far more plausible and unfolded very differently due to three reasons. First, Safavid Iran preceded Mughal India, therefore as a new state it was not in a position to recognize others, but rather it was in need of recognition. Second, Babur was under personal obligation to Shah Isma'il.[9] Third, in spite of his aversion, Babur probably realized that Safavid Iran was far stronger and more stable than he was.[10]

Interestingly, Chaghtai chroniclers, right from the times of Timur, had been stating emphatically that the sway of Timur and his descendants extended over India.[11] However fanciful the statement may be, it shaped the aspirations of Chaghtai princes and Babur's ambitions. Undoubtedly, Babur never thought of himself as less than a *pādshāh*. Though Babur won and lost several battles, he was always a king without a kingdom or in quest of a kingdom.[12] Timurid descent ensured Babur's claim to kingship and political recognition by his contemporaries.

In peninsular India, for Golkonda and other Deccan sultanates, the issue of recognition was far more intricate. The Deccan sultanates shared a similar problem of recognition as they had drawn their sovereign authority from a single but declining Bahmani sultanate. The absence of a unifying authority in north India may have allowed the Deccan successor states to emerge as independent sovereigns. The divisible nature of a former singular sovereign authority, fragmentation of a consolidated territorial jurisdiction and the drawing of walls between the people of one and the same region were all artificial measures that rendered political recognition considerably difficult. Marathi and Kannada-speaking areas were unevenly divided between the Nizam Shahs and Imad Shahs on one hand, and 'Adil Shahs and Barid Shahs on the other. Golkonda's domains were also linguistically quite distinct and diverse, and comprised mainly of Telugu-speaking people in the eastern Deccan. Sultan Quli's efforts to carve a kingdom out of the Bahmani Sultanate in this region had no immediate historical continuity and marked the emergence of a new political entity.[13] In their early years of inception therefore, the Central Asian rulers of these Deccan kingdoms were not necessarily seeking the recognition of their native subjects, but the approval of other Islamic polities around them.

Sultan Quli Qutb Shah's problem of recognition was inexorably linked to forging ties with the Safavids and Mughals. It is worth mentioning here that the Bahmani monarchs had been recognized by the Ottoman Caliphs and by the household of Timur.[14] Perhaps looking upon this as a precedent as well as to forge a religious and ideological affinity, Sultan Quli turned to Safavids, who had begun to send their emissaries to the Deccan. Recognition within the subcontinent was, however, more urgent than acceptance by Safavid Iran. This became imperative once Mughal rule was established in north India, and Sultan Quli Qutb Shah as well as the other Deccan sultans did not delay seeking Babur's approval. Although Babur had set up his government in north India much after the formation of the Deccan sultanates and was a new political contender in India, it would seem that he urgently needed to be recognized by the self-styled sultans of the Deccan. But as Timur's descendent, he was perhaps more likely to be accepted among his peers than those who had carved out states in the Deccan before his arrival.

It may also be kept in view that the Bahmani kingdom, however nominal, was still in existence at the time, which probably prevented the Mughals from recognizing the Deccan sultans. Soon after his conquest of Hindustan, Babur made an observation of the political conditions prevalent throughout the country. Regarding the Deccan, he observed that the Bahmani monarchs were left without authority and their 'great Begs' had laid hands on the entire Deccan and demanded whatever they wanted.[15] This observation clearly indicates that as late as in 932/1526, Babur recognized the Bahmanis, although they were politically weak by then, and regarded the sultans of the Deccan as mere 'Begs'.

Both the sinking Bahmani ruler and the aspiring potentates of the Deccan recognized the political clout associated with Babur's Timurid ancestry and quickly sent their embassies (*rasūl*) with letters expressing loyalty to him.[16] The last of the Bahmani monarchs, Kalimullah, sent a letter to Babur through a confidant, who proceeded on the mission under disguise. Shah Kalimullah informed Babur that unfortunately his old servants (*naukarān-i qadīmī*) in various parts of the Deccan had become exceedingly oppressive and had kept him under surveillance. He requested Babur to come to his rescue and get him released from their oppression. In return he promised to cede Berar and Daulatabad to Babur. The new Mughal emperor could not, however, concede to the Bahmani sultan's request.[17] He had already invited Sayyid Deccani, also known as Shah Tahir to dinner, the *elchi* of the Nizam Shahs, who had called upon Babur earlier. This gesture of courtesy, however, cannot be construed as recognition, because Babur was aware that the Bahmanis were still the sovereign *de jure* in the Deccan. He seems to have politely and tactfully avoided the issue of recognizing the Deccan sultans as independent political sovereigns.

Similarly, Safavid Iran's recognition of the Bahmani Sultanate prevented it from accepting the new Deccan successor states until as late as 924/1518.[18] In Jumada 921/1515, an embassy from Shah Isma'il Safavi arrived at the Bahmani court with a letter and gifts of costly clothes, jewellery and Arabian horses. In addition, he also sent the *tāj-i shāhī*, which was representative of Twelver Shi'ism (*Asna 'Asharī*). Under the influence of Sunni amirs like Qasim Barid,[19] Sultan Mahmud Shah Bahmani seems to have ignored the embassy.[20] According to Tabataba, both the Shah and the military (*sipāh*) of the Bahmani kingdom were by that time Sunnis. Nonetheless, the embassy was a tacit acknowledgement of Bahmani sovereignty in the Deccan. It also showed that the Safavid court did not recognize the independent Deccan states that were now coming into being.

The earliest evidence of a Deccan sultanate embracing Shi'ism and seeking political recognition from Safavid Iran comes from the 'Adil Shahi Sultanate of Bijapur.[21] Isma'il 'Adil Shah had already sent Sayyid Ahmad Haravi to Iran between 914/1508 and 920/1514.[22] Mahmud Shah Bahmani however, had discourteously treated and dismissed the Iranian embassy of 921/1515. The Iranian *elchi*, therefore, then moved towards Bijapur and was received by Isma'il 'Adil Shah, who arranged for his return through Dabhol.[23] Bijapur's courteous treatment of this embassy pleased Shah Isma'il Safavi. It can be surmised that the Iranian *elchi* reported on the political decline of the Bahmanis, the overwhelming domination of Sunni amirs at the court and the autonomy of 'Adil Shah and other Deccani rulers who were anxious for recognition. Thus about two years after his embassy to the Bahmani court in 951/1515, Shah Isma'il Safavi sent another embassy under Ibrahim Beg Turkman to Isma'il 'Adil Shah. This was the first embassy Safavid Iran sent to the new Deccan sultans that arrived at Bijapur in 925/1519. Ibrahim Beg Turkman brought with him precious gifts and a letter, which was a formal declaration of the recognition of 'Adil Shah as *pādshāh*.[24] This event marks a clear beginning of Safavid Iran's recognition of those Deccan sultanates that were also inclined towards the Shi'ite faith.

In Golkonda, Sultan Quli was a bit more scrupulous than Isma'il 'Adil Shah in shifting his political allegiances and only gradually followed the bold steps that other Deccan sultans had taken. As early as 918/1512, he had openly declared his adherence to the Shi'ite faith and dropped the name of Mahmud Shah Bahmani from the *khutbah* (Friday sermon) read

in his provinces. He seems to have keenly observed the Safavid Movement
in the context of the Deccan politics and Indo-Iranian relations.[25] After
the death of Mahmud Shah Bahmani in 924/1518, Sultan Quli too made
a formal declaration of his autonomy and introduced the name of Shah
Isma'il Safavi in the *khutbah* before his name.[26] This was clearly an attempt
on the part of an emerging Deccan Sultanate to please Safavid Iran. It can
be presumed that the Iranian embassy, led by Ibrahim Beg Turkman, sent
to the court of Isma'il 'Adil Shah, would have come to know of Sultan Quli
Qutb Shah's action. By 926/1520, Shah Tahir too arrived in Goa where he
met Sayyid Ahmad Haravi, who had just returned from Iran as an *elchi* of
Isma'il 'Adil Shah to the court of Shah Isma'il[27] and was escorted by a set
of horsemen, deputed by Burhan Nizam Shah.[28]

Sultan Quli deputed his first noteworthy *elchi* to the court of Babur
in the year 932/1526 with a letter felicitating the Chaghtai monarch in
establishing his rule over north India.[29] No evidence, Indian nor Iranian,
is available from the first quarter of the sixteenth century to verify if Shah
Isma'il accorded recognition to Golkonda. Nevertheless by the time of Shah
Tahmasp I, Golkonda had definitely attained the status of a recognized
sultanate in Indo-Iranian relations. However, even during the reign of
Shah Tahmasp I, there is no clear account of official relations between
Golkonda and Iran until 948/1541. By this period, Iranian sources begin
to report the presence of Deccani *elchis* (including ones from Golkonda) at
the Safavid court. These *elchis* presented ornate gifts and in return, they were
favoured with robes of honour, a bejewelled crown, horses and embellished
daggers.[30]

Although the Safavid chronicle *Tārīkh-i 'Ālam-i Ārā-i 'Abbāsī* records the
above mentioned events for the year 948/1541, later sources from Golkonda
seem to suggest diplomatic contact right from the times of Shah Isma'il
Safavi and Sultan Quli Qutb Shah, using the phrase 'the one in Iran and
the other in India' to refer to the exchange between the two states, claiming
that the two had been maintaining amicable relations and exchanging
envoys soon after the establishment of the Qutb Shahi Sultanate. This
could be a retrospective projection of the unfailing connections between
Golkonda and Iran but if true, it can be deduced that Iran recognized
Golkonda before 930/1524, i.e. prior to the death of Shah Isma'il I and
before Babur's arrival in India.[31]

Political Imbalance—The Second Phase

The fourth decade of the tenth century Hijri[32] was marked by many major
events in this trilateral history of relations. Shah Isma'il Safavi's demise in
the year 930/1524 in Iran, the death of Shah Kalimullah Bahmani in the

year 934/1528 in the Deccan and that of Babur in the year 937/1530 in Hindustan changed the course of events in both Iran and Hindustan, and had significant repercussions for Golkonda. At the age of eighty, Sultan Quli Qutb Shah had to find a plausible way to reorient his foreign policies, as the political climate in both Hindustan and Iran was not calm and peaceful and thus, uncongenial for the promotion of diplomacy.

In Iran, Shah Tahmasp was only ten years old when he ascended the throne in 930/1524. The young monarch had to face many difficulties from the very outset of his reign. The immediate trouble was the discord and bloodshed among the Istajlu, Taklu and Shamlu clans of the Iranian Qizilbash upon whom the young sovereign's political stability depended.[33] On the north-eastern frontiers he had to respond to a series of invasions by the Uzbeg chief Ubaid Khan, who had launched six major attacks[34] from the time of Shah Tahmasp's accession until 938/1532.

On the western side of his kingdom, Shah Tahmasp had to resist the aggression of the Ottoman Sultan Suleiman, a rival with whom he would fight at least four major wars.[35] Thus, the turbulent beginnings of Shah Tahmasp's reign did not permit him to entertain peaceful envoys from minor political entities.[36] Moreover, he was always away from his capital, engaged in negotiations with the envoys of warring neighbours. From the second half of the fifth decade of the tenth century Hijri,[37] he stayed at his capital Qazvin and promoted relations with other states.[38]

According to Iskandar Munshi, in the year 948/1542 *elchis* from the great rulers (*salatīn-i 'uzzām*) of the Deccan particularly from Nizam Shah, the *valī* of Ahmadnagar, and Qutb Shah, the *valī* of Golkonda, arrived at the Safavid court.[39] Experienced *elchis*, well-versed in the art of diplomacy, arrived at the Iranian court time and again to profess that their rulers were devotees to the household of 'Ali (*haidar-i-karrār*) and claimed themselves to be Shi'ites of the Twelve Imams. According to Iranian sources, these *elchis* asserted their loyalty and faith to the Safavid ruler with the argument that the *khutbah* was being recited with the names of the Twelve Imams and the Safavid monarch throughout their dominions. These *elchis* were received with all necessary protocol. The Golkonda *elchi* of 948/1542 received, among other things, a bejewelled *tāj* from Shah Tahmasp for Sultan Quli Qutb Shah.[40]

In Hindustan, Humayun, during his early career, showed an ambition to extend Mughal suzerainty over the Deccan. In 942/1535, he captured Ahmedabad and most parts of Gujarat, and intended to lay siege in Burhanpur. This was quite stressful for the Deccan sultans, all of whom requested Humayun in their humble petitions to spare Khandesh.[41] At the same time the Deccan sultans immediately formed a military alliance to defend themselves against Humayun and to protect Miran Muhammad Faruqi of Khandesh.[42] Sultan Quli Qutb Shah was part of this alliance. However, the allied Deccan forces eventually did not clash with Humayun, as he had to face the Afghans under Sher Shah.[43]

The rest of Humayun's tenure was full of turmoil and inundated with political problems. He faced many challenges, lost his kingdom in 947/1540 and fled to Iran. While in Iran, Humayun, because of his deep obligation to Shah Tahmasp, may have had to profess an ostensible acceptance of the Shi'ite faith. This moment of Mughal recession could not have gone unnoticed by Sultan Quli and his contemporary Deccan sultans, which rendered the Mughal sultan virtually ineffective in this relational diplomatic triangle. By the time Humayun had fled, an *elchi* from Golkonda was already in Iran in 1542. Humayun would eventually restore his suzerainty over Hindustan with Iran's help; however, in this moment of Mughal weakness, Golkonda sought to strengthen its alliance with the Safavids.[44]

The intervening tenure of Sher Shah (947/1540 to 952/1545) was short and expeditious. He had neither the time nor the resources to meddle in the affairs of the Deccan.[45] Nor did Sultan Quli, who was in a strong alliance with Iran, show any cognizance of Afghan suzerainty in north India. Sher Shah, who was against the Safavids, tried to work out an international strategy in alliance with the Ottoman Caliph Suleiman and the Uzbeg rulers of Transoxiana, to overthrow the Qizilbash movement and Safavid regime.[46] Although Sher Shah's design for the wholesale disposal of the Safavids by an internationally allied force was never realized, yet the very design should have alarmed Shah Tahmasp and the Deccan sultans. In these circumstances, Shah Tahmasp, exhausted by constant military conflicts, may have bargained for peace with the Uzbegs and the Ottomans. These new political equations thus created the conditions to strengthen relations between Golkonda and Iran. First, Iran may have preferred to have an anti-Afghan Shi'ite ally in the Deccan. Second, Golkonda aspiring to get recognized internationally sought to take advantage of the crisis between the Mughals and Afghans in north India.

During the rest of Sultan Quli's reign and throughout the period of his successors, Jamshid Qutb Shah and Subhan Quli, no account of political and diplomatic relations between Golkonda and Iran is traceable.[47] The relational triangle of politics was, for sometime, broken on account of the Deccan's political disregard for a weaker Hindustan on one hand, and the absence of balanced Mughal-Iranian relations on the other.

The political imbalance in these relations continued till the end of Humayun's reign in 963/1556. The Mughals remained morally obliged to the Safavids early in the reign of Akbar and up to the death of Shah Tahmasp in 984/1576. Shah Tahmasp had reduced Qandahar in 965/1558 when the Mughal emperor was barely fifteen years old. Although obliged to return Qandahar to Iran, Humayun had persistently avoided the issue and in fact, never handed it over to Shah Tahmasp in his lifetime.[48] It appears that even though Akbar wanted to retain Qandahar, his immediate reaction was to not object to Shah Tahmasp's conquest of the city. The young ruler's measured response may have to do with his sense of obligation towards the Safavids, who had aided his father during his exile. Apart from the issue of Qandahar, Shah Tahmasp had also been interfering in Akbar's internal affairs by recommending certain nobles to the Mughal court. Akbar, who was growing stronger, accepted his suggestions but in such a way that led to a stagnation in Mughal-Iranian relations from 972/1564 onwards.[49]

At the age of thirty-five Akbar was a powerful monarch. As soon as Shah Tahmasp passed away he retook Qandahar. Shah Isma'il II had succeeded Shah Tahmasp but reigned for a very short period. He was succeeded by his eldest brother Shah Muhammad Khudabandah Safavi, who was blind, in 985/1577. The twelve years that these two weak Safavids ruled facilitated the rise of the Uzbegs. The powerful Uzbeg chief 'Abdullah Khan, observing the weak situation in Iran, invited Akbar to join him in an alliance against the Safavids with the ultimate object of overthrowing them and dividing Iran between themselves. Akbar was disinclined to accept the proposal given his obligation to the House of Shah Tahmasp, who had helped his father Humayun and also because the Safavids were the descendants of the household of the Prophet.[50] It is likely that Akbar's real interest was in Balkh and Badakshan, his ancestral lands in Transoxiana, which 'Abdullah Khan Uzbeg now held. Akbar was, therefore, probably not pleased with the rise of the Uzbeg chief, although he continued to maintain peaceful relations with him. He could foresee that the rising Uzbegs could upset the balance of Mughal power and their relations with contemporary states.

It was, therefore, in Akbar's interest to protect Iran against the Uzbegs. He may have thought of helping Khudabandah against the unruly Qizilbash nobles and against Ottoman interventions, by extending military aid to him or even by going there himself to rescue the beleaguered Safavid ruler. Although this never happened, the course of events indicated a shift in the balance of power. During Akbar's reign, Golkonda was caught between a weak Safavid Iran and a powerful Hindustan. This imbalance in trilateral relations tended to discourage Golkonda's relations with Iran and marked the beginning of Mughal supremacy over the Deccan.

Ibrahim Qutb Shah, who succeeded to the throne of Golkonda in 957/1550, revised his policies towards both Iran and Hindustan. He does not seem to have entered into relations with Humayun (during his second tenure) or with Akbar until the death of Shah Tahmasp with whom he kept in touch for as long as he lived.[51] During the reign of Khudabandah, Ibrahim Qutb Shah realized that Akbar was extending his authority over the Deccan. Akbar had already received allegiance from Miran Mubarak Shah, the *valī* of Khandesh in 972/1564,[52] and from Murtuza Nizam Shah I, *valī* of Ahmadnagar in 981/1573.[53] With the Mughal frontier expanding, Ibrahim Qutb Shah, frustrated with a weak Iran, summarily sent his *peshkash* to Akbar in 985/1577, at the least to feign allegiance to the Mughals. Ibrahim Qutb Shah sent quite an impressive set of gifts in his *peshkash*, which included a fighting elephant of an unusual size named Fath Mubarak. On 27th Aban (Sha'ban) 985/October 1577, the *elchis* of Qutb-ul-Mulk brought the magnificent beast before Akbar. The animal looked so wild that it seemed impossible to ride it. But Akbar's mahout (*jahān pahalwān-i-ilāhī*) immediately jumped on its back and brought the beast to its knees in no time, to the surprise of the Qutb Shahi *elchis*.[54] Not only Ibrahim Qutb Shah, but all the other Deccan sultans submitted their *peshkash* to Akbar. This *peshkash* appeared to be voluntary rather than obligatory and included mostly gifts but hardly any cash.

Akbar soon realized that this declaration of allegiance was a pretense on the part of the Deccan states that simply wanted to gain time. He put this professed allegiance to test by commanding the Deccan sultans to carry out his orders. In Bahman (Zilqada) 987/December 1579, Akbar issued a *farmān* to the Deccan sultans who were regarded as the landlords (*marzbān*) of the Deccan, to subjugate the Portuguese (*firangīs*) who were hindering Muslim pilgrims on their way to Mecca.[55] This was a part of Akbar's programme of dislodging the Portuguese from their coastal strongholds. At the same time, Safavid Iran may have encouraged Portuguese action against Muslim pilgrims.[56] One may wonder if Golkonda and other Deccan sultanates were collaborating with the Safavids by aiding or ignoring Portuguese activities in the western Indian Ocean. Akbar's *farmān* was issued at the time when Iran was ruled by its weakest ruler Khudabandah, and the Deccan sultans had to stand their ground without any external support. This particular *farmān* had several implications. First, evicting the Portuguese would strengthen Mughal access to Indian ports. Second, it would put an end to Portuguese attempts to control shipping and trade. Third, it would crush Safavid Iran's bold policy of allying with the Deccan sultans and forging an informal alliance with Portuguese seafarers, who were interfering with Mughal trading activities. Lastly, by making the Deccan sultanates responsible for keeping eye on the Portuguese, Akbar wished to monitor the activities of coastal chieftains and foreign traders while testing the loyalties of subordinate regional states.

Regardless of whether or not Akbar succeeded in the above goals, this *farmān* created an atmosphere of fear among the Deccan sultanates. Even Golkonda, the frontiers of which were quite removed from Mughal territories, was so afraid of Mughal power that in less than three months after the issue of the *farmān*, Ibrahim Qutb Shah submitted another allegiance to Akbar. In Muharram 988/1580, he sent his *elchis* with valuable gifts and *peshkash* together with his petition (*'arzdāsht*) asserting his loyalty and attachment to the Mughal court.[57] Abul Fazl observed that though the landlords of the Deccan had resorted to sycophancy (*lābahgarī*) and flattery (*niyāyishguzārī*), they were not proving themselves so obedient in practice. But he also observed that Akbar's acceptance of *peshkash* and gifts relieved some of Ibrahim's anxiety to please the Mughal emperor.[58] Ibrahim Qutb Shah died in the year 988/1580 and was succeeded by his fourteen-year-old son Sultan Muhammad Quli Qutb Shah.

In the second half of the sixteenth century, the asymmetry in Mughal-Safavid relations had clearly favoured Iran. By the middle of Akbar's reign however, in the late sixteenth century, the Safavids were weak and Akbar pushed forward in the Deccan. For Golkonda, this shift meant that the initial phase of recognition allowed it to emerge as a regional, autonomous polity. When the balance of power, in Indo-Iranian relations weighed heavily in favour of Mughal Hindustan, Golkonda was once again in a precarious position as Akbar refused to recognize it even as a regional sultanate. Contemporary Mughal chroniclers describe the Qutb Shahis and other Deccan sultans as *marzbāns* or *hākims*.[59]

But Akbar did not translate his ambitions of bringing the Deccan under his sway through any military action. He deputed eminent, experienced emissaries who advised the Deccan sultans to submit their allegiance to the Mughal emperor. That strategy constituted a series of diplomatic missions from 991/1583 to 1000/1592,[60] during which period Akbar never took military action against the Deccan. Akbar's representatives on such missions, *khushūrs* or *wakhshūrs* (apostles) as they were called, were sent to intimidate the Deccan sultans and preach the inevitability of Mughal rule in their dominions.

In the year 996/1587, Shah Khudabandah Safavi surrendered his throne to his rebellious but promising eighteen-year old son 'Abbas Mirza Safavi, who commanded the confidence of the major Qizilbash sects.[61] This was the beginning of the re-emergence of a powerful Safavid Iran. Akbar surely realized the consequences of Shah 'Abbas I's accession particularly in the context of his (Akbar's) decision to cede Qandahar to the Safavids and mindful of his relations with the Deccan sultanates. He, therefore, expedited his campaigns in the Deccan by resorting to military intervention.[62] Mughal forces had already reached Gujarat as early as in 991/1583.[63] In 999/1590, Akbar deputed Sultan Murad to admonish the landlords of the Deccan since they continued to be defiant.[64] In 1001/1592 Shaikh Abul Faiz Faizi, was sent as *wakhshūr* to the Deccan.[65] The following year, in 1002/1594, Raja Man Singh was sent from Bengal to the Deccan and Sultan Murad was ordered to be ready for launching an attack on Ahmadnagar.[66]

Sultan Murad laid siege to Ahmadnagar in the year 1004/1595 but was resisted by an allied force of the Deccan sultans led by Chand Bibi of Ahmadnagar. An auxiliary force of 2,000 horsemen belonging to Sultan Muhammad Quli Qutb Shah led by Mihdi Quli Sultan Talish also joined the resistance. Mihdi Quli Sultan Talish drove the Mughal forces back for sometime and returned soon after to Golkonda disregarding subsequent developments on the battlefield of Sonepat (Ahmadnagar).[67] The siege ended and the Mughals dictated peace upon the defeated Nizam Shahis.[68] Still, at the end of Akbar's reign, the Mughal army could not fully control the situation and would carry out many more campaigns in the Deccan in the following decades, first under the leadership of Sultan Murad (d.1007/1598) and then, under Prince Daniyal till the destruction of the fort of Asir in the year 1009/1600.[69]

After this treaty, the position of the Nizam Shahs was reduced to that of a Mughal protectorate. The extended frontiers of the Mughal Empire now touched the fringes of Bijapur. Soon after the defeat of the Nizam Shahs, Ibrahim 'Adil Shah was the first to demonstrate submission towards the Mughals. According to Mughal sources, Sultan Muhammad Quli Qutb Shah too, showed an attitude of humility (*niyāzmandī*) and desired, along with other Deccan sultans, the deputation of an ambassador from the imperial court to his sultanate for the maintenance of congenial relations. But Akbar turned a deaf ear to that request for sometime. It may be inferred that Akbar did not immediately concede to their request for the obvious reason that the exchange of diplomats might justify the independent status of Golkonda. However, after a few years, he deputed Masud Beg to Golkonda to stay there as a Mughal political agent keeping an eye on the Deccan courts and imparting the message of Mughal supremacy.[70] In Shawwal 1013/1604, Akbar received *peshkash* from Sultan Muhammad Quli Qutb Shah, which included thirty elephants with golden ancillaries, bejewelled articles, and other rarities from Golkonda.[71] Akbar died in the following year on 12th Jumada II 1014/1605 and was succeeded by his son Nuruddin Jahangir.

In Iran, Shah 'Abbas, who succeeded to the throne in 996/1587, dealt with dissension amongst the nobility, Ottoman military aggression in the west and Uzbeg threats in the east. The development of relations with Hindustan or Golkonda was, therefore, not a priority. Shah 'Abbas first tried to negotiate peace with his main rival, the Ottoman Sultan Murad III, and made an attempt to recover Khorasan from 'Abdullah Khan Uzbeg.[72] Qandahar was then separated from Iran on account of the Uzbeg occupation of Khorasan. As mentioned earlier, Akbar could have easily taken over Qandahar during the reigns of Isma'il II or Khudabandah, but refrained from doing so out of obligation. However, he did not hesitate in annexing Qandahar while Iran was preoccupied with its arch-rivals.[73]

Shah 'Abbas I, ambitious to get stronger, seized the chance to improve relations with Akbar and the Deccan sultans.[74] By the late sixteenth century, Akbar was aging and his son, Jahangir, had rebelled while Shah 'Abbas grew stronger, particularly after his conquests of Khorasan in 1006/1597 and Herat in 1007/1598.[75] It appears that Shah 'Abbas I, a few years after his accession, sent an *elchi* named Asadullah Beg Tabrizi Kark Yaraq as a roving ambassador to the rulers of the Deccan. The title 'Kark Yaraq' (Chief of Ordnance) suggests that he was a military official who may have provided expertise to the Deccan sultans regarding important military matters. Asadullah Beg Kark Yaraq returned to Iran in the year 1005/1596 when Yadgar Sultan Rumlu too had returned from the court of Akbar. Asadullah Beg Tabrizi Kark Yaraq brought back with him numerous gifts sent by the Deccan sultans.[76]

Further details about the letters carried by Kark Yaraq and his mission in the Deccan are not available. Still, two things are definite. First, his deputation confirms Shah 'Abbas I's interest in Deccan affairs even during his troubled early career. Second, the *elchi* would have furnished detailed information regarding the Deccan courts to Shah 'Abbas I.

Qazi Mustafa, Golkonda's Envoy to Iran

In the above context of increasing Mughal intervention in the Deccan, the young Sultan of Golkonda, Muhammad Quli Qutb Shah, began to re-assess the nature and scope of his relations with Iran, especially in consultation with his *peshwā*, Mir Muhammad Mu'min Astarabadi[77] and the Majlis.[78] Ever since his accession, Muhammad Quli Qutb Shah had resisted the Mughals and sought relief only by offering them occasional *peshkash*. He also joined a military alliance with other Deccan sultans to resist them with force. Mughal chronicles note that on the battlefield of Sonepat (Ahmadnagar), the Golkonda army formed the left wing of the allied forces.[79] Safavid Iran always encouraged and appreciated such an alliance. It would also be the last alliance among the Deccan sultans. Mughal observers repeatedly criticized Golkonda's untrustworthy and fickle allegiance.[80] Sultan Muhammad Quli Qutb Shah constantly gauged the military strength of the Mughals on the one hand, and their diplomatic resourcefulness on the other. Like his ancestors, he too, looked towards Iran for help. Iranian diplomatic contacts may have included some sort of military help as well.

Muhammad Quli may not have expected to enter into diplomatic relations with Shah Khudabandah Safavi. He had keenly observed Shah 'Abbas' early years and took his time to evaluate the situation in Mughal Hindustan. Under intense political pressure, he desperately needed external political support. His hopes rested upon Safavid Iran's ascendency. Sultan Muhammad Quli Qutb Shah sent his first embassy led by Qazi Mustafa[81] to the court of Shah 'Abbas I. The Qutb Shahi *elchi* carried a letter from Sultan Muhammad Quli Qutb Shah addressed to Shah 'Abbas I.[82] The letter opens with prayers for the long life of the addressee and a score of beautiful phrases of ceremonial nature along with a few couplets of panegyric. These titles of address cannot just be viewed as conventions of ornate writing and often contain veiled references to contemporary diplomatic relations. For instance, Muhammad Quli concluded his admiration of Shah 'Abbas I by citing an Arabic couplet:

'Laqad tamm-al-kalām bimā aqūlu
Izā mā qultu jadda kum ur rasūlu'

(There ends the talk when I say that,
your grandfather was a Prophet)

At the end of the letter, he wrote a few couplets of praise for Shah 'Abbas I and sought his mercy. The letter ends with prayers for the perpetual existence of the Safavid kingdom and prayers to the Prophet and his household. Such diplomatic correspondence was often embellished with figurative and enigmatic phrases lest the letter be accidentally exposed to Mughal censors. The risk of censorship that Muhammad Quli Qutb Shah expressed indicates that his envoy had proceeded through the trunk route and had therefore to pass through the Mughal Empire on his way to Iran. The Golkonda sultan thus informed Shah 'Abbas I that the insurgents (*ahl-i-tughyān*), a euphemism for the Mughals, had been creating great disturbances for the past several years. This enigmatic reference was to Mughal military aggression in the Deccan from 1002/1593 to 1009/1600.[83] The reason for Mughal hostility, as explained by Muhammad Quli Qutb Shah, was the attachment of Golkonda for the Safavid dynasty. Further, he emphasized that this attachment was an avowed and established fact.

Sultan Muhammad Quli Qutb Shah made a fervent appeal to Shah 'Abbas I to take appropriate action, which would relieve Golkonda and other Deccan sultanates from Mughal oppression. He assured the Safavid ruler that all the Deccan sultans were adhering to the Shi'ite faith and were faithful to Iran.

At the end, Muhammad Quli Qutb Shah recorded his credentials for Qazi Mustafa, the *elchi* and the letter's bearer, and indirectly suggested that the *elchi's* actual mission would be conveyed orally.[84]

No record is available regarding the success and return of Qazi Mustafa. Nevertheless he seems to have conveyed the oral message quite effectively and enlightened Shah 'Abbas I about the situation in the Deccan and Golkonda's political problems. No immediate response from the Safavid monarch is available in the extant epistolary evidence. However, in the year 1012/1604 Shah 'Abbas I sent an *elchi*, Uighurlu Beg Sultan, to Golkonda.

Uighurlu Beg Sultan came to India by sea and landed at the port of Goa in 1012/1604. News conveyers (*manhiyāns*) of the port carried the information about his arrival to the Qutb Shahi court.[85] Sultan Muhammad Quli Qutb Shah honoured his arrival and deputed Mir Ziau'ddin Muhammad Nishaburi to receive the guest in Goa. The royal receptionist entertained the *elchi* in Goa and escorted him up to the borders of Golkonda kingdom with all the necessary protocol. At the border a team of nobles (comprising *amīrs, khāns, akābīr* and *a'yān*) gave the *elchi* a reception and they all moved towards the capital where Uighurlu Beg Sultan was allowed to appear before Sultan Muhammad Quli Qutb Shah at Kala Chabutra.[86]

At this reception, the *elchi* imparted Shah 'Abbas I's message of a long-lasting and sincere friendship with Muhammad Quli Qutb Shah. He then submitted Shah 'Abbas' letter to Sultan Muhammad Quli along with gifts which included a bejewelled *tāj*, a dagger with a belt; 500 full pieces of velvet, *firangī* (European) satin, garments with brocade and fabrics of exceptional quality in a variety of textures and colours, twelve pairs of carpets (*qālīn*) and forty Iraqi horses with bejewelled saddles and other innumerable valuable gifts. In the reception given by Muhammad Quli Qutb Shah, Uighurlu Beg Sultan and the men in his retinue were all favoured with robes of honour and gifts exceeding the prescribed requirements set forth in the Book of Protocol (*kitāb-i tashrifāt*). They were also provided with elegant palaces.[87]

The letter carried by this ambassador is not traceable but the purpose of this embassy is mentioned in contemporary chronicles. The mission of Uighurlu Beg Sultan, according to *Tārīkh-i-Qutb Shāhī*, was to 'express the attachment between the two dynasties and to strengthen their foundations of unity'.[88] Information supplied by Firishtah suggests that one of the missions of Uighurlu Beg Sultan was to establish matrimonial relations between the household of Shah 'Abbas I and Muhammad Quli Qutb Shah by uniting the latter's daughter in marriage with the former's son.[89] Sultan Muhammad Quli Qutb Shah had only one daughter, Hayat Bakshi Begam, and no other heirs. Perhaps the sultan may have not liked to part with his only daughter and in 1016/1607, he celebrated her marriage with his nephew Sultan Muhammad, son of Muhammad Amin, which the Iranian emissary Uighurlu Beg Sultan probably attended, given that he was still in Hyderabad in 1607.

Uighurlu Beg Sultan stayed in Golkonda for over six years and had ample opportunity to observe its internal affairs and the inter-sultanate relations in the Deccan, as well as their policies with the Mughals. Like Asadullah Beg Kark Yaraq, he also held a military rank in Iran and had come to Golkonda with 100 military elites (*ghāziyān-i 'uzzām*) who may have trained the Golkonda army. Over the course of his stay, Uighurlu Beg most certainly witnessed political factions and rivalries at the Golkonda court. Two Iranian veterans, namely, Mir Muhammad Mu'mina's *peshwā* and Mirza Muhammad Amin Shahristani as *Mir Jumla*, fully controlled the administration. Before the *elchi* departed, the unfortunate incident of Nabat Ghat took place in Hyderabad in about 1017/1608.[90] This incident was a debacle in which the *gharībs* (Arabs, Pathans and the Mughals) were ruthlessly slaughtered and their deaths were avenged thereafter by a massacre of the Deccanis, especially those who were in police and military services. Sultan Muhammad Quli issued a *farmān* for the expulsion of the Mughals and others, referred to in *Tārīkh-i Qutb Shāhī* as triflers or troublemakers (*hirzahgard*).[91] An organized revolt of the Deccanis immediately followed this event and sought to overthrow Muhammad Quli Qutb Shah and enthrone his brother Khudabandah.[92] Reports and orders issued about this incident suggest that the Golkonda court disfavoured Deccanis, Pathans, Mughals and Arabs. Iranian *āfāqīs* constituted the majority of the Qutb Shahi nobility. This anonymous Deccan chronicle also notes the 'one thousand enlightened advisors', identifying Iranian courtiers as *hazār shamʻ-i-ārā*[93] who surrounded Sultan Muhammad Quli Qutb Shah, and were possibly those who engineered the incident. It is strange that in the entire event, the name of Mir Muhammad Muʼmin has been scrupulously avoided. As late as 1016/1607, after Hayat Bakshi Begam's marriage with Prince Sultan Muhammad Qutb Shah, the bridegroom was declared as the heir apparent to the Golkonda throne.[94] This required undoing the old aspirant to the throne. It was not unlikely that the entire conspiracy was plotted to remove Khudabandah, who was an obstacle in the way of Sultan Muhammad Qutb Shah. The presence of Iranian *elchi*, Uighurlu Beg Sultan in the Qutb Shahi court while the Nabat Ghat incident unfolded cannot be overlooked, as it provided him with an opportunity to observe court politics and the interventions of migrant Iranians in Golkonda.

Returning to the relations of Golkonda with Delhi after the death of Akbar, it appears that Sultan Muhammad Quli Qutb Shah drastically changed his policy. After Jahangir's accession, all the Deccan sultans, particularly ʻAdil Shah sought Iran's guidance regarding the orientation of their policy vis-à-vis the Mughals. They abstained from sending condolence-cum-congratulatory *elchis* to Delhi without Iran's consultation.[95] They also delayed contact with Iran up to 1018/1609–10.

A Balance of Power—The Third Phase

Jahangir, Muhammad Quli and Shah ʻAbbas I were roughly of the same age,[96] but Muhammad Quli had ascended the throne in the year 988/1589, Shah ʻAbbas I, eight years later in 996/1597, and Jahangir became emperor much later in the year 1014/1605. While a prince, he had entered into correspondence and forged a friendship with Shah ʻAbbas I.[97] Surprisingly, Shah ʻAbbas I as well as the Deccan rulers abstained from deputing envoys to offer condolences upon the death of Akbar and to congratulate Jahangir on his accession, which they ultimately did in the beginning of the sixth regnal year. The obvious reason was the Safavid plan to re-capture Qandahar. Shah 'Abbas I launched his first attack on Qandahar during Akbar's last years and the second one during Jahangir's first regnal year.[98] Jahangir, though he had to respond to many internal disturbances, took immediate and successful measures to save Qandahar. Iranian forces retreated from Qandahar by the middle of the year 1015/1606. Shah 'Abbas I, whose ambitious plan had failed, felt the risk of loosing his good friendship with Jahangir. He therefore pretended to be unaware that Safavid forces were attempting to reduce Qandahar. He sent a letter of explanation to Jahangir through Husain Beg Shamlu and tried to revive his friendship with the Mughal monarch. In 1018/1609–10, Shah 'Abbas I sent his first major *elchi* Yadgar 'Ali Sultan Talish to Hindustan on a much delayed mission to express condolences and congratulate the new emperor.[99]

Therefore, ever since his accession Jahangir experienced the unfraternal and, at times, insulting attitude of his so-called brother Shah 'Abbas I. Besides unfriendly Safavid policies, he also sensed a change in the attitude of the Deccan sultans. Emboldened by their association and diplomatic relations with Iran, the sultans neglected to cultivate relations with the Mughals, and even instigated the Safavids to focus their energies on Qandahar, in order to divert the Mughals from the Deccan. Jahangir first dealt with the issue of Qandahar and then directed his attention towards the Deccan.

On 4th Rajab 1018/23 September 1609, he sent his son Parviz on an expedition to the Deccan.[100] On 6th Zilqada 1018/21 January 1610 he received a report from the *khān-i azam* that Parviz's army was not enough to overcome the allied forces of the Deccan sultans. Jahangir instantly resolved to go to the Deccan. Before Prince Parviz could reach Burhanpur, a petition (*'arzdāsht*) was received from the *Khān-i-Khānān* and other *amirs* saying that the Deccanis had formed an alliance and were ready to mutiny. The Mughal nobles claimed that the situation urgently demanded more forces. But Asaf Khan, elder brother of Nur Jahan and close counsellor to the Mughal king, advised Jahangir to stay in Delhi. Simultaneously, Jahangir received another *'arzdāsht* from 'Adil Khan Bijapuri stating that he would be willing to explain his position to a reliable envoy who could convey his message to the Mughal emperor and that it would be only for the betterment of the rulers of the Deccan. In consultation with his son and the *amirs*, it was decided that there was no need for Jahangir to proceed to the Deccan personally. Reinforcements were sent under his son's command on 17th Zilqada 1018/1 February 1609.[101] This was the beginning of several other reinforcements that were diverted to the Deccan front. The rallying Mughal army harassed the Deccan sultans so much that they could no longer ignore Delhi.

Afraid of Mughal invasion, the sultans of the Deccan entered into a two-fold alliance. The first was a military alliance to meet the Mughal challenge and the second was collaboration in formulating a joint foreign policy. In 1018/1609, Sultan Muhammad Quli Qutb Shah, Ibrahim 'Adil Shah II and Malik Ambar sent their *elchis* to Iran with letters addressed to Shah 'Abbas I.

The same year Shah 'Abbas I called on Muhammad Quli Qutb Shah to relieve Uighurlu Beg Sultan.[102] Before the *elchi* could be relieved however, Sultan Muhammad Quli sent Qambar Ali, a man in whom he had confidence, with gifts comprising Indian jewellery and textiles to Shah 'Abbas I with the aim of strengthening their alliance.[103]

Uighurlu Beg Sultan was relieved and the same year Mihdi Quli Sultan Talish was sent as the return *elchi* from Golkonda[104] with a letter and numerous gifts especially produced over the course of five years. Accompanied by the *elchis* of Bijapur and Ahmadnagar,[105] Uighurlu Beg Sultan proceeded to Iraq.[106]

The letter of Sultan Muhammad Quli Qutb Shah addressed to Shah 'Abbas I was embellished with ceremonial language. The letter re-affirmed the credentials of the return *elchi* Mihdi Quli Sultan Talish who was being sent to Iran as a permanent representative of Golkonda at the Safavid court.[107] It expressed Sultan Muhammad Quli's loyalty and his gratitude for sending over an *elchi* to Golkonda. The letter is in two parts, the second of which is more informal, personal and humble. In it, Sultan Muhammad Quli Qutb Shah requested Shah 'Abbas I to pay special attention to the oral message communicated through Mihdi Quli Sultan Talish. He made an earnest effort to strengthen his friendship with Shah 'Abbas I and requested him to recommend his case to Jahangir in a way as if it was at his own initiative and accord.[108]

The objective of both missions carried by Mihdi Quli Sultan Talish and Uighurlu Beg Sultan, as explained in the letter, was the promotion of strong relations between Muhammad Quli Qutb Shah and Shah 'Abbas I. The Iranian *elchi* returned with a team of *elchis* of the Deccan sultans all of whom had similar goals. According to Iranian sources, the sultans of the Deccan lodged a petition at the Safavid court against Mughal interference in their dominions. The great friendship between the household of Timur and the Safavid family had become stronger than ever before through the relations of Shah 'Abbas I and Jahangir. The Deccan sultans desired that Shah 'Abbas appeal to Jahangir on their behalf. The first thing Shah 'Abbas I did after receiving the *elchis* was to dispatch a letter to Jahangir recommending the cases of the Deccan sultans[109] through an *elchi* named Shah Quli Beg Luk.[110]

Soon after that, Jahangir received Shah 'Abbas I's first major embassy led by Yadgar Sultan Talish in Muharram 1020/March 1611.[111] Shah Quli

Beg Luk also reached Delhi in Safar 1020/April 1611 and delivered Shah 'Abbas I's letter of recommendation to Jahangir.[112]

Shah 'Abbas requested Jahangir to be kind to the Deccan rulers (*hukkām-i-kirām-i 'ālī maqām-i-dakan*) who had the privilege of being in the neighbourhood of a magnificent king like Jahangir. He emphasized the close relationship of the Deccan sultans with Iran and suggested that a favourable attitude might bring peace and popular approval. He further requested Jahangir to overlook their shortcomings (*taqsīrāt*).[113]

Jahangir, who had already dispatched his reinforcements to the Deccan from 1018/1609, entered into negotiations with Ibrahim 'Adil Shah II in 1019/1610 by sending Mir Jamalu'ddin Inju.[114] He was nevertheless displeased and did not seem to have changed his attitude upon receipt of this letter in Safar 1020/April 1611. On 21st Rabi II 1020/23 June 1611, he revised his Deccan strategy and took steps to reinforce it by appointing 'Abdullah Khan as the *subehdār* (governor) of the Deccan and transferred several officials.[115] It is strange that Iranian sources claim that Jahangir gave up his aggressive attitude against the Deccan on receipt of the letter of recommendation.[116] This contention is not tenable given the fact that Jahangir was firm in his policy towards the Deccan. In the meanwhile, Sultan Muhammad Quli Qutb Shah passed away on 17th Zilqada 1020/11 January 1611 and was succeeded by his nephew and son-in-law, Sultan Muhammad Qutb Shah.

Diplomatic Duplicity—The Fourth Phase

The team of the Deccan *elchis* who travelled to Iran in 1018/1609 via the sea route would have reached their destination early in 1019/1610. By that time, the strained relations between Iran and Hindustan were once again turning into a renewed friendship. The Iranian *elchi* Yadgar 'Ali Sultan Talish had reached Delhi and was waiting for an audience from Jahangir who, of course, entertained him only in Muharram 1020/1611. The mediation of Iran sought by the Deccan *elchis* would only have been possible after the re-establishment of formal and amicable relations between Iran and Hindustan. The Golkonda *elchi* was held up at the Safavid court till at least 1023/1614 when the other *elchis* of the Deccan were relieved together with the return *elchis* from Iran.[117]

The news of Sultan Muhammad Quli Qutb Shah's demise had already reached the Iranian court through Mir Muhammad Amin Mir Jumla. Due to differences with the new Golkonda sultan, Mir Muhammad Amin had left for Iran where he reported the details of affairs in the Deccan after the accession of Sultan Muhammad Qutb Shah to Shah 'Abbas I. Unable to find a suitable position in Iran, he would eventually move to the Mughal court to join the services of Jahangir.[118] The Iranian *elchi* had to carry a condolatory-cum-congratulatory message to the new Golkonda sultan. Shah 'Abbas I was aware that Sultan Muhammad Qutb Shah was the nephew and son-in-law of Sultan Muhammad Quli Qutb Shah and had inherited the blood of a Sayyid family from his maternal side. Shah 'Abbas also knew that the renowned scholar, administrator and statesman, Mir Muhammad Mu'min Astarabadi, had educated and trained the young sultan. Iranian *elchi* Uighurlu Beg Sultan obviously brought all these factual details to the knowledge of Shah 'Abbas I.

In the year 1023/1614, after recommending the case of Golkonda and other sultanates to Jahangir, Shah 'Abbas I relieved the *elchis* of the Deccan, except perhaps the *elchi* of Golkonda. Among the team of returning *elchis*, Husain Beg Tabrizi Qapuchi Bashi[119] was sent to Golkonda with letters from Shah 'Abbas I addressed to Sultan Muhammad Qutb Shah[120] and Mir Muhammad Mu'min.[121] Husain Beg Tabrizi left Iran from the port of Hormuz and landed in India at the port of Dabhol, travelling in a large ship driven by the southern winds (*bād-i-junūb*). The port couriers (*munhiyān*) carried the news of his arrival to the Qutb Shahi escort, who was staying there and forwarded the news to Sultan Muhammad Qutb Shah. The sultan deputed *siyādat panāh* (protector of chieftainship) Mir Zain-ul-abidin Mazandarani with necessary funds to receive the Iranian envoy at the port of Dabhol.[122] Mir Zain-ul-abidin Mazandarani received Husain Beg Tabrizi at Dabhol and escorted him to the borders of Golkonda observing all necessary protocol. On the news of their arrival at the borders of the sultanate, the sultan deputed Ambiya Quli Khan with a set of nobles to receive the *elchi* at the Golkonda border. The guest was brought to the capital with all diplomatic etiquette. In the month of Rajab 1023/August 1614, the Iranian Qapuchi Bashi (embassy) met at Kala Chabutra. He communicated the good wishes of Shah 'Abbas I and presented gifts to the Qutb Shah. Among the gifts were a bejewelled *tāj*, a sword, a dagger with belt, 50 horses of a good breed with embellished reins, 3 full pieces of *zarbaft* and several other gifts.[123] The envoy then delivered the letter of Shah 'Abbas I addressed to the Qutb Shahi monarch.

Sultan Muhammad Qutb Shah, after accepting the Iranian presents, bestowed a robe of honour on the *elchi* and favoured the men of his suite, who were around eighty in number, with royal presents (*tashrīfāt-i shāhānah wa in'ām*). They were provided with comfortable buildings as their accommodation. The eighty persons in Husain Beg Tabrizi's entourage were all military leaders (*ghaziyān-i 'uzzām*).[124]

The letter brought by Husain Beg Tabrizi was quite detailed, a total of 450 words, and covered many aspects of relations between Golkonda and Iran. Shah 'Abbas I first offered his condolences upon the death of Sultan Muhammad Quli Qutb Shah and then congratulated Sultan Muhammad

Qutb Shah on his accession. He also made a reference to the 'inherent affinity and an emotional bond of love' he felt towards the late sultan.

He informed Muhammad Qutb Shah that of late he had entered into a peace treaty with the Ottoman emperor, through a mediator, in order to save his subjects from constant war and devastation. Shah 'Abbas I expressed his desire to keep abreast of the affairs in Golkonda and advised Muhammad Qutb Shah to relieve Husain Beg at an early date to expedite the exchange of *elchis*, who would keep them posted with news from both ends. Shah 'Abbas I informed him that he had sent an army to conquer the *vilāyats* of Kich and Makran in southern Iran. This conquest would also enable quick and easy traffic (*taraddudāt*) between Iran and the Deccan. Shah 'Abbas I also informed him that Haji Qambar Ali had narrated the grief he felt upon the death of his uncle, Muhammad Qutb Shah.[125] In the end Shah 'Abbas I desired a close friendship and promised to extend all possible help to the young sultan of Golkonda.[126]

Shah 'Abbas I was acquainted with the fact that Mir Muhammad Mu'min Astarabadi, whom Sultan Muhammad Quli Qutb Shah had appointed as the *peshwā* of Golkonda, was the preceptor of the new monarch, Sultan Muhammad Qutb Shah. He continued as Golkonda's most influential *de facto* administrator and key policymaker. The personality of Mir Mu'min was well known at the Safavid court.

Shah 'Abbas I withdrew his siege of Qandahar and after concluding peace with the Ottoman caliph, he had a moment of relative respite. He was waiting for a more decisive strategy to regain what he had lost. He had to recover much of his territories from the Ottomans and Qandahar from the Mughals. The maintenance of his relations with the Deccan was an important diplomatic measure towards the restoration of Qandahar.

The presence of Mir Muhammad Mu'min in the Deccan was quite promising for the successful execution of Shah 'Abbas I's two-pronged strategy at Qandahar and the Deccan. The time was ripe for a decisive move by Iran. Shah 'Abbas I had already resorted to more intimate relations with the Deccan sultans, especially with Golkonda. As a corollary to the same diplomatic measure he went to the extent of addressing Mir Muhammad Mu'min too. Though the form of Shah 'Abbas I's letter is that of a *farmān*, one may treat it as a letter.

In his letter, dated Ramadan 1022, Shah 'Abbas I addressed Mir Muhammad Mu'min in respectful ceremonial phrases and informed him that he should rest assured of Safavid favour and pay immediate attention to all urgent matters in Golkonda. The Shah wrote that he knew of Mir Mu'min's earlier association with the Safavid court. Since the judicious sultans of Golkonda were devoted to the household of the Prophet, a sincere relationship had developed between the Safavid and Qutb Shahi Houses.

Shah 'Abbas I added that it was for the same reason he held them (Qutb Shahs) in a genuine and deep friendship. In such circumstances, the presence of a veteran like Mir Muhammad Mu'min was a fortunate coincidence.

Shah 'Abbas I further added that he was sending a man of his confidence to offer condolences for Sultan Muhammad Quli Qutb Shah's death and Sultan Muhammad Qutb Shah's succession. The Shah desired Mir Muhammad Mu'min to utmost for the revival of the terms of his attachment with the Safavid court. Mir Mu'min was further advised to handle the situation in such a way as to get the *elchi* relieved earlier so that he would not be held up inordinately, as had been the case before. Shah 'Abbas also desired Mir Mu'min to keep in touch with him through letters and to inform him of Golkonda's needs. The Shah closed the letter assuring Mir Muhammad Mu'min of his boundless royal favours.[127]

Shah Jahan's Subjugation of the Deccan

Conscious of Iranian diplomatic strategy in alliance with the sultans of the south, Jahangir was never ignorant of Deccan affairs. He adhered to Akbar's policy of reducing the Deccan and went on reinforcing his strategy there. In addition to his earlier reinforcements in 1611, he had sent many more in the subsequent years. In the year 1021/1612, he first sent Chin Qilich Khan to set right Portuguese (*firangi*) interference at the port of Surat.[128] He also revised his strategy in the Deccan, where the hasty actions of a certain 'Abdullah Khan had resulted in dissension in the Mughal camp. This had encouraged the Deccan sultans to initiate negotiations with Mughal nobles posted in their domains.[129] It is interesting that in Zilhijja 1021/January 1613, 'Adil Khan ('Adil Shah) submitted his allegiance to the Mughals and proposed that if the Deccan expedition was entrusted to him, he would restore their lost territories to them. Jahangir did not accept the proposal given the unpredicatable political background of such offers.[130]

Late in the year 1024/1615, Malik Ambar led the Deccani armies, including Golkonda's and Bijapur's *lashkars* (troops), into battle with the Mughals but lost decisively.[131] Golkonda and Bijapur felt the risk of Mughal domination until they received guidance and aid from Iran; meanwhile they thought it advisable to maintain peaceful relations with Hindustan. They sent envoys and *peshkash* to the Mughal court. Golkonda sent a *peshkash* that was perused by Jahangir on 21st Mihr (26th Sha'ban) 1025/29 August 1616.[132]

In the same year, Jahangir felt that Prince Parviz could not carry forth the Deccan strategy and he decided to entrust the campaign to Prince Khurram. Prince Khurram who was then assigned the title of Shah, was sent off to the Deccan on 19th Shawwal 1025/20 October 1616.[133]

Prince Khurram handled the Deccan situation with immense tact. He deployed diplomatic pressure rather than military might and succeeded in receiving allegiance from the Deccan sultans. On 29th Rabi I 1026/27 March 1617, Prince Khurram sent Sayyid 'Abdullah Basha, who reached Jahangir's camp at Mandu and delivered the prince's letters informing the emperor that all the Deccan sultans had submitted their allegiance. Jahangir took it as a great step forward and thanked God.[134] Commenting on the prince's successful mission, he had noted that the headstrong, nefarious and rebellious sultans of the Deccan had been duly humbled and were now compelled to recognize their inferior position and pay their dues.[135] Prince Khurram gathered an enormous *peshkash*, an amount the Mughals had never received from any of their contemporary rivals. By 11th Shawwal 1026/2 October 1617, Shah Khurram entered Mandu with the *elchis* and *peshkash* from 'Adil Shah, Qutb Shah and the other rulers of the Deccan. Jahangir warmly received Prince Khurram and favoured him not only with a promotion in his rank but also with an unprecedented title of Shah Jahan.[136]

Jahangir saw the enormous articles of *peshkash* brought from the Deccan and evaluated them. The *peshkash* of Golkonda included a diamond worth Rs.30,000; 150 elephants out of which 3 were equipped with chains and other ancillaries made of gold, and 9 elephants with ancillaries made of silver. These were such fine elephants that at least 20 of them were selected for the emperor's personal use. And 5 of the elephants were of an unusually large size and were very famous.[137] They were valued at one lakh rupees each. Besides these, there were 100 horses of Arabian and Iraqi breed, 3 of them adorned with bejewelled reins.[138]

Shah Jahan's presence in the Deccan worried Bijapur and Golkonda. On account of its geographical location, in comparison with Bijapur, Golkonda had to answer to Mughal aggression through diplomacy rather than belligerence. As an immediate diplomatic measure, Golkonda tried to pacify the Mughals by offering generous *peshkash* to them, but its ultimate loyalty was with Iran. It was high time for Golkonda to send an envoy to Shah 'Abbas I. In 1028/1619, on the occasion of the celebration of Jahangir's fourteenth regnal year, Shah Jahan was presented with a ruby and several other articles in the *peshkash* of Golkonda. An elephant that was received was so magnificent that Jahangir immediately wished to ride it within the courtyard of his palace.[139] Muhammad Qutb Shah had sent his *peshkash* and a letter through his *vakīl*, Mir Mushrif. According to Jahangir, Muhammad Qutb Shah had expressed his sincere loyalty and requested him to send the emperor's portrait, which Jahangir apparently did.[140]

Such were the relations between Golkonda and Hindustan. At the same time, the friendship between Hindustan and Iran was at its height.

Ever since 1020/1611, Jahangir and Shah 'Abbas I had resumed their legendary friendship, which they called fraternity. They had been exchanging fantastic gifts and maintaining a frequent traffic of *elchis*.[141] Yet their minds were never free from diplomatic manoeuvres against each other, even though Jahangir feigned his generosity towards the Safavids and Shah 'Abbas I made elaborate claims of his love for the Mughal emperor.

On 3rd Rabi I 1027/18 February 1618, the aforementioned Mirza Muhammad Amin, the former *Mir Jumla* of Golkonda, reached the Mughal court after a considerable stay in Iran and was retained in Mughal service.[142] The contemporary Iranian sources describe his going over to Jahangir as defection (*farār*), which indicates an attitude of suspicion towards those courtiers who went over to Mughal Hindustan.[143] Undoubtedly, Mirza Muhammad Amin was fully aware of the state of affairs in Golkonda, Bijapur and Iran. His presence would have been of immense use to Jahangir. By the end of the eleventh century Hijri, from 1021/1612 to 1030/1621, all contenders in this diplomatic triangle conceived of a different strategy. The Deccan sultans united against the Mughal army, which was moving further south, while Safavid Iran attempted to recover Qandahar.

Husain Beg Tabrizi Qapuchi Bashi was detained in Golkonda for twenty-eight months. He was released in the middle of the year Zilqada 1025/November 1616. Shaikh Muhammad Ibn Khatun, a member of the Majlis and an eminent scholar and statesman, was sent with him as a return *elchi* to Iran. They proceeded via Burhanpur and on their way, paid their respects to Jahangir on Rabi I 1026/March 1617, when the Mughal emperor was encamped at Mandu.[144] Both the *elchis* reached Iran and called on Shah 'Abbas I at Qazvin in 1027/1618 with letters from Sultan Muhammad Qutb Shah and Mir Muhammad Mu'min addressed to the Shah. They reached at a time when Jahangir's *elchi*, Khan Alam, too had arrived at Qazvin with a large camp. It appears, from the prominence given by Iranian chroniclers to the account of the arrival of Shaikh Muhammad Ibn Khatun, that the Qutb Shahi *elchi* was received with all necessary decorum.[145] Shaikh Muhammad Ibn Khatun was detained in Iran for as long as Khan Alam stayed there. He was received in the year 1029/1620 with necessary ceremonies, along with Qasim Beg Paran Sipah Salar of Mazandaran as return *elchi*.[146] Qasim Beg Paran was entrusted with a double mission: one at the Mughal court and the other at Golkonda. The Iranian *elchi* called on Jahangir at Agra in Khurdad (Rajab) 1030/June 1621 and delivered the letter of Shah 'Abbas I addressed to Jahangir together with gifts.[147]

Shah 'Abbas I, in his letter addressed to Jahangir, declared his intense fraternal loyalty and introduced Qasim Beg Sipah Salar Mazandaran as an old servant of the Safavid family whose forefathers had been serving them for many generations. The Shah instructed that Qasim Beg would inform

Jahangir about the state of affairs in Iran and then proceed to the Deccan. Shah 'Abbas I stated that the main object of sending that letter and *elchi* was to thank Jahangir for forgiving the errors of the great sultans of the Deccan and favouring them with kind attention, which the Shah claimed to have heard. The Shah requested that Qasim Beg be relieved early so that he could proceed to the said sultans and persuade them to be more loyal and obedient to Jahangir. At the same time, the Shah expressed his hope that Jahangir would always be kind to them, as it was expected that great rulers extend favours to their loyal subordinates. The Shah closed his letter by requesting the early dismissal of Qasim Beg and recorded his well wishes for Jahangir.[148] Despite all such recommendations and requests, Jahangir did not relieve the *elchis* of Iran and Golkonda, Qasim Beg and Ibn Khatun respectively, for more than a year and continued with his earlier Deccan policy.

The explanation for Qasim Beg Paran and Ibn Khatun's detention can be found in the context of the contemporary course of events. By this time, Shah 'Abbas I had adopted a policy of professing deep relations with Jahangir by sending him frequent envoys, letters and gifts on one hand, and encroaching on the western frontiers of Hindustan on the other.[149] Iran's military strategy on the north-west frontier was reinforced by a diplomatic strategy in the Deccan, which itself was no less than direct military action as Iran was constantly sending military experts (*ghāziyān-i 'uzzām*) with its *elchis* to Golkonda and the other Deccan sultanates.

Iran's first encroachments on Mughal territories were at Kich and Makran that formed, even according to the Iranian sources, a part of Indian provinces in Thattah.[150] Shah 'Abbas I had already informed Sultan Muhammad Qutb Shah about his decision of reducing Kich and Makran in the year 1023/1614, and he annexed Kich and Makran early in the year 1030/1621.[151] The present *elchis*, Qasim Beg Sipah Salar and Ibn Khatun, had reached Agra through the new route of Kich and Makran. Shah 'Abbas I's annexation of that territory of Hindustan was enough reason for Jahangir to be cautious about allowing a free traffic of envoys between Iran and the Deccan. It was more dangerous especially when a commander like Qasim Beg Sipah Salar was being sent as an envoy. Jahangir had heard the news of Shah 'Abbas I's plans of reducing Qandahar.[152]

At the same time, the Deccan sultans were organizing themselves under the leadership of Malik Ambar while Shah Jahan was busy at Kangra and Jahangir was in Kashmir. Ambar, with an allied force of 60,000 soldiers, attacked the Mughal army, which was staying in Ahmadnagar and its suburbs under the command of Abdu'r Rahim Khan-i-Khanan, and drove them back to Burhanpur. By the end of 1029/1620, Jahangir deputed Shah Jahan again to lead the Deccan campaign. By the middle of the year 1030/1621,

Shah Jahan had defeated the allied Deccani forces and forced Malik Ambar to sign a treaty according to which he was to pay a tribute and reparations for war (*jarīma*).[153] Before deputing Shah Jahan, Jahangir had informed Shah 'Abbas I that the Deccan sultans had rebelled and were not adhering to the covenants agreed upon earlier. He had therefore dispatched Shah Jahan with *lashkars* and artillery for the Deccan campaign.[154]

By this time, Shah 'Abbas I had written another recommendation letter on behalf of the Deccan sultans to Jahangir. Expressing his feelings of boundless love and sincerity, Shah Abbas wrote that it was but natural for them to have a dialogue on matters that the enlightened and erudite Mughal emperor already understood. He therefore took liberty to talk about the great sultans (*salatīn-i-'uzzām*) of the Deccan, who had been submissive (*mutī'*) and paid tribute (*bāj guzār*) to his (Jahangir's) illustrious House. He further stressed that the sultans of the Deccan were the devotees of the Safavid family from times past. From the beginning of his reign, Shah 'Abbas boasted that he had been persistently trying to revive the traditions of his ancestors (a reference to his efforts for popularizing the Shi'ite faith). Recommending the case of the Deccan sultans, he wrote that Jahangir ought to forgive them even if they had done something to offend him, for the sake of a sincere friend like himself (Shah 'Abbas). He requested Jahangir to let the world know that their friendship was so close that they did not even care to loose their territories for each other.[155]

Shah 'Abbas I's recommendations had no effect. Jahangir, in one of his letters, had already informed him about assigning the Deccan campaign to Shah Jahan and also complained about Shah 'Abbas I's intention to reduce Qandahar expressing his utmost surprise.[156] Jahangir had repeatedly received the news of Shah 'Abbas I's intention to take over Qandahar early in the year 1031/1622 from one major Iranian envoy, Zainal Beg, who was residing in the Mughal court at that time.[157] To his complete surprise, Shah 'Abbas I annexed Qandahar on 11th Sha'ban 1031/11 June 1622.[158]

That same year Nur Jahan's manipulations to get her son, Parviz, declared as heir apparent led Shah Jahan to rebel against Jahangir. By that time Jahangir's health had also deteriorated. Such circumstances loosened Mughal hold over the Deccan, at least until 1035/1626, when Shah Jahan withdrew his rebellion, submitted his apologies to Jahangir and was again at the helm of affairs in the Deccan. Jahangir passed away on 27th Safar 1037/28 October 1627 and was succeeded by Shah Jahan.

Sinking Sultanate—The Fifth Phase

From 1030/1620 to 1040/1630, major changes were taking place in Golkonda, Iran, Hindustan and elsewhere, chiefly on account of the deaths of the rulers and statesmen. In Golkonda, Iranian *elchi* Qasim Beg Paran died in 1034/1625.[159] The same year, the great statesman of Golkonda, Mir Muhammad Mu'min, passed away on 2nd Jumada I 1034/31 January 1625.[160] Sultan Muhammad Qutb Shah died on 13th Jumada I 1035/31 January 1626 and was succeeded by his son, 'Abdullah Qutb Shah, who was barely twelve years old at that time.[161]

In Bijapur, Ibrahim 'Adil Shah passed away on 11th Muharram 1037/12 September 1627 and was succeeded by his son, Sultan Muhammad 'Adil Shah, who was only fifteen years old. The Nizam Shahi ruler Murtaza I, weak and subdued, died in 1039/1630. The great Abyssinian military expert of the Deccan, Malik Ambar, passed away on 25th Sha'ban 1035/12 May 1626.[162] The death of this defender of the Deccan removed the first barrier to Mughal advance in northern Deccan and facilitated their aim of expansion further south.

In Hindustan, Prince Shah Jahan, elated with his success in the Deccan campaigns, felt that his prospects for accession to the throne were turning bleak on account of Nur Jahan's manipulations in favour of the inept Prince Shahryar (Parviz). As a measure to keep Shah Jahan away from the helm of affairs, she issued orders for his posting to Qandahar in the year 1031/1622. Shah Jahan refused to comply. His disobedience was treated as revolt and consequently the revolt became a reality. Shah Jahan continued to be a rebel for some time and this gave him the opportunity to travel extensively through India and also to enter into correspondence with Shah 'Abbas I. He also travelled through the territories of Golkonda and Bijapur.[163] He succeeded Jahangir on 26th Jumada I 1037/2 February 1628 when he was thirty-six years old. In Iran, Shah 'Abbas I died on 24th Jumada I 1038/19 January 1629 and was succeeded by his inexperienced and meek grandson Sam Mirza, known as Shah Safi, who was sixteen years old.[164]

At about the same time in Turan, Imam Quli Khan was trying to engineer a trilateral strategy against Iran, joining hands with Jahangir of Hindustan and Murad IV of the Ottoman Empire. He issued letters to them in 1035/1625-26.[165] In the Ottoman Empire, Sultan Murad IV succeeded Sultan Mustafa in the year 1032/1623 at the age of twelve. His *vazir*, Hafiz Ahmad Pasha, had led an expansionist policy in parts of Azerbaijan and Iraq-i-Arab that continued though the first half of Sultan Murad IV's reign. During the ninth year of Murad's reign, Hafiz Ahmad Pasha was assassinated in a mutiny led by the Janissaries. The incident provoked Murad IV to rise against the mutineers and carry forth with Hafiz Ahmad Pasha's policies.

On Iran's western frontiers, Murad IV led campaigns in Irvan and Baghdad. The former was restored to Iran under the earlier treaty of 1555 while the latter was lost forever. The eight years of disturbances from 1032 to 1040/1623 to 1631 led by the Grand Vazir and Sultan Murad IV's concerted military campaigns in the following eight years kept Iran in a state of constant struggle on its western frontiers.[166]

Returning our attention to Golkonda, it is unknown when Jahangir permitted Qasim Beg Paran, the Iranian *elchi*, and Ibn Khatun to proceed to Golkonda. Nevertheless, the two envoys reached Hyderabad by 1032/1623.[167]

Before Muhammad Qutb Shah could enter into any further diplomatic dialogue with Iran, the Iranian *elchi* Qasim Beg Paran died at Golkonda in 1034/1625. Muhammad Quli Beg, the son of the late *elchi*, who had accompanied his father to Golkonda was, of course, present. Since he was a person capable of carrying his father's mission, 'Abdullah Qutb Shah appointed him successor of Qasim Beg.[168]

In the year 1037/1628, Muhammad Quli Beg was relieved along with Khairat Khan, *sar naubat* (chief of kettle-drum), who was sent as the return *elchi* of Golkonda. Muhammad Quli Beg and his entire suite were seen off with all ceremonies according to the Book of Protocol.[169] Gifts comprising jewellery, various types of textiles and a letter were sent for the Iranian ruler. The embassy proceeded to the port of Surat with the aim of sailing through the Sea of Oman. On arriving at Surat, Mughal officials directed them to go to the imperial court at Agra first,[170] where they called on the emperor on 15th Zilhijja 1037/6 August 1628. Shah Jahan honoured Muhammad Quli with robes and Rs.15,000 as an *in'ām*.[171] The two *elchis* then sailed in an English vessel and reached Bandar 'Abbas early in the year 1038/February 1629, where they heard of the demise of Shah 'Abbas I (which had taken place on 25th Jumada I 1038/10 January 1629).[172]

On 29th Sha'ban 1038/13 April 1629, Khairat Khan's letter conveying the news of Abbas I's demise in Farahabad (Mazandaran) dispatched from Bandar 'Abbas was received in Golkonda. Nevertheless, the two *elchis* having communicated the news to Golkonda proceeded to Isfahan and called on Shah Safi and delivered the gifts and the letter, which pleased the new ruler very much.[173]

The letter carried by Khairat Khan was actually addressed to Shah 'Abbas I but was delivered to his successor, Shah Safi Safavi. The style and the tenor of the letter was sober, dignified and reflected a renewed confidence in diplomatic relations. After a detailed ceremonial address, the letter articulated three objectives. First, Golkonda's sultan congratulated Shah 'Abbas I on his recapture of Qandahar. He also expressed his happiness at the Safavid victory and foresaw it as an initial step towards overthrowing Mughal suzerainty, although he mildly protested that the news of the victory had not been communicated to him. Second, 'Abdullah Qutb Shah officially informed the Safavid ruler of the Iranian *elchi* Qasim Beg Paran's death.[174] He commended the *sipāh sālār* (commander-in-chief) for his services and laid out the reasons for sending Muhammad Quli Beg, the son

of the deceased, who was as able an emissary as his father. 'Abdullah Qutb
Shah then recorded Khairat Khan's credentials, stressing that the Iranian
monarch should have full confidence in him. The letter's conclusion was
short wherein 'Abdullah Qutb Shah expressed the traditional attachment
of the two Houses, assured his loyalty, requested Shah Safi's favourable
attention and informed him that the actual message would be conveyed
orally by his *elchi*.[175]

Shah Safi bestowed the Golkonda *elchi* not only with robes of honour
but also with a grant of horses with golden ancillaries and a special assignment of a village (*qariyah*) where the relatives and kinsmen (*aqwām-wa-
avīmāq*) of Khairat Khan had been living in Iran. This assignment was an
in'ām and thus rent-free.[176]

Khairat Khan stayed at Shah Safi's court for at least four and a half
years. He regularly communicated news regarding developments in Iran,
and received gifts and information from Golkonda as well. In the year
1041/1631, 'Abdullah Qutb Shah sent him robes and gifts in accordance
with the Book of Protocol.[177] He was probably relieved of his duties early
in 1043/1633.

The Deed of Submission

Hindustan and Golkonda's relations were relatively cordial during the 1620s.
For the first time a Mughal prince (Shah Jahan) had sent a formal embassy
through Ikhlas Khan Qazvini with a letter to Golkonda in 1035/1626 to
offer condolences upon Sultan Muhammad Qutb Shah's death and
to congratulate 'Abdullah Qutb Shah.[178] The obvious reason was that Shah
Jahan had sought refuge and help from Muhammad Qutb Shah during his
revolt against Jahangir in the preceding years.

Similarly, 'Abdullah Qutb Shah sent a congratulatory letter with *peshkash*
to Shah Jahan that was received on 15th Zilhijja 1037/6 August 1628 at
Agra.[179] Interestingly, Shah Jahan had granted audience to the bearers of
the congratulatory letter and *peshkash* from Golkonda on the same day that
he had allowed an audience to Muhammad Quli Beg and Khairat Khan,
whom he called when they were on their way from Surat to Iran.[180]

The semblance of cordiality and friendliness would not last long, however. Subsequent events testified that both Shah Jahan and 'Abdullah Qutb
Shah were bent upon defeating each other. Shah Jahan increased political
pressure on Golkonda on one hand, forged hasty alliances with the Safavids
and broke ties with the Uzbegs on the other. 'Abdullah Qutb Shah, unable
to stand his ground, was constantly looking towards Iran, instigating it to
crush the Mughals.

Mughal pressure on Golkonda was both military and political, and
quickly began to defy diplomatic decorum. Golkonda paid tribute, but the

Mughals demanded more and more by posting their representatives to collect *peshkash* not only in terms of specific amounts but also in terms of specific articles according to schedules, with instructions to furnish the tributes on specific dates and places.[181]

In Shawwal 1040/1631, Mughal forces, under Muhammad Baqir Najm-i Sani's command, entered the territories of Golkonda, breaching shared borders near present-day Orissa. The Qutb Shahi *sar lashkar* (chief of army), Afzal Khan Tarka, defended Golkonda's territories. Peace was negotiated at the instance of Shah Jahan who issued a *farmān* for the withdrawal of Mughal forces from Golkonda's territories.[182]

The Qutb Shahi *peshkash*, received in 1042/1633, totalled fifty lakh rupees. Although Mughal interference continued in the internal matters of the Deccan sultanates, Shah Jahan also wanted the Shi'ite faith to be abandoned as the official religion and substituted by the Sunni faith and practice. On 10th Muharram 1045/16 June 1635, Shah Jahan issued a *farmān* to Golkonda through 'Abdul Latif Gujarati in which he demanded that (1) the name of the Shah of Iran be dropped from the *khutbah* and the name of Shah Jahan be put in its place (2) the arrears of *peshkash* should be submitted at once in accordance with the statement enclosed. The *farmān* also contained a warning against the Shi'ite practice of condemning the Three Companions of the Prophet. The *farmān* was more than 500 words long and ended with a final warning that in case it was not complied with, Mughal forces would march into Golkonda. The same *farmān* noted that the emperor's lenient attitude towards 'Abdullah Qutb Shah was only due to the services the late Muhammad Qutb Shah had rendered to Shah Jahan. As a token of kindness and favour, Shah Jahan had assigned the governance (*ayālat*) of Golkonda to 'Abdullah Qutb Shah and desired him to execute a Deed of Submission (*inqīyād nāmah*).[183]

Shaikh 'Abdul Latif reached Golkonda on 8th Ramadan 1045/5 February 1636 and was received by Karim Khan and Mir Mu'izuddin Muhammad.[184] He stayed in Golkonda until the end of the year 1045/1636 and returned in Muharram 1046/June 1636 with Shaikh Muhammad Tahir.[185] Qutb Shahi sources describe 'Abdul Latif's mission as less successful and mention the Deed of Submission as a treaty of accord.[186]

The Deed of Submission concluded by 'Abdullah Qutb Shah in Zilhijja 1045/May 1636 was over 450 words and confirmed his absolute submission to the Mughals. Some of its salient features, which the Golkonda sultan agreed to, while swearing on the Koran in the presence of the Mughal political agent 'Abdul Latif, were:

1. The names of Twelve Imams should be substituted with the names of the four orthodox Caliphs and the name of the Iranian monarch

should be replaced with the name of the Mughal emperor in the *khutbah*.

2. Gold and silver coins would be struck with the dies sent by the Mughal emperor.

3. A tribute of 2 lakhs *huns* equal to 8 lakhs of rupees would be remitted to the Imperial treasury from the 9th regnal year of Shah Jahan.

4. 'Abdullah Qutb Shah would prove his sincere friendship with friends of the Mughal empire and an enemy of its enemies.

5. In view of the above terms Emperor Shah Jahan assigned the territories (*nāhiyah*) of Golkonda to 'Abdullah Qutb Shah.[187]

In response to the above Deed of Submission, Shah Jahan recorded a treaty ('*ahad nāmah*), had it inscribed on a gold plate and sent to 'Abdullah Qutb Shah through Khwaja Muhammad Zahid who accompanied Muhammad Tahir, *hājib* of Golkonda. The treaty, dated 7th Rabi II 1046/29 August 1636, is quite brief. The most significant part of this covenant was that Shah Jahan swore an oath to God and His Prophet not to interfere in the affairs of 'Abdullah Qutb Shah and his descendants for as long as Qutb-ul-Mulk adhered to the terms of the Deed of Submission. It was recorded that the covenant would be observed as a *laūh-i-mahfūs* (a guarded tablet).[188]

Secret Relations—The Sixth Phase

While Shah Jahan was forcing his terms upon Golkonda, he was also devising an exceedingly ambitious strategy of re-taking Qandahar from Iran and then conquering his ancestral homeland of Turan. The young Shah Safi was, at that time, engaged in defending the western frontiers from Ottoman invasions. Shah Jahan did not hesitate in taking diplomatic measures for the recovery of Qandahar. He was aware of 'Ali Mardan Khan's discord with Shah Safi and was attempting to manipulate him into such a position where he would have no choice but to cross over to the Mughals. He took over Qandahar in 1047/1638, a year after getting Golkonda to sign the Deed of Submission and communicated his actions to Shah Safi.[189]

Despite military confrontations, the exchange of *elchis* continued between Iran and Hindustan. After the annexation of Qandahar, Shah Jahan sent a letter to Shah Safi for the continuation of amicable relations and offered to pay him a sum equal to the revenue of Qandahar every year. Shah Safi, well aware of Mughal advances in the Deccan, was naturally displeased and provoked further by the Mughal annexation of Qandahar and 'Ali Mardan Khan's defection. Early in the year 1049/1639, he concluded peace with Murad IV at the cost of Baghdad and started serious preparations for the recovery of Qandahar. However, before he could reach Qandahar, he died at Kashan on 12th Safar 1052/16 May 1642 and was succeeded by his son Shah 'Abbas II. Ever since the Mughal conquest of Qandahar their relations with Iran remained strained, and Shah Jahan continued to militarily and politically dominate and direct trilateral diplomatic relations for some years.

Khairat Khan returned to Golkonda accompanied with Imam Quli Beg Shamlu, a state messenger (*yasāwal*) from Iran. They travelled to India via Qandahar and first called on the Mughal Emperor Shah Jahan at Bagh-i Hafiz Rakhna on 21st Ramadan 1043/11 March 1634, while he was on his way to Lahore. In this earlier stage of contact between Shah Safi and Shah Jahan, their formal relations had been quite congenial. Imam Quli Beg Shamlu delivered Shah Safi's letter to Shah Jahan together with several rare and valuable presents. Shah Jahan favoured the *elchi* with a robe of honour and a cash grant of Rs.40,000.[190]

Shah Safi's letter, addressed to Shah Jahan, was brief and restrained, indicating that the Iranian ruler was disinclined to have a favourable policy towards Mughal India. He wrote, 'If I speak, we may digress. I wish to express myself through silence.' With such a scrupulous attitude he requested Shah Jahan to maintain peaceful relations as their ancestors had done. He then informed him that Imam Quli Beg Yasawal was being sent on an ambassadorial mission (*rasm-i-sifārat*) to Sultan 'Abdullah Qutb Shah on account of the old and sincere relations between the two Houses.[191]

On 1st Zilqada 1043/19 April 1634, 'Abdullah Qutb Shah received the news of their arrival at the frontiers of Golkonda with great happiness. Mir Muizu'ddin Muhammad *Mushrif-ul-Mumālik* (Accountant General) received them at the entrance of the kingdom, meeting all the necessary expenditures of the embassy's reception. When the *elchis* and the Chief of Protocol were near the city they were received, under royal orders, by Shaikh Muhammad Tahir, *sar khayl-i-shāhi*, and a grand feast was arranged for the guests. At the third stage, an armed military unit in colourful uniform was sent to give a formal reception to the *elchi* at a place about four miles to the north of the capital. On 17th Zilqada 1043/5 May 1634,[192] 'Abdullah Qutb Shah himself rode to the location to welcome the *elchi*. The place was thus named Khairatabad to commemorate the event. The *elchi* delivered the gifts comprising horses from Iraq, a bejewelled crown, weapons, carpets from Kirman and Jawsaq (near Ray) and several other textiles along with the letter.

The letter brought by Imam Quli Beg congratulated 'Abdullah Qutb Shah on his accession. The sultan spoke to the *elchi* about Shah Safi and the state of affairs in Iran. Mir Muizu'ddin Muhammad was asked to attend upon him. The *elchi* was provided with the garden of Mir Muhammad Amin *Mir Jumla* (who had, of course, left Golkonda long ago[193]) with elephants, horses and other amenities. 'Abdullah Qutb Shah invited him to a banquet arranged in the royal palace. For his maintenance, Imam Quli Beg was assigned the *pargana* of Majahidpur earning him an annual revenue of 2,000 to 3,000 *huns* and a cash grant of 1,000 *huns* with 100 *khandi* (equal to 2,000 maunds) of foodgrains and several other facilities and emoluments.[194] Imam Quli and Khairat Khan were favoured with presents and other honours on many occasions. On one occasion, 'Abdullah Qutb Shah himself paid a visit to the house of Imam Quli Beg.[195]

The Iranian *elchi* had come to Golkonda at a time when Mughal pressure on the sultanate was more than ever before. Little is known about the political and diplomatic activities of Imam Quli Beg in Golkonda but it may be kept in mind that all the events in Golkonda-Mughal relations, before and after the execution of the Deed of Submission, took place while Imam Quli Beg was present in Golkonda. His presence at court, in the middle of all the action, suggests that important decisions about diplomatic relations with the Mughals were not taken without his consultation.

Golkonda does not seem to have sent any envoy to Iran during the stay of Imam Quli Beg Shamlu. Yet there is the possibility that messages were communicated through secret *elchis*. We may assume that Iran was kept informed of the developments in Golkonda, which necessitated the deputation of the second embassy of Asadullah Beg Kark Yaraq who reached Golkonda a year after the Deed of Submission. In the month of Zilhijja 1046/ April 1637, Mirza Asadullah Beg Tabrizi Kark Yaraq arrived at Golkonda with a letter from Shah Safi addressed to 'Abdullah Qutb Shah.[196] The *elchi* was called to the *huzūr* (presence) of 'Abdullah Qutb Shah who favoured him with an audience and a robe of honour. The *elchi* was provided with a magnificent house and other facilities. The nobles and high officials invited him to dinner and entertained him in different ways. Unfortunately the *elchi* was seized by dysentery. The Indian and Iranian physicians tried their utmost to treat him but he passed away after a few days.[197] His brother Mirza Muhammad Jauhari, who was staying at Golkonda, took care of the funeral.[198] Several important Shiʻi nobles attended the funeral.[199] The quick and sudden death of Mirza Asadullah Beg Kark Yaraq did not obviously allow him to play any major role, but as it appears from the title *Kark Yaraq* that presumably he was also to serve as military advisor for the Qutb Shahi armies.

The Royal Pilgrims

Yearning for peace, territorial integrity and internal freedom, Golkonda executed the Deed of Submission, after which, instead of attaining peace, it found itself even more troubled. It could hardly keep up open relations with Iran, as the Mughals seriously objected to such correspondence.

Golkonda therefore resorted to secret contacts with Iran for which some avenues developed through the migration of 'Abdullah Qutb Shah's aunt to Iran.

In the year 1047/1638, after the death of Muhammad Shah, 'Abdullah Qutb Shah's grandmother Khanum Agha and his aunt Shahr Banu, who were related to the family of Shah Ni'matullah Kirmani and thus to the Safavid family, were permitted to proceed on *hajj* escorted by Qazi Zahiru'ddin Muhammad Najafi, who too was perhaps a member of the same House.[200] Vazīr Khairat Khan escorted the pilgrims up to Masulipatam. On 1st Rajab 1047/9 November 1637, they proceeded on the ship of Shaikh Muhammad Malik Shirazi, a renowned merchant, towards Bandar 'Abbas to go first to Iraq-i-Arab and then to Mecca.[201] By that time Sultan Murad IV had captured Baghdad, and the pilgrims had to discontinue their journey and stay at Isfahan, the capital of Safavid Iran.[202] Early in the year 1049/1639, 'Abdullah Qutb Shah gave money to merchants Mirza Muhammad Mashhadi and Khwaja 'Abdul 'Ali Ardestani to purchase certain articles from Iraq-i-Ajam and carry the same to the royal ladies at Isfahan. According to Iranian sources, the royal ladies of Golkonda reached Qazvin in 1049/1640 and were granted audience by Shah Safi.[203] Their journey to Mashhad was a part of their pilgrimage, regarding which 'Abdullah Qutb Shah had sent a letter to Shah Safi that was carried and delivered by Qazi Zahiru'ddin in Qazvin.[204] Shah Safi immediately responded to the letter and informed 'Abdullah Qutb Shah about their safe arrival in Iran and further assured him that they would be royal guests and would be provided with all necessary facilities and could proceed to Mecca whenever they pleased. In that letter, which was sent through Sayyid Muzaffar Murtaza, a person in the royal retinue, Shah Safi added a few sentences to the effect of the renewal of their friendship and desired 'Abdullah Qutb Shah to keep in touch through letters.[205]

Khanum Agha, 'Abdullah Qutb Shah's grandmother, died at Isfahan early in the year 1050/1640 and was buried at Mashhad.[206] 'Abdullah Qutb Shah's aunt, Shahr Banu, who was staying with the royal family of Iran probably remained in Iran for good. Monetary help was being sent to her from Golkonda.[207] Shahr Banu and her nephew Najabat Khan[208] played an important role in the continuation of Golkonda's relations with Iran, serving as conduits for political messages to Shah Safi and subsequently to Shah 'Abbas II, particularly after the defection of Mir Jumla Mir Muhammad Sa'id Ardestani.

Imam Quli Beg Shamlu stayed in Golkonda for about seven years and was perhaps disheartened by the changing atmosphere at court under Mughal influence. In Rajab 1049/November 1639, Imam Quli Beg decided to return to Iran probably without seeking formal permission from 'Abdullah Qutb Shah. He, therefore, set out and encamped at a station outside the city.

'Abdullah Qutb Shah had at the same time decided to proceed on a tour to Masulipatam. He immediately issued a *farmān* regarding the kind of officials who would accompany him which included the envoys. A separate *farmān* was therefore issued to Imam Quli Beg to come back and join the sultan's entourage. The *elchi* was again favoured with presents according to high protocol.[209] He accompanied 'Abdullah Qutb Shah on his journey to and from Masulipatam, which took about two months.[210] Golkonda sources give a very elaborate account of the favours that 'Abdullah Qutb Shah frequently bestowed upon Imam Quli Beg.[211] He was relieved with ceremony and was accompanied by *hakīm-ul-mulk* (Royal Physician), Nizamu'ddin Gilani, as return *elchi* of Golkonda in the month of Sha'ban 1050/November 1640 and proceeded from Dabhol to Bandar 'Abbas. By that time, Hakim Gilani's son had returned from Isfahan and was given a position in the Majlis.[212] The two *elchis* reached Iran in 1051/1641.[213]

While Nizamu'ddin Gilani was staying in Iran as *elchi* of Golkonda, Shah Safi passed away on 12th Safar 1052/2 May 1642[214] at Kashan. Though the news of his death reached Golkonda immediately, it was officially confirmed by Gilani through his letter that reached Golkonda by Zilqada 1052/January 1643.[215] Muhammad Sadiq and Muhammad Tahir[216] from Gilani's retinue brought this letter.

Apparently, 'Abdullah Qutb Shah did not feel the need to send a separate embassy for Shah 'Abbas II's accession since Gilani was already there. He, therefore, issued a *farmān* to *hakīm-ul-mulk* Nizamu'ddin Gilani, early in Zilqada 1053/January 1644 to offer his condolences upon Shah Safi's death and congratulate the new ruler.[217]

Hakim-ul-Mulk stayed in Iran up to at least 1056/1646 and returned to Golkonda sometime before 1063/1653. During the decade after *hakim-ul-mulk's* departure with Imam Quli Beg, there is no evidence of any political envoy being sent from Golkonda to Iran and vice versa. Nevertheless in 1058/1648, Shaikh Muhammad Ibn Khatun, the greatest of Golkonda's diplomats, proceeded for *hajj* from the port of Masulipatam but died in a shipwreck, early next year, in 1059/1649. Ibn Khatun's gifts for Shah 'Abbas II were, however, saved by men in his suite and were carried subsequently to the king, an arrangement made possibly by 'Abdullah Qutb Shah's aunt.[218]

The Last Desperate Effort—the Seventh Phase

Shah Jahan, after compelling Golkonda into submission in 1046/1636 and annexing Qandahar in 1047/1638, was set upon realizing his ambitions in Turan. From here on all his resources were diverted towards Balkh and Badakhshan, which he occupied militarily and diplomatically by 1056/1646.

While Shah Jahan was running his ambitious campaigns in Turan, Golkonda went on submitting *peshkash* to the Mughals but simultaneously expanded its territories in the south with the help of its able prime minister (Mir Jumla) Mir Muhammad Sa'id Ardestani. The newly added territories of *taraf-i Karnātak* (provinces of the Karnatak) enriched Golkonda with their diamond mines, developed harbours and additional amount of *peshkash* from the peasantry and merchants. In the meantime, Shah Jahan's campaigns in Turan cost him much more than his earlier estimates. Above all, he lost Qandahar as well as Balkh and Badakhshan by 1059/1648. The failure of Shah Jahan's foreign policy represented the defeat of his territorial ambitions in the north-west and left him politically isolated.[219] Relations with Iran would remain strained for the rest of his reign. He re-initiated his campaigns in Qandahar through his sons, who had by now gained military experience. In the year 1064/1653, Prince Aurangzeb was again sent as the viceroy of the Deccan, which marked the beginning of a new phase in this relational history. As Jahangir had inherited Akbar's generosity, Aurangzeb had inherited Shah Jahan's ambitions. He immediately observed the changing situation in the Deccan where he had come after an interval of ten years.

The first significant event that occurred during the second tenure of Aurangzeb's viceroyalty was the conflict between 'Abdullah Qutb Shah and his Prime Minister, Mir Jumla Mir Muhammad Sa'id Ardestani, and the latter's defection. The immensity of *Mir Jumla's* riches, his military acumen, his political command and his powerful contacts with Iran, European merchants, and some princes of the Karnatak[220] all placed him in a unique position. 'Abdullah Qutb Shah was both envious and afraid of Mir Muhammad Sa'id, who had resolved to cross over to a more hospitable and lucrative camp. Prince Aurangzeb gave him a warm reception without any delay. After receipt of a letter from Mir Jumla, Prince Aurangzeb addressed 'Abdullah Qutb Shah in a letter (*yarlīgh*) dated 2nd Rabi I 1066/20 December 1655, informing him that Mir Muhammad Sa'id had been assigned a *mansab* of 5,000 *zāt*/5,000 *sawār*, the highest rank in the Mughal nobility. Therefore, he should be relieved without delay and sent to the Mughal court with his son and dependents along with Mir Abul Qasim and Sayyid 'Ali, who had carried the letter. 'Abdullah Qutb Shah was further warned of an attack in case he chose not to comply with imperial orders.[221] 'Abdullah Qutb Shah did not attempt to detain Mir Muhammad Sa'id, instead he imprisoned his son Muhammad Amin, violating the specific orders contained in Aurangzeb's letter. It justified, according to the Mughals, an invasion of which he had been forewarned. Prince Aurangzeb issued reminders to 'Abdullah Qutb Shah advising him to release Muhammad Amin immediately.[222] 'Abdullah Qutb Shah did not comply with any of the orders and the Mughal army, under Prince Sultan Muhammad Akbar, marched towards Hyderabad and laid siege to Golkonda fort by 5th Rabi II 1066/22 January 1656.[223] Interestingly, Hakim-ul-Mulk who had called on Prince Sultan Muhammad Akbar to present gifts and to initiate negotiations on behalf of 'Abdullah Qutb Shah, was detained in the Mughal prince's military camp (*urdū*) until Muhammad Amin was released.[224]

Prince Aurangzeb had already left Aurangabad on 3rd Rabi II/20 January and arrived at Hyderabad in thirteen days. Negotiations continued till the end of Jumada II during which Muhammad Amin and his mother were released and sent to the Mughal camp with their belongings. 'Abdullah Qutb Shah paid heavy amounts in *peshkash* in accordance with the terms of peace or as war indemnity and gave his daughter in marriage to Sultan Muhammad.[225] The marriage took place on the morning of 18th Jumada II 1066/3 April 1656 as per the Hanafi tradition of Muslims.[226]

During the course of the siege and negotiations, a few skirmishes had taken place between the Mughal and Qutb Shahi forces, which provoked the Mughal army to start plundering Hyderabad city.[227] Mughal and Golkonda sources record the account of the Mughal siege of Golkonda, their devastation of Hyderabad city and the details of their exploits.

Abdullah Qutb Shah's Letter to Shah 'Abbas II

Early in the year 1067/1656, Prince Aurangzeb began his campaign against Bijapur with Mir Muhammad Sa'id, whom the Mughal emperor had now entitled as Mu'azzam Khan. Sultan 'Abdullah Qutb Shah, who had anticipated a highly probable Mughal advance towards Golkonda, addressed Shah 'Abbas II in a letter dated Rabi II 1067/January 1657, informing him about the details of the Mughal invasion led by Prince Aurangzeb in the preceding year and the probability of a repetition of the same. He also requested Shah 'Abbas II to suggest some ways for strategic diplomacy.

This diplomatic letter comprising about 1,400 words was perhaps the most intrepid action ever ventured upon by any of the Qutb Shahi sultans. After a brief ceremonial opening, 'Abdullah Qutb Shah wrote that Shah 'Abbas II was the promoter of the faith of the Twelvers (*Asna 'Asharī*) and had inherited the disposition of the Prophet of Islam. He would, therefore, be ever victorious. As usual he emphasized the ancestral affinity of the two Houses and expressed his personal devotion to the Safavid household. He recalled that during the reign of late Shah 'Abbas I, whenever the Mughals oppressed Golkonda the late Shah rescued it either through mediation or by the demonstration of his forces.

'Abdullah Qutb Shah expressed his regret that he could not enter into formal relations with the Shah. The Mughals always kept an eye on activities in Golkonda, and any correspondence between Golkonda and Iran could provoke them, therefore he had resorted to secret contacts.[228]

He informed Shah 'Abbas II that during the year 1065/1655 he had to face many troublesome challenges and to deal with another such incident was beyond his capacity. The most significant of those events was the defection and revolt of Mir Muhammad Sa'id (Mir Jumla).

Interestingly, the Golkonda Sultan referred to Shah Jahan as mere Sultan Khurram and charged him with the breaking of earlier treaties. He informed Shah 'Abbas II that Sultan Khurram deputed Prince Aurangzeb with a cavalry of 30,000 to invade Golkonda while Muhammad Sa'id, conniving with him, had proceeded from the other side with a cavalry of 6,000 and an infantry of 70,000 mustered from Karnatak.[229] He then narrated the details of how the Mughal army had plundered the city of Hyderabad and then laid siege to Golkonda fort. As the siege was prolonged and no help was in sight, 'Abdullah Qutb Shah had to negotiate peace, which was concluded upon the payment of twenty lakhs of *huns* (equivalent to 300,000 *tomans*) and a matrimonial alliance (*musāhirat*). Moreover, the province of Karnatak which was captured and brought under Qutb Shahi sway after fighting for many years and spending crores of rupees, had been assigned to Muhammad Sa'id by Shah Jahan as *in'ām*.[230]

'Abdullah Qutb Shah further wrote that *Mir Jumla's* mischief had not come to an end. On 14th Rabi II 1067/20 January 1657, *Mir Jumla* was again reported to be advancing speedily with a cavalry of 30,000 to capture Hyderabad, Bijapur and the Qutb Shahi province of *taraf-i-karnātak*. He added that a great calamity had fallen upon him, the state of affairs was out his control and he felt helpless. He made an appeal to the religious spirit and the paternal disposition of Shah 'Abbas II with the hope that he would not allow the Mughals to oppress Golkonda. His kingdom, where the sacred call of *'aliyun waliullah*[231] had echoed for over 170 years, the place that many Shi'ite immigrants had chosen as their abode, deserved Safavid protection.

Finally he expressed his willingness to pay the expenditure of the forces that would be employed on the borders of Qandahar for putting out the spark of mischief (*sharāreh-i sharārat*), no doubt referring to the Mughals.[232] 'Abdullah Qutb Shah promised he would remit the necessary funds at a proper time through the *vakīls* of his private estate (*khāssah sharīfah*). In the meanwhile, he was sending a few presents and a list through Miranji to ensure that the letter was not delivered without due ceremony.[233]

'Abdullah Qutb Shah's Letter to his Aunt Shahr Bano

'Abdullah Qutb Shah thought it was inadequate to invite Shah 'Abbas II's attention to his pitiful situation. Fear-stricken, he anticipated that an even greater catastrophe might compel him to flee from Golkonda. He, therefore, quickly wrote to his aunt Shahr Banu, who was in Iran, to request Shah 'Abbas II to make necessary arrangements in case he needed to escape.

'Abdullah Qutb Shah addressed his aunt with great respect and much ceremony and mentioned Shah 'Abbas II with numerous praiseworthy titles. He again stressed the devotional attachment of the Qutb Shahi family to the descendants of the House of Shah Safi, who were the ultimate saviours of Golkonda.

He informed her that Shah Jahan, at the instigation of the most unfaithful Mir Muhammad Sa'id, had thrown all his treaties and pacts into oblivion and had developed enemity towards him. The sultan's well-informed aunt would have heard by now that Shah Jahan had sent his son Aurangzeb with a huge army that had mercilessly plundered the city of Hyderabad less than a year ago.[234] That year (1067/1657), he sent another 30,000 to 40,000 horsemen under Prince Aurangzeb and Mir Muhammad Sa'id while 'Abdullah Qutb Shah received help from nowhere. If, however, the Golkonda sultan could not withstand the situation he would seek refuge at the Safavid court. He, therefore, requested his aunt to supplicate Shah 'Abbas II to issue a *farmān*, as was done during the times of the late Shah Safi, addressed to the Dutch (*Valandah*) and the English (*Angrez*) captains with binding instructions to arrange the sultan's escape. A reliable person should be sent whenever he intended to proceed to Iran to make all necessary arrangements for his safe voyage.[235]

The two letters were dispatched between 14th Rabi II 1067/20 January 1657 and early Jumada I 1067/February 1657 and may have been sent together with Mir Miranji.[236] 'Abdullah Qutb Shah's mention of Shah Jahan as Sultan Khurram in a letter addressed to Shah 'Abbas II, whose father Shah Safi was called *farzand* or son by the Mughal emperor was quite peculiar. It speaks of 'Abdullah Qutb Shah's immense dislike of the Mughals and the extreme frustration that had led him to search desperately for alternatives. On one hand, he appealed to Shah 'Abbas II's religious sentiments to crush the Mughals offering to meet the cost of war at Qandahar and, on the other hand, he made arrangements for his escape to Iran.

The Golkonda sultan was clearly ill-informed. His statement that Aurangzeb and Mir Jumla were advancing towards Golkonda earlier in the year 1067/1656 was either a product of his apprehension or a ploy to provoke Shah 'Abbas II. Second, his desire to send his armies on the borders of Qandahar was superfluous, as Iran had already re-taken Qandahar in 1059/1648. His complaint about Shah Jahan's assignment of the Karnatak provinces to Mir Muhammad Sa'id was also insubstantial since 'Abdullah Qutb Shah had already executed a Deed of Endowment (*waqf nāmah*) in favour of Mir Muhammad Sa'id while he was in his service. He had himself irrevocably declared Muhammad Sa'id Ardestani and his descendants as perpetually in charge (*mutawalli*) of the southern parts of his kingdom.

The sultan did not regain his confidence even after Shah Jahan lost his campaigns in both Qandahar and Turan and his sons began an ugly contest for succession.

Shah 'Abbas II's Reply to 'Abdullah Qutb Shah

Shah 'Abbas II, with much political acumen, clearly perceived the changing situation in Golkonda as well as in Hindustan. Late in 1067/1657, or early next year, he replied to 'Abdullah Qutb Shah. The essence of the letter is briefly cited here.

After a ceremonial address, Shah 'Abbas II acknowledged the receipt of 'Abdullah Qutb Shah's letter. He then wrote that a true friendship was put to test when one of the friends was in distress and needed help. He assured the sultan that his cooperation with Golkonda would exceed the help and cooperation extended by his forefathers, along with ever increasing love and affection. He advised 'Abdullah Qutb Shah to learn to stand his own ground and to stand united with friends. He prompted the Golkonda sultan to exploit the situation created by the Mughal war of succession.

The bearer of the Qutb Shahi letter had passed away in Iran; therefore, Shah 'Abbas II sent the reply through someone else (*falān*) and desired that he should be relieved early.[237] The contention that Shah 'Abbas II seized the opportunity offered by the war of succession to entice the Deccan sultans against the Mughals, urging them to sink their differences and assuring them that he was prepared to move his own forces against the Mughal empire, lays too much emphasis on sectarian solidarity and cannot be substantiated through epistolary evidence.[238] Shah 'Abbas II also did not mention *Mir Jumla* who was on good terms with the Safavid family. There is no evidence if he had sent any military aid to Golkonda or took any special action on the borders of Qandahar. He took a keen interest in the matter only to aggravate the contest of Shah Jahan's aspiring successors. He helped Murad by sending military aid and Dara Shikoh through diplomatic encouragement.[239]

On 7th Zilhijja 1067/6 September 1657, Shah Jahan fell ill. Though his illness continued for a short period, he proceeded to Akbarabad in about a month. By 20th Muharram 1068/18 October 1657, several rumors had led his sons to start the struggle for succession. Dara Shikoh, the eldest son, was present in Delhi and seized the chance to suppress the news at court and master the situation. Aurangzeb left his expedition in the Deccan to his son Muhammad Mu'azzam and proceeded to Akbarabad apparently to see his ailing father, but actually to establish his claims to the imperial throne. He controlled a large part of the Mughal army that was being used in the Deccan campaigns.[240] He put these forces to use in the war of succession but was compelled to loosen his grip over the Deccan. This provided a renewed lease of life to Bijapur and Golkonda.

Before the war of succession was concluded and Aurangzeb had entered Akbarabad, Dara Shikoh wrote to 'Abdullah Qutb Shah on 2nd Jumada II 1067/8 March 1657, assuring him on behalf of Shah Jahan that the imperial government had no intention of annexing Golkonda.[241] Dara's letter was perhaps a source of consolation for 'Abdullah Qutb Shah.

On 6th Sha'ban 1068/29 April 1658, Prince Sultan Muhammad Akbar wrote a detailed letter to 'Abdullah Qutb Shah informing him about his success in defeating the Imperial army sent by Dara Shikoh under Jaswant Singh.[242] Again on 4th Safar 1069/22 October 1658, Prince Sultan Muhammad Akbar informed 'Abdullah Qutb Shah about Aurangzeb's victory over Dara Shikoh[243] and the latter's flight to Thattah. He also informed him that Aurangzeb's forces were pursuing Dara Shikoh in the north-west. Such reports provided the Golkonda sultan with some time to breathe, and yet assured Aurangzeb's rise as the emperor of India. Golkonda had to, therefore, reorient its foreign relations. Aurangzeb defeated his brothers and declared himself successor to the imperial throne of India on 1st Zilqada 1068/1669/21 July 1658. The enhanced responsibilities of an imperial government further disengaged his mind from his former preoccupation of the Deccan campaign. Throughout the rest of 'Abdullah Qutb Shah's reign, he had very few occasions to dabble in Golkonda's affairs, as the sultanate continued submitting *peshkash* in cash and kind to the Mughals.[244] From a letter of Aurangzeb addressed to 'Abdullah Qutb Shah on 24th Zilqada 1074/8 June 1664, informing him about the appointment of Prince Muhammad Mu'azzam (Shah Alam Bahadur Shah), it becomes evident that Aurangzeb was quite happy with 'Abdullah Qutb Shah and desired him to be regular in sending yearly *peshkash*. He assured 'Abdullah Qutb Shah of all his favours.[245]

Golkonda-Mughal relations progressed smoothly until 1075/1665 when Raja Jai Singh (Mirza Raja) concluded peace with Shivaji who handed over the keys of twenty-four forts to Mughal chiefs, under the famous Treaty of Purandar. This alliance between the Marathas and the Mughals left Bijapur and Golkonda feeling more insecure. Moreover, the treaty stopped the spirited Shivaji from his advances further north. Instead he diverted his campaigns against Bijapur and Golkonda. That naturally led to the alliance of the two sultanates to defend themselves against the Marathas. In Rajab 1076/January 1666, 'Abdullah Qutb Shah sent an auxiliary force of 6,000 horsemen and 25,000 footmen led by Neknam Khan (Riza Quli Beg) to join the Bijapur army led by Sharza Khan and fight against the allied Maratha-Mughal forces at Bijapur. Peace was, however, concluded after much killing and a disastrous siege of five months, in Zilqada 1076/1666 to the loss of both parties.[246] Shortly afterwards the alliance between Shivaji and the

Mughals was dissolved and the relations between the two became hostile again. In the year 1079/1669, Shivaji made a secret visit to Golkonda and assured enormous military aid to 'Abdullah Qutb Shah.[247] Yet the Mughals reacted more strongly against Shivaji than against Golkonda. It appears that the rest of 'Abdullah Qutb Shah's career was relatively undisturbed by the Mughals. He does not seem to have entered into any political or diplomatic contact with Shah 'Abbas II or his successor Shah Suleiman Safavi.

Iranian Envoy Muhammad Muqim in Golkonda

As discussed earlier, Shah 'Abbas II's letter was communicated secretly, the name of its bearer concealed and references to the Mughals were made enigmatically. Shah 'Abbas II, who had closely observed the developments in Hindustan, believed that the war of succession among the sons of Shah Jahan would prevent the Mughals from holding onto Golkonda. As a matter of fact, Aurangzeb had been immediately distracted from his investments in the various strongholds of Bijapur in 1067/1658 when the war of succession broke out. Shah 'Abbas II, therefore, found an opportunity to openly send an envoy to the Deccan with a letter that was explicitly against the Mughals. Shah 'Abbas II sent the letter with Mirza Muhammad Muqim Kitabdar (Librarian) of *khāssah-i sharīfah* (Crown Lands). Neither the date of the letter nor the *elchi*'s departure from Iran or his arrival in Golkonda were recorded. Nevertheless, he was seen in Golkonda on 2nd Muharram 1072,[248] although he was expected to have reached there earlier in 1068 or 1069/1659 or 1660.[249] Mirza Muhammad Muqim Kitabdar had to carry Shah 'Abbas II's letters to both Golkonda and Bijapur.

Shah 'Abbas II's letter to 'Abdullah Qutb Shah is almost similiar to his previous letter but unique for its openness, confidence and its detailed narration. It suggests that it was written when the war of succession was at its height and Shah 'Abbas II was expecting the disintegration of Mughal power.

The letter began with glorified ceremonial phrases for 'Abdullah Qutb Shah and acknowledged the receipt of the sultan's previous letter. He spoke highly of the love and unity between the two Houses and admired the contents of 'Abdullah Qutb Shah's letter.[250] Shah 'Abbas II commented that Mughal violation of earlier treaties had put the integrity of Hindustan's ruler and his sons into serious doubt. 'Abdullah Qutb Shah's report on the promise-breakers who had risen to oppress and plunder Golkonda was justified in the light of the age-old ties between their dynasties. It was just to seek Safavid help against deserters and those averse to Shi'ism. Such enemies should be thoroughly disabled and dislodged. Shah 'Abbas II assured 'Abdullah Qutb Shah that the situation in Golkonda was not yet lost and there was still time to respond. He assured him that all help would be made available and advised him to be confident of a great victory in the near future.

Regarding Hindustan, he observed that the Mughal Empire's super-structure would come down definitely as it stood on different pillars, each of which had been shaken by the war of succession. The fall of Mughal power was, therefore, inevitable. He advised 'Abdullah Qutb Shah to stand by 'Adil Shah, as had their ancestors. He emphasized that religious sentiments and political consciousness also united the Deccan sultanates.

In the end he recorded the credentials of *elchi* Mirza Muhammad Muqim Kitabdar who would carry the oral message to 'Abdullah Qutb Shah, informing him about the state of affairs in Iran. Shah 'Abbas II further desired an early dismissal of his *elchi* along with all open and secret messages.[251]

Shah 'Abbas II's observation was based on up-to-date information but it lacked balance in respect of both Hindustan and Golkonda. His effort to unite the sinking sultanates of Golkonda and Bijapur to rise against the Mughals was unrealistic. Moreover, there is no evidence of his extending any substantial help to those sultanates. Similarly his prognosis of the Mughal Empire's downfall based on the war of succession was swiftly nullified by Aurangzeb's rapid rise through drastic measures.

Aurangzeb was busy in establishing his government in other parts of the empire and, therefore, could not pay much personal attention to the Deccan sultanates. However, he never neglected the affairs in Golkonda. The Mughal intelligencers or news writers (*waqāi' navīs*) were present in parts of Golkonda and Bijapur. 'Abdullah Qutb Shah and his *āmirs* treated the Mughal news writers of Hyderabad well and availed their services when needed. They had been conveying information regarding the Iranian *elchi* Haji Mirza Muhammad Muqim Kitabdar's day-to-day activities to the Imperial Court.[252]

No specific information on Mirza Muhammad Muqim's official reception in Golkonda is traceable. Nevertheless, he stayed there for a considerable time. 'Abdullah Qutb Shah sent him gifts like fruits and a *sarāpā* (or robe) on numerous occasions.[253] During his stay in Golkonda, Muhammad Muqim kept in contact with Budaq Sultan, the Iranian *elchi* at Aurangzeb's court. On 11th Muharram 1072/27 August 1661, he requested a Mughal news writer to make necessary arrangements to escort two persons from his suite named Murtuza Quli and Ilah Quli to accompany Budaq Sultan who had reached Delhi on 3rd Shawwal 1071/22 May 1661.[254] Emperor Aurangzeb was pleased, as Iran had recognized his accession while Shah Jahan was still alive. He did not raise any objection to the traffic of envoys between Iran and the Deccan sultanates. Many minor *elchis* from Iran arrived in Golkonda and joined Muhammad Muqim. On 23rd Safar 1072/8

October 1661, a person from Iran arrived in Golkonda from Masulipatam and joined Muhammad Muqim's retinue. The Iranian *elchi* sent twenty-five barrels (*tablah*) of Iranian fruits to 'Abdullah Qutb Shah, who favoured him with a robe of honour upon reception. Sultan 'Abdullah then sent for Muhammad Muqim through Ibrahim Beg, *sar naubat*, who showed the elchi to his palace (*haveli*) in Hyderabad. He also treated the *elchi* to betel (*pān*). On the same occasion he conferred cap-a'-pie (*sarāpā*) on two persons from Muhammad Muqim's entourage, who had recently arrived from Iran.[255]

Shah 'Abbas II had been sending gifts to 'Abdullah Qutb Shah through Haji Muhammad Muqim, carried by different parties from Iran to Golkonda, either through Masulipatam or Surat. On 6th Sha'ban 1073/7 March 1663, a person was reported to have entered the city of Aurangabad. He was an agent of Muhammad Muqim and had brought six Iraqi horses through the port of Surat. The same person proceeded with this horses to Golkonda on 22nd Sha'ban 1073/23 March 1663.[256]

Mirza Muhammad Muqim was expected to communicate news from Golkonda to Iran, but from a letter of Shah 'Abbas II it appears that the *elchi* was somewhat negligent in the performance of his duties.[257] Probably in the year 1076/1665, Shah 'Abbas II, while he was in Mazandaran for a hunt, addressed Muhammad Muqim who was in Golkonda. The Shah addressed him with kind regards and informed him about his delightful engagements in Mazandaran. He then mildly complained that an experienced servant like Muhammad Muqim had not communicated a letter reporting the state of affairs in Golkonda and about the health of that sultan.[258] He then ordered Muhammad Muqim either to return immediately to Iran after obtaining permission from 'Abdullah Qutb Shah (whose name is missing) or to send a detailed report about his (Sultan 'Abdullah's) health and the state of affairs in Golkonda about which Shah 'Abbas II was very concerned. He closed the letter demanding that the *elchi* bring two nice female elephants along with two mahouts with him when he returned to Iran.[259]

The date of Muhammad Muqim's return from Golkonda is not traceable. By the year 1076/1667 Shah 'Abbas II was unhappy with Aurangzeb, but he died in Rabi I 1077/1668 in Mazandaran and was succeeded by his son, Shah Suleiman.[260] 'Abdullah Qutb Shah, failing in health and dejected by circumstances, was probably not pleased to relieve the Iranian *elchi*. He was was further distraught because of his mother's, Hayat Bakshi Begam, death on 28th Sha'ban 177/3 February 1667. He himself died on Muharram 1083/21 April 1672. After Sultan 'Abdullah's death, political relations between Golkonda and Iran came to an end, even though his successor, Sultan Abul Hasan Qutb Shah, would make a feeble effort to reestablish the relations by turning to earlier diplomatic precedents.

Diplomatic Hoax—The Last Phase

Abul Hasan Qutb Shah ascended the Qutb Shahi throne soon after 'Abdullah Qutb Shah's death in Muharram 1083/April 1672. He was the third son-in-law of Sultan 'Abdullah, and his accession had received the strong support of Sayyid Muzaffar Mir Jumla. The news of his accession was carried to Aurangzeb together with his *peshkash*, and a petition requesting the validation of his succession and recognition of his government.[261] Aurangzeb, who was proceeding to Hasan Abdal (in Kabul) on an expedition to punish the Afghans, responded to the petition by issuing a *farmān* that said:

1. According to early treaties concluded with 'Abdullah Qutb Shah the entire territory of Golkonda, after his death, would be annexed to the Mughal Empire.
2. Nevertheless in view of the loyalty and faithfulness of Abul Hasan, 'Abdullah Qutb Shah's dominions were being assigned to him on account of the emperor's inherent generosity.
3. The assignment was subject to Abul Hasan's adherence to the laws of allegiance and loyalty.
4. The sultan should avoid any alliance with Shivaji and should not extend any sort of help to him.
5. He should remit a *peshkash* amounting to forty lakh rupees every year to the imperial treasury.
6. He should seek royal favours with his loyal services and suitable gifts.
7. He should record a treaty with the above conditions and swear on the Koran in the presence of Abdur Rahman (son of Islam Khan), the bearer of the *farmān*, and Khwaja Osman, the Mughal envoy then present in Golkonda.[262]

Abdur Rahman sent the *farmān* to Golkonda together with the imperial forces on 6th Shawwal 1084/4 January 1674.[263] Because of the new circumstances prevailing in Golkonda, the execution of the treaty was slightly delayed. In the meanwhile, Abdur Rahman was appointed as the *Bakshi*[264] of the Deccan, after the death of Fath Khan.[265] On 9th Safar 1086/25 April 1675, Abul Hasan Qutb Shah signed the treaty following all the instructions contained in *farmān*.[266]

He observed the treaty's terms for barely two years before revising his policy towards the Mughals under Shivaji's counsel. The veteran Maratha military leader reached Hyderabad and held a meeting with Abul Hasan Qutb Shah on shared political problems in Safar 1088/March 1677. Madanna Pandit, who was the *peshkar* (accountant) of Golkonda, also attended this meeting. Shivaji succeeded in his mission of drawing Golkonda into an alliance with him to defend themselves against the Mughals and also in collecting a 'huge amount and a strong force of soldiers' from Golkonda.[267] The transaction did not go unnoticed by the watchful Mughals. The *subehdār* (governor) of the Deccan, Bahadur Khan Kukaltash, received the news when he was in Pathri. He immediately moved to Hyderabad via Kandhar and exacted 'heavy fines' from Abul Hasan.[268] Soon after arriving in Hyderabad, Bahadur Khan Kukaltash received a letter from Shaikh Minhaj who had been appointed by Abdur Rahman to assess Gulbarga's revenue.[269] Shaik Minhaj wrote that the time was right to capture the fort, and requested that an army be sent up to a location where he could guide it further.[270] Before Bahadur Khan Kukaltash could take action, Diler Khan and Abdul Karim (Bahlul Khan) sent a petition to Aurangzeb that Bahadur Khan Kukaltash was forging a secret alliance with Abul Hasan, Sikandar 'Adil Shah and Shivaji. They stressed their boundless loyalty assuring the emperor that Hyderabad could be annexed to the Mughal Empire if a reasonable force was sent to aid them. Aurangzeb summoned Bahadur Khan Kukaltash in Jumada 11 1088/August 1677. Diler Khan and Abdul Karim led the Mughal army to Malkhed on the border of Golkonda.[271] Muhammad Ibrahim Khalilullah Khan Sipah Salar, *sar khayl* of Golkonda, mounted a defence and made them retreat. They entered into a peace treaty.[272]

Abul Hasan issued a Deed of Victory (*fath nāmah*), praising the good services of Khalilullah Khan, which was probably circulated to all important outposts of his kingdom as is evident from the text of the Deed.[273] In 1089/ 1678, Aurangzeb returned from his long stay at Kabul and reached Ajmer. The same year, Prince Muhammad Mu'azzam was called to Ujjain from the Deccan and Bahadur Khan Kukaltash was again sent as the *subehdār* of the Deccan.

Meanwhile, Prince Muhammad Akbar, the youngest son of Aurangzeb, revolted at the instigation of the Rathore.[274] Though he found a respite under Sambhaji's protection, Khan Bahadur Kukaltash and Prince Muhammad Mu'azzam chased him away. He had been roaming in different parts of the Deccan until his ultimate flight to Iran.[275] During this chase, Prince Muhammad Mu'azzam wrote a letter to Abul Hasan to arrest Prince Akbar if he happened to enter his territories. Abul Hasan dutifully replied, assuring him that he would do his utmost to arrest the rebel prince, if he entered Golkonda's boundaries.[276]

In Ramadan 1092/September 1681, Aurangzeb left Ajmer for the Deccan with the aim to set things right himself. He reached Aurangabad in Zilqada 1093/November 1682. The rise of Akkanna and Madanna in Golkonda and their imprisonment of Sayyid Muzaffar in 1094/1683 were two important events reported to the emperor. Mir Hashim, son of Sayyid Muzaffar, was in the imperial service. He made a detailed representation against the unwholesome activities of the two brothers (Akkanna and Madanna), who had got his father demoted from the position of *Mir Jumla* to *vakīl-us saltanat* and then had him imprisoned. He requested the emperor to take necessary action for his release.[277] At the same time it was reported that Abul Hasan had taken back Ramgir and other *sarkārs* that had been annexed to the Mughal *subah* of Zafarnagar. Aurangzeb deputed Bahadur Khan Kukaltash to restore the territories that had been taken illegally.[278]

The same year, Mirza Muhammad, *mushrif-i-ghusl khānah* (inspector of baths), was sent to Abul Hasan to collect certain jewels and enter into a dialogue with the sultan. In the course of the discussion with him, Abul Hasan revealed his desire to be called the *pādshāh* of Golkonda.[279] Soon after Mirza Muhammad Mushrif's return, Mughal forces led by Prince Muhammad Mu'azzam and Bahadur Khan Kukaltash reached the frontier of Golkonda near Bijapur's borders where they were faced by a large Golkonda army under the command of Muhammad Ibrahim Khalilullah. Golkonda rejected the terms of peace offered by Prince Muhammad Mu'azzam and war ensued.[280] Golkonda's army was defeated but not chased out; as a result, Aurangzeb warned Bahadur Khan Kukaltash and Prince Mu'azzam for their negligence.[281]

The Golkonda forces again challenged the Mughal army early in the year 1095/1684 and were chased up to Hyderabad. Madanna's group in the Qutb Shahi court sought to defeat Muhammad Ibrahim Khalilullah, the *sipāh sālār* (commander-in-chief) of Golkonda. Their differences increased to such a point that Muhammad Ibrahim Khalilullah deserted Golkonda and crossed over to Aurangzeb's camp. This defection created a state of anarchy and the Mughal army plundered the city of Hyderabad.[282] Abul Hasan shut himself up in the Golkonda fort and submitted his apologies to Aurangzeb, seeking Prince Muhammad Mu'azzam and his son, Prince Muizuddin's mediation.[283] Golkonda's men put Akkanna and Madanna to death and their severed heads were sent to Aurangzeb to subdue his anger.[284] Sayyid Muzaffar was, of course, released earlier in 1094/1683.[285]

Abul Hasan lost many strong men of his retinue. Through Prince Mu'azzam and Bahadur Khan Kukaltash's mediation he had some respite, but he could not conclude peace with the Mughals. Aurangzeb was determined to overthrow the Golkonda sultanate and its sultan was conscious of the forthcoming catastrophe.[286] He made a last desperate effort to invite the sympathies of Iran to hold off the situation.

Abul Hasan's Letter to Shah Suleiman Safavi

Abul Hasan had some connections (of an indirect nature) with Shah Suleiman Safavi. Presumably, he had kept in touch with the Kirmani family who had shifted from Golkonda to Isfahan during 'Abdullah Qutb Shah's reign.[287] A few years before, he had addressed Sahib Kuchak, Ni'matullah's daughter who was in Iran, asking her to request Shah Suleiman Safavi to make arrangements for the safe voyage of members of Ibrahim Khalilullah, the *sipāh sālār*'s household, from Isfahan to the ports of Iran.[288]

Abul Hasan does not seem to have entered into any direct political correspondence with Shah Suleiman Safavi until 1095/1685, when he addressed the Shah in a detailed political letter that was carried to him secretly. The letter opened with more than 100 ceremonial phrases addressing Shah Suleiman Safavi. Even in this section, much emphasis was laid on the Shah being the Chief Khalifa of Allah and a great promoter of the Shi'ite faith. He then recorded his devotion with the usual argument about the ancestral ties of the Qutb Shahi and Safavi Houses. He added that there had never been any break in the relations of Qutb Shahs with the Safavids and that their unswerving devotion to each other was known throughout the world.

Abul Hasan maintained that the Sultanate of Golkonda had once been under the rule of the enemies of 'Ali (*khawārij*).[289] The Qutb Shahi sultans introduced and popularized the Shi'ite faith throughout the sultanate and had the names of the Safavid rulers and their dynasty included in the *khutbah*. The Golkonda Sultanate had always been protected from mishaps due to this reason. He reminded Suleiman that whenever any enemies encroached upon the sultanate, Safavid rulers always took action to repel them or intervened through diplomacy or force.

Before actually reporting Golkonda's affairs to Shah Suleiman, Abul Hasan offered his tactful apologies for failing to contact the Iranian ruler earlier. He complained that excessive infiltration by the most unwanted Mughals had disturbed the peace and tranquility of the Shi'ite abode (*dar-ul-mum'inīn*), namely, Hyderabad city.[290]

Returning to his main concern, he wrote that the ruler of India (Aurangzeb), finding Sikandar 'Adil Shah a minor and the writer of this letter (Abul Hasan) deprived of Safavid favours, had started staying in the Deccan with his enormous army and heavy artillery under the pretense that he had come to subjugate of the son of Shivaji (Sambhaji) and to chase his own son Akbar.[291] But the truth was that the Mughal emperor planned to annex the *vilāyats* of Golkonda and Bijapur. Sultan Abul Hasan argued that one of the main reasons for Mughal aggression was the ancestral devotion of those two Deccan sultans to the Safavi House. In spite of a treaty (*'ahad nāmah*) previously agreed upon by all parties, the Mughals had continued to encroach upon Bijapur and Golkonda. Abul Hasan also made a reference here to the armies under Diler Khan, *sipāh sālār*, and Bahlul Khan Afghani Bijapuri that had intended to plunder Hyderabad six years earlier but were successfully defended by the Golkonda army's Shi'ite leadership.

He added that under the pretense of blocking Sambhaji's passage, Aurangzeb was posting his army at various places throughout the territories of Bijapur. He took liberties for such actions under a guise of friendship. He constantly asked Abul Hasan for military and financial help. Moreover, he was enticing the *amirs* and *vazīrs* of Golkonda with offers of high ranks as this was a key-device for his success.[292] Abul Hasan attempted to make Shah Suleiman believe that the Mughals wanted to overthrow Golkonda and Bijapur for their Shi'ite disposition and loyalty towards Iran. He even argued that once the Deccan sultanates were overthrown, Aurangzeb might plan to conquer Iran. Abul Hasan asserted that like his predecessor, he thought of himself as a representative (*nāib*) of the Safavids in Golkonda. He, therefore, deemed it urgent to make a report of these events so that Iran would extend aid for repelling the enemy. Abul Hasan further added that it was an established tradition of the Safavid rulers to help any ruler they found overwhelmed by an enemy, regardless of the fact whether such a ruler was a friend or not. The stories of such help by the Safavids were recorded in the annals of world history.[293]

In the end, Abul Hasan expressed his hopes that those who had helped even their enemies should not neglect their friends, or else in a few short years the sound of the holy phrase '*aliyun waliullah* would no longer be heard in Golkonda.[294] The letter and oral message were also sent to Shah Suleiman's harem. Presumably, this letter was also delivered to Sahib Kuchak, the daughter of Ni'matullah.

There is no evidence if Shah Suleiman Safavi responded to the appeal of the sinking Sultan of Golkonda. Mughal aggression increased until the Golkonda Sultanate was overthrown, annexed to the Mughal Empire and Abul Hasan was taken a prisoner on 24th Zilqada 1098/21 September 1687.

NOTES

1. Shakeb, 'The Black Sheep Tribe from Lake Van to Golkonda', *Itihas*, Journal of the Andhra Pradesh Archives, vol. III, no. 2, July–December 1975, pp. 35–80.
2. Henceforth all these kingdoms together shall be referred to as the Deccan sultanates. For the predecessor of these Deccan sultanates, see the work of H.K. Sherwani on the Bahmanis, *The Bahmanis of the Deccan: An Objective Study*, New Delhi: Munshiram Manoharlal, 1985 [hereafter Sherwani (B)].
3. Regarding Sassanian roots in the household of 'Ali and thus in household of the Safavid rulers see Abu Ja'far Muhammad Ibn Jarir al Tabari (*c.* 838–923); *Akhbār u'rrusūl wa'l Mulk* I, pp. 25, 45–51; Browne IV, p. 18. It may further be noted that from his mother's side, Shah Isma'il inherited the blood of Aq Quyunlus and the Greeks, see Browne III; p. 407; IV, p. 47; Sarwar, pp. 23–5.
4. This river is also known by its classical name Jaxartus.

5. For the nature of Islam in Iran see Chapter 3.
6. Firishtah I, pp. 598–9; *H.S.* III, pp. iii, 44–9.
7. The lady's veil was a taunt against Shah Isma'il's maternal side that hailed from the Aq Quyunlu tribe, and the bowl, a taunt against his father who was a dervish. There was an exchange of sarcastic verses between Shaibani Khan and Shah Isma'il. The Uzbeg chief argued that Shah Isma'il's lineage did not entitle him to a monarchy while the Safavid ruler proclaimed military superiority over him. Rashidu'ddin Fasluhah, *Tārīkh-i-Rashīdī* (English translation), pp. 232–3; *H.S.* III, IV, pp. 54, 56; *A.A.A.*, pp. 27–9; Sykes II, p. 160.
8. *H.S.* III, IV, pp. 76–80; *A.A.A.*, pp. 31–2; Sykes II, p. 162.
9. For details of relations of Shah Isma'il with Babur see R.I., pp. 5–18.
10. As specified earlier, states have been treated as persons in this discussion. Therefore names of states and the names of their rulers have been used interchangeably throughout this study.
11. *H.S.* III, pp. 44–9.
12. It may be noted that Babur was a sovereign *de jure* of Farghana in 899/1494, *B.N.*
13. Sultan Quli's career commenced in the personal retinue of Mahmud Shah Bahmani where he had the title of Khawas Khan before he rose to the position of *tarafdār* of Tilangana in 901/1495, *B.N.* For Sultan Quli see *T.Q.S.*, fol. 19(b) *Burhān*, p. 155; Firishtah I, p. 719; Sherwani (B), p. 377.
14. Recognition of Sultan Muhammad Shah Bahmani (1358–75) by the Abbasid Caliph al-Mu'tadid [see Firishtah I, p. 542; Shewani (B), p. 87] and Firoz Shah's recognition by Timur (Firishtah I, pp. 598–9) may be referred to as a few instances.
15. *B.N.*, p. 482.
16. Firishtah I, p. 729.
17. Sherwani (B), pp. 283–5.
18. Iran's recognition of the Bahmani kingdom upto 921/1515 was established by the arrival of Shah Isma'il's *elchi* in the court of Mahmud Shah Bahmani. No further Safavid emissaries were sent to any of the Deccan sultans before 925/1519. The death of Mahmud Shah Bahmani in 924/1516 provided new prospects for the Deccan sultans to assume autonomy.
19. Both Firishtah, vol. II, pp. 32–3 and Tabataba, p. 162 state that Mahmud Shah Bahmani wanted to entertain the Iranian *elchi* with all necessary protocol but his court politics, dominated by Qasim Barid, prevented him from doing so. The discourteous behaviour of Mahmud Shah Bahmani need not necessarily be construed to mean he was anti-Shi'i as some of his closest nobles, except Barid ul-Mulk and Imad ul-Mulk, were Shi'i.
20. *Burhān*, p. 162.
21. As early as in 908/1502, Yusuf 'Adil Shah invited a grand meeting of all Deccan *tarafdārs* and nobles wherein he made an official declaration of his adherence to the Shi'i faith and his decision to make it his kingdom's religion. Sayyid Ahmad Haravi, one of the Shi'i nobles who attended the meeting, was later sent to the court of Shah Isma'il as an *elchi* of 'Adil Shah. Firishtah II, pp. 17–18. Also see Chap. 3, pp. 93–120.

22. It is possible that Sayyid Ahmad had been to Iran much before 914/1508, probably in the year 910/1504 or so (see Firishtah I, pp. 19–22).

23. Firishtah II, pp. 23, 32–3.

24. According to Firishtah II, p. 33, Isma'il 'Adil Shah exclaimed upon the arrival of the Iranian *elchi*, 'Now the monarchy (*shāhī*) has come to my House (*khandān*)'. He ordered his army to wear a red crown with twelve folds to receive the *elchi*.

25. Firishtah I, p. 724; Firishtah II, p. 329.

26. According to Firishtah II, pp. 329, 350, Sultan Quli introduced the names of the twelve Imams in his *khutbah* in 918/1512 and dropped the names of the first three Caliphs gradually. Later when he heard of the Shah Isma'il Safavi's accession, he entered the Safavid ruler's name before his own. Qutb Shahi sources are silent about this action. Nevertheless, the name of Shah Isma'il was included in the *khutbah* in Golkonda after the Sultan Quli Qutb Shah's assumption of autonomy, which he did only after Mahmud Shah Bahmani's death in 924/1518 (*T.Q.S.*, fol. 25).

27. Firishtah II, pp. 23, 32–3.

28. *Burhān*, p. 254.

29. Firishtah I, p. 729.

30. *A.A.A.*, p. 89.

31. *Hadīqat*, pp. 80–1.

32. 931 to 940/1524 to 1534.

33. *A.A.A.*, pp. 35–7; Sykes II, p. 164.

34. He invaded on six occasions: first, in the year 930/1524; second in 931/1525 twice in 935/1529; fifth in 937/1530 and for the sixth time in 938/1531. By his third invasion he delivered a major setback to the Qizilbash but was defeated in 938/1531 in the sixth expedition. *A.A.A.*, pp. 37–49.

35. These wars were fought in the years 940/1533; 941/1534; 955/1548 and 961/1553. *A.A.A.*, pp. 49–59; Sykes II, pp. 164–5.

36. From the way in which Iskandar Munshi has narrated Shah Tahmasp's receiving *elchis* of different states, it appears that the ruler's early years did not permit him to entertain minor entities. The description of their embassies has been relegated to the end of the section regardless of the sequence of their arrival. *A.A.A.*, pp. 87–9.

37. 941/1534 to 950/1544.

38. *A.A.A.*, pp. 87–9.

39. Iskandar Munshi seems to have mixed up Gujarat and Deccan. In his text (*A.A.A.*, pp. 87–9) he has mentioned Ahmedabad Patan instead of Ahmednagar. He has also mentioned the name of Hyderabad with Golkonda but the city of Hyderabad was not founded by the time these *elchis* from the Deccan reached Iran in the middle of the sixteenth century.

40. Ibid. There is no evidence if Sultan Quli had received the *tāj* even earlier than Shah Isma'il. Further the *tāj* was definitely representative of Twelver Shi'ism. On its possible political significance, see Chap. 3, pp. 96–7.

41. Firishtah I, p. 402.

42. P.M. Joshi, 'Khandesh', *History of the Medieval Deccan*, vol. I, Chap. IX, pp. 506–7.
43. Firishtah II, p. 558.
44. For Humayun's career before he fled to Iran, see the work of S.K. Banerji, *Humayun Badshah*, vols. I–II, Oxford University Press, 1938. For his journey and stay in Iran, see the memoirs of Jauhar Aftabchi, *Tazkirat-ul Wāqi'āt* and for his later career with reference to his relations with Iran, see R.I., Chap. III, pp. 22–40. Also see *A.A.A.*, pp. 73–6.
45. For Sher Shah's career see K. Qanungo's *Sher Shah* (Calcutta, 1921) and Ni'matullah al-Harawi's *Makhzan-i Afghānī*.
46. *Muntakhab (B)*, pp. 369–70; R.I., pp. 202–3.
47. The reigns of Jamshid (950/1543 to 957/1550) and Subhan Quli (957/1550) were short and plagued with conflict and rivalries within the Golkonda court. These two sultans may not have been able to enter into a formal relationship with Iran.
48. R.I., Chaps. III and IV, pp. 22–55.
49. *A.N.* II, p. 237.
50. R.I., pp. 51–5.
51. R.I. (93) informs about Ibrahim Qutb Shah's letter and Mustafa Khan Ardestani who was sent to the Safavid court. The author has given the description of these letters in his calendar in Document Numbers: 295, 296, 297 and 298. These letters were not accessible at the time of this study. Further, a modern Urdu scholar of Hyderabad, Hakim Syed Shamsullah Qadri, states that when Ibrahim Qutb Shah realized that Nizam Shah (of Ahmadnagar) developed relations with the Safavids, he too sent an embassy to Shah Tahmasp and made Khurshah (the former renowned *elchi* of Nizam Shah, then in Golkonda) accompany his *elchi*. In 971/1561 Khurshah returned to the Qutb Shahi court accompanied by a return *elchi*, named Qutb Beg Qurji, *Tārīkh: A Quarterly Journal of History and Archaeology*, vols. I–II, April–June 1929, p. 118.
52. In Muharram 972/1565, Miran Mubarak Shah submitted his allegiance and sent *peshkash* to Akbar through the dignitaries close to the emperor. He also gave his daughter in marriage to Akbar, *A.N.* II, p. 230.
53. Meanwhile, other Deccan sultans were also beginning to feel pressure from Akbar. In Rajab 981, after the return of Muhammad Husain Mirza and others from Daulatabad to Gujarat, Akbar deputed Mir Muhammad Muhsin Razvi Mashhadi to the Deccan to advise Nizam-ul-Mulk of Ahmadnagar and deliver the message of Akbar's inviolable sovereignty. Nizam-ul-Mulk received Muhsin Mashhadi with respect but did not concede to the mission. Mir Muhsin Mashhadi informed the Mughal emperor that the Deccan was suffering from lawlessness and instability and suggested that it was the right moment to conquer it (*A.N.* III, pp. 77–8). In Isfand 984/1577, Akbar sent a force under the leadership of Shahbuddin Ahmad Khan with instructions that diplomatic dialogue should be used to bring the Deccan rulers to their senses. If the regional sultans reacted aggresively, they would be undone but full care should be taken of the Deccan's populace (*A.N.* III, p. 197).
54. *A.N.* III, p. 221.

55. The Portuguese had begun to occupy the ports on the coastal south, especially in Goa from the early sixteenth century. During the reign of Akbar they interfered with Mughal seafaring and blocked Muslim pilgrims on their way to Mecca. Akbar, in his earlier efforts, did not succeed in subduing them. For Safavid interference see R.I., pp. 50, 53. For Mughal actions regarding Portuguese see *A.N.* III, pp. 280, 486, 491, 496.

56. Ibid.

57. *A.N.* III, p. 297.

58. Ibid.

59. *Marzbān* meant a landlord, a general of the borderlands, a governor on the borders of a hostile country or a landed proprietor. Official Mughal historian, Abul Fazl, uses this as a general term of reference for the Deccan sultans. The other term *ḥākim*, meant a governor who is generally appointed by a supreme sovereign authority and does not have an independent status.

60. In 981/1573 Mir Muhsin Razvi Mashhadi (*A.N.* III, pp. 77–8); in 984/1576 Shahbuddin Ahmad Khan (ibid., p. 197); in 993/1584 Khan-i-A'zam (ibid., pp. 464–5); in 994/1585 Mir Abu Turab (ibid., pp. 489–90); in 999/1590 Shahzadah Sultan Murad (ibid., p. 598); the same year Abul Faiz Faizi, Abul Fazl's elder brother (ibid., pp. 596–7) was deputed as Akbar's *wakhshūr* to communicate the message of Mughal supremacy. Faizi left Lahore on 24 August 1591 and returned to court in May 1593 and was absent from court for approximately 21 months.

61. Shah 'Abbas I's mother, Iqwan Sultana, engineered the plot to enthrone her son and was also joined by Mihdi Quli Sultan Talish who shortly afterwards defected and fled to Golkonda by 995 or 996 AH. (*A.A.A.*, pp. 269–70), where he was employed as military chief. He would later command the Qutb Shahi forces on the battlefield of Ahmadnagar against the Mughal army, led by Prince Murad, in the year 1004/1595.

62. In the year 1002/1594 (check date against text) Raja Mansingh/Man Singh was deputed to the Deccan. Akbar ordered Sultan Murad who was ready to lead a campaign (*A.N.* II, pp. 647–8). On 5th Isfand 1004/1595, more Mughal forces moved towards Ahmadnagar (ibid., p. 696). On 1005/1596, Murad defeated the allied Deccan forces led by Chand Bibi of Ahmednagar (ibid., p. 717).

63. *A.N.* II, p. 420.

64. Ibid., p. 598.

65. Ibid., p. 639.

66. Ibid., pp. 647–8.

67. Ibid., pp. 698–700, 718–19; *Burhān*, pp. 605–14; Firishtah II, pp. 174–9.

68. Tabataba has provided a detailed supplement on the terms of this dictated peace concluded with Chand Bibi, *Burhān*, p. 625.

69. *A.N.* III, p. 780.

70. Ibid., p. 782.

71. Ibid., p. 838.

72. *A.A.A.*, pp. 270–4; Sykes II, pp. 173–4; Browne IV, p. 104. It may be noted that General Farhad Pasha led the Ottoman campaigns in Iran. The Uzbeg

Chief Abul Mu'min Khan laid siege to Mashhad during the third regnal year of Shah 'Abbas I, *A.A.A.*, pp. 274–7.

73. R.I., pp. 57–61. Riazul Islam has given an account of Akbar's recovery of Qandahar in great detail.

74. Shah 'Abbas I sent at least two major embassies to the Mughal court. One was led by Yadgar Sultan Rumlu in 999/1590 and the other by Minuchihr Beg in the year 1007/1598; both were well received by Akbar and relieved by the return *elchis*, Mirza Ziau'ddin and Mir Ma'sim, respectively. The latter was relieved by Shah 'Abbas in 1013/1604 without much 'ceremony'. For details see R.I., pp. 55–67. At same time, when Shah 'Abbas I had sent Yadgar Sultan Rumlu to the Mughal court, he had also dispatched Asadullah Beg Kark Yarak to the Deccan.

75. *A.A.A.*, pp. 379–80.

76. Iskandar Munshi mentions that Asadullah Beg Tabrizi Kark Yaraq performed the duties of an ambassador to the Deccan sultanates. The letters which he carried form Shah 'Abbas I to the Deccan sultans, particularly the one addressed to Qutb Shah have not survived. There is no evidence if he was accompanied by any return *elchi* from Golkonda, *A.A.A.*, p. 362.

77. For the life and role of Mir Muhammad Mu'min see Chap. 3, pp. 102–3.

78. The Majlis was an institution in the Safavid government. It was a sort of king's privy council. A Majlis naturally assumed a stronger position when the monarch was a minor. The Qutb Shahi Majlis seems to have become stronger and selective during the reign of Sultan Muhammad Quli Qutb Shah in consultation with Mir Muhammad Mu'min. Mir Muhammd Mu'min invited the finest intellectuals from Iran like Shaikh Ibn Khatun, Muhammad Amin and others who trained other Qutb Shahi elites to participate in the Majlis.

79. *A.N.* II, p. 719.

80. Ibid., pp. 717–18, 782.

81. Qazi Mustafa was probably an eminent noble capable of carrying out a diplomatic mission. But this name is not traceable in the contemporary records of Golkonda.

82. *Makatib (Z)*, fols. 409(a) to 411(a).

83. See fn. 62.

84. *Makatib (Z)*, fol. 411(a).

85. His name has been spelt variably by different scribes who wrote the anonymous *Tārīkh-i-Sultān Muhammad Qutb Shāh*. The codex before us (MS. no. 23, S.A.A.P.) reads as Ughuryu. Some other readings are Ughuzlu, Ughurlu, etc. In the letter of Sultan Muhammad Quli Qutb Shah addressed to Shah 'Abbas I in *Makātīb (Z)*, fols. 408 b to 409 this name reads as Ughurlu. This spelling is the same as a codex of *T.Q.S.*, fol. 279(a) preserved in the Salar Jung Museum (MS. no. 85, Tarikh, SJM & L). His full name, in the light of above sources, is Uighurlu Beg Sultan. From the titles with which Sultan Muhammad Quli Qutb Shah addresses Uighurlu Beg Sultan, it appears he held a fairly high rank of Yuzbashi in the private estate (*khāssah-i sharīfah*) of Shah 'Abbas I. Briggs in vol. III, Appendix, p. 475 reads his name as Oghzloo, which is wrong.

86. *T.Q.S.*, fol. 127.
87. Ibid.
88. *T.Q.S.* does not record the text of this letter.
89. Firishtah II, p. 342; Zor's contention (*Hayāt-i Mir Mu'min*, p. 59) that Muhammad Quli Qutb Shah was preparing to send his daughter to Iran, stems from the fact that Firishtah concluded his account before the marriage of Hayat Bakshi Begam and naturally before the departure of the Iranian *elchi* from Golkonda, may be correct. Riazul Islam's statement of Shah 'Abbas I's arrangement for a matrimonial alliance with the Qutb Shahi family is a bit ambitious, R.I., p. 93.
90. *T.Q.S.*, f. 130.
91. Ibid.
92. Ibid., f. 131(a); The account contained in *T.Q.S.* alleging that Prince Khudabandah's revolt was engineered by Shah Raju, a descendant of Sayyid Muhammad Gesudaraz, is untenable because Shah Raju was born in 1002/1593 in Bijapur (see his work *Zād-ul-Mawāhiddīn*, fol. 2(a), MS. 272 preserved in the Idara-i Adabiyat-i-Urdu, Hyderabad). Shah Raju migrated to Hyderabad during the reign of 'Abdullah Qutb Shah (Bilgrami, pp. 74–5). The contents of *T.Q.S.* respecting Shah Raju therefore appear to be a later interpolation.
93. *T.Q.S.*, fol. 131.
94. Also see Sherwani (Q), p. 293.
95. The letter of 'Adil Shah sent by Mir Khalil Khushnawis along with the team of the Deccan *elchis* in 1018/1609 clearly states that they had abstained from sending congratulatory-cum-condolatory *elchis* to Jahangir until they received instructions to do so from Iran.
96. Jahangir was born in 978/1570; Muhammad Quli in 974/1566; Shah 'Abbas I in 978/1570.
97. For an account of Jahangir's relations with Shah 'Abbas I see R.I., Chap. V, pp. 68–96.
98. Ibid., pp. 65, 68.
99. *Tuzuk*, pp. 94–6; *I.N.*, pp. 34–7; *A.A.A.*, p. 552; R.I., p. 70.
100. *Tuzuk*, pp. 75–6; *I.N.*, p. 26.
101. *Tuzuk*, pp. 78–9; *I.N.*, p. 31.
102. A reference to Shah 'Abbas I's *farmān* addressed to Muhammad Quli Qutb Shah ordering the return of Uighurlu Beg is included in Muhammad Quli's letter carried to Iran by Mihdi Quli Sultan Talish. See Pl. 2, *Makātīb (Z)*, fols. 408(b) to 409 (a).
103. *T.Q.S.*, fol. 127 (b).
104. For his deputation as return *elchi* see *T.Q.S.*, fol. 127(b). For more on Mihdi Quli Sultan Talish see *A.A.A.*, pp. 255–70. Mihdi Quli Sultan Talish was the son of Hamza Khalifa, a renowned noble of Talish, Qarabagh, a Qizilbash of the Istajlu clan (ibid., p. 269) and held an important position in the nobility of Shah Muhammad Khudabandah (ibid., p. 248). He joined the conspiracy of Iqwam Sultanum, mother of Shah 'Abbas I, which was engineered with the cooperation of several groups of Qizibash in the year 996/1587 for enthroning

Shah 'Abbas I and dethroning Khudabandah. Though Mihdi Quli was a much trusted figure in the plot, he defected from Iqwam Sultanum and fled to Golkonda (*A.A.A.*, pp. 269–70).

105. Mir Khalilullah Khushnawis was the *elchi* of 'Adil Shah, Habash Khan of Nizam Shah and Malik Ambar.

106 *T.Q.S.*, fol. 127(b). Here the word Iraq obviously stands for Iraq-i-Ajam, which had the major ports of Safavid Iran including Bandar Abbas. This suggests that Golkonda *elchi* proceeded to Iran via the maritime route.

107. Muhammad Quli Qutb Shah relied heavily on Mihdi Quli Sultan Talish and may have wanted him to be his permanent representative at the Safavid court. But the antecedents of Mihdi Quli Sultan Talish, like his defection from Iqwam Sultanum's faction and his arrival in Golkonda as a fugitive and unceremonial return to Iran before confrontations with the Mughals were over, suggest that his services as diplomat were not sought after. He does not seem to have occupied any remarkable position in the Qutb Shahi Majlis or nobility. All these facts suggest that Muhammad Quli Qutb Shah proposed his detention at the Safavid court with a view to keep him away from Golkonda. Uighurlu Beg Sultan probably carried out the actual mission. There is no mention of Talish's return to Golkonda in Indian or Iranian sources. Both the sources are silent about his subsequent career.

108. For the full text of the letter see *Makātīb (Z)*, fols. 408(b) to 409(a).

109. *A.A.A.*, p. 612.

110. *Makātīb (Z)*, fol. 382–3.

111. *A.A.A.*, p. 552; *Tuzuk*, p. 94; *I.N.*, p. 34; R.I., p. 70.

112. Ataki, fol. 409(a). Bod. MS. 101, fol. 370 as cited by R.I., p. 95, fn 1.

113. For the text of the letter see *Makātīb (Z)*, fol. 382.

114. According to Jahangir, Mir Jamaluddin Husain Inju was sent to the Deccan at the request of 'Adil Shah and that all the Deccan rulers (*dunyādār* as he refers to them) had full confidence in him. He reached Bijapur on 22nd Sha'ban 1019/1610 and was given a reception a few miles from the city by 'Adil Shah himself (*Tuzuk*, pp. 85–9).

115. *Tuzuk*, pp. 98–9.

116. *A.A.A.*, p. 612. Shah 'Abbas I wrote many other letters recommending the cases of the Deccan sultans. In one of his letters he thanked Jahangir for conciding to his recommendations and made a complaint that Jahangir had again deputed some *amirs* who were oppressing his friends in the Deccan, *Makātīb (S)*, fols. 161(a) to 162(a).

117. Among the *elchis* of the Deccan there were—Mir Khalilullah Khushnawis of Bijapur who was relieved by Shah Quli Beg Zek; Habash Khan, the *elchi* of Nizam Shah and Malik Ambar, was replaced with Darwish Beg Mar'ashi, who served as return *elchi* together with Husayn Beg Qapuchi Tabrizi of Golkonda in the year 1023/1614. Darwish Beg Mar'ashi passed away in Shiraz on his way back to the Deccan. His son Muhammad Beg then carried the mission. All these *elchis* were led by Mir Khalilullah Khushnawis but only Husain Beg Tabrizi eventually reached the Deccan in 1023/1614, *A.A.A.*,

p. 612; *T.Q.S.*, fol. 143(b). The others were held up due to unfavourable weather and were relieved again in the year 1029/1620 when another batch of the envoys of the Deccan was sent, *A.A.A.*, p. 670.

118. *A.A.A.*, p. 623.

119. Husain Beg's name has been mentioned variably in different codices. Though 'Husain Beg' is common in every text, his designation and native place are somewhat confusing and indicated as Qaichaji Bashi Tabrizi, spelt in a variety of ways in different codices. *T.Q.S.*, S.A.A.P., MS. 23, fol. 143; *T.Q.S*, Tarikh, SJM & L, MS. 85, fol. 309(a); *A.A.A.*, p. 612; *Hadīqat*, p. 81; R.I., p. 95.

120. For the text of the letter see *T.Q.S.*, fol. 144.

121. For the text of the letter see *Hadīqat*, p. 193 and Zor, *Hayat-i Mir Mu'min*, pp. 122–3.

122. *T.Q.S.*, fol. 143(a).

123. Ibid., fol. 143(b).

124. Ibid.

125. Little is known about Haji Qambar 'Ali. His name has been mentioned both by Muhammad Quli Qutb Shah and by Shah 'Abbas I, in *T.Q.S.*, fol. 127(b) and fol. 144(b). Muhammad Quli sent him to Iran in the year 1018/1609 (ibid., fol. 127). He was probably in Golkonda at the time of Muhammad Quli's death in 1020/1611 and in Iran before 1023/1614, when he reported to Shah 'Abbas, ibid., fol. 144(b). It is likely that Haji Qambar Ali was a merchant, frequently travelling between Iran and Golkonda and was respected by the rulers on account of his status.

126. For the text of the letter see *T.Q.S.*, fol. 144.

127. Ibid.

128. *Tuzuk,* p. 114.

129. Ibid., p. 115.

130. Ibid.

131. Ibid., p. 154.

132. Ibid., p. 164.

133. Ibid., p. 168; I.N., p. 62.

134. Ibid., p. 189.

135. Ibid.

136. *Nishān* of Shah Jahan dated 1st Rabi II 1032/23 January 1623, H.A.K.C. Document No. 3, S.A.A.P. Also Ziauddin Ahmad Shakeb, *Mughal Archives: A Descriptive Catalogue of the Documents Pertaining to the Reign of Shah Jahan,* Hyderabad, 1977. This *nishān* records the assignment of the title of 'Shah Jahan' to Prince Khurram with his seal, *Amal* I, p. 108; *Tuzuk,* pp. 195–6.

137. The names of these elephants have been detailed in *Tuzuk,* p. 199.

138. Ibid.

139. *Tuzuk,* p. 267; *I.N.,* p. 87.

140. Ibid., p. 273.

141. For the details of these relations see R.I., Chap. V.

142. *Tuzuk,* pp. 234–6; *I.N.,* p. 77 also see fn 126.

143. *A.A.A.*, p. 623.

144. *Tuzuk,* p. 185.

145. *A.A.A.*, p. 663.
146. Ibid., p. 670. *A.A.A.* records the names of this *elchi* as Qasim Beg but the rubrics given in the codex at the beginning of his letter read his name as Qasim Beg Paran. *Makātīb (Z)*, fol. 399 and the *Hadīqat*, pp. 80–1 attest to the same reading.
147. *Tuzuk*, p. 338; *I.N.*, p. 183; *Makātīb (Z)*, fol. 399.
148. *Makātīb (Z)*, fol. 399.
149. R.I., pp. 80–3.
150. *A.A.A.*, p. 674; R.I., p. 81.
151. Ibid.
152. *Tuzuk*, pp. 351–2.
153. *Tuzuk*, p. 337; I.N., p. 125. For a detailed account of Shah Jahan's subjection of the Deccan in 1030/1621 see Sherwani (Q), p. 392.
154. *Makātīb (S)*, fols. 3(a) to 4(b); *Tuzuk*, p. 358.
155. For the full text of the letter see *Makātīb (S)*, fols. 161(a) to 162(a).
156. *Makātīb (S)*.
157. *Tuzuk*, pp. 350–2.
158. Ibid., pp. 352, 356–60, 396.
159. *Hadīqat*, p. 82.
160. For a full discussion on the exact date of the death of Mir Muhammad Mu'min see Zor, p. 175.
161. *Hadīqat*, p. 28, the Mughals were also conscious of his being too young; *'Amal* VI, p. 313.
162. *Tuzuk*, p. 420; *I.N.*, p. 189.
163. Ibid., pp. 381–2, 386–8, 391.
164. *A.A.A.*, pp. 757–8.
165. R.I., pp. 90–1.
166. Lane-Poole, pp. 217–20; *A.A.A.*, p. 744; B.P. Saksena, pp. 214–5; Abdur Rahim, 'Mughal Relations with Persia', *Islamic Culture*, vol. 9, no. 1, 1937.
167. *Hadīqat*, p. 82.
168. *Makātīb (Z)*, fol. 626; *Hadīqat*, p. 82.
169. See Appendix A, Section 3.
170. It appears from Mughal sources, the two *elchis* went to Agra at their own accord (*P.N.* I, pt. I, p. 226; *'Amal* I, p. 312) whereas according to Golkonda sources the two *elchis* were called for by Shah Jahan from Surat to Agra, who gave them a letter as well as an oral message to be delivered to Shah 'Abbas I, *Hadīqat*, p. 83. The Mughal sources do not mention Shah Jahan's letter and oral message to Shah 'Abbas sent through this embassy. Undoubtedly, Shah Jahan had sent a letter through them, *Nuskha-i-Jāmi–i-Murāsilāt ul Albāb* in the British Museum, MS. Add 7688, fols 231(b) to 232(a) as cited by R.I., p. 116, fn 3.
171. *P.N.* I, p. 226; *'Amal* I, p. 312.
172. *Hadīqat*, p. 83; *E.F.I.*, 1624–5, pp. 9, 300, 302, 321. The date of Shah 'Abbas I's death given in *Hadīqat*, p. 83 as AH 1037 is wrong.
173. *Hadīqat*, p. 84.
174. For the full text of the letter see *Makātīb (Z)*, fol. 626.

175. Ibid.
176. *Hadīqat*, p. 85.
177. Ibid., p. 127
178. Ibid., p. 32.
179. Golkonda sources do not mention this mission whereas Mughal sources have all recorded it. *P.N.* I, p. 227; *'Amal* I, p. 313.
180. Ibid.
181. There are many instances: Shaikh Muhiu'uddin, the Mughal agent, brought *peshkash* from Golkonda accompanied by Wafa Khan, along with a letter of allegiance, *P.N.* I, pp. 366–7; *Hadīqat*, p. 127. Shah Ali Beg, the Mughal *hājib*, was in Golkonda in 1041/1632 when the pressure for *peshkash* was still there, *P.N.* II, p. 125. In Muharram 1044/1635, Qutb ul-Mulk was warned again for *peshkash*. Ibid., pp. 144–5, 153–4. In Shawwal 1045/1636, Abdul Latif and Khan Jahan were sent to Golkonda for bringing *peshkash* and the Deed of Submission. Similar events are seen even after the Deed of Submission. See *P.N.* I, pp. 177, 184–200, 208, 211–15; and *P.N.* II, pp. 99, 101, 216, 222, 355, 432.
182. *P.N.* I, p. 373; *Hadīqat*, pp. 93–7.
183. Ibid., p. 130; *'Amal* II, p. 148.
184. *Hadīqat*, p. 169.
185. Ibid., p. 175.
186. Ibid.
187. For the full text of *inqīyād nāmah* see Talqani, no. 47; *P.N.* I, pt. II, p. 178; *'Amal* II, p. 188; Sherwani (Q), p. 436.
188. For the text of this covenant (*'ahad nāmah*) see Talqani No. 63; *P.N.* I, pt. II, pp. 210–11. 'Abdullah Qutb Shah would later refer to this *'ahad nāmah* emphatically after two decades when his kingdom would once again be in jeopardy, in 1067/1656.
189. For Shah Jahan's coup of Qandahar and his ambitions in Turan see. R.I., Chap. VI, pp. 97–123; Abdur Rahim, 'Mughal Relations with Persia and Central Asia', *Islamic Culture*, vol. 9, no. 1, 1937.
190. *'Amal* I, p. 626, II, 1–2; *P.N.* I, pt. II, p. 8.
191. For the full text of the letter see *Makātīb (Z)*, fol. 306.
192. Riazul Islam has miscomputed the duration of their journey from Bagh-i Hafiz Rakhna to Golkonda. According to him 'the two envoys saw Shah Jahan in Ramazan 1043/March 1634, handed him a letter from Shah Safi and proceeded on their way to Golkonda, where they arrived about a year later' (R.I., p. 116). As a matter of fact it took only one month and few days and not a year. It should be noted that though *Hadīqat*, p. 156, records their arrival in the section pertaining to the events of AH 1044, it clearly specifies that the *elchis* arrived in Golkonda in the month of Zilqada of the 'aforementioned year' which was 1043/1634.
193. *A.A.A.*, p. 623.
194. *Hadīqat*, pp. 157–8; for the weight of *khandi* see Chap. 4, p. 138.
195. Ibid., p. 185.

196. *Hadīqat*, p. 189. The text of the letter is not available. As a matter of normal practice, the real message might have been communicated orally while the letter only recorded the emissary's credentials.

197. Ibid. Asadullah Tabrizi Kark Yaraq was already quite old at this time, as he had come to Golkonda once before in 1000/1591, during the reign of Sultan Muhammad Quli Qutb Shah. His second visit was forty years later.

198. According to Mirza Nizam'ddin Ahmad Shirazi (*Hadīqat*, p. 189), Mirza Muhammad Jauhari, brother of Asadullah Tabrizi Kark Yaraq, had previously been in the retinue of Mughal noble, Zamana Beg Mahabat Khan (d.1634), and had been staying in Golkonda as *hājib* of Mahabat Khan. After the death of the latter, Mirza Muhammad Jauhari joined service under 'Abdullah Qutb Shah.

199. Ibid. He was buried at the cemetery of the city, Daira-i Mir Mu'min.

200. Muhammad Amin, the brother of Sultan Muhammad Quli Qutb Shah and the father of Sultan Muhammad Qutb Shah, had married Khanum Agha, the daughter of Mir Maqsud 'Ali, a Tabataba Sayyid. Another daughter of Mir Maqsud 'Ali was married to Mir Qutbu'ddin Ni'matullah Dashtaki Shirazi, who was a member of the family of Shah Ni'matullah Kirmani. Shah Muhammad, the husband of Shahr Banu ('Abdullah's aunt) and the son-in-law of Khanum Agha, died in the year 1047/1638 and his son, Shah Khawandkar, married the daughter of *Malik-ut tujjār* (Chief of the Merchants) and also died earlier in 1045/1636. After the deaths of these persons, Khanum Agha and her widowed daughter Shahr Banu decided to go on *hajj* (*Hadīqat*, pp. 206–7). Qazi Zahiru'ddin and his son Mir Miran, being from Najaf were probably members of the Kirmani family, a branch of which had settled in Najaf, and Mir Miran was a frequently adopted name in their house (see *Tuzuk*, pp. 150, 193–4).

201. *Hadīqat*, pp. 209–10.

202. Ibid., p. 206.

203. *Khuld-i Barin*, V, fol. 74a = *Zail-i Tārīkh-i 'Ālam-i Ārā-i 'Abbāsī*, pp. 235–6 as cited in R.I., p. 118, fn 3. Riazul Islam has further discussed the variations of this date from different sources.

204. *Makātib (Z)*, fol. 628.

205. For the text of the letter see *Makātib (Z)*, fol. 628. It should be noted that the rubrics given in the beginning of the letter are wrong, according to which it is misattributed to Shah 'Abbas II.

206. *Hadīqat*, p. 289.

207. Ibid.

208. Najabat Khan was probably an official title and not a personal name. He was a descendant of Shah Ni'matullah Kirmani (Talqani, no. 44) and may have been the son of Qutbu'ddin Ni'matullah Dashtaki, see footnote 201. He had communicated the messages of 'Abdullah Qutb Shah to Shah Safi (Talqani).

209. *Hadīqat*, p. 230.

210. Ibid., p. 256.

211. Ibid., pp. 238, 246, 268, 272.
212. Ibid., p. 272.
213. *Khuld Barin*, V, fols. 78(b) to 9(a) = *Zail-i Tārīkh-i 'Ālam-i Ārā-i 'Abbāsī*, p. 250, T. Sultani, fols. 435(a–b); *F. Safaviyya*, fol. 51(a), as cited by R.I., p. 118, fn 5.
214. The date of his death had been recorded in Golkonda as 13th Safar. *Hadīqat*, p. 312.
215. Ibid., p. 313.
216. Ibid., p. 295; for the full text of the letter see *Shajar*, fol. 392(b). Shaik Muhammad Tahir was the nephew of Ibn Khatun, *Hadīqat*, p. 295.
217. *Hadīqat*, pp. 311–19; *Shajar*, fol. 392(b). Riazul Islam's contention (R.I., p. 118) that neither of the Deccan powers could send the usual congratulatory embassy to Iran on Shah 'Abbas II's accession is therefore not correct.
218. Talqani, Letter no. 21; *I.T.W.*, p. 160 and also *Dabistān*, p. 204 as cited by Qadri (I), p. 61.
219. For the Shah Jahan's next strategy at Qandahar and Turan and his subsequent relations with neighbouring rivals, see R.I., Chap. VI, pp. 97–123.
220. For the life of Mir Jumla see the work of Jagdish Narayan Sarkar, *The Life of Mir Jumla*, especially its Appendix D, p. 302, details the arrest of Mir Muhammad Amin by 'Abdullah Qutb Shah.
221. *'Amal* III, p. 213; For the full text of the letter see Talqani, Letter no. 70.
222. Aurangzeb's letter of warning in this respect is in Talqani, Letter no. 71, and a similar letter written by Sultan Muhammad in Talqani, Letter no. 89.
223. *'Amal* III, p. 224.
224. Ibid.
225. Ibid., p. 228.
226. Ibid., p. 229.
227. Ibid., pp. 223–4.
228. There are scores of newsletters (*waqāi'*) recorded by Mughal intelligence in Golkonda during the reign of Shah Jahan and Aurangzeb still preserved by the SAAP, and they show how the Mughals kept themselves informed of the state of affairs in Golkonda and Bijapur, *S.W.D.*
229. While 'Abdullah Qutb Shah furnished exact figures of the Mughal forces to Shah 'Abbas II, contemporary Mughal sources do not give the strength of their army.
230. This charge was clearly untrue as 'Abdullah Qutb Shah had himself assigned the province of Karnatak to Muhammad Sa'id when he was in Golkonda.
231. Meaning: 'Ali is the friend of Allah'.
232. Talqani, Letter no. 1.
233. This Miranji is expected to be the aforementioned Mir Miran, son of Qazi Zahiru'ddin Najafi, who had gone to Iran with 'Abdullah Qutb Shah's aunt. Mir Miran was appointed a member of the Majlis when his father was sent to Iran. *Hadīqat*, p. 209.
234. 'Abdullah Qutb Shah's statement regarding the plunder of Hyderabad city and particularly his own possesions appear to be exaggerated. Similarly, the mention of the Sayyid ladies being dishounoured by infidels and

Afghans also appear to be hyperbole to urge Shah 'Abbas II to act against the Mughals.

235. The Mughal sources record that the Mughal army had been provoked as a result of mischief made by the Golkonda army, but every care was taken to protect the inhabitants of Hyderabad and especially the city palace of 'Abdullah Qutb Shah. *'Amal* III, pp. 223–4.

236. 'Abdullah Qutb Shah's letter addressed to Shah 'Abbas contains a reference to Aurangzeb's departure from Aurangabad on 14th Rabi II 1067. But the letter itself is undated. The second letter addressed to his aunt is dated as 'early Jumada I 1067'. Therefore, the two letters were written within the span of two to three weeks after 14th Rabi II and in every likelihood were written and sent together early in Jumada I 1067/1656.

237. For the text of the letters see *I.T.W.*, p. 12. Riazul Islam's contention (R.I., p. 122) that this letter was a draft which would have probably not been communicated is perhaps based on the omission of the names of persons in the text of the letter, instead of which a reference is made by saying so and so (*falān*). It may be noted that the word *falān* is never written when the letter is drafted. Epistolarians use the word to obviate probable implications while making their epistolography (*inshā*') accessible to general public.

238. R.I., p. 122. Riazul Islam's references are based on 4 letters, 2 addressed to 'Abdullah Qutb Shah and 2 to Adil Shah (*I.T.W.*, pp. 12, 45, 48). The above letters of Shah 'Abbas II were all replies to the letters of Qutb Shah and 'Adil Shah. 'Abdullah Qutb Shah's letters have already been discussed in the previous section and suggest that 'Abdullah Qutb Shah did not have the confidence to fight against the Mughals at this precarious stage. Moreover, Shah 'Abbas II never committed to his plan to invade Hindustan in these letters. He only advised the Deccan rulers to wait and take advantage of the Mughal war of succession. Lastly, the author has confused Shah 'Abbas II's two letters addressed to 'Abdullah Qutb Shah (*I.T.W.*, pp. 12, 45) as brought by Mirza Muqim. For the letters brought by Mirza Muqim see below.

239. For his military aid to Murad, *I.T.W.*, p. 8 and for Dara Shikoh, *I.T.W.*, p. 5.

240. *'Amal* III, pp. 263–88; *K.K.* II, p. 5; *Dilkasha*, pp. 15–19.

241. For the text of the letter see Talqani, Letter no. 80.

242. Talqani, Letter no. 81. For the war with Jaswanth Singh see *Dilkasha*, pp. 18–19.

243. *Dilkasha*, p. 27; Letter of Prince Muhammad Sultan in Talqani, Letter no. 83.

244. There are many reports regarding the submission of *peshkash* by 'Abdullah Qutb Shah to the Imperial Treasury; the correspondence between 'Abdullah Qutb Shah and his son-in-law, Prince Sultan Muhammad, contains interesting reference to the payment of *peshkash* during that period. See Talqani, Letters no. 83, 91, 92, 93. Similarly, the Mughal *waqāi'* of Hyderabad dated 1st Muharram 1072/1661, 9th Muharram 1072/9 April 1662, 4 Shawwal 1072/13 May 1662 and 7th Shawwal 1072/1662 contain information regarding several instalments of *peshkash* in cash and kind that 'Abdullah Qutb Shah sent to the Mughal court; also see *S.W.D.*, pp. 1–20.

245. Talqani, Letter no. 76.

246. *K.K.* II, pp. 191–6; *Dilkasha*, pp. 46–8; for an excellent account of the treaty of Purandar and its impact on Bijapur and Golkonda see Sherwani (Q), pp. 448–9.

247. *K.K.* II, p. 220.

248. *S.W.D.*, p. 4.

249. From the letter's content two things are clear. First, it was written when the war of succession had not yet concluded. Second, Shah 'Abbas II was prone to aggravate the situation. In such circumstances Muhammad Muqim Kitabdar may have left Iran during the war of succession and reached Golkonda during the same period or immediately after.

250. For his letter carried to Bijapur see *I.T.W.*, p. 48.

251. For the full text of the letter, see *I.T.W.*, pp. 45–8 and also with minor textual variations in *Makātīb (S)*, fol. 3(b).

252. *S.W.D.*, pp. 4, 7, 12, 52–3.

253. Ibid., pp. 4–5.

254. For the details of the embassy of Budaq Sultan at the Delhi court see R.I., pp. 125–7, 232. The *elchi*'s name has been mentioned as Budaq Beg in Mughal chronicles. See *K.K.* II, p. 124; Kazim, *'Ālamgīr Nāmah*, pp. 607–9. But in the Mughal newsletters his name was recorded as Budaq Sultan (*S.W.D.*, p. 7). Similarly, the Iranian sources too make a mention of his name as Budaq Sultan (*I.T.W.*, p. 82). R.I., pp. 125–7 relied on Indian chronicles and mentioned the name of the *elchi* as Budaq Beg, which is not adopted here.

255. All these details have been ascertained from the Mughal newsletters dated 23rd Safar 1072/8 October 1661; also see *S.W.D.*, p. 12.

256. Ibid., pp. 52–3.

257. *I.T.W.*, p. 68.

258. The names here are again obviously suppressed due to the strained relations of Iran and Hindustan.

259. For the text of the letter see *I.T.W.*, pp. 68–9.

260. For details of these disgruntled relations and Shah 'Abbas II's death see R.I., pp. 127–9.

261. *K.K.*, pp. 235–6; *Dilkasha*, pp. 94–5.

262. For the *farmān*'s text see *Zafrah*, pp. 35–8.

263. *Dilkasha*, p. 95; Shah Nawaz Khan, *Ma'āsir-ul Umarā*, p. 37.

264. Officer-in-charge of military administration and intelligence. *Mughal Archives*, vol. I, 354.

265. *Dilkasha*, p. 106.

266. For the text of the treaty (*'ahad nāma*) see Talqani, Letter no. 9; *Zafrah*, pp. 38–9. The letter records the date of its execution on 8th Safar.

267. *Dilkasha*, p. 88. For a detailed discussion of Shivaji's aforementioned visit to Hyderabad see Sherwani (Q), pp. 636–7.

268. *Dilkasha*, p. 89.

269. *S.D.A.R.*, p. 113.

270. *Dilkasha*, p. 113.

271. Ibid., p. 116.

272. Ibid., p. 117.
273. Talqani, Letter no. 15.
274. *K.K.* II, p. 264, presumably referring to the Rathore leader Durgadas, who took Prince Muhammad Akbar to the court of Sambhaji.
275. *K.K.* II, pp. 284–90; R.I., p. 131.
276. Talqani, Letter no. 18.
277. *K.K.* II, pp. 292–3.
278. Ibid.
279. Ibid., pp. 294–5.
280. *K.K.* II, p. 296.
281. Ibid., p. 299.
282. Ibid., pp. 305–6; *Dilkasha,* pp. 146–7. The latter source records this event under the year 1096–1097 whereas the former records them under the events pertaining to 1095.
283. *K.K.* II, pp. 307–8; *Dilkasha,* p. 147; Talqani, Letter nos. 2, 3, 11, 19, 22, 24.
284. *K.K.* II, p. 308; *Dilkasha,* p. 148.
285. *K.K.* II, p. 313; *S.D.A.R.,* p. 152.
286. *K.K.* II, p. 313.
287. See previous discussion of the royal pilgrims from Golkonda in Iran.
288. Talqani (A), Letter no. 5.
289. *Khawārij* or the Kharijites formed the earliest religo-political sect of Islam. Once supporters of the Fourth Caliph 'Ali, they later turned into deadly opponents and rose in an armed uprising against him (Hitti, p. 246).
290. Here Abul Hasan mentions the Mughals in most loathsome terms, noting they had the nature of vultures and owls. Though he belonged to the Chisti Sufi order, he vehemently stressed his faith in the Shi'ite creed, which clearly served a political purpose.
291. Shivaji had already passed away by the year 1091/1680. Abul Hasan seems to be referring to Sambhaji.
292. This complaint of Abul Hasan is ratified in Mughal records. See *S.D.A.R.,* pp. 25, 35, 126.
293. This was obviously a reference to Tahmasp's help to Humayun.
294. For the letter's full text, see Talqani (A), Letter no. 25.

3

Ties of Religion and the Traffic of Ideas

TIES OF RELIGION and the traffic of ideas between Safavid Iran and Golkonda were a natural corollary of the diplomatic and political relations discussed in the previous chapter. Several of the emissaries who travelled between the two states were also learned religious scholars and missionaries.

Specific historical conditions had produced a unique relationship between religion and the state in both Iran and the Deccan. Neither the Safavids nor the Qutb Shahs were ancestrally Shiʻi. They came to adopt the Shiʻite faith under very different circumstances. This chapter covers the foundation of Safavid Shiʻism in Iran, the earliest instances of Shiʻism in the Deccan and how it evolved in Golkonda as a result of its relations with Safavid Iran. It traces the ways in which Safavid Shiʻism was propagated symbolically in the Deccan sultanates. The Qutb Shahs were not the first to introduce Shiʻism in the Deccan. At the Bahmani court in the fourteenth century, Mir Fazlullah Inju (d.1394)[1] of Shiraz was the Shiʻi preceptor and prime minister to Feroz Shah Bahmani. In the early sixteenth century, Shah Tahir (d.1549) arrived in the Deccan during the reign of Shah Tahmasp and served under the Nizam Shahi dynasty of Ahmednagar. The Qutb Shahs of Golkonda absorbed such pre-existing influences. Select personalities such as Mir Muhammad Muʼmin and Shaikh Muhammad Ibn Khatun who were Shiʻi missionaries, became powerful in the court. This chapter also presents a brief cross-section of the religious practices and institutions that were implanted in the Deccan from Safavid Iran.

As a result of this migration of learned elites, aspects of statecraft and intellectual production were closely linked to religion and religious ideologies. The second part of this chapter covers the areas of administration, education and philosophical ideas that travelled between the two states. The majority of evidence presented here comes from the library of the Qutb Shahi court that received, replicated and preserved books from

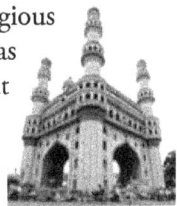

Iran and elsewhere. In this chapter, a range of manuscripts on subjects like the education of princes, medical practices and treatises on ethics and philosophy that had made their way to the Deccan are introduced. The presence of the works of Iranian scholars and philosophers indicates that Golkonda's courtly elite encountered and incorporated religious and intellectual thought from Safavid Iran. The reception of these works beyond the court is, however, more difficult to measure. These ideas were bound to have interacted and contrasted with diverse, pre-existing local religious cosmologies and ways of thinking already present in the Deccan. The traffic of ideas was not a simple process of transfer from one place to another, but the social and demographic conditions of each polity determined how ideas were received and changed.

Although diplomatic ties and the exchange of letters and gifts symbolically linked the two Shi'i states, two completely different sets of circumstances had brought both into being. One of the key factors that gave an impetus to the Safavid revolution was religion. This movement did not introduce a new religion as such, but was rather a sectarian upsurge led by the leaders of Shi'ite faith under the supreme leadership of Shah Isma'il Safavi. Though sectarian, it was so radical and omnivorous that it hardly left any aspect of Iranian thought and society unaffected. Religion and politics were so akin in the Safavid movement as to appear as two dimensions of one and the same fact. Initially, the Safavids faced their greatest political challenge from external enemies, rather than internal constituents. Over time, the ideological foundations of the Safavid dynasty were consolidated further by quelling hostile factions among the nobility, by purging out dissenting Sufi orders and projecting itself as an absolute political sovereign to rival states.

The situation in Golkonda was somewhat different (though the relationship between religion and politics manifested a somewhat similar tendency as in Iran). The first and foremost factor of this disparity was inherent in the Deccan's heterogeneous subject population, which adhered to many different faiths, as discussed in the introductory chapter. While in Iran the Safavid movement enveloped all of society and affected it to the core, its operation in Golkonda was restricted to the monarch and nobility. In Iran, when the Safavids came to power, the Sunni Muslim population was predominant, and they were not adherents of multiple religions. In Golkonda, even the nobility was not unanimous in its support for the Safavid movement as Deccanis, Sufis and the indigenous elements refused to embrace it. When it first emerged in the early sixteenth century, an unrecognized Golkonda state experienced a political vacuum as a result of a weakened Bahmani monarchy. At the same time, weakened Sufi institutions (*khānqāh*) created a space for a new religious leadership. This gap allowed Iranian migrants to bring religious thought and ideas to the newly formed sultanate.

Foundations of State and Religion in
Iran and the Deccan

Though Safavid Shi'ism embraced the central tenets of the Shi'ite faith, it had its own peculiarities. The controversy on the issues of Caliphate and Imamate was initially of a political nature but took on a strong religious character in Iran and Iraq. By the period of this study, the issues of Caliphate and Imamate were highly debated chapters of history not just in theory but also in the everyday practices of Shi'ism. The religiosity of history and historicity of religion were intertwined in the psyche of Shi'ite society and such religious sentiments were often mobilized for political motives.

By the close of the fifteenth century and the beginning of the early sixteenth century, socio-political and economic conditions in Iran paved the way for the development of a host of potentates throughout the country with no strong unifying central authority.[2] Another noticeable factor contributing to the Shi'ite revolution was the changing relationship between the Sufis and the state throughout the Muslim world during the fifteenth century. Early during that century Sufis had great influence over the state, but subsequently that domination was first reduced to a compromise between the two in which both were unified. Sufi institutions were slowly dismantled and ultimately converted to Shi'ism in Iran.[3] In the Deccan on the other hand, the Sufis were firmly entrenched in court politics in the beginning but progressively distanced themselves from the court. Three instances of the families of Sayyid Muhammad Gesudaraz of Gulbarga (d.825/1422), Shah Ni'matullah of Kirman (d.831/1428) and of Shah Safiuddin of Ardabil (d.735/1334) show how contemporary rulers yielded to the spiritual and political influence of Sufis. In the case of Muhammad Gesudaraz, this change in the relationship with the court over different generations was most apparent. His most immediate descendants distanced themselves from the rulers. After that however, later generations in this lineage grew worldly-wise and accepted positions in court. Monarchs granted large appanages to Sufis and their disciples that were generally given to the most important sections of the elite. The Sufi *khānqāh* and the court were, therefore, interlocked in a mutually dependent relationship.[4]

Ties between Sufi households and sultans were often strengthened through matrimonial alliances. Such intermarriages facilitated the exchange of gifts and often served as a conduit for diplomatic missions between the two regions. The importance of these alliances and the mobility with which they operated across Iran and the Deccan is most evident in the activities of household of Shah Ni'matullah Kirmani.[5] The Safavi and Kirmani families in Iran entered into matrimonial relations from the times of Shah Tahmasp. Khadijah Sultan Begam, the third daughter of Shah Tahmasp, was married to Shah Ni'matullah, son of Mir-i-Miran Yazdi, and after her death, Tahmasp's

eighth and widowed daughter Khanash Begam was married to the same
Shah Ni'matullah. Sabiyah Sultan Begam (often identified as Safiyah Sultan
in many codices of *Tārīkh-i 'Ālam-i Ārā-i 'Abbāsī*), the daughter of Isma'il
Mirza, was married to Shah Khalilullah, the younger son of Shah Ni'matullah
Yazdi.[6] A daughter of Shah Ni'matullah Yazdi born to Khanash Begam was
married to Sultan Muhammad Mirza.[7] The descendants of Shah Safiuddin
of Ardabil also entered into matrimonial relations with the household of
Aq Quyunlu chiefs, as Shaikh Junaid Safavi had married the sister of
Uzun Hasan. Shaikh Haidar Safavi married Uzun Hasan's daughter named
Halimah Baki Aqa or Alam Shah Begam.[8] After they arrived in the Deccan,
Ahmad Shah Vali Bahmani (d.1436) gave his daughter in marriage to Shah
Habibullah and his granddaughter to Shah Muhibullah. Both were the
grandsons of Shah Nuruddin Ni'matullah Kirmani.[9] Among the descendants
of Sayyid Muhammad Gesudaraz, Husain Shah Wali (d.1657 or 1626)[10]
has been reported to have married the daughter of Ibrahim Qutb Shah.[11]
'Abdullah Qutb Shah's daughter was married to Abul Hasan, a disciple of
Sufi saint, Shah Raju (d. 1096/1684).[12]

Since the Safavids claimed to be Sayyids and had been mystic preceptors,
they were in a position to work out grounds for the divine sanction of
their political suzerainty. Not immediately after the foundation of the
dynasty but in a later period, Safavid *mujtahids* like Mir Muhammad Baqir
Majlisi (d.1111/1698) would go to the extent of presenting two sayings or
traditions (*ahādīs*) of the Prophet predicting the appearance of the Safavid
dynasty which would eradicate infidels in the east, particularly in the
areas stretching from Jazira to Multan, with their capital at Gilan. Several
codices of this treatise by Baqir Majlisi, *Kitāb-i-ghaīb-wa-huzūr*, were copied
in Golkonda and Bijapur and are still preserved in various institutions
and by families of Hyderabad.[13] Although the traditions presented by
Mir Muhammad Baqir Majlisi are not approved by any Sunni sources, in
this treatise he traced the first tradition to Imam Muhammad Bin 'Ali Baqir
and the second to Imam Ja'far Bin Muhammad Sadiq. To substantiate this
claim, Majlisi traced the chain of this tradition to the *Kitāb-i-ghaībat* of
Abu Khalid Kabuli who referred it further back to Muhammad Bin Ibrahim
al-Numani. Muhammad Baqir Majlisi's interesting treatise dealt with two
issues, namely the disappearance (*ghaīb*) of the Twelfth Imam and the
appearance (*zuhūr*) of the Safavids, with an intention to assign a greater
divine sanctity to the Safavid family.[14]

Religion and politics were two dimensions of the Safavid state's uni-
versalist and expansionist ambitions and the regime therefore used different
methods to popularize its version of Shi'ism.[15] Apart from its ideological
aspect, the devices for popularizing Shi'ism in other states were diverse, for
example the deputation of *elchis* of different categories to contemporary

polities with letters professing the Shi'ite faith, and gifts including a *tāj* or crown/cap. Although the tradition of sending a *tāj* belonged to the Sufis in the past, the Safavids, also embraced it, but modified its colour and shape to suit their unique symbolic purpose.

The Safavid *tāj* had twelve scallops, each of which represented one of the Imams and was not an invention of the Safavid household. The Sayyids of Iran had distinguished themselves by wearing a *tāj* with twelve scallops to indicate their descent from the Twelve Imams on one hand, and of their belief in the rightful claim of 'Ali and his descendants to the institution of Caliphate on the other. As early as 8311/1428, Shah Ni'matullah had sent a *tāj* with twelve scallops with the title of *valī* to Ahmad Shah Bahmani.[16]

The Safavid *tāj* was different from that of the Kirmanis in the details of its shape but it had twelve scallops based on the earlier, pre-Safavid pattern. Nevertheless its peculiarity was its red colour. As noted earlier, the Safavid nobility and army were called Red Heads or Qizilbash on account of their red caps.[17] The first instance of Shah Isma'il sending the *tāj* to the Deccan occurs in the year 921/1515 when he sent it as a token of his invitation to the Shi'ite faith to Mahmud Shah Bahmani who refused to accept it.[18]

Safavid monarchs also developed the practice of honouring their eminent guests by crowning them with a *tāj* so as to compel them to accept Shi'ism, as Shah Tahmasp did in the case of Humayun.[19] They had also sent a *tāj* to the Qutb Shahs, though it is not known if it was sent more than once to the same ruler. Yet many of the Qutb Shahi monarchs had received a *tāj* from Iran. Again it is not certain if the crowns of the Qutb Shahs were the same as the ones received from Iran or their own. However, Golkonda's acceptance of the *tāj* sent by the Safavids was a symbolic expression of stronger ideological ties between the two.

The most meaningful evidence of the religio-political attachment of Golkonda with Iran is provided by the recitation of the Shi'ite *khutbah* expressing the Qutb Shah's allegiance to the Safavids. Thus the *khutbah* had two aspects, one religious and the other political. Religiously, it required the inclusion of the names of Twelve Imams replacing the names of four orthodox Caliphs. Sultan Quli incorporated it in the year 918/1512 when he was still a provincial governor (*tarafdār*) of Tilangana.[20] Politically, he included the name of Shah Isma'il Safavi, probably after dropping the name of the Bahmani monarch in the year 924/1518, after the complete collapse of the Bahmani kingdom.[21] This *khutbah* was followed by all the Qutb Shahi sultans until 'Abdullah Qutb Shah was forced by Shah Jahan to execute the Deed of Submission (*inqīyād nāmah*) in 1045/1636.[22]

Shi'ite Influence in the Deccan

The Qutb Shahs were not the first advocates of Shi'ism in the Deccan. In fact, they were the last even among the other sultans succeeding the Bahmanis, to declare themselves as Shi'i. The nucleus of the Shi'ite faith and tradition in the Deccan dates back to the times of Feroz Shah Bahmani who followed some Shi'ite traditions[23] at the instance of his Shi'i preceptor, Mir Fazlullah Inju.[24] Inju was quite close to Firoz Shah not only because he was the king's preceptor but also because he was later appointed prime minister.

The rise of Shi'ite influence in Bahmani society was mainly due to the influx of *āfāqīs* from the times of Ahmed Shah Bahmani (825/1422). He was the first Bahmani monarch, who, probably as advised by his *āfāqī* friend Khalaf Hasan Basari, neglected the Sufis of the Deccan and invited Shah Ni'matullah Kirmani from Mahan.[25] Though Shah Ni'matullah could not accept his invitation on account of old age, he conferred upon him the mystic title of *vali* and accepted him as his disciple (*murid*).[26] Two of Shah Ni'matullah Kirmani's grandsons named Habibullah and Muhibullah Kirmani reached Bidar by 834/1430 and entered into matrimonial relations with the royal family. Habibullah Kirmani, being elder, occupied the Sufi seat of his family in Bidar. Though the other Sufi saints of Bidar like Sayyidul Sadat Muhammad Hanif, Abul Faiz Minallah Muhammad Muhammad ul Husaini and Shaikh Ibrahim Multani were invited to important state functions, they had reservations about politics. The other Sufis of Gulbarga, Bijapur and Daulatabad were more detached from affairs of the court. This situation placed the Kirmani family in a dominant position.

The changed relationship between religion and politics in the Bahmani kingdom provided a channel for previously suppressed Shi'ite elements to come forward with greater political ambitions. This resulted in an extra-ordinary influx of *āfāqīs* who were Shi'is from Iran and Arabia.[27] Those *āfāqīs* soon dominated the Bahmani elite. Needless to say, the Bahmani elite consisted of two parties—the Deccanis and the *āfāqīs*—who were hostile to each other. The Bahmani monarchs had the difficult task of maintaining an equilibrium between these two elements. The great Bahmani *vazir* Mahmud Gawan was a victim of this conflict.[28] The Deccani-*āfāqī* conflict continued throughout the Bahmani period until five of its provincial governors assumed autonomy and three of them subsequently declared themselves to be Shi'i.[29]

While such was the situation in the Deccan, the state of affairs in Iran was entirely different. There the Turkmen tribes struggled against each other at different stages. In the first order, the Qara Quyunlus fought against Chaghtais; in the second they fought against Aq Quyunlus and in the third stage, the Aq Quyunlus were undone by an alliance of various Turkmen clans, on the basis of tribal principles, under the leadership of Shah Isma'il Safavi.[30]

We may therefore infer that throughout the fifteenth century the political aspirations of the Shi'is were expressed in one way or the other by many of the Sayyid families who had until then been either Sufi or Sunni.[31] It was in the second stage that Shah Isma'il openly and formally proclaimed Shi'ism in Iran. The rulers of the Deccan, including the Qutb Shahs, followed this declaration.

It is interesting to note that in the middle of the fifteenth century, religious authority was assumed by a monarchy in the Deccan. At the end of the same century, religious leadership in Iran assumed political authority. In any case, it was a union of religion and politics, which manifested itself in a peculiar character of being a religious politics and a political religion at the same time.

Religion of the Qutb Shahs

The traditional religion of Qutb Shahs was the one that their Qara ancestors had adhered to ever since their conversion to Islam.[32] Obviously the religion first embraced by them near the Oxus was based on the Sunni faith. But ever since their settlement at Lake Van and particularly with the rise of Qara Muhammad and Qara Yusuf, they appear to have been more pre-occupied with war than religion. Nurullah Shustari observed that the general conduct and attitude of the Qaras, except that of Mirza Ispand, usually violated the edicts of Islamic tradition (*shari'ah*).[33] Jahan Shah's banishment of Shaikh Junaid and the grandfather of Shah Isma'il Safavi is evidence of his disregard for the Sufis of a great order or, at the least, his brazenness towards political leaders from a competing, religious background. The Qaras did not show any remarkable religious inclination except that Jahan Shah became a disciple of Shah Naimuddin Ni'matullah Yazdi, a descendant of Shah Ni'matullah Kirmani, and gave his daughter in marriage to him.[34] After Jahan Shah, the Qara Quyunlus fell victim to the Aq Quyunlus who were the disciples of the Safavid household, which by then was assuming a Shi'ite character. Moreover, the political rise of the Safavids brought the Kirmani and Safavid families closer through matrimonial ties. Sultan Quli Qutb Shah, who was brought up in an atmosphere of Aq domination, would have undoubtedly been overwhelmed by its complete devotion to the Safavid household. It was perhaps in such a milieu that he embraced the Shi'ite faith.

Some of the ladies of Qara family like Arayish Begam and Auraq Sultan, daughters of Qara Iskandar, had an inclination towards certain aspects of the Shi'ite faith.[35] Sultan Quli was the first person in the line (though quite late) who declared himself a Shi'i, claiming that he had been adhering to that faith even before Shah Isma'il initiated his movement.[36]

Whatever might have been the faith of the Qaras or even of Sultan Quli during his early career, there is no doubt that he considered the Shi'ite faith as the state religion ever since he assumed autonomy in the Deccan.[37] It is worth mentioning that Sultan Quli made a claim of being Shi'i only after the rise of Shah Isma'il in Iran.[38] Moreover, he was not the first of the Deccan sultans to declare his adherence to the Shi'ite faith as he was following the precedent of the 'Adil Shahs.[39] By the year 944/1537, Burhan Nizam Shah too had joined the common faith of Bijapur and Golkonda. From this point on, there developed a shared socio-religious attitude among the Deccan sultanates, resulting in a uniform foreign policy, especially towards Safavid Iran.

The foundation of Golkonda-Iran relations and the relative weakness of the former allowed a heavy influx of Iranian elites in Golkonda, who exercised great influence over the court. All the Qutb Shahs adhered to Shi'ism.[40] This was emphatically professed in their correspondence with the Safavids of Iran, in which they claimed that they had been adhering to the faith of the Safavid household and had been doing their best to further the aspirations of the Safavid movement.[41] As a preliminary measure they had declared their sultanates *dār us salām* (peace territory) as against *dār ul harb* (war territory).[42] It was due to their efforts that the Shi'ite doctrinal phrase '*aliyun vali ullah* echoed throughout the Golkonda Sultanate. After the execution of the Deed of Submission, Shi'ism officially ceased to be the state religion of Golkonda, which placed 'Abdullah Qutb Shah in a dilemma regarding his relations with Iran. He continued to adhere to the Shi'ite faith privately. In the year 1072/1661, he sent Razi Danish as his vice-pilgrim (*nā'ib-uzzīyārah*), assigning him an annuity of a few thousand *tomān tabrizī* for the course of his lifetime. The vice-pilgrim was to pay visits to the holy shrine of Imam 'Ali Reza and perform all the necessary rituals every morning.[43] It is worth noting that even the last Golkonda sultan, Abul Hasan Qutb Shah, who was disciple of the Sufi saint Shah Raju, also claimed his adherence to the Shi'ite faith in his letter addressed to Shah Suleiman Safavi.[44]

Religious Missionaries

Under Safavid patronage, Shi'ism spread through the deputation of missionaries and learned elites to other polities. In Iran there developed a number of schools (*madrasahs*) that produced scholarly *mujtahids*[45] who successfully spread their mission in Iran and carried it to India, especially to the Deccan. Some of the *mujtahids* were also astute diplomats and they acquired important positions in Golkonda and other Deccan sultanates. A few of such personalities are introduced here.

Shah Tahir

The first of the Shi'i missionaries who reached the Deccan after the Safavid Revolution was Shah Tahir. He landed at Dabhol (Goa) in the year 926/1520.[46] He was not a state missionary formally deputed by Shah Isma'il, but an émigré who had left Iran after earning the displeasure of Shah Isma'il. The Shah had become suspicious of whether Shah Tahir was actually adhering to the *Asna 'Asharī* (or *Ja'farī*) version of Shi'ism or not.[47]

Shah Tahir was a Sayyid, a descendant of the Isma'ili sultans of Egypt. His genealogy went back to Abul Qasim Muhammad bin 'Abdullah al-Mihdi. After the fall of the Fatimid dynasty, his ancestors went to Khwand, a village in the vicinity of Qazwin in the year 567/1171. During the last quarter of the ninth century Hijri, Shah Tahir succeeded to the Sufi seat of his ancestors. Because of Shah Isma'il Safavi's dislike and destruction of other mystic orders in his dominions, Shah Tahir chose to migrate from Iran. He had a charismatic personality and was an accomplished scholar and a skillful missionary.[48]

Shah Tahir had no official status when he arrived in the Deccan. He was not deputed as a Safavid diplomat nor did he represent any Shi'i organization. He was on his own. However, he was successful in forging ties between the court and religious elites in the Deccan sultanates. The confidence that Burhan Nizam Shah I commanded in him can be judged from an incident when, as early as in the year 932/1526, Shah Tahir was sent as a political representative to the court of Babur.[49] He played an important role in mediating in the conflicts between the sultans of the Deccan. For instance, in the external policies of Golkonda he mediated between 'Ali Barid and Sultan Quli Qutb Shah, when the former in alliance with Ibrahim 'Adil Shah I encroached upon Golkonda's territories in the year 941/1534. The negotiation was so successful that 'Ali Barid handed over the keys of Medak Fort to Sultan Quli without any further resistance.[50]

As a Sunni sultan, Burhan Nizam Shah was rather indisposed to accept the Shi'ite faith even though he willingly accepted the political and diplomatic services of Shah Tahir. Shah Tahir made Ahmednagar the centre of his activities where he developed a wide network among the nobility and the Muslim populace, participating in a series of public debates, group discussions and dialogues (properly termed as *munāzirah*) with opponents who were Sunnis. His achievement as a missionary may be judged from the conversion of Burhan Nizam Shah to Shi'ism in 944/1537. A miraculous incident regarding the conversion is described in *Tārīkh-i Firishtah*. 'Abdul Qadir, the sultan's beloved son, was seized by high fever. Despite every possible treatment his health deteriorated and Burhan Nizam Shah lost all hope of his son's survival. In order to cure him, Shah Tahir took the opportunity to request Burhan Nizam Shah to pray to the holy Imams and to promise to introduce their names in the *khutbah*. Assuming that his son's recovery was impossible, Burhan Nizam Shah conceded to Shah Tahir suggestions. That same night 'Abdul Qadir recovered from his illness. This incidence tilted the scales and led Burhan Nizam Shah to promote the Shi'ite faith in his dominions.[51] Besides the sultan, it is said that Shah Tahir's missionary efforts also led to the rapid conversion of Sunnis from all ranks, sometimes at the rate of 3,000 persons per day. It was through his efforts that the names of the first three Caliphs (*ashāb-i sulāsah*) were dropped and the names of the Twelve Imams were included in the *khutbah* at Ahmednagar.[52]

The news of this great socio-religious change in Ahmednagar brought about by Shah Tahir and his rising influence in the Deccan reached the court of Shah Tahmasp in Iran. The Iranian monarch did not hesitate in making use of an effective missionary like Shah Tahir. He, therefore, addressed him through a *farmān* in the year 949/1542 appreciating his valuable services. Shah Tahmasp encouraged him to propagate the Twelvers' faith in the Deccan.[53] Again in Rabi I 954/May 1547, Shah Tahmasp addressed Shah Tahir, of course in reply to his letter, through a *farmān* sent with Khurshah bin Qubad-ul-Husaini of Nizam Shah who was returning from Iran. Shah Tahmasp lauded the valuable services that Shah Tahir had rendered to the cause of the Safavid movement in the Deccan. His mission had upheld and furthered the movement both in its religious and political aspects. Shah Tahmasp acknowledged his services and never failed to encourage him to intensify his mission.[54]

Shah Tahir wielded enormous influence in the Deccan as well as in Iran. His accomplished scholarship, political acumen, and social network placed him in a position from where he could effectively influence the conduct of different rulers as well as do missionary work among the populace in the Deccan. This he continued to do until his death in 956/1549.[55]

Mir Muhammad Mu'min

The most important person who played a distinct role in the socio-political life of the Golkonda Sultanate was Mir Muhammad Mu'min. He was born in Astarabad in 960/1552. He was the nephew of the renowned scholar Amir Fakhruddin Sammaki and a student of Sayyid Nuruddin al-Musavi al-Shustari. He was appointed as preceptor of Sultan Haidar, son of Shah Tahmasp Safavi. However, the prince died young and Shah Isma'il Safavi II ascended the Iranian throne after the death of Shah Tahmasp.[56] Mir Muhammad Mu'min migrated to Golkonda in 989/1581, a few months after the death of Sultan Ibrahim Qutb Shah. He entered Qutb Shahi services under Sultan Muhammad Quli and rose to the highest post of *peshwā* by about 994/1585.[57]

As *peshwā*, or prime minister, he was responsible for the formulation of all state policies. As a member of the Safavid court, Mir Mu'min had already apprenticed as an administrator, and this training and experience clearly helped him in Golkonda. All important decisions regarding internal and external matters like appointments of persons to key posts, the deputation of *elchis* and the appointments of persons in the Majlis were taken by him or at least in consultation with him. He was the second most important noble at Golkonda court; the first was Mir Jumla Mir Kamaluddin Mustafa Khan Ardestani.[58]

Both Iranian and Golkonda sources unanimously attest that Mir Muhammad Mu'min furthered Shi'i doctrine in Golkonda. He adopted a three-fold strategy to achieve this goal. First, since he was a scholar of considerable stature, he encouraged Shi'i scholarship in Golkonda by inviting or entertaining intellectuals from Iran.[59] Second, he increased the strength and influence of Shi'i elements among the Qutb Shahi elite. Third, he set up *'āshūr khānahs* and other Shi'i institutions in the city and other parts of the sultanate. Shah 'Abbas II, who entered into correspondence with him on religio-political issues, appreciated his distinct role in spreading Shi'ism in the Deccan.[60]

Shaikh Muhammad Ibn Khatun

Shaikh Shamsuddin Abu Ma'ali Muhammad Bin Ali Bin Khatun al-Amuli, often identified as Ibn Khatun by historians, was another figure who played an important role in shaping the policies of the Golkonda Sultanate.

He was born in a village called Ayans located in the hilly area of Amol. He received his education at Mashhad and Isfahan under the renowned scholar Shaikh Bahauddin Muhammad Bin Husain al-Amoli (d.1031/1621).[61] He reached Golkonda in about 1009/1600 where, after sometime, he was entertained by Sultan Muhammad Qutb Shah and gradually attained the position of royal secretary (*dabīr-ul-mumālik*). In 1025/1616, he was sent to the court of Shah 'Abbas I as a return *elchi* of Golkonda accompanying the Iranian *elchi*, Husain Beg Qapuchi Bashi.[62] After a four-year stay in Iran, he returned to Golkonda and was appointed *peshwā* of the sultanate during the reign of Sultan 'Abdullah Qutb Shah. He was the last person to hold that supreme position after Mir Muhammad Mu'min in 1038/1629. Again in the year 1058/1648, he proceeded on *hajj* from the port of Masulipatam but died in a shipwreck near the port of Mocha in 1059/1649.[63]

Ibn Khatun was an eminent scholar, a skillful administrator and a politician and diplomat. He played a significant part in balancing the external policies of Golkonda. Most of the members of the Majlis, during the times of 'Abdullah Qutb Shah, were appointed at his instance. Alongside his administrative and political activities he ran his own school (*madrasah*) and entered into academic discourses with scholars and intellectuals every day.[64] He attended all the important cultural functions and was accessible to common people outside the court.[65] His wide range of activities influenced the political elite, the intellectuals, the literati, diplomats and even Golkonda's subjects. Ibn Khatun worked to popularize the Shi'ite faith in all such circles. His most significant contribution was his books relating to various aspects of Shi'i doctrine.[66]

One of Ibn Khatun's works, *Kitāb al-Imāmah*,[67] focusing on the issue of the Caliphate and Imamate, can be found in the library of Golkonda. The debate on the foundations of early Islam and the divergent interpretations by Shi'i and Sunni scholars on these key issues preceded Safavid Shi'ism by many centuries.[68] The terms '*amir-ul-muminīn*' (Commander of the Believers) and '*khalifatullah*' (God's Caliph) are two titles used interchangeably in Islamic literature. The institution of the Caliphate served as the head of a state as well as a divine agent of governance.[69] Sunnis had submitted their allegiance to the dynastic caliphs since the time of the Umayyads,[70] despite the fact that the institution of the Caliphate came into being as a result of a combined process of selection and election. Sunnis accepted the first four orthodox Caliphs as the rightly guided (*rāshidūn*) and legitimate successors of the Prophet. Shi'ite scholars or *mujtahids* on the other hand, who enunciated on religious doctrines, refused to accept these dynastic Caliphs, right from the times of the first orthodox Caliph Abu Bakr, as legitimate authorities. Instead, they placed this authority in the Imamate. According to them, God designated an Imam, who was inherently innocent (*ma'sūm*), a member of the household of the Prophet, and therefore the only rightful and legitimate successor to the Prophet. In *Kitāb al-Imāmah*, Ibn Khatun articulated these disagreements citing earlier authorities, seeking to delegitimize the first three Caliphs[71] and support the rightful successor of 'Ali.[72]

Shaikh Ibn Khatun's efforts to popularize the Shi'ite faith in Golkonda were somewhat similar to that of Mir Muhammad Baqir Majlisi in Iran. He was not only a missionary himself but was more of an organizer of missionaries. The influx of *mujtahids*, scholars, men of letters and other intellectuals from Iran to Golkonda encouraged by Shaikh Muhammad Ibn Khatun was far greater during the time of 'Abdullah Qutb Shah than in earlier periods.

Popular Shi'ism in Golkonda

While the *mujtahids* were trying their best to influence the indigenous elite with Shi'ism, the sultans too, sought their guidance to promote the Shi'ite faith among the populace in urban and rural areas. Like most other religions, Shi'ism too flourished with different periodical rituals and festivals in Golkonda. Popular Shi'ism in Golkonda mostly consisted of rituals, patronized by the sultans.

Golkonda society, which comprised Sunnis, Brahmanical Hindus and Lingayats, already had a series of rituals, some of which were patronized by the state from ancient times.[73] Among the Sunni festivals, *Shab-i-bārāt*, *Milād-u'nnabi* and various *Urs* were the chief socio-religious festivals patronized by the sultans. *Milād-u'nnabi* was celebrated once a year[74] but the *Urs* of hundreds of saints were celebrated all through the year.[75] Non-Muslims celebrated Diwali, Holi and Dusshera with grand processions. The Sunnis adopted various elements of these local rituals in their celebrations of *Shab-i-bārāt*, *Milād* and the *Urs*. These Sunni and Hindu rituals were shared by both communities. It was in this pre-existing context of popular religious practices that Shi'ite public festivals and rituals were introduced, some of which were adapted from Safavid Iran.

Muharram

In view of the above circumstances it was important for the Qutb Shahs to develop a popular Shi'ism that resembled pre-existing practices of Sunnis and non-Muslims. They instituted *'āshūr khānas* and *imāmbārās* of various sizes in the city and in almost every village. They spent enormous amounts on the celebration of the mourning rituals from first to the tenth of Muharram every year. All sorts of pleasure-seeking activities, music and slaughter of animals, eating of *paan* and hairdressing were officially prohibited throughout the sultanate. All the nobles, officials and servants were provided with black garments from the government's wardrobe (*jamādar khānah*). More than 1,000 lights were lit in *'āshūr khānas* and symbolic standards (*'alam*) representing the martyrs of Karbala were installed in them. Shi'i preachers (*zākir*) would give lectures in praise of the innocent Imams and condemn the first three Caliphs. The ambassadors of Iran, Hindustan and other Deccan sultanates would attend public commemorations of Muharram.[76]

Muharram was observed similarly throughout the sultanate at all ports, forts and villages. Its expenditure was met from government treasury. This popularized Shi'i traditions among Sunnis and Hindus, who would also take a special bath, dress neatly and prepare sherbet during Muharram. The name of Husain became very popular and was adopted even by non-Muslims.[77] Muharram would last until the twentieth of the next month, Safar, with several subsidiary rituals, which would attract residents of cities and villages throughout the sultanate. Various elements of such rituals were also interesting and bore some resemblance to local devotional practices, such as moving around the fire during Holi and processions carrying sacred standards like those seen in Dusshera. State patronage made these celebrations grander than those organized privately.

Milād U'nnabi

In Golkonda, the birthday of the Prophet of Islam (*Milād-u'nnabi*) was celebrated as a state function and on a grand scale. It had become a very interesting festival during the times of Sultan Muhammad Quli Qutb Shah, but since it mostly represented a Sunni tradition Sultan Muhammad Quli's successor, Sultan Muhammad Qutb Shah, prohibited both its official and private celebrations. 'Abdullah Qutb Shah revived the festival with unprecedented pomp and glory. The revived *Milād* festival acquired a diplomatic significance and was attended by ambassadors, scholars and artists from various parts of the world, especially from Iran.[78]

Shab-i bārāt

Shab-i bārāt was celebrated on the night of fifteenth Sha'ban with many rituals and entertainments in Golkonda. Lavish illuminations and fireworks were arranged. The monarchs themselves took part in the festival. Sultan Muhammad Quli Qutb Shah, who was fond of this festival, also composed poems in praise of *Shab-i bārāt*.[79] In addition to these festivals, there were some other occasions that forged a symbolic link between Golkonda and Iran, such as *Jashn-i Nauroz*, *'Eid-i Ghadīr* and *Chahār Shambeh*, in praise of which Sultan Muhammad Quli Qutb Shah also wrote verses in the Dakani.[80]

The city was named Hyderabad after the name of Haidar ('Ali).[81] The famous edifice of Charminar was a duplicate of a similar monument with a similar name in Yazd and represented the form of a ceremonial Shi'ite standard called *ta'zīyah*.[82] All surviving Qutb Shahi buildings have distinct Shi'ite motifs, which we also find in other artifacts such as textiles, metalwork and carpets now preserved in museums.

All such techniques and symbols may have been effective enough to promote a strong sense of a shared Shi'ite faith across rulers and subjects. Yet, there were several elements among the Golkonda elite who were antagonistic to Shi'ism and Iranian domination. There were instances when the Iranian or Shi'i and Deccani or Sunni elements clashed with each other, leading to discord amongst the nobility.[83]

TRAFFIC OF IDEAS

A century and three-quarters of connections between Qutb Shahi Golkonda and Safavid Iran was an extension of a much longer history of Indo-Iranian cultural relations. This exchange was not altogether new. Pre-existing conditions and influences in both Iran and Golkonda had shaped intellectual life. In both societies, Shi'i Islam encountered and fused with different indigenous schools of thought. In Iran, Zoroastrian[84] thought shaped religion while Hellenistic ideas influenced philosophy and medicine. In Golkonda,

Iranian intellectuals and philosophers encountered diverse local religious cosmologies. In both regions, indigenous and foreign ideas had sustained quite a long history of synthesis, blending and mutation.

Ideas in Golkonda were of as many types as there had been castes and tribes in the subcontinent, profoundly influenced by Brahmanism, Buddhism, Jainism and Hinduism, the cult of the Lingayats and ultimately, Christianity and Islam. By the period of this study, most of the above influences had lost their distinctiveness, though Brahmanism, Hinduism and the Lingayat sects had survived. Right from the advent of Islam in India and the Deccan, ideas from Central Asia that had already absorbed features of Hellenistic and Zoroastrian thought arrived here and shaped the spheres of humanities and physical sciences. The Bahmani kingdom, especially from the times of Feroz Shah and subsequently under Mahmud Gawan, played a leading role in importing such thoughts and values. But the Telugu-speaking areas of the Deccan were not completely under Bahmani sway. Sultan Quli Qutb Shah had thus advanced the claim that he was the first to introduce Islam in the Telugu-speaking regions. As the Qutb Shahi dynasty was consolidated, more migrants from Iran, who were learned elites, administrators, doctors, philosophers, etc., arrived and a complex synthesis of ideas and practices took place. While the number of fields shaped by the traffic of ideas is wide, this section discusses the structure of administration, different fields of education and philosophy between the two regions.

The Arts of Administration

The structure of administration in Golkonda was a combination of Indian and Iranian systems. The Qutb Shahs had inherited broad regional, agrarian, economic and commercial administration from the Vijayanagar Empire. Structurally, official personnel, practices and procedures were initially a continuation of the Perso-Bahmani system that Sultan Quli Qutb Shah modified much later.[85] During the reigns of subsequent rulers, a heavy traffic of administrative personnel and ideas from Iran transformed the institutional, procedural and personnel structure of Golkonda.

The administrative institutions at the centre in Golkonda displayed Iranian characteristics. Such institutions included both consultative bodies as well as administrative agencies. The highest consultative body in Golkonda was the Majlis,[86] an institution that had its roots in Iran from previous centuries.[87] Apart from this consultative body of administrators, the political elite and literati, the institutions of *peshwā* and *Mir Jumla* were the highest administrative offices. It is doubtful whether the two posts ever existed in Iran but both were immensely important in Golkonda. The office of the *peshwā* in Golkonda, which was originally a religious one in Iran, also had political and administrative responsibility.[88] The office of *Mir Jumla* was unique to Golkonda and had similar responsibilities as the office of *peshwā* but excluded the religious leadership. Below them, the offices of *sar khayl* (Head of Regiments/Lieutenant), *Sar Lashkar* (Brigadier of Army), *Hājib* (Chamberlain), *Dabīr-ul-mulk* (Royal Epistolarian), *Mushrif-ul-Mulk* (Auditor General), *Sipāh Sālār* (Commander-in-Chief), *Silāhdār* (Chief of Ordinance), *Qāzī* (Judge), *Āmil* (Revenue Collector), *Tahvildār* (Keeper), *Shāh Bandar* (Keeper of Port), *Qilādār* (Keeper of Fort) down to *Massāh* (Land Surveyor) and *Zamīn Paīmā* (Land Measurer) were posts of Iranian origin, both in nomenclature and functions.[89] Besides the institutions of civil and military administration of the sultanate, the institution of the royal palace was also an amalgam of Indian and Iranian courts.[90]

Although Golkonda's administration did not have the elaborate documentation procedures and large paper administration of the Mughals, all important administrative decisions and official and private transactions were recorded on paper. Persian was the official language; however, important documents, like *farmāns*, were issued in regional Indian languages. The great numbers of Iranians in administration led to an increase in Persian administrative terminology and practices in Golkonda, to the extent that it had a distinct impact on Telugu and Kannada in many respects.[91]

The administrative documents issued through the agencies (*parvānagī*) of eminent administrators, the various deeds and bonds executed at the office of the *Qāzī*, procedures of governing and protecting public and private transactions, the Books of Protocol (*tashrifāt*), the Rules of Majlis (*Qānūn-i Majlis*) and other important documents clearly exhibit an Iranian influence.

Iranian personnel, politicians or diplomats, international traders or eminent scholars, expert physicians, engineers, architects, poets, painters or craftsmen of high intellectual calibre and experts of war or civil and military administration, served as a channel for the traffic of administrative ideas. On occasions, due to the exceptional talents and capacities of such administrators, special posts had to be created in Golkonda. The post of *peshwā*, a combination of religious and political leadership, was created for the multifaceted personalities of men like Mustafa Khan, Mir Muhammad Mu'min and Ibn Khatun. The presence of naturalized and Golkonda-born Iranians served as a permanent channel for the influx of men and ideas from Iran.

Education

By the sixteenth century, the education system of Iran had assimilated Arab, Hellenistic and indigenous elements in its structure and spirit. The Safavids inherited this pre-existing structure and set it in a new direction by producing Shi'i divines or *mujtahids*. Changes in the education system were introduced to promote Safavid ideology.[92]

Colleges (*madrasahs*) were instituted in Golkonda during the reign of Qutb Shahs and facilitated the diffusion of ideas and knowledge that had originally developed in an Iranian environment. First, there was the medical college, *Dār-ul-shifā*, established by Sultan Muhammad Quli Qutb Shah.[93] Then, notable colleges in Golkonda such as *Madrasah-i-Ibn Khatun* and *Madrasah-i Hayat Bakshi Begam* were also set up. The curriculum taught at the *madrasah* of Ibn Khatun included detailed courses of reflective (*ma'qūlāt*) and narrative (*manqūlāt*) branches of knowledge. The curriculum comprised the commentaries of Koran (*tafāsīr*), the traditions of the Prophet (*ahādīs*), Islamic jurisprudence (*fiqh*), philosophy, logic, mathematics and Arabic and Persian literature.[94]

Among those who trained at these Golkonda colleges was the renowned historian Mirza Nizamuddin Ahmad Shirazi, author of *Hadīqat-us-Salātīn*, who acknowledged revising this important court chronicle under Ibn Khatun.[95] Similarly, the historian and scholar, 'Ali Bin Taifur Bistami, too, was proud of being Ibn Khatun's student.[96] 'Ali Bin Taifur Bistami was the son of Taifur Bin Muhammad of Bistam who was an eminent scholar. Bistami was a versatile scholar and contributed a number of books on history, literature, mysticism, ethics and lexicography. He was in Golkonda during the reigns of 'Abdullah Qutb Shah and Abul Hasan Qutb Shah.[97] The eminent diplomat and Qazi of Golkonda, Zahiruddin Muhammad Najafi,[98] and his son Mir-i-Miran, who rose to the position of Royal Epistolarian (*Dabīr-ul-mulk*)[99] and Muhammad 'Ali Jabal Druzi, the author of *Majma' ul amsāl* were among Ibn Khatun's other students. Muhammad 'Ali hailed from Jabal Druz, Isfahan. He reached Golkonda in 1054/1644 and joined the retinue of Ibn Khatun at whose instance he compiled a thesaurus of Persian proverbs with illustrative examples.[100]

The curriculum for the education of princes was somewhat different and comprised the following subjects in addition to curricula meant for students of religion and medicine:

1. The art of governance (*qawā'id-i-jahāndārī*)
2. Administration of justice (*ma'dalat-wa-nisfat*)
3. World affairs (*ādāb-i-gītī*)
4. The Regulations of Majlis (*qānūn-i-majlis*)
5. Court procedure (*diwān dārī*)
6. Royal customs (*marāsim-i-pādshāhī*)
7. Military organization and training (*ihtimām-i-'asākir*)[101]

The medium of instruction was Persian and the books of syllabi were both in Persian and Arabic. These were mostly written in Iran and most of the teachers were Iranians. Among the tutors of 'Abdullah Qutb Shah there were men like Mir Qutbuddin Ni'matullah Shirazi. Among others were *sādāts* like Mirza Sharif Shahristani, Khwajah Muzaffar Ali, and Maulana Husain Shirazi.[102] There were perhaps a few exceptions like Mullah Wajhi who was a Deccani. Such institutions suggest that Iran was the primary source of religious and political education of courtly elites in Golkonda.

Medical Knowledge

The curricula of medicine in the medical college of *Dār-ul-shifā* and the results of education imparted there may be gauged from the wealth of medical literature produced in Golkonda. The treatises on medical practices indicate what was being taught in the medical colleges as well as rules of hygiene, manuals for maintaining good health and prescriptions for different ailments. Not just works of Greek or *Ūnānī* medical systems, but also the works of Indian (*hindī*) physicians and medicinal systems must have shaped medical practices in Golkonda. Although little direct evidence has survived, with such a diversity of medical knowledge systems, Graeco-Arab and Indian medical systems would have undoubtedly influenced each other. The Greek system found its way into Golkonda through two channels: first through the Iranian physicians (*hakīms*) and second through the European physicians, who too had derived their medicinal knowledge from Graeco-Arab traditions but had developed it further.[103] The Qutb Shahs officially invited many of these doctors, both Iranian and European. A brief list of those *hakīms* who had contributed to the diffusion of Graeco-Arab medicine in Golkonda, either as exceptionally skillful clinicians or as medical scholars, is given here. In cases where the date of death is not available in the sources, each individual has been identified with the sultan under whose reign they served.

Mir Muhammad Mu'min

The renowned Qutb Shahi *peshwā*, Mir Muhammad Mu'min, was interested in the promotion of medical research. There is no evidence of him personally indulging in clinical practices but his interest in medical knowledge may be presumed from his patronage of certain texts. He patronized several medical scholars and encouraged medical research.[104]

Shamsuddin

Hakim Shamsuddin 'Ali al-Husaini hailed from Jurgan (Gorgan).[105] He was attached to the court of Muhammad Quli Qutb Shah (d.1020/1612). He encouraged many medical research projects taken up by eminent physicians.[106]

Hakim Safiuddin Muhammad

He hailed from Gilan and was appointed as the court physician of Muhammad Quli Qutb Shah (d.1020/1612). He was a specialist in aphrodisiac medicine.[107]

Taqiuddin Muhammad

He was the court physician of Sultan Muhammad Qutb Shah (d.1035/1626) and was an expert pharmacologist.[108]

Ibn Imad Ruzbihan Isfahani

He was an administrator and a member of the renowned Ruzbihan family of Isfahan. The encyclopedic range of his interests made him indulge in medicine as well. He was interested in pharmacology and made some contributions to it. He held the position of *sar khayl* under Muhammad Qutb Shah (d.1035/1626).[109]

Hakim Isma'il

He was attached to the court of 'Abdullah Qutb Shah (d.1083/1672) and served as consultant physician.[110]

Hakim Gabriel

Hakim Gabriel was an Armenian and followed the Nestorian faith of Christianity. He was the court physician of 'Abdullah Qutb Shah. He died in Golkonda in the year 1045/1635.[111]

Hakim Nizamuddin Gilani

Hakīm-ul-Mulk Nizamuddin Gilani was perhaps the greatest of the medical scholars of Golkonda. He was a native of Gilan and was student of Bahauddin Amuli (d.1031/1621) and Shamsuddin Muhammad Baqir Damad (d.1040/1630). He completed his education and received a degree in various branches of medicine and philosophy on 14th Sha'ban 1023/9 September 1614. When he first came to India, he joined the retinue of the Mughal noble Zamana Beg Mahabat Khan known as *khān-i-khānān*. In the year 1044/1634, when Mahabat Khan died, he intended to leave for Iran, but was invited by 'Abdullah Qutb Shah and appointed as the Royal Physician in place of late Hakim Gabriel.[112]

Hakīm-ul-Mulk contributed to the promotion of Graeco-Arab medicine in Golkonda in many ways. He served Golkonda as a physician, a scholar, a statesman and an ambassador.

Hakim 'Abdul Jabbar

He hailed from Gilan and was the court physician of 'Abdullah Qutb Shah in the year 1049/1639. He was also appointed as *Munshī-ul-Mumālik* (Royal Epistolarian).[113]

Mirza Abul Qasim

He hailed from Shiraz and was attached to the court of Shah 'Abbas II. He was invited to Golkonda by 'Abdullah Qutb Shah in 1076/1665.[114]

Karim Yazdi (d.1075/1664)

Hakim 'Abdul Karim of Yazd was a renowned physician and was attached to the court of Shah Safi Safavi. Sultan 'Abdullah Qutb Shah invited him to Golkonda, where he remained until his death in 1075/1664. His son Mirza Muhammad Ibrahim died in a shipwreck while he was taking his father's body back to Iran.[115]

Khulqi Shustari (d.1047/1637)

Mullah Khulqi Shustari visited Golkonda twice during the reign of Muhammad Quli Qutb Shah. During his second visit in about 1027/1618, he was appointed as professor in the medical college, *Dār-ul-shifā*. For over twenty years he taught medicine and subjects like mathematics and other reflective (*ma'qūl*) and descriptive (*manqūl*) disciplines. He was also appointed as a member of the Majlis by 'Abdullah Qutb Shah. He died at Golkonda in 1047/1637.[116]

Studies in different branches of medicinal science were encouraged in Golkonda, and were carried out either directly by taking up a research project or by translating authoritative Arabic works into Persian. All the classical works like that of Avicenna (Ibn Sina), Rhazes, Zainuddin Attar and the fundamental medicinal theories of Hippocrates and Galen had been imported to Golkonda, and were used for both educational purposes and as reference works in hospitals.

Golkonda imported the traditional medical system of Iran and introduced it on a large scale in the sultanate. The scientific interests of Golkonda's *hakīms* appear to have been centred around pharmacology, though some attention was paid to pathology, therapeutics and hygiene. The contemporary Iranian physician and surgeon Hakim Shifai (d.1627) had shown considerable interest in anatomy, physiology and surgery. However, from available evidence and surviving works, it seems Golkonda's physicians did not have much interest in those subjects. There are a few casual papers relating to anatomy, which cannot be treated as original or profound. Nevertheless, such papers are helpful in tracing how aspects of Graeco-Arab medicine, both in theory and clinical practice, were introduced in Golkonda.

In the discipline of pharmacology, Graeco-Arab methods of assaying simple and compound drugs were discussed. For this purpose, drug ingredients that originated in Central Asia and the Levant were introduced. The introduction of such drugs was a natural corollary of Persian translations or commentaries of the works originally produced in other parts of the Islamic world. In respect to simple drugs the following facts were generally observed:

1. The Arabic name of the drug ingredient and its Persian or Indian equivalent if it could be obtained by scientists.
2. The general description of botanical, mineral or animal essences that constituted a new drug.
3. The colour, taste, smell and the nature of the substance as liquid, solid or viscous.
4. Its chemical and physical reactions to air, water, fire and earth.
5. Its reactions on the human body when combined with other simple drugs.
6. Complements that could increase or neutralize its effect.

Every drug ingredient, which was extracted from a vegetable, animal or mineral source, was treated as a simple ingredient until it was artificially mixed and processed with one ingredient or more.[117] The process of making compound drugs by grinding, heating, burning, distilling, squeezing, etc., were all introduced through the pharmacopeia of compound drugs.

An enormous range of recipes that made different kinds of compound medicines to cure diseases were imported from Iran and tried in Golkonda. Galen as well as Avicenna and Attar were taken as the ultimate authorities on medicine and whenever a Golkonda physician found that his findings conformed with their theories, he would record in his anthology that his experiment was in keeping with the canon (*qānun*) or *minhaj*.[118]

Standardized medical prescriptions were not possible without a standard system of minute weights. However, during the seventeenth century, the issue of weights and measures had become complicated and confusing. This difficult problem was solved by Mir Muhammad Mu'min in Golkonda who contributed *Risālāh-i-Miqdāriyāh*, a valuable manual of all minor and heavy weights in use.[119] Aside from pharmacology, attention was paid to ocular and aphrodisiac medicines. It was for the latter category that manuals from the Indian medical system on aphrodisiacs and sex were rendered into Persian.[120]

The clinical records of Graeco-Arab pathological prescriptions and therapeutic treatments in Golkonda have been lost due to the recent redevelopment of old hospital sites. However, a few anthologies, still in manuscript form, indicate the methods adopted by the *hakīms* of Golkonda. Physicians kept the following factors in view while diagnosing a disease:

1. The physiology and the disposition of the patient.
2. The syndrome of the disease.

3. Special observation of the internal and external organs and the point of trouble.
4. Category of disease in the light of the therapeutic manuals of Avicenna and other authorities.[121]

They emphasized sound habits and hygiene. Hygienic slogans for the upkeep of health were formulated and manuals for maintaining health were written with great detail on subjects such as upkeep of the body by following strict hygienic principles, precautions to be taken during the changing seasons, sex and food habits and the use of aphrodisiac medicines, liquor and rich diets.[122]

Medical Institutions

Apart from the private medical institutions maintained by various *hakīms*, there is evidence that at least one major institution named *Dār-ul-shifā* was established by the Qutb Shahs. *Dār-ul-shifā* was a hospital with a medical college and several other ancillary institutions like hostels, mosques, caravanserais and baths. The entire complex (some parts of which still survive) appears to have been constructed over an area of about ten acres. It was a two-storey building, set on a plinth area of 15,000 sq. ft. with a square open yard inside. The complex had the following sections:

1. Rooms for physicians of different ranks and an area for out-patients.
2. A dispensary with rooms for storing and processing medicine.
3. From the ruins of the building, it appears that the complex had 140 rooms with verandahs for inpatients.
4. The mosque outside the hospital building still exists.
5. Medical colleges (*Madrasah-i-Dār-ul-shifā*).
6. Caravanserais for ailing people and travellers coming from distances.
7. Baths attached to caravanserais.

All the above institutions from hospitals to the baths were provided with efficient staff. The physicians had a double function of attending to the clinic and imparting education to medical students. This institution was constructed by Sultan Muhammad Quli Qutb Shah by 1004/1595–6.[123] Royal physicians would normally attend court and later proceed to the hospital near the royal palace. Moreover, knowledge of medicine was not the exclusive prerogative of professional *hakīms*. Administrators like Mir Muhammad Mu'min, Ibn Khatun and even the monarchs took an active interest in supporting new medical research.

ETHICS AND PHILOSOPHY

Much like medical knowledge and education, ethics and philosophy in the Islamic world too came about as a synthesis of Graeco-Arab ideas. The influence of Hellenistic ideas on Muslim thought has been discussed and well documented through the study of Greek literature that was rendered into Arabic from the ninth century onwards.[124] The arrival, adoption and reception of these disciplines in India had a long history but underwent some changes during the period of this study. A natural corollary of the fusion of Greek and Islamic thought was the appearance of a number of new scholastic thinkers in a composite Muslim society of Arab, Iranians and Turks from Transoxiana to Cairo. This new intellectual renaissance was responsible for the development of various disciplines like ethics, logic, philosophy, theology, mysticism, mathematics, astronomy, medicine, rhetoric, art and architecture. The educational system, ethical and scholastic philosophy, medicine and other sciences introduced by the Iranians in the Golkonda Sultanate were not purely Iranian in character as they were an amalgam of all the above influences.

It need not be stressed that Aristotelian and Platonic thought had been fundamental to the foundation of politics, ethics, logic, and philosophy in the Islamic world. Their names and ideas had reached Golkonda through various disciplinary channels. Moreover, the names of Hellenistic physicians, astronomers, mathematicians and others occur frequently in the works of the lexicographers of Golkonda who included them with many variations in their Persian lexicons.[125] Such Hellenistic names were in Arabicized and Persianized forms with variations, making it difficult to find their Anglicized forms. A biographical dictionary entitled *Tazkirat-ul Hukamā* written by Ismail bin Ibrahim Tabrizi[126] during the times of Abul Hasan Qutb Shah contains these and many other names with brief introductions. Presumably this is a Persian translation of some earlier Arabic work, but also contains the names of many Greek thinkers, physicians, mathematicians, poets and grammarians.

There were two types of ethical works in Golkonda and Iran—Grecian and Sufi. Three important works, which correspond to different stages of ethics, had tied together the structure of Hellenistic thought with the guidance provided in the Koran and *sunnah*. Ethics (*makārim-ul-akhlāq*), briefly referred to as *akhlāq*, was basically Hellenistic and its main source was Aristotle's *Nicomachean Ethics*. This discipline was more Greek in character in its early stage, as in the *Akhlāq-i-Nāsirī* of Nasiruddin Tusi (d. AD 1274), in the Mongol period.[127] There was more Islamic thought in the work of Jalalu'ddin Dawwani (d.908/1502–3) in his *Lawāmi' ul ishrāq fi makārim il akhlāq*, popularly known as *Akhlāq-i-Jalālī*, during Ottoman times.[128] The third stage of *akhlāq* came with the Iranianization of its essentially Graeco-Islamic character as seen in works like *Akhlāq-i-Muhsinī* of Husain Va'iz Kashifi (d.910/1504–5).[129] Ethical works of all these three stages had reached Golkonda. However, it was in the third phase in both Iran and Golkonda that ethics also bore some marks of a Shi'ite influence. These works were written as parables and anecdotes arranged according to the moral laws of Islamic jurisprudence (*fiqh*), further supplemented by some of the Prophetic traditions (*hadīs*). The ethical propositions were in the forms of aphorisms and maxims in brief but effective wording. The parables and anecdotes related to the early characters of Iranian history or the immaculate Imams, while others referred to Arab Islamic authorities and Hellenistic characters.

Ethics, in its earlier Graeco-Islamic stages, embraced two wings of theoretical (*nazarī*) and practical (*'amalī*) knowledge on issues like morality, civilization, statecraft, psychological problems, the development of personality, rules for a proper living and, above all, the complicated issue of epistemology. However, in its earliest stage, the important issues were treated separately in the form of treatises on each individual topic. Such treatises produced in Golkonda are randomly scattered and if put together, they may provide a better picture of the growth and reception of ethical literature in the sultanate.[130] It may be noted that *fiqh* literature that focused on social behaviour and grew especially in this period was more Islamic and less Hellenistic in its character. This was a result of the Safavid movement's drastic process of ideological revisionism from a Shi'ite point of view. These works were received and read by Golkonda's intellectual and courtly elite.

The most creative product of the intercourse of Islam with Hellenism was perhaps the development of scholastic philosophy and the schools that began from the period of the Abbasids (AD 750) onwards.[131] Among the main scholastic movements were the *Mu'ttazilah* (Rationalists), the *Mutakallimīn* (Speculationists), the *Ash'arite*, *Ishraqiyūn* (Illuminationists), *Falsafah* (Philosophers) and others.[132]

The Qutb Shahs brought Muslim scholastic thought to the soils of Golkonda and the courtly elite earnestly took part in such philosophic discussions. The main themes of discussion taken up by the scholastic groups were:

1. The 'Being'
2. View of atom
3. The reality of motion
4. God and his corporeality and attributes
5. The theory of Eternal (*qadīm*) and Originated (*hadīs*)
6. The beatific vision (*tajallī*) of Allah
7. The reality of human action

There were these and many other subjects of serious discussion. Although the list of Muslim scholastic thinkers is extensive, those whose thoughts were especially appreciated in Golkonda include Muhammad bin Ya'qub Kulayni (d. 329/941),[133] Shaikh Mufid (d. 413/1022),[134] Sayyid Murtaza 'Alam ul Huda (d. 436/1044),[135] Nasiruddin Tusi (d. 672/1274),[136] Jamaluddin Mutahhar (d. 726/1325),[137] Sa'aduddin Taftazani (d. 791/1389),[138] Sayyid Sharif Jurjani (d. 816/1413),[139] Mullah Alauddin 'Ali Qushchi of the ninth century Hijri,[140] Jalalu'ddin Dawwani (d. 908/1502–3)[141] and Sadruddin Shirazi (d. 1050/1640).[142]

The thoughts of all these thinkers could be traced back to Nasiruddin Tusi and to Hellenism. Some of them went to the extent of arguing that Aristotle was a prophet.[143] The authorities representing Shi'ite commentaries of scholastic philosophy who received much attention in Golkonda were Sayyid Murtaza Alam-ul-Huda and Mullah Sadruddin Shirazi.[144]

The first important work introducing scholastic thought was the *Tabsirat-ul-'awām fī ma'rifat-i maqālāt-ul-ānām* by Sayyid Murtaza Alam ul-Huda (d. 436/1044), who was the great-grandson of the seventh Imam Musa-al-Kazim.[145] Alam ul-Huda introduced various scholastic groups and made it clear that the ideas of the earliest Muslim thinkers like Avicenna Abu Nasr Farabi and others owed much to Socrates, Plato, Aristotle, Ptolemy, Galen, Pythagoras and many other Hellenistic and Egyptian thinkers.[146] He evaluated the main tenets of different schools of thought.

A significant contribution to the introduction of scholastic philosophy was made by Muhammad Amin bin Muhammad Sharif Astarabadi (d.1033/1623–4) who was an eminent scholar and the founder of the Akhbari school. His *Dānish Nāmah-i-Shāhī* is an important treatise, which can be found in the Qutb Shahi library.[147] The preface of this text recounts the meeting of the author with Shaikh Muhammed Ibn Khatun while the latter was in Iran as an envoy of Qutb Shahs. Although he did not visit the Deccan, Muhammad Amin contributed *Dānish Nāmah-i-Shāhī* especially for Muhammad Qutb Shah and sent it through Shaikh Muhammad Ibn Khatun. This work contains valuable information on the religious ties as well as the traffic of ideas between Golkonda and Iran. He contributed the work to be a guide for the community called *firqah-i-nājiah* (sect of the delivered) who sought renunciation and hence, the right path.[148] He classified scholastic thinkers into *Ishraqiyyīn* (Illuminationists), Sufis, *Mutasharriyīn* (Legalists) and *Mutakallimīn* (Speculationists). He further classified *Mutakallimīn* as *Asha'irah*, *Mu'ttazilah* and *Usūliyīn* (Principalists). He also introduced the groups of *Mashshayīn* (Peripatetics)[149] and *Akhbariyyīn*. His information is based on numerous authorities cited above.[150]

Muhammad Amin contended that the *Mutakallimīn* based their thoughts on rational thinking (*afkār-i 'aqliyah*) and introduced a new discipline called *kalām*. The *Mashshayīn* (Peripatetics or Aristotelians), according to him, were the followers of Aristotle, *Ishraqiyyīn* were Platonists.[151] He neither fully praised scholastic philosophy nor totally dismissed it. He proposed a criterion of allowing only those thoughts and ideas that conformed to the sayings of immaculate Imams and the traditions (*ahādīs*) received through them. According to him the followers of the immaculate Imams too indulged in scholastic philosophy but the Imams always advised them to abstain from *kalām* and *fiqh* as both were based on rational observations (*anzār-i 'aqliyah*). Thus, to indulge in philosophy, subject to such restrictions on thought, was the way of Akhbaris. His approach stimulated speculative and philosophical thinking on one hand, but always contained it within the received traditions of the Imams on the other. Muhammad Amin further added that such restrictions on thinking would be imposed on Akhbaris until the time the hidden Imam would reappear.[152]

The issues on which the *Akhbariyyin* differed from other scholastic thinkers and Sufis was the question of 'Being' (*wujūd*), the existence of God, freewill and the nature of human action. They held that the subjective approach of general scholastic thinkers on 'Being' as Unity could not be approved without the sanction of the traditions laid out by the holy Imams. They believed that 'Being' was constituted of God and the Universe, which were two separate realities.[153] Muhammad Amin further discussed 'Being' with reference to conception and perception. He ultimately concluded that the objective reality of the universe was visual and original whereas the subjective reality was reflective, imaginary and secondary.[154] The Akhbaris discarded the conception of *wahdat-ul-wujūd* according to which God could not be personified and understood Him as the beginning and the end of 'Being'.[155] Scholastic thinking therefore represented a contrast with that of the Sufis.

A corollary of the above discussion was the controversy over the reality of human action, which according to scholastic thinkers was the manifestation of divine will. Man, therefore, was not ultimately responsible for his actions. Amin held that *Ash'arites* especially tended to exonerate man from his responsibility of right or wrong. The Akhbari thinkers were opposed to this contention and advanced a series of arguments to support a notion that man was created by God and so were his actions. Man's actions therefore could not be a reflection of divine will.[156]

While the presence of such a treatise illustrates the traffic of ideas between Safavid Iran and Golkonda, it is difficult to measure the reception and use of these works beyond the courtly elite. Iranian Shi'i learned circle, who had migrated and settled in Golkonda, would have no doubt debated these philosophical and ethical issues. But unlike Safavid Iran, where Shi'ism dominated intellectual and educational activities, the religious and social atmosphere of the Qutb Shahi court was different. Given that the religious milieu of Golkonda was more transparent and the contenders in it more diverse than Safavid Iran, reading such treatises as evidence of Shi'i ascendency in the Deccan would fail to account for pre-existing Sunni, Sufi and non-Muslim ways of thinking. Perhaps the ideas of Shi'i intellectuals in the Deccan also evolved in this new environment, beginning to look different from their homeland in Safavid Iran. The increasing interest of select Shi'i elites in doctrinal debates and theology happening in Iran was no doubt integral to that dynasty's ideological project. But in Golkonda, these debates occurred in a society where Sufis had always dominated the religious atmosphere. Ideas on ethics and philosophy would have undoubtedly interacted with but not necessarily fused easily with existing Sufi and non-Muslim ways of thinking in Golkonda.

CONCLUSION

As stated in the beginning of this chapter, when the Qutb Shahs came to power, the teachings of Islam as well as Shi'ism had already been introduced in the Deccan. The Koran and the traditions of the Prophet of Islam served as the fundamental guide for the conduct of society. The universal character of these two was elucidated and made adaptable to different societies by learned elites and religious missionaries. The mainspring of Islam was not entirely unknown to the Telugu-speaking society before the Qutb Shahs. Even before the Bahmani days, many Sufi saints had settled in what was later to become the kingdom of Golkonda. Their shrines became the seats of Sufi teachings and their work was continued by their successors (*khalifahs*).[157] The Bahmani court saw the arrival of personalities like Fazlullah Inju and other Shi'i officials who occupied important positions alongside Sufis. By the early sixteenth century, Shi'i missionaries such as Shah Tahir arrived in the successor states of the Bahmani kingdom such as Ahmednagar. These individuals translated and preached the central tenets of Islam and wielded influence over the ruling elite.

The salient features of Islam such as monotheism, eschatology and justice as introduced and propagated by the Qutb Shahs existed alongside local religious cosmologies, be it Sufi or non-Muslim ways of thinking. The monotheism of Sufis embraced the idea of the Unity of Being (*wahdat-ul-wujūd*). Shi'ite doctrine, brought from Iran, disallowed the mystic conception of Unity and instead, emphasized the separateness of God and Man. Different sects of Indic religions such as the Vira Shaivite Lingayats, prominent in the Deccan, too had notions of the oneness of God. Differences also existed on eschatology and notions of a life hereafter. The Iranian scholars of Golkonda like Muhammad Muqim bin Kamaluddin Husain,[158] Ali bin Taifur Bistami[159] and the anonymous author of *Usūl-i-Khamsah* paid special attention to the propagation of Islamic eschatology and contributed considerable literature, projecting it as a very important issue. While the evidence of interaction with indigenous traditions is not found directly in sources, we may inductively reason that Iranian scholars at the least would have had to observe and understand Golkonda's pre-existing religious traditions. This may explain instances in such treatises where they went to the extent of exploring theories of transmigration.[160]

There is a sizeable volume of literature related to the interpretation of the Koran, the traditions (*hadis*) and jurisprudence (*fiqh*) produced in Golkonda or imported from Safavid Iran, which may reveal many more specialized aspects of the intellectual history of the Deccan. This chapter has sampled a few of the instances wherein ideas and books travelled from Safavid Iran to Golkonda. It has shown how the movement of personnel laid the foundation of the administrative structure of Golkonda on an Iranian pattern. Several of these administrators were in turn, also educators and religious missionaries. They supervised the field of education and established institutions of religious as well as medical learning. The wide range of ethical and philosophical debates of this period had a precedent in pre-existing ideas both in Iran and Golkonda. While debates on the social conduct of man, the nature of 'Being', etc., had a much longer history in all parts of the Islamic world, in the sixteenth and seventeenth centuries as a result of the Safavid movement, these ideas were transformed and articulated from a distinctly Shi'ite point of view. It has been argued here that the context of the dissemination of these ideas needs to be understood as specific to the social conditions of Iran and Golkonda. Safavid Iran no doubt served as a symbolic model and a political ally of Golkonda. However, the migration of Iranian personnel to the Deccan was not without competition. While diplomatic relations and select courtly elites were firmly embedded in the exchange of religious knowledge, the reception of these ideas is less clear and hardly unambiguous.

The aim of this chapter has been to move away from a straightforward political history of relations between Golkonda and Safavid Iran taken exclusively from Persian court chronicles to survey other types of historical materials such as educational curricula, medical and religious manuscripts, lexicons and compendiums. Political and diplomatic ties did not translate into an easy and smooth transfer of ideas that changed either society overnight. Further investigation of religious learning in Golkonda, rather than a simplistic appraisal of Shi'i identity in the Deccan, would require a close study of treatises on different religious disciplines and areas of learning. These ideas can then be measured and evaluated for their engagement with Sufis, Sunnis and other pre-existing modes of intellectual thought in the Deccan.

NOTES

1. Sherwani (B), p. 78.

2. The first large-scale devastation in fifteenth-century Iran started with the rise of Timur and the decline of the Ilkhanids, which was followed by age-long hostility between the successors of Timur and Qara Quyunlus. The third stage of conflict was between Aq Quyunlus and Qara Quyunlus and then between Aq Quyunlus and Safavids, which again involved Turkmen tribes and Iranian potentates. See Sykes II, Chapter IV. For an account of the economic foundations of the conflict paving way for Safavid absolution, see Lambton, Chapters IV and V, pp. 77–128. For the antecedents of the struggle over political authority between the nomadic-military elite (Turks) and urban-settled elite of eastern Anatolia and Iran (Tajiks), see John E. Woods, *The Aqquyunlu: Clan, Confederation, Empire*, University of Utah Press, 1999.

3. Roger Savory, *Iran under the Safavids*, Chaps I and II, Cambridge: Cambridge University Press, 2007; Andrew J. Newman, *Safavid Iran: Rebirth of an Empire*, London: I.B. Tauris, 2006, pp. 1–49.

4. Sayyid Muhammad Gesudaraz of Gulbarga was not pleased by the fact that his descendants accepted powerful positions in the royal court (an account of the saint's displeasure has been recorded by his grandson Abul Faiz Minallah of Bidar in his *Shawāmil ul Jumal fi Shama'il ul kumal*, fol. 194, preserved with the Sajjada Sahib of Rauza-i-Shaikh, Gulbarga, Karnataka). Large appanages were granted to his descendants earlier by the Bahmanis and later by the Qutb Shahs and 'Adil Shahs (more than hundred documents of such grants are preserved in Khusro Husaini Collection, S.A.A.P). Also see Richard M. Eaton, 'The Court and the Dargah in the Seventeenth Century Deccan', *Indian Economic and Social History Review*, vol. 10, no. 1, 1973, pp. 50–63.

5. Terry Graham, 'The Ni'matu'llāhī Order under Safavid Suppression and in Indian Exile', in *The Heritage of Sufism: Late Classical Persianate Sufism (1501–1750)*, ed. Leonard Lewisohn and David Morgan, vol. III, Oxford: Oneworld Publications, 1999, pp. 165–200.

6. *A.A.A.*, pp. 103, 164.

7. Ibid., pp. 100, 108.

8. Browne IV, p. 47.

9. *Burhān*, p. 81; Firishtah I, p. 635. Also see Muhammad Suleiman Siddiqui, *The Bahmani Sufis*, p. 83, Idara-i Adabayat-i Dilli, 1989.

10. See the two dates given for the death of Husain Shah Wali in Sherwani, p. 254, fn. 204.

11. A.J. Malkapuri, *Mahbūb-i Zilminan*, pp. 337–42; Sherwani (Q), p. 203.

12. Talqani, Letter no. 39; *Zamimah*, fol. 182(b); *Zafrah*, p. 34.

13. Two copies of this manuscript are preserved in the SJM & L, Hyderabad, MS. no. 67, 'Aqaid-wa-Kalam.

14. Ibid.

15. Browne IV, Chap. VIII; Malcolm I, pp. 500–3.

16. The *tāj* of the Kirmanis sent to Ahmad Shah had twelve scallops and was of green colour, Firishtah I, p. 634.

17. The tradition of red *tāj* of the Qizilbash movement was also adopted by some of the rulers of the Deccan especially Yusuf 'Adil Shah who made the red *tāj* a compulsory part of the dress of his army, Firishtah II, p. 33.

18. *Burhān*, p. 162; also see Chap. 2.

19. Aftabchi, p. 64; R.I., pp. 30–1.

20. Firishtah II, p. 329; also see Chap. 2.

21. Ibid., pp. 329–30.

22. Also See Chap. 2, 'The Deed of Submission'.

23. Early during his career he was faced with a matrimonial problem of having more than four wives, which was not permissible under Sunni traditions. Mir Fazlullah Inju justified the action through Shi'ite traditions, which became a subject of debate and discussion, Firishtah I, pp. 587–8.

24. Fazlullah Inju was born into the renowned Inju family of Shiraz. *Injū* or *anjū* was a sort of land grant category of Crown lands, such land was the same as *khālisah*. It was assigned to a Taba Taba Sayyid of Fars named Abul Miyaman Hasan by Abaqa (d. 680/1282) and Arghun (d. 690/1291), the son and grandson of Mongol ruler, Hulagu. The same land grant continued in the name of his son, Qutbuddin Ahmad, under the category of *injū*. The descendants of Qutbuddin have since then been known as Inju Sayyids but were originally Taba Taba Sayyids, see Lambton, pp. 78–9. Fazlullah Inju was educated under the renowned scholar Sa'aduddin Taftazani who lived from 722/1322 to 791/1389. He was in due course appointed as the preceptor to the Bahmani princes, Feroz Shah and Ahmad Shah, and became prime minister during the reign of Feroz Shah. See Firishtah I, Chapter on Firoz Shah Bahmani.

25. Firishtah I, pp. 633–4; *Burhān*, pp. 54, 65.

26. Firishtah I, p. 634.

27. See a detailed account of such influx of *āfāqīs* over many generations in Sherwani (B), pp. 191, 223.

28. The event of Chakan was a clear example of the seriousness of Deccani-*āfāqī* conflict, *Burhān*, pp. 81–4; Sherwani (B), pp. 240–3. Also see Sherwani's discussion on the party system in the Bahmani court, Sherwani (B), Chap. VIII. For Gawan's death see Firishtah I, pp. 691–3; *Burhān*, p. 130; Sherwani (B), pp. 335–6.

29. Among the five sultans of the Deccan succeeding the Bahmanis, three declared themselves Shi'i. They were the 'Adil Shahs, the Nizam Shahs and the Qutb Shahs. The Imad Shahs and Barid Shahs remained Sunnis.

30. Minorsky has made an excellent analysis of the tribal principle of alliance and dis-alliance and has treated the Safavid Revolution as the third stage of the Qara Quyunlu and Aq Quyunlu conflict and Turkmen domination. *Tazkirat-ul-Mulūk*, tr. and ed. V. Minorsky, p. 30; Lambton, p. 106. Also see Shakeb, 'Black Sheep Tribe from Lake Van to Golkonda', pp. 35–80.

31. The careers of Shaikh Junaid and Shaikh Haidar Safavi in Iran clearly demonstrate this trend, Browne IV, p. 47. Similarly, Shah Khalilullah Kirmani, son of Shah Ni'matullah Kirmani, showed a haughty attitude towards the monarch, Mufid, pp. 44–6. His son Habibullah fell a victim in this game of politics, *Burhān*, pp. 92–4.

32. See Shakeb, 'Black Sheep Tribe', pp. 35–80.
33. *Majālis*, see section relating to Qara Quyunlus.
34. Mufid, p. 53.
35. According to Nurullah Shustari those two ladies or rather the entire tribe was Shi'i. The observation is based on the simple evidence that the inscriptions on the rings of those two ladies were indicative of their love of 'Ali and his descendants, *Majālis*, see section relating to Qara Quyunlus. This seems to be a rather far-fetched inference.
36. *T.Q.S.*, fol. 25(a).
37. Ibid., fol. 25(a), 26(a).
38. Firishtah I, pp. 329–30.
39. Ibid.
40. The seals and a number of epigrams of the Qutb Shahs confirm that they adhered to the Twelver (*Asna 'Asharī*) faith.
41. Ibid.
42. Obviously the non-Shi'ite world and especially the Mughal Empire were referred to as *dār-ul-harb*. For the theoretical significance of *dār ul harb* (war territory) and *dār us' salām* (peace territory), see Hitti, pp. 136–8. Also see E.J. Brill, *Shorter Encyclopaedia of Islam*, ed. H.A.R. Gibb and J.H. Kramers, vol. 3, 1953, p. 69.
43. The full text of the *farmān* issued in this report by 'Abdullah Qutb Shah has been given by Talqani, Letter no. 41.
44. Talqani (A), Letter no. 25. See Chap. 2, 'Sinking Sultanate—The Fifth Phase'.
45. For a better appreciation of a *mujtahid* and his function called *ijtihād*, as the way it was practiced differently by Shi'i and Sunnis, see Taftazani, pp. 144, 166–7; Browne IV, Chap. VIII; Hitti, pp. 399, 441. Also see Khalid Ansari, *Ijtihād*, Bhopal, 1951. For the development of *madrasahs* in Safavid Iran, see Mufid, pp. 654–9.
46. *Burhān*, p. 254; Firishtah II, pp. 22–3, 201, 203. Sherwani has pointed out a discrepancy about Shah Tahir's arrival, who according to Firishtah, arrived at Ahmednagar in 928/1522 and according to Tabataba, in 926/1520, Sherwani (Q), p. 73, fn. 102. As a matter of fact there is no contradiction in the statements of Tabataba and Firishtah, as the former clearly states that Shah Tahir set out from Iran through the sea route early in the month of Jumada I 926/1520 and reached Dabhol at Goa the next week, while Firishtah states Shah Tahir arrived at Ahmednagar in 928/1522. Shah Tahir spent the intervening period in the territories of Bijapur.
47. *Burhān*, pp. 253–4; Firishtah II, pp. 22–3. Sherwani has perhaps missed Tabataba's detailed account of Shah Tahir earning the displeasure of Shah Isma'il and leaving Iran at the advice of Mirza Shah Husain Isfahani, despite his observation: '*Burhān* says that he was sent as an envoy to Ahmednagar by the Safavi Monarchy', Sherwani (Q), p. 73, fn. 102; also see Hidayat Hossein, 'Shah Tahir of the Deccan', *New Indian Antiquary*, vol. 2, 1939, pp. 460–73.
48. Firishtah II, pp. 213–26; *Burhān*, pp. 251–68. For the history of Isma'ilis, see Hitti, p. 446.

49. See Chap. 2, 'Recognition—The First Phase of Relations'.
50. For details see, *T.Q.S.*, fols. 48(b) to 49(a); Firishtah II, p. 330; Sherwani (Q), p. 34.
51. Firishtah II, pp. 218–22.
52. Ibid., pp. 212, 223.
53. *Burhān*, p. 280.
54. Ibid., pp. 290–1.
55. There is much controversy about the date of his death. We agree with Sherwani on this issue. Sherwani (Q), p. 73, fn 102.
56. *A.A.A.*, p. 109.
57. *Hadāiq*, fol. 187(b).
58. Firishtah II, p. 342.
59. For the life of Mir Muhammad Mu'min and his scholarly patronage see Zor, *Hayāt-i Mir Mu'min*. Devare has also given a good account of Mir Muhammad Mu'min's patronage of Iranian intellectuals, Devare, pp. 168–77.
60. See Chap. 2.
61. Nasrabadi, p. 159; *Dabistān*, p. 203; *Shuzūr* II, p. 395; *Rauzat*, pp. 21–2; *Nujūm*, p. 77; *Mahbub-ul-Albāb*, p. 110; also Qadri (I), p. 214.
62. See Chap. 2.
63. *Dabistān*, p. 204. A manuscript entitled *Kashkol* preserved as MS. no.16, SJM & L. records the date of his death on fol. no. 10 as Tuesday 5th Jamadi I 1059/19 January 1649. On these folios there are transcriptions of the letters of Kazim Karim Iraqi who was by that time serving as *dabīr* in Golkonda. See Ethe, p. 683.
64. *Hadīqat*, pp. 151, 167.
65. Ibid., pp. 164–5.
66. Qadri (I), p. 217 lists five of his books (1) *Sharh-ul-Irshād Azhān fi Ahkām ul Imān* (2) *Sharh-i-'Arba'īn* (3) *Sharh-i Jāma'-i-'Abbāsī* (4) *Takmilah-i-Jāmi' 'Abbāsī* (5) *Kitāb-ul-Imāmah*. See Appendix (i): Evaluation of Sources.
67. Ibn Khatun, *Kitāb al-Imāmah*, MS. no. 10, Manaqib, SJM & L.
68. Taftazani, Chaps. XVI and XIX. Bukhari, *A'ssahih* part 29 *Kitāb-ul-Ahkām*; Muslim, *A'ssahih* vol. 5 *Kitāb-ul-Amārah*; Tayalisi, *Musnad*, Tradition No. 926.
69. Patricia Crone and Martin Hinds, *God's Caliph: Religious Authority in the First Centuries of Islam*, Cambridge: University of Cambridge Oriental Publications, 1986, pp. 4–23.
70. Taftazani, pp. 145–6.
71. Abu Bakr (r. AD 632–34), Umar (r. AD 634–44) and Usman (r. AD 644–56).
72. Along with Ibn Khatun's *Kitāb al-Imāmah*, there is an anonymous work contributed during the times of Sultan Muhammad Qutb Shah on the issue of the Imamate. See Anonymous, *Usūl-i-Khamsah-i-Imāmiyah*, MS. no. 11, 'Aqaid-wa-Kalam, SJM & L.
73. There are many poems of Sultan Muhammad Quli Qutb Shah, composed in Dakani, that clearly reflect the sultan's interest in these festivals, *Kulliyāt*,

pt. I, pp. 35–148. Also see Fryer I, pp. 276, 277; Fryer II, p. 79; *Hadīqat*, pp. 48, 67.

74. Ibid.; For *Milād-u'nnabi* see *Hadīqat*, p. 59; *Kulliyāt*, pp. 11, 35.

75. There are many manuals of *Urs* entitled *Kitāb ul I'rās* preserved in OMLRI and SJM & L. These manuals contain lists of all those saintly personalities whose *I'rās* were celebrated in the Deccan. It may also be noted that *Urs* was a festival that was not necessarily celebrated only at the place where a saint's tomb existed. It was also celebrated in absentia, for those saints buried in other parts of India and the Middle East.

76. *Hadīqat*, p. 54. The topo sheets of the Survey of India indicate *'āshūr khānas* at almost every village of the area which was once under Golkonda Sultanate.

77. Ibid., pp. 57–8.

78. Ibid., p. 59.

79. *Kulliyāt*, pp. 87–96.

80. Ibid., pp. 63, 75, 129 and pp. 17, 22 of its supplement.

81. Talqani, Letter no. 25; also see Chap. 2.

82. The Charminar of Yazd was constructed in 720/1348, see Mufid, pp. 150, 492, 558, 655. Although Sherwani expresses disagreement with this hypothesis, Sherwani (Q), pp. 304–5.

83. *T.Q.S.*, fol. 113; also see Chap. 2.

84. Alessandro Bausani, *Religion in Iran: From Zoroaster to Baha'ullah*, Bibliotheca Persica Press, 2000.

85. See Sherwani (Q); Chap 1, 'Foundations of the State', pp. 10–12.

86. *Hadīqat*, pp. 44–6; also see Chap. 1.

87. The word *majlis* is of Arabic origin and was adopted by the Persians during the Sassanian period. This has been referred to in Firdausi's *Shah Nāmah*, for the council in ancient Iran. This word is presumably an Arabic equivalent of archaic Persian word or *kankāsh*.

88. The word *peshwā* literally means a leader. It has been largely used in Iran in the sense of a religious leader. In Golkonda too this was partially a religious institution which is confirmed by the additional title *Muqtadā* and *Murtazā-i-Mumālik-i-Islām* given to *peshwās* like Mir Muhammad Mu'min and Shaikh Muhammad Ibn Khatun, *Hadīqat*, pp. 3, 11, 33.

89. *Passim.*

90. The Majlis of Daulat Mahal (*Hadīqat*, pp. 167, 226) were much like the employees of the *khāssah-i sharīfāh* of the Iranian monarch. Similarly the tutors of princes called *mullahs* (*Hadīqat*, pp. 9–12) and the royal physicians called *hakīm-ul-mulk* appear to be very important offices of the royal retinue. Similar posts existed in contemporary Iran.

91. Persian and Arabic words are found in Telugu endorsements on official documents of Golkonda, see Qutb Shahi documents of K.H.C, S.A.A.P.

92. Browne IV, pp. 353–4, 367–80.

93. *T.Q.S.*, fol. 111(a); *Hadīqat*, p. 210; Bilgrami, p. 25. See section on 'Medical Knowledge and Education'.

94. *Hadīqat*, p. 151.

95. *Hadīqat*, p. 4.

96. *Hadāiq*, fol. 201(a).

97. The list of his work is too detailed to be cited here. Most of his works, compilations and translations were at the instance of the monarchs. For his ancestry, see *Nujūm*, p. 94 and *Shuzūr*; for his life and work see, *Hadāiq*, MS. no. Tarikh 213, SJM & L and preface to his translation of *Makārim-ul-Akhlāq*, MS. no. 22, Akhlaq, SJM & L. Also see Qadri (I), pp. 77–81, Siddiqua, pp. 88, 135–9.

98. *Hadīqat*, p. 167.

99. He was first appointed as *qazi* of cantonment and the member of the Majlis and lastly, became *dabīr* in 1047/1637. *Hadīqat*, pp. 167, 209; K.H.C., Doc. 44, S.A.A.P.

100. His work is found in different libraries under various titles as *Jāmi' ut tamsīl*, *Jāmi' ut tamāsīl*, *'Ajaib-ul-Amsāl and Majma' ul amsāl*, see MS. no. 76, Lughat, SJM & L, and I.O.L. MS. No. 2209. This has been published from Tehran in 1278/1861 and from Bombay in 1290/1873.

101. *Hadīqat*, pp. 12–13, 20.

102. Ibid., pp. 9–13.

103. There were many European physicians who visited Golkonda and practised there. The Venetian physician Manucci has recorded an account of his medical service in Golkonda. Pieter de Lange was a Dutch surgeon employed by 'Abdullah Qutb Shah at a monthly salary of Rs.800. The French traveller Tavernier was his guest during his stay at Golkonda, Tavernier, p. 232. Cyril Elgood, *A Medical History of Persia and the Eastern Caliphate: From the Earliest Times Until the Year A.D. 1932*, Cambridge University Press, 1951, pp. 348–92. For an authoritative account of the Greek origin of Arab Medicine, see Ibn Usaibiyah, *Uyūn al-Anba fi Tabaqāt al-Atibbā*, Cairo, 1882 and *H.M.P.*, Chap. LXVII, pp. 1332–48.

104. A copy of *Ikhtiyarāt-i Qutb Shāhī* (MS. no. 13, Tibb, SJM & L), based on the first part of *Ikhtiyarāt-i Badī'* of 'Ali b. Husain Husaini (d.1403), was produced in Golkonda.

105. He translated the *Tazkirat-ul-Kuhhālīn* of 'Ali Ibn Isa, an occultist of the Abbasid period (see Hitti, pp. 368–9). Codex of the translation is preserved as MS. no. 49, Tibb, SJM& L.

106. According to Qadri (I), p. 191, he was one of the authors of *Ikhtiyarāt*.

107. Hakim Safiuddin Gilani, *Tazkirat-u'shshahwāt*, MS. no. 868, Tibb, OMLRI.

108. Taqiuddin Muhammad Amoli, *Mizān ut Taba'i Qutb Shāhī*, MS. no. 266, Tibb, SJM & L.

109. *Hadīqat*, pp. 33, 113–14, 131.

110. Ibid., p. 103.

111. Ibid., p. 167; Qadri (I), p. 81; Bilgrami, p. 151. There is ambiguity about the date of his death.

112. For the political career of *Hakīm-ul-Mulk*, see Chap. 2, 'The Royal Pilgrims'.

113. *Hadīqat*, p. 259.
114. Talqani, Letter no. 22.
115. Talqani, Letter no. 37; *Makātīb (Z)*, fol. 629; Mufid, p. 408.
116. *Hadīqat*, p. 210.
117. For simple drugs *Ikhtiyarāt* is the best work, also see *Nafāyis*, Chaps. 6 and 7; *Khirqah*, vol. VI, Chap. 10.
118. Kahin Attar was a Judo-Egyptian pharmacist who wrote his famous *Minhāj-ud-dukkān Wa Dastūr-ul-A'yān*, a manual of drugs in about AD 1260 in Arabic, see Hitti, p. 685; Siddiqa, pp. 100–3.
119. See Chap. 4, 'Commercial Contacts'.
120. Regarding literature pertaining to aphrodisiac medicine produced in Golkonda, see *Tazkirat-u'shshahwāt* of Hakim Safiuddin Gilani, MS. no. 868, Tibb, OMLRI; *Shajarah* treatise no. 91; Hakim Shamsuddin bin Nuruddin's *Zubdat-ul-Hikam*, Chap. IV, Section 13, MS. no. 277, Tibb, SJM &L. Muhammad Amin Jami of Golkonda translated the Sanskrit text *Kuka Shāstra* into versified Persian and titled it *Lazzat-unnisa* at the instance of Sultan 'Abdullah Qutb Shah, *Tarjumah-i Kuk Shāstar*, MS. no. 208, Tibb, SJM & L.
121. For literature regarding pathology and therapeutics produced in Golkonda see Anonymous, *Makhzan-i-Tibb-i-Qutb Shāhī*; Gilani, *Shajar* treaties no. 19, 73; Shamsuddin 'Ali al-Husaini al-Jurjani, *Tarjumah-i-Tazkirat-ul-Kuhhālīn*. Also see *Nafāyis*, Chaps. 3–8.
122. For literature on hygiene produced in Golkonda see *Zubdat-ul-Hikam* by Nuruddin, *Zubadat*; *Shajarah*, articles 89, 100 to 102. Also see Siddiqua, pp. 98–109.
123. *T.Q.S.*, fol. 111(a); *Hadīqat*, p. 210; *Zafrah*, pp. 12–13; Bilgrami, p. 25.
124. Franz Rosenthal, *The Classical Heritage in Islam*, University of California Press, 1975.
125. *Burhān-i-Qāti'* of Muhammad Husain Burhan compiled in Golkonda in 1062/1651 contains the names of scores of Greek thinkers as on pages 58, 62, 66, 78, 90, 116, 138, 141, 174, 182–3, 195, 200, 284–5, 298, 354, 369–70, 386, 473, and 613. Names that frequently appear are of thinkers like Socrates (*Suqratis*), Plato (*Aflatūn*), Aristotle (*Arastū*) and physicians such as Hippocrates (*Buqrat*), Asclepius (*Asqaliyūs*) and Galen (*Jalinus*). MS. no. 8, 9, Lughat, SJM & L.
126. *Tazkirat-ul Hukamā*, MS. 744, Jadeed, OMLRI.
127. For the importance of Tusi's work in Mughal India, see Muzaffar Alam, *The Languages of Political Islam 1200–1800*, University of Chicago Press, 2004, pp. 46–53.
128. Bakhtiyar Husain Siddiqi, 'Jalal al-Din Dawwani' in *H.M.P.*, vol. 2, pp. 883–8.
129. See special issue of *Iranian Studies*, vol. 36, no. 4, 'Husayn Va'iz-i Kashefi, December 2003.
130. The best of the work relating to ethics produced in Golkonda is perhaps *Tuhfah-i-Qutb Shāhī* of 'Ali bin Taifur Bistami. Among other ethical works produced in Golkonda reference may be made to *Dastur-ul-'Amal-i-Salātīn*

preserved at Khuda Baksh Library at MS. no. 2037 and *Risālah dar Akhlāq*, preserved as MS. no. 22, SJM & L.

131. For the Graeco-Islamic character of scholastic philosophy, see Arnold, pp. 239–82; Hitti, Chap. XXX.

132. For a survey and evaluation of these and many other Muslim schools of philosophy, see *H.M.P.*

133. *Danish*, fol. 4(a); for general information about him, see Browne IV, p. 405; *H.M.P.*, p. 936.

134. *Danish*, fol. 4(b); ibid.

135. Ibid.

136. *Danish*, fol. 13(b); *Tuhfah* is a commentary on Tusi's *Tajrid-al-'Aqāid* written by Zainu'ddin Badakhshi in Golkonda. For further information about Tusi, see Browne IV, p. 405, *H.M.P.*, pp. 568, 655, 883.

137. *Tuhfah*, fol. 3(a); *Danish*, fol. 4(b); *Khirqah* III, Section 23; for further information about Mutahhar see Browne IV, p. 54; *H.M.P.*, pp. 397, 800, 906 footnote.

138. *Danish*, fol. 4(a); for his life and work, see the translation of his *Sharhul 'Aqāid u'nnasafiya* with an introduction by E.E. Elder, *A Commentary on the Creed of Islam*, New York: Columbia University Press, 1950. Also see Browne III, p. 354, *H.M.P.*, pp. 646, 1360.

139. *Danish*, fol. 18(a). Also see Browne III, p. 355; *H.M.P.*, pp. 907, 1051, 1360.

140. *Tuhfah*, fol. 3(a); Browne III, p. 386. Also see *H.M.P.*, p. 936.

141. *Tuhfah*, fol. 3(a); Browne IV, pp. 83, 231, 427; *H.M.P.*, pp. 884, 887–8.

142. *Tuhfah*, fol. 3(a); Browne IV, p. 429; *H.M.P.*, Chap. XLVIII.

143. See *Khirqah*, pt. V, in which Ibn Imad has cited a few sayings (*ahādīs*) of the Prophet in which he supposedly identified Aristotle as a Prophet. Also see *Dānish*, fol. 3(b); *Tabsirah*, fol. 2(b) to 8(b).

144. *Tuhfah*, fol. 3(a).

145. Browne IV, p. 405.

146. *Tabsirah*, fols. 2(b) to 8(b).

147. Muhammad Amin bin Muhammad Sharif Astarabadi, *Dānish Nāmah-i-Shāhī*, MS. no. 54 'Aqaid, SJM & L.

148. *Danish*, fol. 1(b).

149. *H.M.P.*, pp. 907, 923, 1331.

150. *Danish*, fol. 3(a).

151. Ibid., fol. 3(b).

152. Ibid., fol. 4(a).

153. Ibid., fols. 6(a) to 8(b).

154. Ibid., fols. 18(a) to 24(a).

155. Ibid., fol. 28(b).

156. Ibid., fols. 56(b) to 59(a).

157. Even today shrines of such Sufis exist in Hyderabad, Cuddapah, Rajahmundry, Warangal and Kaulas. For details see relevant district gazetteers.

158. See his treatise, *Dar Tahqīqī-i Ma'ād Wa Hashr-i-Ajsād*, Persian MS. no. 1792, Bodleian.

159. Bistami too contributed a special treatise on eschatology entitled *Risālah-i-maʿsūmiyah*, which deals with the subject according to the Shiʿite point of view.

160. For the development of the ideas of transmigration and reincarnation in Iran, see *Tabsirah*, fols. 51(b) to 54(a). Among the Iranians in Golkonda, we find instances where ideas of incarnation and transmigration are expressed in poetry, such as in the work of Adai Yazdi, see Nasrabadi, *Tazkirah-i Nasrābādī*, pp. 291–2.

4

Commercial Contacts

Introduction

THE ECONOMIC RELATIONS of Golkonda with Iran formed an important component of complex commercial trade and political relations in the Indian Ocean during the sixteenth and seventeenth centuries. Sources in English, Dutch and Portuguese offer significant details on the economic conditions of south India, though studies from these materials rarely use Persian manuscripts to construct the history of commercial linkages. This chapter supplements primary and secondary materials on economic relations between Golkonda and Iran with treatises in Persian on subjects of trade such as weights and measures, currencies and tracks the activities of Iranians traders available in Persian chronicles. While this discussion does not directly address production, consumption, entrepreneurship, and labour, it draws inferences from existing sources about these economic activities. It can be deduced that Golkonda served as a commercial bridge for Iran's import trade, and its capital was used to purchase commodities which were carried to other parts of the Indian Ocean, especially South-East Asia. The Deccan therefore served as a transit point for Iranian, Indian and European merchants where goods and currency were exchanged and further traded to South-East Asia. Second, this chapter collates data on currencies, weights and measures, and statistics on quantities of goods traded between Iran and Golkonda. From the available evidence, it concludes that while political relations and markets fluctuated, the participation of all merchants—Indian, European and Iranian—seemed to have been fairly competitive in this period. Golkonda's growing overseas, especially textiles, attracted merchants from Japan to England. European factories in the East had fewer commodities of their own and capital for investment, but they played a considerable role in organizing international markets. This chapter considers a wide range of trade-related matters such as transportation and communication, freight trade, currencies and exchange, weights and measures, taxes and the structure of markets in both Golkonda and Iran.

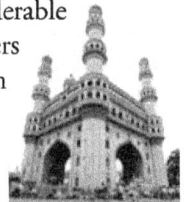

Transportation and Communication

Maritime traffic between the two countries was conducted by ships of various sizes and standards which were manufactured in Golkonda or were sailed in from Holland, Denmark, Portugal and England. European factories in Golkonda provided or organized large-scale maritime transport facilities as a part of their trade along coastal South Asia and the East Indies. Their interest in freight trade led them to hire ships from private sources and sometimes to hire ships from the administration of Golkonda.[1]

Golkonda was a major ship-manufacturing centre. Its shipbuilding industry flourished at Narsapur Peta about 30 to 36 miles from Masulipatam.[2] Golkonda ships, carrying loads varying from 600 to 1,000 tons and in some cases even 1,500 tons, sailed out to various coasts of the far East and as far as the Red Sea and Iran in the West.[3]

There is scarce evidence of any major shipbuilding industry in Safavid Iran, yet Iran had many well-developed ports. Under the influence of the Portuguese, the first such port was Hormuz, which became a centre of overseas trade between the East and West. A good number of Hindu (Gentile) merchants had settled there.[4] Hormuz became a flourishing international bazaar of spices, drugs, silk cloth, fine Persian tapestry and horses, which were supplied to India.[5] In the middle of the seventeenth century, Shah 'Abbas II encouraged the English to overthrow the Portuguese. As a result, Hormuz was almost plundered and Bandar Abbas developed as the greatest Iranian port. Maritime traffic between Golkonda and Iran was subsequently dominated by the English and partly by the Dutch, whose ships were preferred by the people of both regions because of their safety and reliability.[6]

The land route via Qandahar and the Mughal Empire was not convenient for the Iran-Golkonda traffic while the sea route offered a safe and comfortable alternative such that 'persons had just to get into a ship at Masulipatam and then disembark at Bandar Abbas'.[7] Golkonda chronicler Nizamuddin Shirazi asserts that the maritime traffic was active throughout the whole year from the port of Masulipatam.[8] The statement seems rather exaggerated, as during the heavy monsoon season between June and September, ships as a rule, did not ply between the Persian Gulf and the Golkonda coast.[9]

Freight Trade

Various types of ships, cargoes and ladings, operating through many commercial centres, carried out a thriving maritime trade through the south-eastern archipelago in the Indian Ocean, crossing the Persian Gulf and entering the Red Sea and then pushing northwards to Europe and England. This circuitous route formed a characteristic feature of the sea-going trade in this period. Part of this traffic included the lucrative freight trade, which was organized by businessmen of Golkonda, Iranian merchants and European factors. European factories were constituted by small bands of merchants who set up their businesses in foreign markets with some capital, which once established, made large profits. Money and entrepreneurship were not their only assets; their ships and cargo too were important trade factors. Data regarding the contribution of the above agencies in the development of the Golkonda and Iran freight trade cannot be furnished without material information about the role of Iranian businessmen. Yet, a general evaluation leads one to infer that, though fluctuating throughout the period, the role of all the participants was fairly competitive. Freight trade between Golkonda and Iran was higher compared to passenger transportation, with commercial commodities constituting the majority of the payload of maritime transportation. Freight trade between Golkonda and Iran received new impetus for three reasons: first, the English had established themselves in Indian Ocean trade; second, the Portuguese faced a setback in the Iranian bazaar in AD 1622;[10] and lastly, the Dutch opened a factory in Gombroon (Bandar Abbas) in the 1630s.[11]

In the 1650s, freighting of goods and passengers from the Coromandel to Persia yielded the Dutch a profit of 13,020 florins. The profit made by the English must have been at least equal to that if not higher. Information regarding freight trade profit made by Indians, Iranians and other private Western traders is scarce. It may be inferred that the annual approximate freight profit on the total freight trade between Golkonda and Iran would have been more than three times the profit the Dutch earned in 1652 through one of their agencies, Jan Company.[12]

Freight had several components. Three of the most important of these were capital value, the nature of consignment and distances. The rate of freight varied from commodity to commodity.[13] Freight trade also affected the price level as the prices on imported and exported goods were fixed to cover freight charges.[14] Like any other item, freight trade between Golkonda and Iran was governed by several factors and manifested a considerable fluctuation.[15] Instances of boom and slump were present throughout the period,[16] and on some occasions trade completely ceased. There are instances when the duties on freight were consolidated and paid annually in a lump sum, such as the agreement between Wemmer Van Berchem and 'Abdullah Qutb Shah which was fixed at 3,000 *pagodas* per year. There were, of course, more informal ways of gaining access to ports, and traders often had to please the authorities with gifts.[17]

Larger ships, usually carrying passengers, sailed between Coromandel ports and Bandar Abbas.[18] The establishment of Dutch factories also contributed to the development of freight trade especially after 1640. Dutch ships regularly carried both passengers and goods between Golkonda and Iran.

Sometimes freight trade was so profitable that it made up for the losses of capital potential from Iran.[19]

Currencies and Exchange

In the bazaars of coastal Golkonda and Iran, coins from many parts of the world were exchanged. There, one could find florins and stuivers of Holland, ducats of Hungary, rials of Spain, rixdollars of various countries, cubangs of Japan in addition to a number of old and new silver and gold coins of Golkonda, Iran and Mughal India.

The domestic coins of Golkonda, both gold and silver, were struck after the names of the Rayas of Vijayanagar and the Mughal emperors respectively. The Qutb Shahs struck only copper coins (*fulūs*) in their names. The gold coins of Golkonda were of varying weights and denominations, and were all referred to by a broad term, *hun*,[20] but for the convenience of this discussion they may be categorized as *pagodas* of higher value and *fanams* of lower denominations.[21]

The first category, *pagodas*, were of the same metallic value though the older coins were considered more valuable and were therefore exchanged by paying a premium on the new coins. From all the types of *pagodas*, the most sought after was the *hun sivā rāyā*, which served as standard money especially for accounts, such as the pound in England or *tomān* in Iran. Shah Jahan and Aurangzeb preferred to receive their *peshkash* in this coin.[22] Although it was current in Golkonda[23] (with the name of the king Sri Pratapa Sadasiva Raya on one side and the legend of Shiva and Parvati on the other), we cannot assume that this coin was always used in actual exchange.[24] It is interesting to note that the Mughals also had a gold coin called *ashrafi* or *mohur*, but it seldom served as an actual coin of exchange or accounts. Instead the rupee and the *'abbāsī*, both silver coins of middle denominations, were used for these purposes.[25] This naturally resulted in the money of Hindustan and Iran being lighter compared to the *hun* of Golkonda. The rupee's value had changed ever since Sher Shah Suri introduced it in Hindustan.[26] Shah Jahan brought it to Golkonda where it was minted there under the terms of the Deed of Submission. But it was never considered a Qutb Shahi coin.[27]

The currency of Golkonda, particularly the *hun*, was in use at its metallic value. With the rise in the price of copper during the second half of the seventeenth century, the price of gold was affected and consequently also the value of the gold coin. It is interesting to note that a currency, which had no extra token value over its metal, went down on account of the change in the metallic price without showing any resistance to the strength of its token value. The Qutb Shahs, whose coins were made of copper, were apparently not able to maintain the value of gold coins current in their sultanate. This may have been one of the consequences of farming out revenue administration and the

TABLE 4.1: Iranian coins and their values

	£	sh.	d.
shāhī	0	0	4
mahmūdī	0	0	8
'abbāsī	0	1	4

NOTE: 2 *shāhī* = 1 *mahmūdī*; 2 *mahmūdī* = 1 *'abbāsī*.

collection of commercial taxes through intermediary elites in their kingdom.[28] Nevertheless, to keep to the point of discussion, the value of a *hun sivā rāyā* officially remained between five to three rupees. But moneychangers charged a premium from 14 to 70 per cent.[29]

The other category of gold coins was *fanam*, which was smaller than the *hun*.[30] The relation between *hun* and *fanam* varied form place to place. A *pagoda* in Masulipatam was exchanged with fifteen *fanams*, in Nizampatam with sixteen *fanams*, thirty-two in Madras and in Hyderabad for twelve.[31] The *hun* and *fanam* had a changing value in relation to the sterling. Nevertheless, the prevalent rate of exchange of one *pagoda* was 2 sh. (shillings) and that of *fanam* was 3 ds. (pennies or pence).[32]

Among silver coins, mention may also be made of *nevels* (8–9 *nevels* = 1 *fanam*);[33] *tār* (4–5 *tār* = 1 *nevel*)[34] and *kāsū* (12 *kāsū* = 1 *tār*). The copper coins called *fulūs* were not found in international exchange, even theoretically in the minutest fraction of accounts.[35]

The biggest standard gold coin in Iran was the *tomān*, which was equal to £ 3-sh. 5-d. 6.[36] According to Fryer it was an imaginary coin like a pound, which was good 'to reckon'.[37] The actual coin of exchange was a gold Venetian, either brought from Venice or the Ottoman Empire.[38] The indigenous coin of exchange minted and current in Iran during the visit of Bowrey and Fryer was a silver coin called *'abbāsī*, valued at 1 sh.-d. 4,[39] and other small coins called *mahmūdī*,[40] worth d. 8, and *shāhī*, worth d. 4.[41] The Iranian coins and their values are shown in Table 4.1.

The *shāhī* of Iran was worth a little more than a *fanam* of Golkonda, i.e. 3 *shāhīs* = 4 *fanams*. Fifty *shāhīs* made a *tomān*. In addition to the gold and silver coins, there were brass coins of names and denominations as shown in Table 4.2.

The first two coins, *pice* and *ghaz*, were 'nominal' and not real coins,[42] and were in use as coins of account for minor fractions. Besides Persian ones, coins of almost all contemporary polities were exchanged in the Persian Gulf.

The exchange value of the coins of Golkonda, and Hindustan showed a constant tendency to be devalued throughout the seventeenth century. During the time of Jahangir, a *tomān* was worth Rs.30[43] but its price increased to 42 rupees[44] during the reign of Aurangzeb. Similarly a *tomān*, worth 6⅔ *huns*[45] during the times of 'Abdullah Qutb Shah, appreciated to 8⅓ *huns*[46]

TABLE 4.2: Denomination of brass and silver coins

BRASS

2 *pice*	=	1 *ghaz*
2 *ghaz*	=	1 *ghaz-i begī*
2 *ghaz-i begī*	=	1 *bīstī*
5 *ghaz-i begī* or 2½ *bīstī*	=	1 *shāhī*

SILVER

2 *shāhī*	=	1 *mahmūdī*
2 *mahmūdī*	=	1 *'abbāsī*
2 *'abbāsī*	=	1 Surat rupee

NOTE: 3 *shāhī* = 4 *fanams* of Golkonda.

during the reign of Abu'l Hasan. By the close of the period of this study, the currency of Golkonda and Hindustan showed a downward trend, whereas, the currency of Iran gained theoretical stability.

The European gold coin, the Venetian, a common medium of exchange in all markets between Iran and Golkonda, was imported from Iran into various bazaars of Hindustan in huge quantities.[47] English currency also played a role in Golkonda-Iran monetary transactions after the East India Company displaced the Portuguese on the Golkonda coast and in Iran. Apart from several other intermediary currencies the prevalent rates of exchange between *hun*, *tomān* and the rupee may be tabulated in Table 4.3 in terms of their pound value.

The rates in these tables broadly cover the fluctuations that took place at different times and in various places. It may be noted that Golkonda, Iran and Hindustan had *tomān* and *ashrafī* as their highest coins of account, whereas in Golkonda the heavier series of *pagodas* or *huns* as well as *fanams* of different denominations were all made of gold and served both as money of account as well as actual legal tender. Therefore, in actual practice, Golkonda maintained a heavy uni-metallic gold currency which was exchanged with the lighter Mughal rupee, the Iranian *'abbāsī*, the Dutch florin and the British sterling. As a matter of principle, the lighter money gradually drove the heavier out of circulation. There was a steady outflow of Golkonda *huns* to Iran, Hindustan and European countries.[48]

The Structure of Golkonda Bazaar

The Golkonda Sultanate gained considerable influence in the world market at the beginning of the seventeenth century for two main reasons. In the initial phase, during the times of Sultan Quli Qutb Shah, Golkonda's territories

TABLE 4.3: Rates of exchange in Golkonda and Hindustan

		£		sh.		d.
(a) GOLKONDA						
tār	=	0	–	0	–	0.007
nevel	=	0	–	0	–	0.033
fanam	=	0	–	0	–	3
hun	=	0	–	8	–	0
(See above and notes 31 to 36)						
(b) IRAN						
pice	=	0	–	0	–	0.2
ghaz-i	=	0	–	0	–	0.4
ghaz-i begī	=	0	–	0	–	0.8
bistī	=	0	–	0	–	1.6
shāhī	=	0	–	0	–	4
mahmūdī	=	0	–	0	–	8
abbāsī	=	0	–	1	–	4
tomān	=	3	–	6	–	6
(c) HINDUSTAN						
pice	=	0	–	0	–	0.37
Silver rupee	=	0	–	1	–	7 (to 0.2.3)
ashrafī or Gold *mohur*	=	2	–	3	–	9

only included the Gingelly coast, but after the reduction of Vijayanagar by Ibrahim Qutb Shah on Safar 987/May 1579, the major southern coastline of Coromandel was annexed.[49] Second, European merchants, who had proven effective agents in the development of trade in Golkonda, had not set up any of their major establishments in Golkonda by 1613. In this early period, even the Portuguese, who had a commercial hold on Hormuz and coastal Iran as well as on the Malabar coast, had little interest in the eastern Coromandel, which did not fall directly under the purview of their administration.[50] The Dutch factories, in particular the Jan Company, were established in Coromandel in 1025/1616,[51] and the British merchants were established in Golkonda as early as in 1026/1617.[52] Of course, there is evidence of the presence of Iranian merchants in Golkonda well before 1008/1600 though the actual details of their business are not available. Persian chronicles mention the names of Iranian and Golkonda merchants who were assigned grand titles such as *malik ut tujjār*. However, mention of such merchants is generally made in terms of their socio-political affairs and the volume of their trade is rarely recorded.

The structure of the Golkonda bazaar was a loose but colossal complex of specialized industries and raw agricultural and mineral commodities, which could be bought at the dealer's counter or directly acquired at their source. The bazaar was governed by the principle of free trade, making it accessible to merchants from all over the world.[53] Three factors governed the structure of bazaar throughout the period of this study. Firstly, in their revenue administration, the Qutb Shahs adhered to the principle of farming out provinces, districts and further subdivisions to the nobles of various ranks in a hierarchical order.[54] The system gave a great deal of autonomy to each noble within his jurisdiction. Second, the open and productive bazaar of Golkonda encouraged European merchants to establish their factories, which in turn played an important role in organizing their business. These entrepreneurs were encouraged both by the nobility and the government in view of their own interest. There were, however, moments of discord between local elites, foreign merchants and the administration.[55] The alien merchants, particularly the Dutch and the English, played an important role in organizing industrial and agricultural production. The third factor was the indigenous *sahūkār* and middlemen who played an indispensible role both in financing and organizing business.[56] In spite of the above conditions, the bazaar of Golkonda in its very nature was a producers' bazaar catering to a large-scale export trade all over the contemporary world from Japan to England.

Weights and Measures in Golkonda

In Golkonda, as in Iran, commodities were weighed rather than measured. All ordinary goods other than clothes were sold by weight. Nevertheless, measures of capacity were also present but were not seen in international transactions.[57] The units of heavy and minute weights were different in denomination despite casual analogies in nomenclature.

(a) *Heavy weights*: The Golkonda bazaar had many systems of heavy weights. The indigenous system too had some regional variations. Various indigenous units of measure can be converted to the European avdp. or avoirdupois system of weights based on a pound which was equal to 16 ounces. The most popular system of heavy weights is shown in Table 4.4.

A *tolā* was an important unit both in Golkonda and Hindustan. It was a common denomination, though variable in standards, both in the systems of heavy and minute weights. In actual practice it was a large denomination in the scale of minute weights but a small denomination in the scale of heavy weights. Its weight in the Mughal systems, both minute and heavy, was uniform as each *tolā* was comprised of 12 *māshās* or 185.5 grains avdp. and each *māshā* was 8 *ratis* or *gungchīs*. (A *gungchī* = 1.932 grains

TABLE 4.4: Units of heavy weights

3 *tolā*[58]	= 1 *pollam*[59]	=	$\dfrac{0.075 \text{ lbs. Dutch}}{0.08175 \text{ lbs. avdp.}}$	= 35.425 grams
24 *tolā* or 8 *pollam*	= 1 *ser*	=	$\dfrac{0.6 \text{ lbs. Dutch}}{0.654 \text{ lbs. avdp.}}$	= 283.40 grams
5 *ser*	= 1 *viss*	=	$\dfrac{3 \text{ lbs. Dutch}}{3.27 \text{ lbs. avdp.}}$	= 1 kg. 417 grams
8 *viss* or 40 *ser*	= 1 *maund* Masulipatam	=	$\dfrac{24 \text{ lbs. Dutch}}{26.16 \text{ lbs. avdp.}}$	= 11 kg. 865 grams
20 *maund*[60]	= 1 *kandy* or 1 *bahār*[61]	=	$\dfrac{480 \text{ lbs. Dutch}}{523.2 \text{ lbs. avdp.}}$	= 237 kg. 320 grams
littel[62]	=	=	$\dfrac{288.073 \text{ lbs. Dutch}}{314 \text{ lbs. avdp.}}$	= 136 kg. 428 grams

(This was especially used for weighing indigo.)

parra (Bimlipatam)	=	=	$\dfrac{45 \text{ lbs. Dutch}}{49.05 \text{ lbs. avdp.}}$	= 22 kg. 249 grams
last (Bimlipatam)	= 72 *parra*	=	$\dfrac{3240 \text{ lbs. Dutch}}{3531.6 \text{ lbs. avdp.}}$	= 1,602 kg.
parra (Pullicat)	=	=	$\dfrac{48 \text{ lbs. Dutch}}{52.32 \text{ lbs. avdp.}}$	= 23 kg. 731 grams
last (Pullicat)	= 80 *parra*	=	$\dfrac{3840 \text{ lbs. Dutch}}{4275.6 \text{ lbs. avdp.}}$	= 1,979 kg. 377 grams

NOTE: The *last* and *parra* measures were used for weighing rice and wheat. These weights have been discussed by Raychaudhuri from Dutch sources.

avdp. or 3.5 *jaū*.) A *tolā* in Golkonda had variable standards in different scales. In the scales of minute weighs it was equal to 9 *māshās* or 139.104 grains avdp.[63]

(b) *Minute weights*: The unit of minute weights was required to measure precious metals, stones and drug ingredients. The system in vogue in Safavid Iran as well as in Golkonda was a complex of Arabic, Persian, Greek and Indian systems. The best treatise on the subject is *Risālah-i-Miqdāriyah* contributed by Mir Muhammad Mu'min, the *peshwā* of Golkonda at the instance of Sultan Muhammad Qutb Shah.[64]

Out of a series of about fifty units of minute weights, Mir Muhammad Mu'min tried to provide exact weights of at least twelve. For each unit he quoted equivalents in alternate terms, each based upon an authority. Indication of equivalents to the details of minute fractions suggests that Mir Mu'min's system was not homogeneous as it represented assorted artificially synthesized units of heterogeneous systems. Mir Mu'min was a competent scholar, aware of contemporary standards, and produced the results of his research to Muhammad Qutb Shah. Thus, one can take this treatise as an authority on the contemporary weights of Golkonda and Iran.

The smallest basic unit according to Mir Mu'min was a *habbah* equal to one *jaū* or a barley grain.[65] Higher units were therefore, as tabulated below:

TABLE 4.5: Units of minute weights

2 *habbah*	= 1 *tassūj*	= 1.444 grains	= 0.0907 grams
2 *tassūj*	= 1 *qirāt*	= 2.888 grains	= 0.1814 grams
2 *qirāt*	= 1 *dānak*[66]	= 4.976 grains	= 0.3624 grams
6 *dānak*	= 1 *diram*[67]	= 29.856 grains	= 2.1768 grams
17 *qirāt*	= 1 *misqāl*[68]	= 50.396 grains	= 3.0838 grams
63 *qirāt*	= 1 *istār* or *tolā*[69]	= 182.000 grains	= 11.7936 grams
7½ *misqāl*	= 1 *uqīyah*[70]	= 377.970 grains	= 23.1285 grams
12 *uqīyah*	= 1 *ratl*[71]	= 4535.640 grains	= 277.5420 grams
2 *ratl*	= 1 *maund* (*man*)	= 9071.280 grains	= 555.0840 grams
1⅞ *maund*	= 1 *kailajah*	= 17008.650 grains	= 1040.7825 grams
3 *kailajah*	= 1 *makkūk*	= 51025.950 grains	= 3122.3475 grams
50 *maund* or 100 *ratl*	= 1 *qintār*	= 453564.000 grains	= 27754.20 grams

The standards of minute weights as defined in Table 4.5, particularly the units of high denomination, had a commercial value in the wholesale transaction of precious metals and drugs in the international markets of Iran and Golkonda. Both precious metals and drugs constituted a significant item of commercial commodities transacted between the two markets under study. The units of low denomination had commercial value in rare cases. Also, invoices of jewels and jewellery, whether transacted as commercial goods or gift articles, contained full particulars of the weights or articles even to the details of *surkhs*.[72]

(c) *Measures of Length*: All sorts of textiles including carpets were measured both in Iran and Golkonda with cubit and *gaz* of variable standards.[73] In Golkonda measures were of almost the same denomination as in Iran, but of a more natural standard.[74] The main measures length in Golkonda were:

a cubit or *hasta*   =   18.7 inches
a *gaz*   =   33.5 inches[75]

The above standards were chiefly used in Masulipatam. Textile pieces of similar quality and size were also sold by counting in scores. A score was called a *corge*.[76] In addition to the above measures of length in Golkonda, there were other systems adopted by foreign merchants from Portugal, England, France, Holland and Denmark within their own business organizations.

Export Commodities of Golkonda

The Golkonda bazaar provided a wide variety of consumer goods and raw materials to fulfil the needs of local consumers as well as for export. The actual volume of exports cannot be worked out with mathematical exactitude yet an attempt will be made to assess the average annual volume of export trade. Some of the commodities exported from Golkonda to Iran are first introduced here in broad categories:

1. *Textiles*: Golkonda was one of the largest centres of textile industry in the contemporary world. It manufactured a wide variety of plain and patterned textiles and knitted pieces. Patterned cloth was both printed and woven. Although the primary material was cotton, the production of silk and satin did not lag far behind. The names of numerous varieties of Coromandel textiles are scattered throughout Tamil, Telugu, Kannada and other literature of the Deccan dating from the times of the Vijayanagar Empire. Golkonda inherited a few vestiges of that enormous industry. Some of the common types of cloths manufactured there included fine Salampores, Percullaes Izarees, Oringall Beteelaes (Warangal Beathila), Allejaes, Saderunches, Collowaypoos, Sazarguntes, Romalls, Gungarees (Dangri) and Sali Cloth.[77] The main centres were at Masulipatam, Pulicat Negapatam, etc. The colourful patterns and exquisite texture of Golkonda textiles were admired throughout the contemporary world from Japan to England, which imported these textiles. All kinds of plain and printed textiles and hosiery were exported to Iran.[78]

2. *Dyestuff*: Golkonda also produced a few varieties of dyestuffs that were extracted from natural sources and used to make red, blue and yellow. The natural agents, chey root and indigo that made red and blue respectively, were produced in ample quantities in various parts of Golkonda.[79] These dyestuffs were a major export commodity. Indian

merchants monopolized the Iranian market to such an extent that the Dutch could not trade in them.[80] The quantity of indigo exported every year was between 300 and 400 *bahārs*. The average volume of indigo exported to Iran may be judged from casual information provided in Dutch sources. By the year AD 1644, the average supply of indigo to Iran was 44,000 lb. The profits on indigo were high, and although the many varieties of indigo sold at different rates, some qualities fetched a gross profit of 234 per cent. There was great competition in the export trade between the native merchants and the European factors.[81]

3. *Furniture*: Golkonda also produced very beautiful woodwork, such as chests of drawers, escritoires (writing cases), tables and chairs of ebony, wrought and inlaid with tortoise shell and ivory, which were in great demand in Iran and elsewhere.[82]

4. *Gunpowder and Saltpetre*: Golkonda produced a considerable quantity of saltpetre, the production of which was primarily organized by the Dutch and English companies at Coromandel. In 1026/1617, it exported gunpowder to all Asian bazaars.[83] The demand for gunpowder was great and constant in Iran.[84] Masulipatam was a major gunpowder and cordage-manufacturing centre.[85]

5. *Iron and Steel*: Golkonda had appreciable deposits of iron and other minerals such as chromite, coal and manganese required in the development of iron and steel industries.[86] Pig iron, iron bands, iron bars as well as cannon balls formed an important export commodity. The export trade of iron and steel was not regular, but demand for it increased in the Eastern archipelago and Iran after 1043/1634, yielding a gross profit from 80 to 100 per cent.[87] Slow transportation from mines to bazaar on the backs of oxen slightly increased its price, but it was a cheap commodity sold in terms of *littel*.[88] As there was a significant import trend of iron and steel for making weapons, it suggests that Golkonda and Iranian officials exchanged military technology as well.[89] Statistics for two years furnished in Table 4.6 may explain this:

TABLE 4.6: Exports of iron and steel to Iran

Year	*Quantum of steel pieces exported to Iran in littels*	*Quantum of iron pieces exported to Iran in littels*
1634	6,684	9,600
1635	15,440	9,039[90]

6. *Precious Minerals*: Golkonda was famous for its abundant mineral deposits.[91] Diamond mining was a developed industry in the region.

Its diamonds and rubies were exported all over the world. The industry was under the control of the administration and strengthened its export trade. There is no specific data about the export of Golkonda diamonds to Iran as a commercial commodity, yet there is mention of Golkonda diamonds being sent to Iran as gifts. Rubies from Golkonda were exported to Iran in large quantities and sold there at great profit.[92]

Besides a great variety of textiles and woodwork, Golkonda also exported many other commodities which were either raw or semi-processed goods catering to meet the needs of Iranian consumers. These included tobacco and paan, which were exported to Iran as many people there had become addicted to these stimulants.[93] The great demand for Golkonda tobacco abroad led the sultan to issue orders discouraging export of tobacco.[94]

Golkonda Exports to Iran

There are many statements pointing to the fact that there was regular trade between Golkonda and Iran, yet no material data provides a complete quantitative sequence. One reason for this is that the agencies organizing export trade were numerous and, at times, hostile to each other. Moreover, native Golkonda and Iranian merchants do not seem to have maintained a record of their business transactions. Similarly, the role of many private European traders has also been left unrecorded. Data partially bearing evidence to the volume of business between Golkonda and Iran in particular, is embedded in the extensive records of the English East India Company and the Dutch factories. According to a Dutch estimate of 1062/1652, there was an annual traffic of a 100,000 florins from Coromandel to Iran.[95] Between 1055/1646 to 1096/1684, the value of cargo exported from Golkonda to Iran with its ratio to the total export trade of Golkonda is furnished in Table 4.7 in terms of florins.[96]

The statistics given in Table 4.7 reveal one aspect, namely, the volume of the export trade of Golkonda with Iran. It is interesting to note that the actual capital potential supplied by Iran was greater than the capital value of goods she received from Golkonda. In other words, Iran was supplying surplus capital to Golkonda, which was mainly on account of the Dutch and the English factors' capacity to organize business in various regions of the Indian Ocean. The surplus capital exceeding four or five times the average may be seen from a comparative cross-section in Table 4.8.

The surplus capital obtained from Iran and initially invested in Golkonda was first diverted to the various regions of the Eastern archipelago where goods from Golkonda were exchanged for other commodities required

TABLE 4.7: Value of exports from Golkonda to Iran vis-à-vis
total trade 1055/1646–1096/1684

(A florin = a *Sikka* rupee)

Year	Total Export from Coromandel (Value in florins)	Coromandel Export to Iran (Value in florins)	Ratio
1646	1,846,709	117,744	2 : 31
1647	1,444,253	137,592	2 : 21
1648	1,449,180	49,429	2 : 59
1649	1,948,319	57,692	1 : 36
1650	1,733,108	176,928	1 : 10
1651	1,781,942	91,698	1 : 19
1652	2,245,680	147,173	1 : 15
1653	1,567,597	32,035	1 : 49
1654	1,383,663	45,598	1 : 30
1655	1,616,524	41,944	1 : 39
1656	1,288,065	118,649	2 : 21
1659	1,680,333	157,598	3 : 32
1664	2,570,474	–	
1665	2,681,007	154,909	1 : 17
1666	2,654,026	63,341	1 : 42
1668	2,120,131	153,331	1 : 14
1671	1,789,960	75,045	1 : 14
1672	2,299,999	125,172	1 : 18
1673	1,495,905	300,000	1 : 5
1676	1,784,084	116,037	3 : 46
1677	631,340	114,334	2 : 11
1680	2,319,941	80,918	1 : 29
1683	2,863,787	116,321	1 : 25
1684	3,407,927	106,049	1 : 32[97]

TABLE 4.8: Surplus capital between Iran and Golkonda

Year	Capital supplied by Iran (Value in florins)	Value of goods exported by Golkonda to Iran (Value in florins)	Surplus Capital	Ratio
1646	384,569	117,744	266,825	3 : 1
1647	538,048	137,592	400,456	4 : 1
1648	492,569	49,429	443,140	10 : 1
1654	309,305	45,598	303,707	7 : 1
1656	200,000	118,649	81,351[98]	2 : 1
TOTAL				26 : 5
AVERAGE				5 : 1

by Iran. In that way Iran served as a powerful financing agency supplying capital to the organizers of the South-East Asian bazaar. It is for the same reason that the commercial ships leaving Coromandel for Iran sailed through Batavia and Aceh.[99] There are instances when apart from surplus capital supplied to Golkonda, considerable capital potential was exported by Iran to Golkonda, regardless of any return export by the latter. Table 4.9 provides a cross-section of Iran's capital supply to Golkonda when the latter did not export anything to Iran:

TABLE 4.9: Iran's capital supply to Golkonda

Year	Capital (in florins) supplied from Iran to Coromandel	Goods exported from Golkonda to Iran
1657	588,135	–
1658	628,627	–
1660	616,947	–
1661	519,060	–
1664	500,000	–
1669	13,545[100]	–

This clearly shows that the Golkonda-Iran commercial relations were not merely bilateral. Golkonda served as a commercial bridge for the import trade of Iran with other regions of the Indian Ocean. Golkonda thus occupied a key position in Iranian foreign trade carried out in the East. No doubt at the same time, Iran occupied a similar position in the westward trade of Coromandel.

Commercial Taxes

Foreign merchants in Golkonda had to pay certain commercial taxes, which can be categorized as informal and formal and secondly as direct and indirect. Nobles and *dalāls* (middlemen, both native and Iranian), who controlled the bazaars, levied many informal taxes. The Dutch factor Schorer and other foreign merchants give interesting details about some of these informal taxes.[101] Schorer specifically records that, in spite of the payment of formal taxes in compliance with the formal agreement with the king of Golkonda, alien merchants had to present various gifts to the harbour master (*shahbandar*) and other persons of authority. That was all done to 'secure friendship', with the governor in particular, whose cooperation was essential in carrying out business.[102] The middleman of Golkonda was an informal partner in the business organizations run by Europeans and others on the Coromandel coast. They charged a fee for providing skilled labour, such as chint printers, or unskilled labour, which may have involved the kidnapping of juveniles for slavery and other similar activities.[103] Another important agency that imposed informal taxes was that of the moneychangers who exchanged money at higher rates, although officially all foreign coins were to be exchanged at their metallic value in Golkonda.[104] It is interesting to note that, according to the English and European factors, Iranian merchants in Golkonda constituted a privileged class that had good relations with the administrative authorities and could therefore avoid most of such informal taxes.[105] Such remarks are, however, debatable, for the obvious reason that while Iranians were exempted from formal taxes, they had to pay heavy informal taxes in the form of presents to the rulers and nobles.

The formal commercial tax was mainly categorized as *zakāt*, which was collected at different places at different rates on different commodities under royal edict. So it formed a regular source of state revenue. There were many kinds of *zakāt*, which can be classified into different categories. Nevertheless, it was imposed on all the import and export goods at flat rates at the harbour. A sort of *zakāt* was also collected on the commodities sold in the inland bazaar of Golkonda. It was generally assessed by the nature and the quantum of goods.[106] In some cases, it was assessed by the number of workmen employed, especially in the case of diamond mining.[107]

Though the producer paid the taxes directly, their incidence was mainly on the consumer. The exorbitant rates of interest, the high rates of exchange of currencies, and the freight duty all tended to raise the price level. The liberty to divert the entire incidence of tax to the consumer was, of course, not absolute, as it was affected by the consumer's behaviour in the bazaar; on occasions, the consumer refused to purchase commodities for years. It was due to this mechanism of supply and demand that the incidence of taxes on the producers and consumers was divided in uncertain proportions.

There are instances where a rise in taxes created a slump in the bazaar and royal ordinances had to be issued to waive or write off the *zakāt*,[108] which could lower the prices, encouraging rapid consumption and an active bazaar.

In addition to the usual taxes, including tolls and octroi, duties had to be paid at the rate of 4 per cent (viz., 2 per cent on entering and 2 per cent on leaving) on the capital value of all consignments contained in a shipment. There were anchorage charges as well.[109]

Abatements

There are instances of allowing discounts and abatements on Golkonda merchandise for export ranging from 7½ to 26 per cent on bulk purchases, especially of textiles.[110] Although it is difficult to say as to whether an abatement was allowed at all times and on all goods as a routine practice, there is no doubt that the practice was governed by certain conditions prevalent in the bazaar. One of the main factors was competition. The merchants of Masulipatam tended to offer attractive discounts to steady their sale in competition with the goods of Petapoli. Abatements were allowed in cases of faulty goods as the standard of packing and storage was not always satisfactory and purchasers inspected goods very closely.[111] It was also implemented on account of the role of the broker in the bazaar who was efficient in prompting bulk disposals of Indian merchandise, especially to overseas merchants. It must be kept in mind that brokers had intimate knowledge of the bazaar on issues, such as the varieties and prices of commercial goods, and they could also serve as procuring agents for goods from different manufacturers. The brokers, known as *dubhāsh*, were normally native persons conversant in two or more languages, usually Persian, the language of the mercantile and administrative elite, and possibly one European language, used in international markets. They also probably spoke Telugu.

Import of Specialist Labour and Materials

The commercio-economic aspects of relations involved the traffic of specialized labour that in turn was responsible for further strengthening of these ties. Among the categorizes of skilled labour—architects, engineers, and artisans[112]—can be especially mentioned as they constructed a number of buildings of varied designs and for numerous purposes scattered all over the kingdom of Golkonda. No doubt, Golkonda's architecture was a blend of Indo-Persian techniques and aesthetics. Iranian designs could not be adequately adopted in Golkonda without the import of some of the construction material as well. Details of the ingredients added to the construction materials, which was normally mixed with lime, and can only be understood through the process of a chemical analysis. This analysis may further reveal the use of Iranian techniques, if not definitely Iranian substances. Nevertheless, in the architectural pattern of Golkonda, Iranian materials were distinctly seen in its *kashi kari* worked on the exteriors and its colourful enamels used in the baroque of interiors. Kashi and enamel work appear in Golkonda throughout the period of the Qutb Shahs. Their wide use can be judged from the size and location of various buildings in Hyderabad, Srikakulam (Sicacole), Masulipatam and other places. The fort of Golkonda and the Qutb Shahi tombs were thoroughly clad from top to bottom with Kashi tiles. Similarly, the interior of these edifices were decorated with enamelled rococo. The enamels of variable tints and shades had an unusual glow and durability.

Although Kashi tiles and its related materials and the enamels for rococo were present in huge quantities, there is no evidence that they were manufactured in Golkonda. This material was imported from Iran as it was manufactured there.[113] Buildings with Kashi exteriors and interiors were either the palaces of kings and nobles or religious buildings and do not seem to have been constructed for the general public. Thus, their use did not require a mass-scale civil engineering project and manufacturing. It is likely that these materials were imported from Iran as and when required. There is no building such as *Chihil Sutūn* (Fourty Columns) in Golkonda, but the colours of *Chihil Sutūn* may be seen in the vestiges of its buildings.[114]

The other aspect of such imports, as mentioned above, was the inflow of architects, civil engineers and artisans from Iran and Iraq. No doubt there were indigenous and Deccani technicians in Golkonda, such as Hussain Shah Wali.[115] Elaborate inscriptions worked out in various styles of Persian and Arabic script are the work of expert Iranian calligraphers and inscribers. Among such inscribers, the names of Jalal-uddin al Shirazi, Husain Shirazi, Mir 'Ali, Isma'il bin Arab Shirazi, Lutfullah Tabrizi and Baba Khan may be mentioned here.[116] Similarly, the industry of books and bookbinding required both men and materials which were imported from Iran, if not on a large scale at least in sufficient quantities for training local artists and setting up their workshops in Golkonda.[117]

Slavery and the Slave Trade

Slavery was an accepted part of social life in the sixteenth and seventeenth centuries. There was a brisk market for slaves both in Golkonda and Iran. We find in Golkonda that the royal household and the aristocracy not only had Indian slaves but slaves from overseas as well—Turkmen, Abyssinians and Georgians, etc.—some of whom had a respectable position in the master's household.[118] There are instances of Iranians purchasing Parsi, Hindu (*jentews*), Banjaras and other slaves in India and moving them to Iran.[119] It is strange that Iranian sources are generally silent about Indian settlements in various parts of Iran. Nevertheless, there had been a considerable traffic of slaves as a commercial commodity between the two states. Famines and other natural hazards gave impetus to the slave trade in Golkonda, where children were sold for 4 to 5 *pagodas* each to secure food, whereas in good times their price rose to 12 and 14 *pagodas* per slave.[120] A study of the traffic of slaves in the sixteenth- and seventeenth-century Asian bazaars reveals that it tended to be from West to East rather than the reverse. The export of slaves does not seem to have had direct patronage from the state.

On occasions, slave trade was found to be more profitable than trade in cloth, especially for the Dutch.[121] The slaves of Turk and Abyssinian origin brought to Golkonda were brave soldiers, who are honourably mentioned in Persian chronicles. They also had a marginal place in the grand Majlis of Golkonda.[122]

Structure of the Iranian Bazaar

Data regarding the structure of the Iranian bazaar is rather scarce. Nevertheless, considering its overseas export trade to Golkonda, it may be asserted that the Iranian export market was basically industrial in character. Safavid Iran had many industries, each with a history dating back to pre-Islamic times. Craft organizations were mostly hereditary. The families of the manufacturers had attained a universal reputation for their artistic achievements, fulfilling the requirements of local consumers as well as catering to vast Eastern and Western bazaars. Unlike Coromandel, the presence of Europeans in the markets of Iran was less prominent and pervasive. Iranian industries were exceedingly localized and protected by landlords, who sourced raw commodities from areas nearby. However, there were a few industries for which some raw materials were imported from other countries, such as iron and dyestuffs that were bought from Golkonda. Iran had to import raw materials for large-scale industries to meet the demand within the country, such as weapon manufacture and cotton textiles. Apart from these, the localized industries produced highly specialized luxury articles like carpets, silk, enamelled pottery, embroidered shawls, brocades, Kashi tiles, books, paintings and medicines, etc. Painters, designers, calligraphers, engravers, artists and architects had a leading role in almost every industry. Iranian shops, displaying Iranian industrial products like textiles, ceramics glass, metalwork, specimens of exquisite *jild sāzī* (bookbinding), were veritable art galleries.

Besides specialized industrial goods, Iran maintained a very steady market of cash currencies and their exchange. The geographical location of Iran turned her into a great centre in which contemporary cash species of the East and West were exchanged. In the particular context of trade relations between Golkonda and Iran, the former was essentially a producer's bazaar for regions across the world, while the latter was the bazaar of cash species providing finances to the entrepreneurs of maritime traffic, especially between the Persian Gulf and the Eastern archipelago.[123]

Golkonda does not appear to have ever supplied capital to the bazaars of Iran, whereas there are instances of the reverse happening. Moreover, the volume of merchandise exported from Iran to Golkonda was surprisingly small which was probably on account of the nature of export goods. Golkonda's exports were mostly produced in response to the demand for necessities from all classes of Iranian society, while the goods exported from Iran to Golkonda chiefly served the needs of the nobility. Therefore, the size and price of the commercial exchange between the two was hardly comparable. The exquisite luxury goods of Iran, normally required by the nobility and the privileged classes, generally augmented her capital investment in foreign trade or served as a medium of exchanging currencies.[124]

The capital procured from Iran augmented the export trade of Golkonda, though not necessarily with Iran. From the records of the Dutch and English factories it becomes evident that the investment of Iranian capital in Golkonda was not aimed at a return business. Its object was to enhance the capital potential by an initial investment in the producers' bazaar of Golkonda from where they were able to procure a handsome consignment, which was in steady demand in the other regions of Indian Ocean, the Middle East and Europe.

Export Commodities of Iran

1. *Carpet Industry*: The carpet industry of Iran had a long history going back to the sixth century or even earlier and it flourished during the reign of the Safavids as well.[125] The varieties of carpets (*qālīn*) have been variably classified by both manufacturers and art historians. It formed an important article of Iran's export trade and was in demand by the sultans and the nobility of Golkonda. The export agencies were both indigenous and European. Luxury articles were an effective instrument for augmenting the capital potential of the Dutch and English factors who could purchase carpets on their route with a slight diversion to the Persian Gulf, sell them off in the bazaars of Malabar and Coromandel or even further inland to the nobility of Bijapur and Golkonda and then amass capital for investing in the export trade of Golkonda to other parts of the Indian Ocean.

2. *Metal Industry*: The metal industry too had a long history in Iran and it developed further under the Safavids. Metals like silver, gold, copper, lead and their enamels were used for manufacturing utensils, boxes, jewellery and related articles, which showed exceptional artistry and were wrought by engraving, embossing, moulding, inlaying and other such techniques.

   The most significant metal industry was that of ordnance. Safavid Iran produced a wide variety of weapons made of steel, which were decorated with almost all the artistic techniques we find in jewellery, utensils or even books.[126] During the eleventh century Hijri, one 'Abdullah Isfahani (Tabrizi) attained a reputation as an expert in manufacturing ordnance.[127]

3. *Textile Industry*: Safavid Iran's textile industry had a classical history; it made strides in manufacturing fabrics of exquisite texture and a variety of patterns. Most of the patterned cloth bore woven designs and very few of them were printed. The material was mainly silk and wool, and cotton as well. The most important of the textiles

were satin (*atlas*), velvet (*makhmal*), linen (*kattan*), brocade (*zarbafi*), and silk (*abrisham*). The main centres of such textile industry were Tabriz, Herat, Isfahan, Kashan, Rasht, Mashhad, Qum, Sava, Sultania, Ardestan and Sherwan. Rasht was famous for its silk industry and Tabriz for patterned textiles. Brocading was adopted in variable degrees in almost all of the textiles mentioned here. Safavid textiles preserved in Iranian museums and other institutions show elaborate artistic skill and labour. They are by no means less artistic and expressive than Safavid paintings.[128] In many cases, the name of the artist too was printed or wrought on the texture of the cloth. The industry ran in collaboration with the pattern designers or *naqqāsh* who also contributed to painting, woodwork, metallic industry, the decoration of ordnance, architecture, bookbinding and carpet industries.[129]

4. *Ceramics*: The Iranian ceramic industries can be classified into pottery (*zurūf*) and the tile industry (*kār-i-khazaf* or *kār-i-kāshī*). Pottery was an art that the Iranians learnt and borrowed from the Chinese, and then adapted the ceramic patterns to suit their taste.

The manufacturing of coloured tiles too was an ancient industry in Iran, the output of which was exported to Golkonda in large quantities. It was a type of ceramic glazed with colourful enamels, processed and mixed with powder extracted from inner crust of shells. Those tiles were used to cover the exterior of buildings, afforded an infinite scope of decorative patterns and had architectural merits. Iranian tiles were of various kinds depending on their substance and scope of patterns. Kashan was the biggest centre while the other centers were Sava, Sultanabad, Isfahan and Daghistan.[130]

There is no recorded data regarding the export of *khazaf* to Golkonda but the Golkonda fort and many other huge buildings still have patches of Iranian tiles suggesting that an enormous volume of tiles was exported to Golkonda from Iran. Since the data regarding the trunk route traffic is extremely sparse, it is presumed that Iranian tiles, the production centres of which were mostly located in the north, were carried to the Deccan through the trunk routes laden on camels, mules and horses accompanied by artisans.

5. *Books and Bookbinding* (sahhafi): Paper was a developed industry by the time of Safavids. Books were recorded mostly on paper and also on parchment (*pustak*). There is no doubt that the task of translating important Arabic books and producing religious literature in Persian was aimed at popularizing Safavid Shi'ism in Iran. Therefore, books were produced on an enormous scale and the industry of books and bookbinding made progress during the sixteenth and seventeenth centuries. That industry too, developed in collaboration with calligraphers and pattern designers (*naqqāsh*). The libraries

of Golkonda had an enormous collection of books manufactured
and bound in Iran. There are instances when the Mughal princes
requisitioned such books from the Qutb Shahi library. From the
industrial point of view, books manufactured in Safavid Iran were
a costly commodity in view of their masterful calligraphy, marginal
patterns, the quality of their ink and paper, the fine leather material
of their binding and use of gold and other mineral colours.[131]

6. *Glass Industry*: Iranians knew the arts of molding glass as well as
cutting flint glass (*billor*). The glass-cutting industry had started
developing from the tenth and eleventh centuries. Unlike the other
industries, the glass industry was less developed, especially with
respect to its artistic accomplishment, yet its progress was by no
means negligible under the Safavids. Glass utensils were decorated
either by painting or cutting, or by both. The important centres of
glass industry were Shiraz, Hamadan, Nishapur, Rey and Sava.[132]

Apart from these major industries there were many minor ones that
added to the volume of Iran's export trade. Besides industrial goods, precious
metals like silver and pearls, horses and fruits were in a constant demand
in Golkonda and were exported from Iran.[133]

Weights and Measures in Iran

Iranian practice tended more towards weighing commercial commodities
than measuring them. There were various systems of weights and measures
indigenous and alien, old and new in Safavid Iran. The standards for bulk
measurements of heavy commodities were different from those for weighing
precious metals and medicinal ingredients.

General commodities like food grains, metals, woods, spices and even
liquids were sold by weight.[134] The lowest unit of heavy weight was a *misqāl*
and the next immediate higher unit was a *man* (*maund*), which represented
different standards from place to place in the country. The predominant
units in vogue are tabulated in Table 4.10:[135]

TABLE 4.10: Predominant units of measure in Iran

1 *misqāl*	=	73 grains or 1/6 ozs. avoirdupois (avdp.)[136]	=	4.703 grams
120 *misqāl*	=	1 *khark man* 1lb. 4 ozs.	=	566.991 grams
5 *khark man* or 600 *misqāl*	=	1 *tabrizī man* 6 lbs. 4 ozs.	=	2 kg. 334.955 grams
2 *tabrizī man* or 1,200 *misqāl*	=	1 *shāhiman* = 12 lbs. 8 ozs.	=	5 kg. 669.910 grams

In Iran, cubits and *gaz* used for carpets were different from those used for measuring cloth, and is tabulated in Table 4.11:

TABLE 4.11: Units of measure for cloth and carpets

(a)	*gaz* for cloth	=	37.5 inches
	cubit for cloth also called King's cubit	=	36 inches[137]
(b)	*gaz* for carpet silk and finer items	=	27 inches
	cubit for carpets, etc.	=	18.25 inches

Some of the pieces of textiles and carpets[138] were also counted in terms of pairs (*juft*).

Export Trade of Iran

Iran had a worldwide export trade that shaped the cultural and economic life of many countries. The coastal market of Iran was sufficiently open and accessible to merchants of different nations, thus making it the biggest centre of monetary exchange in Asia. European factors too played a leading role in organizing her external trade and maintained records of their accounts.[139] They took an interest in Iran's export trade chiefly with the object of procuring capital. Generally, specialized Persian goods such as pearls, silver and cash spices were all the components of their capital potential diverted

TABLE 4.12: Iranian exports to Golkonda from 1646 to 1669

Year	Capital supplied to Golkonda by Iran (in florins)	Total capital supplied to Golkonda by Iran and other regions (in florins)	Ratio of Iranian capital in relation to the total capital
1646	384,569	1,876,667	1 : 5
1647	538,048	1,856,974	1 : 3
1648	492,569	2,194,080	1 : 3
1654	309,305	2,845,500	1 : 10
1656	200,000	1,200,000	1 : 6
1657	588,135	1,921,319	1 : 3
1658	628,072	2,358,849	1 : 4
1659	139,629	2,476,864	1 : 18
1660	616,947	1,745,122	2 : 5
1661	519,060	1,443,839	1 : 3
1664	500,000	1,450,073	1 : 3
1669	13,545	1,823,154	1 : 130
1676	160,879	1,847,471	1 : 11[140]

to the South-East Asian market. A cross-section from Dutch sources shows the capital value (in terms of florins) of Iranian exports to Golkonda in the course of about a quarter of a century from 1055/1646 to 1080/1669, together with its ratio in relation to the total capital imported by Golkonda from various regions.

The above statistics are restricted to the activity of a single Dutch establishment, the Jan Company. It also shows intervals in commercial activities—the export of capital from Iran was held up during times of war as in the years 1058/1649 to 1064/1653 and 1075/1665 to 1079/1668.[141] However in times of peace, capital was exported from Iran, which constituted from a minimum of 1 : 18 to 2 : 5 of the total capital imported by Golkonda from Iran. The prevalent average ratio was 1 : 3.

Special Purchases

Indian, Iranian and European merchants maintained the traffic of commerce between Golkonda and Iran. Yet, there were occasions when those merchants or agents made special purchases for the sultan or the nobles under special orders. Table 4.13 shows some instances of such purchases during the reign of 'Abdullah Qutb Shah.

TABLE 4.13: Purchases of Iranian merchants for Golkonda sultan, 'Abdullah Qutb Shah

Year	Name of the commercial agent	Amount of purchases	Commodities required
1049/1639	Mir Tajuddin Qumi	4,000 *huns*	Miscellaneous
1049/1639	Shah Hasan Riyas	4,000 *huns*	Miscellaneous
1049/1639	Mirza Muhammad Mashhadi	2,000 *tomāns*	Miscellaneous
1049/1639	Khwaja Abdul 'Ali Ardestani		Miscellaneous[142]
1053/1642	Muhammad Sadiq and Tahir		(1) Horses (2) Textiles
1053/1642	Muhammad Sadiq and Tahir	(b) 500,000 *huns*	Textiles[143]
1067/1656	Muhammad Sabir	(a) 500 *huns* (b) 12,000 *qirāns*[144]	*Qalamkār* of Shiraz medicines

Iranian merchants commanded respect in the courts of Golkonda and Iran. They sometimes carried political messages and court news such as Hajji Qambar 'Ali who conveyed the news of the death of Muhammad Qutb Shah to Shah 'Abbas I.[145]

There were occasions when insolvent Iranian businessmen, like Mir Muin-al-din Muhammad Shirazi, were helped by the Golkonda sultan with the grant of a subsistence allowance.[146] Sometimes the Shah himself took personal interest in an Iranian merchant who found it difficult to recover his dues in the Golkonda market. We have the case of Shah 'Abbas II who sent a letter to 'Abdullah Qutb Shah with Hakīm-ul-Mulk, the Qutb Shahi envoy, recommending the case of an Iranian merchant named Khwaja Muhammad Ibrahim, son of Haji Muhammad Sultan, who found it difficult to recover certain amounts payable to him by the merchants of Golkonda. The Shah wished that 'Abdullah Qutb Shah help him in the recovery of his funds.[147]

CONCLUSION

The commercial relations of Golkonda with Iran have been outlined in this chapter to suggest a few key features of systems of trade, markets and commodities. Trade relations of these two regions were part of the larger nexus of commerce in the Indian Ocean. We may infer that the flow of capital from Iran to Golkonda facilitated the purchasing of goods from other trading centres of the Indian Ocean, especially from South-East Asia for Iran. Both polities saw the competitive participation of European, Indian and Iranian merchants. Freight trade aided the exchange of commodities while passenger traffic was also frequent between these states. The systems of weights and measures and currencies surveyed in the chapter, although diverse in the markets, were not entirely standardized. The units and standards for heavy and minute weights and measures of length have been ascertained from published evidence from European sources, travel accounts and unpublished Persian manuscript sources. Although the participation of non-European merchants in Golkonda's administration is apparent in Persian chronicles, data for the exact volume and share of their business is elusive.

NOTES

1. Master I, pp. 36, 243; II, pp. 36, 236, 283.
2. *Relations*, p. 63. The industry was localized at Narsapur Peta as it had abundant natural resources; Master II, p. 36.
3. *Relations*, p. 36; Bowrey, pp. 103–5, Pl. VIII; Purchase I, p. 308.
4. Wilson A.T., p. 108.
5. Purchase II, p. 173.
6. For details on the English and Portuguese rivalry see Hunter I, Chapter II, pp. 60–2 and for the reliance of Qutb Shahs on the English, see Chap. 2, section titled 'Sinking Sultanate—The fifth phase', pp. 54–9.
7. *Hadīqah*, p. 526.
8. Ibid., pp. 247–8.
9. Danvers I, p. 299; *Relations*, p. 61.

10. *A.A.A.*, pp. 689–92; *Hadīqat*, p. 225; Hunter I, p. 329.

11. Raychaudhuri, p. 87.

12. Ibid., pp. 88, 133.

13. Master I, p. 214; II, p. 363.

14. Master I, pp. 139–40.

15. Ibid., pp. 181, 184, 198; E.F.I., p. 174.

16. The maritime traffic between Golkonda and Iran was not always uniform. The Dutch and the English data show heavy traffic in some years and no traffic during other years.

17. *Relations*, pp. 64–5.

18. Master II, pp. 100, 390.

19. Raychaudhuri, p. 133.

20. According to Yule and Burnell, the word *hun* was perhaps derived from the Kannada word *huno*, meaning gold. There were *huns* of several denominations current in the Deccan such as the *hun deva rāyā* weighing from 26.1 to 52.9 grains; *hun sivā rāyā* weighing from 26.1 to 53.03 grains; *huntirimolī* (Tirumala) weighing from 25.7 grains to 26 grains and the *hunharī harī* weighing from 5.7 to 26.7 grains. *Huns* weighing from 25 to 26 grains or so can be taken as half *huns*. There were many other *huns* like *jutor, mailapurī, nellorī, adhonī, dhārwār, ambarshāhī, tubakī, chaul* and *portuguesī*, etc. See *S.W.D.*, pp. 128–36.

21. This categorization is based on the discussions of Moreland on Golkonda currency. *Relations*, pp. 91–3; Moreland, p. 183.

22. Talqani, Letter no. 67. The covenant (*'ahad nāmah*) executed by Shah Jahan in favour of 'Abdullah Qutb Shah equates the amount of *peshkash* in terms of *hun sivā rāyā*.

23. The word *pagoda* is interpreted in contemporary records in three senses: (i) a temple, (ii) an idol and (iii) a coin or a *hun*. It is in the last sense that the term is used in this chapter. For a detailed discussion on the term, see Hobson-Jobson and also Appadorai II, pp. 709–11.

24. *Hun sivā rāyā* was struck by Sadasiva Raya the king of Vijayanagar who ruled from AD 1543–1576. For further details on *hun sivā rāyā*, see T. Smith, *Catalogue of the Coins in Indian Museums* I, p. 324, Pl. XXXI; W. Elliot, *The Coins of Southern India*, p. 152, Fig. 100; Bedyabinod I, serial nos.1, 5, register nos. 20771, 21481, 96; *S.W.D.*, pp. 7, 34, 75, 132–3.

25. For the value of *ashrafī* see Habib, pp. 380–2, 384–7; *S.W.D.*, p. 32; for a discussion on observations of it by Europeans and its value in exchange, see the words *ashrafee, xerafine* and *mohur* in Hobson-Jobson. In the Mughal pacts and agreements with Golkonda and monetary references in correspondence with Iran the term of reference is always rupee and not *ashrafī*.

26. For an interesting history of the rupee see Hobson-Jobson; also see Habib, pp. 380–94, 398.

27. Talqani, Letter no. 67. The Mughal gold and silver coins, *dirhams* and *dinārs*, as mentioned in the covenant were actually *ashrafī* and rupees.

28. There is much evidence of the Qutb Shahs farming out administration and commerce. *Relations*, pp. 11, 32, 54–5, 57, 81–2; *S.W.D.*, p. 17.

29. Tavernier II, p. 71; E.F.I., XII, p. 327; I, p. 262; IV, p. 277; *Relations*, pp. 92–3.

30. For the origin of the word *fanam* and its various other forms see Hobson-Jobson; for its minting see Master I, pp. 72, 213; for its value ibid., pp. 254, 277 and Master II, p. 254; Fryer I, pp. 106, 139, 143, 149; Bowrey I, pp. 4, 14, 115; for Moreland's discussion see *Relations*, pp. 61, 93–4. Also see Appadorai II, pp. 713–15; Joshi, 'Coins'.

31. *Relations*, pp. 93–4; Bowrey, p. 114; and Joshi, 'Coins'.

32. Bowrey, p. 114; Fryer II, p. 132. This rate was not constant. For fluctuations in the exchange rate of *pagodas* or *huns* and *fanams*, see references cited in fn. 30.

33. *Nevel* according to Moreland was the coin, which was referred to as 'cash' by English merchants, *Relations*, pp. 55, 61, 94–5. Cash according to Hobson-Jobson included sundry coins; also see Joshi, 'Coins'.

34. Regarding *tār* see *'tara'* in Hobson-Jobson, Bowrey, p. 281; Fryer I, pp. 143, 149. Also see Moreland's observations on it, *Relations*, pp. 55, 94, 95 and Appadorai, pp. 38, 717.

35. For a detailed introduction to the copper coins of Golkonda see Abdul Wali, *Qutub Shahi Coins*, Moreland's discussion, *Relations*, p. 94, and also Joshi, 'Coins'.

36. Hobson-Jobson; Fryer II, p. 139; III, pp. 152–3, 200; Master I, pp. 176–8; II, p. 387. Mufidi informs us that a *tomān* was equal to ten *huns* (p. 90) or thirty rupees (p. 169), during the times of his visit to Golkonda. Though he has made a reference to the times of Mir Jumla Muhammad Amin who was in Golkonda during the reign of Muhammad Quli Qutb Shah, yet the exchange value given by Mufidi must have been based on his personal knowledge as he visited Golkonda in the year 1084/1673. He also mentioned various types of *tomāns* as *tumān-i-tabrīzī*, *tumān-i-shāhī*, *tumān-i-kāpkī*, etc.

37. Fryer II, p. 152.

38. Ibid.

39. Thevenot, pp. 25–6; Bowrey, p. 114; Master I, pp. 184, 387. For its value, see Master II, pp. 258, 290–1. According to Mufidi one *'abbāsī* was the equivalent of 15 *dinārs*; later the rate changed to one *'abbāsī* equalling 45 *dinārs* because merchants purchased textiles at Yazd and made payments in terms of *'abbāsī*, Mufidi, p. 205. The rise in the price of *'abbāsī* was due to the manipulation of Haji Muhammad Baqir Beg, Shah 'Abbas II's *vazīr* at Jehram. The said *vazīr* melted the coins and dismissed the moneychangers (Shroffs) early in the year 1078/1667, Mufidi, pp. 204–5.

40. Sherwani has levelled a criticism against Joshi saying, 'Dr Joshi is not correct when he says that the *mahmūdī* was a Persian coin; it was in fact a coin which was struck in Gujarat', see Sherwani (Q), p. 572. Joshi may have been unaware of the fact that *mahmūdī* was a coin of Gujarat, but it was adopted in Iran at such a large scale as if it were a currency native to Iran. For details see Fryer II,

p. 139; III, pp. 151–53; *S.W.D.*, p. 35; For the pound value of *mahmūdī* during the seventeenth century, see discussion below.

41. Fryer II, p. 139; III, pp. 152–3.
42. Fryer, p. 407.
43. *Tuzuk*, pp. 199–200.
44. Mufidi, pp. 91, 169.
45. Talqani, Letter no. 1.
46. This *hun* value of *tomān* has been worked out with the help of its pound value given by Fryer III, p. 152.
47. Manucci II, p. 418. This was the only example of gold brought by Europeans in a huge quantity. It was a part of their capital, which they invested throughout South and South-East Asia, including Golkonda.
48. The payments of Golkonda to Hindustan, Iran or European factories were made in *pagodas*, whereas in Hindustan in rupees and to Iran and other European countries in florins or Venetians. Raychaudhuri, p. 140; Manucci II, p. 418.
49. *T.Q.S.* fol. 98(a); Briggs III, p. 438.
50. Raychaudhuri, p. 2.
51. Ibid., p. 28.
52. Hunter II, p. 83.
53. *Hadīqat*, p. 251; *Relations*, pp. 64–5.
54. *Relations*, pp. 11, 32, 54–5, 57, 81–2, 92; Master II, p. 113; Raychaudhuri, pp. 7, 144.
55. Master II, pp. 155, 179–80; Bowrey, pp. 81, 83.
56. *Relations*, pp. 78, 82; Raychaudhuri, p. 12; *Hadīqat*, p. 251.
57. There is no mention of measures of capacity in international transactions.
58. For the weight of a *tolā* in Golkonda, see discussion below.
59. From inscriptional sources, Appadorai confirms a *ser* of 24 *tolā* or 8 *pollam*, each *pollam* to comprise 3 *tolā*, Appadorai II, p. 784. Nevertheless his equation with Troy weights is not verifiable.
60. The above weights are based on the information furnished by Schorer who visited Golkonda in the year AD 1614, *Relations*, Chap. XXXVII, p. 52, which Appadorai II, p. 784, also confirms. Moreland held the data to be authoritative and he tested it through various invoices as well as 'The Book of Weights of India'. Ibid., pp. 87–8.
61. For the origin of the words *maund* or *bahār* and their variations, see Hobson-Jobson.
62. Moreland suggests that Littel was the local corruption of the Arabic word *ritl*. For further details see *Relations*, pp. 61, 91; Raychaudhuri, p. 223.
63. In the scale of heavy weights, the value of a *tolā* in Golkonda has been judged by Moreland as either 175 or 182 grains (Dutch) which were equal to 191 and 199 grains avdp. respectively, *Relations*, p. 90. But working out the value of lower denomination from the value of higher denomination of variable standards may not lead to a satisfactory result. The basic units are not expected to be reciprocal to the changes in higher denominations. Mir Muhammad

Mu'min equated some of the Golkonda weights with Indian minute weights. A *tolā* according to Hodivala was about 185.5 grains avdp. which has been discussed and confirmed by Habib, pp. 367–8. The same has been taken as the basis of above discussions correlated with Mir Mu'min's equation of a *ghungchī* with 3.5 *jaū*.

64. Some of the important equivalents, in addition to those already given in table, shall be shown in respective footnotes. Another contemporary work, *Mizān ut tabaʾi Qutb Shāhī* by Taqiuddin Muhammad bin Sadruddin ʿAli, contains a chapter introducing about 60 units of minute weights. That work too does not furnish any satisfactory system as such.

65. It may be noted that the entire system is based on the smallest unit *jaū* or *habbah* (a gram) in Golkonda whereas according to Abul Fazl a *habbah* was equal to 2 *jaū*. *Jaū* was not a basic unit but comprised of thousands of infinitesimally smaller units called *zarrah*, *Āʾīn* I, p. 37. Nevertheless a *jaū* or *habbah* was smaller than a *rati* or *ghungchī* or *surkh*, the basis of Indian weights, 8 of which made one *māshā*. According to Mir Mu'min, a *ghungchī* was equal to 3.5 *jaū*. See *Miqdārīyah*, fol. 2 (b); *Āʾīn* I, p. 16; Hobson-Jobson.

66. This unit was pronounced as *daniq* in Arabic and as *dānak* or *dang* or *dānug* in Persian and Indo-Persian.

67. Same as *dirham* in Arabic and Persian.

68. The weight of a *misqāl* was equal to 68 *habbah* or *jaū* or 68 4/7 *jaū*. This denomination was most popular in Iran. According to Fryer, 6 Miscolle (*misqāl*) were equal to one ounce, Fryer III, p. 151. For various calculations of *misqāl*, see Hobson-Jobson, p. 568.

69. This is the second instance where Mir Muhammad Mu'min equated a unit of Perso-Arabic weight with unit of Indian weight. The weight of a *tolā* in Golkonda is a subject of much debate.

70. Mir Muhammad Mu'min has equated *istār* with 252 *jaū* or 5 *dirhams* and 3 *qirāt* or 3.5 *misqāl* and 3 *qirāt* or a *tolā*. In view of the *rati* value of *jaū*, i.e. 3.5 *jaū* = 1 *rati*, this *tolā* should be of 9 *māshās* only, instead of 12 *māshās*.

71. Also pronounced as *waqīyā*. It was equated with $1^{2/3}$ *istār* or 510 *jaū* or $10^{5/7}$ (or $^5/_8$) *dirhams*. A *ratl* was further equated with 90 *misqāls* or $127^{4/7}$ *dirhams*, which was equal to $24^{2/7}$ *istār* or *tolās*.

72. This is a characteristic *maund* of minute weights namely to weigh precious metals and drugs. It should not be confused with heavy *maunds* of Iran or Golkonda. Talqani, Letter no. 1 has an invoice of an ʿAdil Shahi *peshkash* submitted to Aurangzeb and describes the weights of diamonds and other precious stones in terms of *surkhs*, establishing the use of minor weights in domestic transactions. *S.W.D.*, pp. 23–4.

73. A cubit is a word obscure origin and probably an Indo-Portuguese corruption of the Portuguese word *covado* or cubit. See *covid* in Hobson-Jobson. In contemporary traveller's accounts the word was spelt in many ways as *Covad, Cobde, Cobdee, Coveld* in Hobson-Jobson; and as *Cubido, Cobides* in *Relations*, p. 88.

74. The cubit of Golkonda also bore an indigenous name as *hast* or *hath*, a measure of length 'from the elbow to the tip of the middle finger' (see *haut*

in *Hobson-Jobson*). That natural unit was based on a minor system as 8 *jaū* (barley corn) = 1 *angūl* (breadth of a finger), 24 *angūl* or 2 span = 1 *hath* or cubit, 2 *hath* = 1 *gaz*.

These natural units were in vogue throughout India. See *covid, haut* and *gaz* in Hobson-Jobson; Bowrey, p. 218.

75. *Relations*, p. 88; Master I, p. 272; II, pp. 167, 376.
76. Master, p. 101.
77. Ibid., p. 144; Bowrey, p. 71; Joshi, 'Textile'.
78. Bowrey, p. 71; *Relations*, p. 80, fn. 2; E.F.I. 1630–33, p. 289, 1634–36, p. 48, 1637–41, pp. 40, 42, pp. 103–4; Joshi, 'Textile', 2, *I.H.C.*, 1942.
79. Some of the important indigo producing areas were Kondaipally, Masulipatam, Nagalwancha, Sandrapatla, Game, Gelupondy (Jalipudi), Ecour (Ellore). *Relations*, p. 79; Raychaudhuri, pp. 10, 163–4; for cheyroot see *Relations*, pp. 35, 54–5, 77, 80; for yellow see, *Relations*, p. 54, fn. 2.
80. Raychaudhuri, pp. 163–4.
81. Ibid.
82. Bowrey, p. 71.
83. *Relations*, pp. 52, 64; Bowrey, p. 285, fn. 5; Raychaudhuri, p. 169.
84. Raychaudhuri, p. 170.
85. *Relations*, p. 64.
86. Census A.P. Map no. 6.
87. *Relations*, pp. 34, 37, 59, 61; Master I, p. 253; II, p. 113; Raychaudhuri, p. 174.
88. *Relations*, p. 34.
89. It may be noted that the Iranian chief of ordnance Asadullah Kark Yaraq visited Golkonda in the year 1046/1637. See Chap. 2, 'Political Imbalance—The Second Phase', pp. 34–41.
90. *Relations*, p. 79; Raychaudhuri, pp. 163–4, 174.
91. A vast diamondiferous strata existed in Golkonda where important gem fields (*khānī* or *gānnī*) had been discovered in the early medieval period. During the Qutb Shahi period, there are notices of diamond mines in the Godavari Valley, the lower Krishna Valley, in the *sarkār* of Guntur, Vijayawada, Golapally, Malavelly, Perthial, Ustapally (between Vijayawada and Hyderabad), Kollur, Kanuparti (on the left bank of Pennar), Cuddapah, which was referred to as *kān-i-almās* in Qutb Shahi documents and Gutti. For details of diamonds and diamond mining in Golkonda see *Relations*, Chap. XVIII, p. 30 fn 38; also see Shukla, M.S., *A History of Gem Industry in Ancient and Medieval India* (Part I—South India); *S.W.D.*, pp. 1–20.
92. *Relations*, p. 63.
93. Bowrey, pp. 30, fn. 2, 97, 35, fn. 1, 303.
94. Ibid., p. 107.
95. Raychaudhuri, p. 134.
96. 1 florin = 1 *Sikka* rupee = Sh. 2–d. $3^{1/2}$
The value of a florin has been indicated by Raychaudhuri as:
1 *rial* of eight = $2^{2/5}$ florins (Raychaudhuri, p. 131)

According to Sir Richard Carnac Temple the value of a *Sikka* rupee was:

1 rial of eight = $2^{2/3}$ *Sikka* rupee (Master II, p. 303).

This leads to an easy inference that a florin was equal to exactly a new or *Sikka* rupee of the Mughals. The *rial* of eight referred to here was the contemporary Spanish dollar.

While working out its pound value, Raychaudhuri (p. 224) has indicated a florin to be worth a little less than sh. 2 which is not correct as Sir Richard Temple has more correctly indicated the pound value of a florin as sh. 2–d. 3 ½ (Master II). For *Sikka* rupee see, Habib, p. 382.

97. Raychaudhuri, pp. 141–3.
98. These statistics too have been taken from Dutch sources given by Raychaudhuri, pp. 133–8, 141–3.
99. Raychaudhuri, p. 87.
100. Ibid., pp. 133, 138.
101. Raychaudhuri, p. 144; Tavernier II, p. 318.
102. *Relations*, p. 65.
103. For the role of middlemen, see *Relations*, p. 64; Raychaudhuri, pp. 11–12; H. Terpstra, *De Vestiging Van De Nederlanders san de Kust van Koromandel*, pp. 42, 103–14.
104. *Relations*, pp. 16, 91–3; Raychaudhuri, pp. 135–6, 185–6.
105. *Relations*, Chaps. XVI, XVII, pp. 64, 78; Bowrey, p. 72; *Hadīqat*, pp. 23–4, 204.
106. *Relations*, pp. 52, 54–5, 64; *Hadīqat*, p. 251; Master I, pp. 70–5, 212; II, pp. 160, 178, 200; Bowrey, pp. 107, 112, fn. 2.
107. Master I, p. 89.
108. *Hadīqat*, p. 251; *Relations*, p. 64. There are several notices in the E.F.I. and Dutch records as well as Persian chronicles and documents which indicate that Golkonda, on many occasions exempted import trade from various tolls and duties broadly termed as *zakāt*. Regarding the nature of *zakāt* and the controversy whether the Mughals adopted this institution from Golkonda, see Habib, pp. 65–7.
109. *Relations*, pp. 52, 54. These are the prevalent rates of duty on incoming and outgoing ships. These could be higher and in some cases were in addition to anchorage fees. Such duties could be paid in cash or kind.
110. Master II, p. 144.
111. Quality of goods was scrutinized by the purchasers who examined the details of the thread, fineness of weaving, and the casual curl in the texture and faulty articles were discarded. Master II, p. 149.
112. Golkonda architecture owed much to the civil engineers (*mi'mār*), architects (*tarrah*), engravers (*naqqāsh*) and stonemasons (*hujjār*) from Iraq (which was a part of Safavid Iran) in collaboration with their Indian counterparts. Such artists were further helped by surveyors (*massah*) and land measurer (*zamīn paīmā*). *Hadīqat*, pp. 203, 215; *H.M.P.*, p. 1092.
113. *Hadīqat*, p. 235. For the details of Kashi work in Iran, see Sana, pp. 54–6; *H.M.P.*, p. 1185.

114. Mosaic pieces of Kashi can still be seen on the western wall of the tomb of Neknam Khan. Small pieces of the same, which have escaped denudation, can be seen on all other royal tombs and in various parts of Golkonda fort. Similarly the enamel decoration can be seen in the interior of Hayat Bakshi Begam's tomb.

115. Husain Shah Wali, descendant of Sayyid Muhammad Gesudaraz of Gulbarga and the son-in-law of Ibrahim Qutb Shah, was the engineer of Hussain Sagar and Ibrahim Sagar water reservoirs. He died in the year 1068/1657.

116. It is interesting to note that the artists were permitted to inscribe their names on the margins of epigrams. These names can be found on various inscriptions, many of which have been published by Bilgrami.

117. Specimens of books calligraphed and bound in the Persian style and manufactured in Iran or Golkonda can be seen in Salar Jung Museum and Library, Oriental Manuscripts Library and Research Institute and the Manuscript Library of State Archives, Hyderabad, and many other institutions in India and abroad. Even at the time of this study there were a few families in Hyderabad who had inherited the art of Safavid bookbinding from their ancestors who lived in Golkonda.

118. For a detailed study of the economic aspect of slavery in medieval India, see Appadorai, pp. 313–22.

119. Herbert, as cited by Wilson, A.T., *The Persian Gulf*, p. 213.

120. Barbosa II, pp. 13, 125; Raychaudhuri, p. 165; Appadorai I, pp. 316–17.

121. Ibid., p. 165.

122. *Hadīqat*, p. 45.

123. *Relations*, pp. 38, 52, 60–1; Bowrey, pp. 71, 289; Master I, p. 454; II, p. 36; Raychaudhuri, p. 182.

124. Raychaudhuri, p. 12.

125. For the carpet industry of Iran, see Ross, *Persian Art*; Sykes II, pp. 203, 206; *Hadīqat*, p. 217; also see Sanai, pp. 150–71 and Ahmed Zaki Beg, 'Al-absita-wa's sajājid' published in *Assiqāfiyah*, Egypt, 14 March 1939.

126. For detailed information on the metal industry in Safavid Iran, see Ross II, pp. 2514–5; III, 2501–3, 2558; Sanai, pp. 265–73; Sykes II, p. 207.

127. Sanai, p. 270.

128. Pope III, pp. 2121–5, 2129, 2239, Ackerman, 'A biography of Ghiyath the Weaver', published in *The Bulletin of the American Institute of Persian Art and Archaeology*, vol. VII, New York, 1934; *Cotton in Medieval Textiles of the Near East*, Paris, 1937; Sanai, pp. 241–51; *H.M.P.*, p. 1188.

129. For detailed information on *naqqāshī* during the Safavid period see Pope III, pp. 1824, 1885–6, Zaki Muhammad Hasan, 'A'ttaswīr fil islām ind-al fars'; Zaki Muhammad Hasan, 'A'ttaswīr wa'l laūn ul Musawwirīn fil Islām' published in *Nawāhī Majidah min siqāfat fil islāmiah*, ed. by Abdul Wahhab 'Uzzam, Egypt, 1938; Sanai, pp. 118–42; *H.M.P.*, p. 1121.

130. H. Riviere, *La céramique dans l'art musulman* (1913); H. Wallis, *The Godman Collection: Persian Ceramic Art Belonging to Mr. F. Du Cane Godman*; Dimand, *A Handbook of Mohammedan Decorative Arts*, New York, 1930; Sanai, pp. 220–5; *H.M.P.*, p. 1185.

131. For the art of *muzahhab kārī* or the decoration of the folios of books under Safavids see *A.A.A.*, pp. 12–127; T. Arnold, *Painting in Islam*, p. 239; Sanai, pp. 72–7. For book industry, see M. Agha Oglu, *Persian Book Bindings of the 15th Century*, University of Michigan, 1935; Arnold and Grohmman, *The Islamic Book*, 1929; Sanai, pp. 143–49. For calligraphy of the Safavid period, see Mufidi, pp. 396–403, 511; Pope II, pp. 1732–3.

132. For details of the glass industry in Safavid Iran, see C.J. Lamm, *Glass from Iran in the National Museum Stockholm*, Uppsala, 1935; Sanai, pp. 274–84.

133. *S.W.D.*, pp. 12, 51, 53.

134. Fryer III, pp. 150–1.

135. Ibid.; Fryer has shown the pound value of Iranian units of weights as below:

'A Maund Shaw is	12	–	Five eights
A Maund Tabreze is	06	–	and a half
Charack	01	–	and a quarter

their lowest weight is a miscolle (Misqal) nearest our Ounce whereof':

6		an Ounce
96		a pound
600	make	a Maund Tab
1200		Maund Shaw, or the King's Maund

The above table shows a slight anomaly in the equation. The correct equation should be:

A Maund Shaw is	12	–	and a half pounds
A Maund Tabrizi is	06	–	and a quarter pounds

136. Further as Fryer has equated the weight saying 'Miscolle nearest our Ounce' and as he was an Englishman, the units would be in avdp.

137. Fryer II, p. 139, III; pp. 151–2.

138. Ibid.

139. Data regarding export trade of Iran to Golkonda is scattered in Dutch, Portuguese and English factory records.

140. Raychaudhuri, pp. 133–8.

141. E.F.I., pp. 1670–77; II pp. 134–5. For instance, the period of Mughal interference after the Deed of Submission and the defection of Mir Jumla, see Chap. 2, pp. 64–5.

142. *Hadīqat*, p. 226.

143. *Shajar*, fol. 392(b). The missive indicates 'Abdullah Qutb Shah ordered these purchases when Hakim-ul-Mulk was staying in Iran. Hakim-ul-Mulk was instructed to supervise the purchase. The horses and textiles were meant for the royal stable and wardrobe (*jāmdār khānah*) of Golkonda. The amount of 5 lakh *huns* was meant for purchasing garments of 'Abdullah Qutb Shah himself.

144. Talqani, Letter no. 20. There is no authentic reference to *Qirān* in contemporary commercial records. Nevertheless a *Qirān* was an alternate name for the rial. A *Qirān* was a silver coin, 1/10 of which made a *tomān*. See Lambton, p. 409.

145. *T.Q.S.*, fol. 127(b) and fol. 144(b); also see Chap. 2, 'A Balance of Powers—The Third Phase', pp. 44–7.
146. *Hadīqat*, p. 252; 'Abdullah Qutb Shah sanctioned a grant of one *hun* per day to him.
147. *Makātīb (Z)*, fol. 629.

5

Conclusion

THE POLITICAL, DIPLOMATIC, ideological and commercial aspects of relations discussed in the preceding chapters of this book lead us to draw inferences on the ambitions of regional sultanate such as Golkonda and its ties with large empires, namely, Mughal India and Safavid Iran.

First, it may be observed that although regional states aspired and struggled for their autonomy and were structurally decentralized in their administration, in some instances they did harbour ambitions to expand territorially and consolidate their power, in the manner of empires. When north India lacked a strong political centre and until the reign of Akbar, the Deccan sultans were more or less autonomous. This autonomy was not threatened until Akbar began his campaigns in south India and realized that the southern sultans would remain defiant and seek the help of Safavid Iran. The latter was itself a political upstart that sought to entrench a new religious and ideological policy while facing constant threats from its more powerful and well-established neighbours such as the Ottoman Empire, the Uzbegs of Transoxiana and the Mughals of Hindustan. The survival of Safavid Iran depended, at times, on distracting these three rivals to prevent them from allying with each other. Although the Deccan sultanates constituted just one component of Safavid Iran's larger diplomatic world and its commitment in real terms towards these regional polities was rather volatile, this alliance nonetheless engendered a calculated opposition towards Mughal Hindustan for more than four centuries. The conflict of the Deccan with Hindustan caused enormous losses of lives and resources. It was perhaps also the indirect reason why the Mughals ultimately lost their north-western province of Kabul to Iran at the same moment when they annihilated the Deccan sultanates of Golkonda and Bijapur.

The rulers of Golkonda, like other Deccan sultans, were nobles of the Bahmani court who had assumed autonomy. It was therefore difficult for them to get their dominions and their independence recognized by other contemporary polities. Safavid Iran came forward to recognize them in a

contradictory manner, as autonomous states on one hand, but as theoretical dependencies of Iran on the other. That situation prevented the Qutb Shahs from fully establishing themselves in the Deccan as the Mughals had done in Hindustan.

Growing political relations with Iran, adoption of Shi'i dispensation and the influx of highly skilled Iranian elites set Golkonda apart from the Mughal Empire. Although Safavid Iran made tall promises to the Deccan sultanates, there was little military aid and diplomatic support. There were even instances when Golkonda had to purchase diplomatic support which was equivalent to the cost of war between Iran and Hindustan. Given the limits of Safavid Iran's symbolic support of the Deccan sultanates (not to mention its more pressing military and diplomatic concerns with other larger states), one will find that the political convictions and diplomatic démarche of Golkonda were at times unrealistic and ambitious.

The second important aspect of relations was economic. The Qutb Shahs had inherited a very strong and highly productive agrarian, industrial and fiscal base from the Vijayanagar Empire. Local administration was farmed out to a nobility of foreign stock that also had mercantile interests in the Persian Gulf and other parts of the Indian Ocean. Powerful Iranian merchants played a considerable role in promoting Golkonda's overseas trade, while competing with the Dutch and the English. Golkonda served as an international bridge for the overseas trade of the East and the West from Holland to Japan and as such it was a very important centre for the exchange of international money. That exchange was both direct and indirect. Golkonda maintained a single currency, both theoretically for accounts and practically in its bazaar, which had a gold standard. Other polities maintained their gold currency only theoretically for accounts and used silver coins for exchange. Safavid Iran maintained brisk commercial relations with Golkonda. It supplied highly specialized goods to the Deccan while purchasing raw materials for its own industries. Iranian goods imported by Golkonda included carpets, silk textiles, brocade, books, Kashi tiles and arms, whereas Golkonda exported cotton textiles, dyestuffs, diamonds, iron and steel to Iran. Commercial contacts between the two states were maintained not only by Iranians but also by European merchants.

The third and most significant aspect of relations was ideological, which had a lasting influence on social, intellectual, and cultural life in the Deccan. Migrant learned elites, who had arrived in the Deccan from Iran, engaged in philosophical debates while encountering pre-existing modes of thought that had had a long presence in peninsular India. While religious treatises and commentaries offer a window to study intellectual ties, they cannot be understood in isolation, without the broader political context of these polities that sets this enquiry's larger framework. An Indo-Islamic culture had already taken its roots in the Deccan during the Bahmani period, which apart from Sunni, Sufi and Shiʻi traditions had also incorporated Zoroastrian and Hellenistic elements. These elements intensified further under Qutb Shahi rule, especially in the areas of philosophy, medicine, and administration. These innovations bore upon public works projects including the *Dār-ul-shifā* hospital, number of madrasah (schools), *caravānserāis* (inns), public baths, and a complex network of high roads that connected Indian Ocean port cities to agrarian areas—all of which benefitted the diverse populace of the south-eastern Deccan.

Appendix I
Evaluation of Sources

THIS STUDY OF RELATIONS between two political entities like Golkonda and Iran is based on sources not only from Golkonda and Iran but also from Mughal India, Transoxiana, the neighbouring Deccan sultanates of Bijapur and Ahmednagar and, European sources in English, Dutch and Portuguese. There are also native sources in Tamil and Telugu. Some of these sources have been directly used in this study and others indirectly. Here we introduce the most frequent and important sources, primarily in Persian, used in this study.

GOLKONDA SOURCES

POLITICAL HISTORY

Many historians of the sultanate recorded the political history of Golkonda, though some earlier works like *Marghūb-ul-Qulūb* have not survived. Among the existing works, three chronicles form the basis of this study.

Tārīkh-i-Qutbī

Tārīkh-i-Qutbī, popularly known as *Tārīkh-i-Elchī-Nizām Shah* by Khurshah bin Qubadul Husaini (d. 972/1565), is a contemporary work that deals with the history of the Deccan sultanates and Safavid Iran. The author was attached to the court of Burhan Nizam Shah and was sent to Iran as an ambassador. Shah Tahmasp received him at Ray in 952/1545. He remained in Iran for about nineteen years, until 971/1563. It is during this period that he wrote this universal history. It has one complete section on each of the five Deccan sultanates. After returning from Iran, he joined service under Ibrahim Qutb Shah and dedicated this work to him. This work supplies valuable information on the early political history of Golkonda as well as Iran.

Tārīkh-i-Qutb Shāhī

Tārīkh-i-Qutb Shāhī is the work of an anonymous author completed in Golkonda in 1027/1617. The actual title of the book is *Tārīkh-i-Sultān Muhammad Qutb Shāh*. It is an abridged version of a very elaborate official chronicle that was not approved of by the sultan. The author of the original work as well as the one who

abridged it were in the Qutb Shahi service and made their contributions at the instance of the sultans.

This chronicle refers to some earlier sources that no longer exist, e.g. *Marghūb-ul-Qulūb* and *Tārīkh-i-Mahmūd Shāhī* from which the author quotes long extracts. The author of *Marghūb-ul-Qulūb*, Sadr-i-Jahan Mullah Husain Tabasi, claimed to have obtained information regarding the ancestry of the Qutb Shahs personally from Sultan Quli Qutb Shah, which the author of *Tārīkh-i-Qutb Shāhī* has borrowed.

The work has an epilogue dealing with the ancestry of the Qutb Shahs, their descendants from Sultan Quli Qutb Shah onwards to the end of the first five years of the reign of Sultan Muhammad Qutb Shah. Historians unanimously consider the *Tārīkh-i-Qutb Shāhī* to be a unique and authentic source for the history of Golkonda. This work has been used as a basic source throughout this study.

Hadīqat-us-Salātīn

The *Hadīqat-us-Salātīn* by Mirza Nizamuddin Ahmad bin 'Abdullah Sa'idi Shirazi is a contemporary and authoritative history of the reign of 'Abdullah Qutb Shah from the beginning of his rule to the end of 1053/1643. It is comprehensive history, which reflects on Golkonda culture and the religion of the nobility, with frequent references to the Iranian influence in the court. It has detailed information on Golkonda-Mughal relations. There are casual references to Dutch, Danish and English merchants settled at Masulipatam.

There is no such authentic chronicle for the rest of the reign of 'Abdullah Qutb Shah and Abul Hasan Qutb Shah. For this period one has to resort to the Mughal, European or later sources. One interesting later source is the anonymous *Zamīmah-i-Tārīkh-i-Qutb Shāhī* added at the end of a copy of the *Tārīkh-i-Qutb Shāhī* (Tārīkh no. 680 OMLRI). This supplement is partially based on *Hadīqat-us-Salātīn* and partially on local traditions collected by the author during the eighteenth century. Though it is full of anecdotes, it cannot be entirely overlooked.

Among later chronicles, *Tārīkh-i-Zafrah* by Girdhari Lal Ahqar written in 1785 is also a sound work. It cites many documents that shed light on Golkonda-Mughal relations and an estimate of expenditure during the reign of Abul Hasan Qutb Shah.

There are many other later works of scholars like Ghulam 'Ali Azad Bilgrami and Abul Qasim Mir 'Alam that contain useful information. Similarly some books like *Dabistān* by Zulfiqar bin Azar Sasani, *Shuzūr ul Iqyān*, *Nujūm-us-sama'* by Muhammad Ibn Sadiq Ibn Mehdi, *Kashf-ul-Hijab wal Astār* by Sayyid I'jaz Husayn and *Mahbūb ul Albāb* of Khuda Baksh have many useful details about diplomats and scholars mentioned in this study.

CORRESPONDENCE

The letters of the Qutb Shahi sultans addressed to the Shahs of Iran are rather scattered. The letters of early rulers are found either in Iranian sources like *Makātīb-i-Zamanah-i-Safaviyah*, or in chronicles and other Golkonda works like *Tārīkh-i-*

Sultān Muhammad Qutb Shah, *Shajar-i-Dānish* of Hakim Nizam-ul-Mulk Gilani or *Hadāiq-u's Salātīn* of 'Ali Bin Taifur al Bistami.

However, there are collections of letters like *Makātīb-i-Sultān 'Abdullah Qutb Shah*, which include his correspondence with Mughal rulers and princes. Two very significant collections of correspondence of 'Abdullah Qutb Shah and Abul Hasan Qutb Shah are introduced here:

Munsha'āt-i-dabīr-ul-mulk

This is a collection of the correspondence of 'Abdullah Qutb Shah with Mughal emperors and princes, and Safavid rulers of Iran drafted by Haji 'Abdul 'Ali Talqani, the Royal Epistolarian of 'Abdullah Qutb Shah from 1655 onwards. The copy before us is in the author's own handwriting–preserved in the private collection of late Nawab Inayat Jung. It may be noted that a copy of the same is preserved in the British Museum as *Inshā-i-'Abdul 'Ali Tabarizī* (no. add. 6600). This copy has been very carefully edited by Sayyid 'Abbas Husain Musavi, son of late Nawab Inayat Jung, under the title of *Muktūbāt-i-Sultān 'Abdullah Qutb Shah*. This edition, which has not been published, has a useful supplement (*mulhiqāt*) containing replies to letters by 'Abdullah Qutb Shah, which have been collected from different authentic sources.

Munsha'āt-i-munshī-ul-mulk

'Abdul 'Azim Talqani, the son of Haji 'Abdul 'Ali Talqani, was the court epistolarian during the reign of Sultan Abul Hasan Qutb Shah. Its original copy in the author's handwriting is preserved in the private collection of late Nawab Inayat Jung. Like *Munsha'āt-i-dabīr-ul-mulk*, this too has been edited by Sayyid 'Abbas Husain Musavi, son of late Nawab Inayat Jung, but remains unpublished. This edition has been referred to in this study.

RELIGIOUS LITERATURE

Religious and ideological literature flourished alongside court histories and diplomatic correspondence. Some works are specialized, some focus on specific topics, while others are general and comprehensive.

Sirāt-ul-mustaqīm wa dīn-i-qawīm

This is one of the earliest works professing Shi'ite creed in Golkonda. It was written during the reign of and dedicated to Sultan Ibrahim Qutb Shah. The author's name has not been indicated, yet it may be pointed out that Iranian theologian Mir Muhammad Baqir Damad (d.1041/1631–2) contributed a work with a similar title. This scholarly work is an example of the transmission of Safavid ideology in the Deccan. It has detailed sections about Muslim theology, prophethood and Imamate from a Shi'ite point of view. It has boldly criticized the mystic concept of the Unity of Being (*wahdat-ul-wujūd*) and many other propositions of scholastic thinkers that were not in line with Shi'ite views. This work has been taken as an important source for Chap. 3 on the ties of religion and traffic of ideas between Golkonda and Iran.

Āyāt ul Ahkām

The *Āyāt ul Ahkām* of Shah Qazi Yazdi is an important manual of *fiqh*. It deals mainly with two issues—faith and forms of worship and social contacts and transactions—from a Shi'ite point of view. About forty chapters deal with the subject, first in the light of provisions in the Koran and then with reference and relation to several Imamiyah Traditions. It was written in Golkonda in 1021/1612 and was dedicated to Sultan Muhammad Qutb Shah.

Tarjumah-i-Qutb-Shāhī

The Traditions of the Prophet were recorded by many expert traditionalists, most of who were Sunnis. Shi'ite Traditions preserved in the household of the Prophet were called *ahādīs-i-Imāmiyah*. Much attention was paid to collect and complete Imamiyah Traditions during the Safavid period. The *Arba'īn* of Bahau'ddin Amoli (d.1031/1632) is a standard manual of Imamiyah Traditions written in Iran during the reign of Shah 'Abbas I. Shaikh Muhammad Ibn Khatun translated the *Arba'īn* with explanatory notes under the title of *Tarjumah-i-Qutb Shāhī* and dedicated it to Sultan Muhammad Qutb Shah. The manuscript before us (no. 10, Hadis Imamiyah, SJM & L) is dated 1024/1615. It was taken to Iran by Shaikh Muhammad Ibn Khatun in 1027/1618. He showed the translation to Bahau'ddin Amoli who recorded his attestation on its last folio. The manuscript was subsequently preserved in the royal library of Golkonda. It is an important evidence of Shi'ite traditions in Golkonda.

Usūl-i-Khamsah-i-Imāmiyah

The *Usūl-i-Khamsah-i-Imāmiyah* is a brief but comprehensive scholarly treatise dealing with the five fundamental principles of the Shi'ite creed: (1) Unity of God, (2) Justice, (3) Prophethood, (4) Imamate and (5) Resurrection. The author is anonymous till date.

The work was contributed during the reign of Sultan Muhammad Qutb Shah. The authorities to which it refers include the Koran, the Hadis, the sayings of Imams, Aristotle, Avicenna, Isamuddin Israili, Tabari, Ibn al-Arabi, Nasiruddin Tusi, Abdu'r Rahman Jami.

Sharh Jāmi'-i-'Abbāsī

This is a commentary of Bahau'ddin Amoli's *Jāmi'-i-'Abbāsī* by Burhan Tabarizi, written at the instance of Shaikh Muhammad Ibn Khatun. Burhan Tabarizi was the famous lexicographer who wrote the *Burhān-i-Qāti'*. *Jāmi'-i-'Abbāsī* was a manual to help Iranian Shi'is regulate their faith and everyday conduct. This commentary suggests Golkonda's learned elites did not delay in introducing these concepts into the Deccan.

Kitāb-ul-Imāmah

This enormous work of Shaikh Muhammad Ibn Khatun Amoli was written in 1058/1641 during the reign of 'Abdullah Qutb Shah. As is evident from the title, it deals with the most controversial subject of Imamate from a Shi'ite point of view. It touches upon every possible aspect of this polemic and has evaluated the views of all the important authorities. This work by a Golkonda scholar is quite exhaustive when compared to other works on this subject produced in Iran.

Faūzu'najāt

This comprehensive work on the issue of Imamate was written by Muizuddin Ardestani in Golkonda in 1058/1648 and dedicated to 'Abdullah Qutb Shah. The issue of Imamate has been dealt with from a Shi'ite point of view. It has chapters introducing the lives of all Twelve Imams. The treatment of the subject is scholarly and the tone of the author similar to a preacher.

Tuhfat ul Gharā'ib

Tuhfat ul Gharā'ib is a Persian rendition together with a commentary on the famous Arabic work *Masa'il* by 'Abdullah bin Salam. The translation and commentary is by 'Ali bin Taifur al Bistami. It contains some parables of the Prophet and 'Ali.

Nikāt-i-Dawām-i-Dūdmān-i-Qutb Shāhī

This small treatise, written by Husain al-Husaini al-Yazdi in 1054/1644, emphasizes that the Deccan sultans upheld the Shi'ite faith from the times of the Bahmanis. It has a section on the religious policy of Qutb Shahs and a section sanctifying the Qutb Shahs with reference to the prophecies of Shah Ni'matullah Kirmani.

Regarding works on Islamic eschatology with a Shi'ite viewpoint produced in Golkonda or imported from Iran, mention may be made of a treatise entitled *Dar Tahqīq-i-Ma'ād Wa Hashr-i-Ajsād* written by Muhammad Muqim bin Kamaluddin Husain during the reign of 'Abdullah Qutb Shah, and *Risālah-i-Ma'sumiyah* of 'Ali bin Taifur al Bistami. In addition to these works there are chapters in other larger works such as *Dānish Nāmah-i-Shāhī, Usūl-i-Khamsah-i-Imāmiyah, Haqq-ul-Yaqīn* by Mir Muhammad Baqir Majlisi.

Ideological and Ethical

Some of ideological and ethical subjects have been partially discussed in religious literature. The following works deal exclusively with ethics and scholastic philosophy:

Tuhfah-i-Shāhī 'Atiyah-i-Ilāhī

It is the Persian rendition with detailed commentary on the *Tajrīd* of Nasiruddin Tusi (d. 672/1274) by Zainuddin 'Ali Badakshshi bin 'Abdullah during the reign of Sultan Muhammad Qutb Shah to whom it is dedicated. Tusi's *Tajrīd* was a masterly work of scholastic philosophy and became a favourite for several generations of commentators and writers. Badakshshi's commentary is quite stimulating and by no means inferior to any of the commentaries on Tusi written in contemporary Iran.

Khirqah-i-'Ulamā

The *Khirqah-i-'Ulamā* by Ibn Imad Ruzbihan Isfahani is a work of encyclopedic range written in Golkonda during the reign of Sultan 'Abdullah Qutb Shah. Ibn Imad, who had travelled vastly and had contacts with contemporary scholars, wrote on a variety of subjects. The six volumes of his work deal with subjects such as:

1. *Tafsīr*
2. *Hadīs*
3. *Fiqh*
4. Ibn-i-Babwayh's philosophy of 'Being'
5. (a) Scholastic philosophy and theology
   (b) Prophethood
   (c) Imamate
   (d) Resurrection
6. A range of disciplines from ethics, statecraft to games, etc. This work has been used at many stages of this study.

Nafā'is ul funūn fi 'arā'is ul 'uyān

This is a famous encyclopedia of sciences and religion. It was compiled by Muhammad bin Mahmud Amoli during the eighth century Hijri. 'Abdullah Qutb Shah had it inscribed beautifully in the year 1035/1625 at Hyderabad. The copy from his royal library has been used in this study. It deals with many subjects and disciplines.

Majmū'ah-i-Qutb Shāhī

Majmū'ah-i-Qutb Shāhī is a small treatise dealing with ethical issues. It was contributed by an anonymous author during the reign of 'Abdullah Qutb Shah. It is preserved under the title of *Jung-i-Qutb Shāhī* in the Buhar Library.

Dastūr-ul-'amal-i-Salātīn-i-Qutb-Shāhī

An anonymous author wrote this small manual of ethics, extracted from *Akhlāq-i-Nāsirī* and other works, for the rulers and the nobles of Golkonda. Another such work, titled *Tuhfah-i-Qutb Shāhī* by 'Ali bin Taifur al Bistami during the reign of 'Abdullah Qutb Shah, is preserved at Oxford (Bodleian Library MS EB i 1471).

Makārim-i-Akhlāq-i-Tabrasī

This is a Persian translation of *Makārim-i-Akhlāq-i-Tabrasī* by 'Ali bin Taifur al Bistami in 1061/1651.

Risālah dar Akhlāq

This too is an ethical treatise contributed by an anonymous author during the reign of Sultan Abul Hasan Qutb Shah. It attempts at providing a practical manual of ethics.

MEDICINE

Some of the treatises on medicine are contained in works like *Khirqah-i-Ulamā* and *Nafā'is ul funūn*, which are more general in their scope. A few significant specialized works are introduced here:

Zubdat-ul-Hikam

It was contributed by Shamsu'ddin bin Nuru'ddin and is a complete manual of hygiene written in Golkonda during the reign of Sultan Muhammad Quli Qutb Shah. About thirty-five of its chapters deal with such subjects as (1) essential conditions for health (2) care during changing seasons (3) care about various parts of body like ears, nose, eyes, throat, liver, etc. (4) diet: including cereals, vegetables, sweets, liquor, etc.

Ikhtiyārāt-i-Qutb Shāhī

The *Ikhtiyārāt-i-Qutb Shāhī* is partially based on the famous manual of medicine, *Ikhtiyārāt-i Bad'i* of 'Ali b. Husain Husaini (d.1403), and was produced in Golkonda at the instance of Sultan Muhammad Quli Qutb Shah. It deals with simple as well as compound drugs. Another anonymous work, entitled *Makhzan-i-Tibb-i-Qutb Shāhī*, has been attributed to Golkonda by Dr. Zor. It is a detailed pharmacopoeia.

Tibb-i-Farīdī

The *Tibb-i-Farīdī* of 'Abdullah Tabib was written during the reign of Sultan Muhammad Quli Qutb Shah. It is a brief but comprehensive manual of medicine dealing with hygiene, therapeutics and pharmacology. It frequently makes references to Hippocrates, Pluto and Galen.

Mizān ut taba'i Qutb Shāhī

This is a complete pharmacopoeia of compound and simple drugs available in India and elsewhere in the Middle East written by Taqiuddin Muhammad bin Sadruddin during the reign of Sultan Muhammad Qutb Shah. The author also has detailed chapters on diets and general hygiene.

Risālah-i-Miqdārīyah

This has been written by Mir Muhammad Mu'min and covers the issue of weights and measures, which had commercial as well as religious significance. The standard for all weights, especially minute weights, was disputed. The main reason for this controversy was that the sixteenth- and seventeenth-century international bazaars of Asia had overlapping series of weights introduced by Arabs, Greeks, Romans, Egyptians, Turks and Iranians, Indians and others. This created confusion of values and denominations, and even of pronunciation. The confusion seriously affected activities in pharmacies, and commercial and religious transactions. Sultan Muhammad Qutb Shah, realizing the seriousness of this situation, desired Mir Muhammad Mu'min to exhaustively research and furnish an authentic and workable system. *Risālah-i-Miqdārīyah* was the result of that research, based on classical authorities as mentioned in its preface. Mir Muhammad Mu'min worked out a complete system of about 13 weights in addition to which he calculated the value of 49 weights of other nomenclatures or denominations, which were variably used in India, Iran or elsewhere in the East. He also discussed measures of length. This scholarly treatise has been made full use of in Chap. 4 on Commercial Contacts.

Risalah-i-Gilānī

The contribution of Hakim-ul-Mulk Hakim Nizamu'ddin Gilani was multifaceted. Three of his works, *Risalah-i-Gilānī, Majmū'ah-i-Hakīm ul Mulk* and *Shajar-i-Dānish*, have survived.

Risalah-i-Gilānī is a pharmacopoeia, while *Majmū'ah-i-Hakīm ul Mulk* is a collection of about 14 small treatises on the use of substances like tobacco, honey, and subjects such as prognostication and traditions. His *Shajar-i-Dānish* is a work of encyclopedic scope. It comprises 108 treatises, some of which were written by him while he collected others. These treatises also include political correspondence between 'Abdullah Qutb Shah and Shah 'Abbas II. Other treatises relate to pharmacology, therapeutics, theology, religious polemic, scholastic philosophy, ethics, etc.

ARCHIVAL SOURCES

The documents of Golkonda are scattered in different institutions. These documents are of different types relating to various administrative levels. Most of them are *farmāns*, witness deeds or deeds of transaction. A number of such documents are preserved in different family and private collections in the State Archives, Andhra Pradesh. Similar collections are still preserved with various Sufi families of Gulbarga, Bidar and Hyderabad. Such archival sources have been used throughout this study.

Another important source are the Mughal archives pertaining to the reign of Shah Jahan and Aurangzeb, numbering about 1.5 lakhs of documents preserved in the State Archives, Andhra Pradesh. These documents account for Mughal strategy and administration in the Deccan from 1628 to 1707 and thus furnish graphic data on the third dimension of this trilateral study. These archives also include Mughal intelligencers' reports on Golkonda. Such reports have been found crucial for the study of political and diplomatic relations, commercial contacts and even in working out an accurate map of Golkonda.

OTHER DECCAN SOURCES

The history of medieval Deccan cannot be studied without two chronicles: *Tārīkh-i-Firishtah* and *Burhān-i-Ma'āsir*, written in Bijapur and Ahmednagar respectively. These chronicles provide basic political history and also have valuable data on the socio-cultural and religious aspects of the Deccan. The biographical details of various intellectuals and learned elites of the Deccan are also contained in them.

Tārīkh-i-Firishtah

Firishtah was born in 960/1552 at Astarabad. His father was employed in the Nizam Shahi court of Ahmednagar. He migrated to the Deccan while quite young. His father Hindu Shah was subsequently appointed as the preceptor of Prince Miran Husain, son of Murtaza Nizam Shah. Both Firishtah and his father remained in the services of Murtaza Nizam Shah (972/1564 to 996/1587) and later during the reign of Miran Husain, 997/1589. In the year 998/1590, Firishtah went to Bijapur where he was appointed the court historian by Ibrahim Adil Shah. It was during this period that Firishtah completed his work *Gulshan-i-Ibrāhīmī*, which is popularly known as *Tārīkh-i-Firishtah*, a general and comprehensive history of India from earlier times till 1015/1606. The account of the earliest period is weak. For the early Muslim period, his sources are the same as those of *Tabaqāt-i-Akbarī*. Firishtah also made use of *Tārīkh-i-Bināakatī, Mulhiqāt-i-Tabaqāt-i-Nāsirī* by Shaikh Ainuddin Bijapuri, *Sirāj-uttawārīkh* by Mulla Muhammad Lari, *Tārīkh-i-Haji Muhammad Qandharī*, and *Favāid-ul-Fuvād*, etc. The most significant parts of this work for the purpose of present study have been the third section on the Deccan sultans, the fourth, fifth, sixth relating to the rulers of Gujarat, Malwa and Khandesh and the eleventh relating to the Portuguese occupation of Malabar.

Tārīkh-i-Firishtah has an excellent account of the Bahmani Sultanate and its five succeeding dynasties in the Deccan up to 1015/1606. Though there are minor anachronisms here and there which are indicative of weak editing, Firishtah is plain, direct and an unavoidable source. *Tārīkh-i-Firishtah* has been used throughout this study.

Burhān-i-Ma'āsir

Sayyid 'Ali Taba Taba, the author of *Burhān-i-Ma'āsir*, hailed from Iraq and had come to Golkonda during the reign of Sultan Muhammad Quli Qutb Shah while he was leading the campaign of Naldurg. Due to some reasons he could not stay in Golkonda and moved to Ahmednagar where he wrote *Burhān-i-Ma'āsir* at the instance of Burhan Nizam Shah. He completed the events up to 1003/1594. His son Abu Talib completed it in 1038, bringing it to the end of Battle of Sonepat in 1009/1600. The work basically deals with the Bahmanis and with the Nizam Shahs of Ahmednagar. It contains valuable information on the inter-state relations of the Deccan sultans, Shi'i beginnings in the Deccan, the early career of Sultan Muhammad Quli Qutb Shah, early Shi'i missionaries in the Deccan and Mughal aggression against Ahmednagar.

IRANIAN SOURCES

POLITICAL HISTORY

Iranian sources covering political and diplomatic aspects are varied. These works include chronicles, genealogies and biographical accounts (*tazkirahs*).

Matla' us Sa'dain

Kamal-ul-din Abdu'r Razzaq was born at Herat in 816/1430. He was called Samarqandi because Samarqand was the birthplace of his ancestors. His father Jalal-ul-din Ishaq was a judge and chaplain in Shahrukh's army. In 1841/1437–8, after the death of his father, Shahrukh took Abd-u'r Razzaq in his retinue in view of the standards of the latter's work.

In 845/1441–2, Abul Qasim Babur sent Abdur Razzaq on an ambassadorial mission to Vijayanagar for three years. He continued to be in active service of the Chaghtai princes from Shahrukh to Abu Sa'id and then retired to a private life. His only formal engagement was that he was in-charge of the *khānqāh* of Shahrukh in Herat till his death in 887/1482. He travelled vastly in Iran and its neighbouring regions from the Oxus to the Tigris and from Arax to Sind. He had living memory of the dramatic rise and fall of Qara Quyunlus.

His work, *Matla' us Sa'dain*, is a unique scholarly contribution to the history of Timur and his descendants. The three volumes cover the pre-Timurid and post-Timurid period respectively. The most complete and contemporary copy pertaining to the Timurid and post-Timurid period and containing an account of the rise and fall of Qara Quyunlus is preserved in the State Archives, Andhra Pradesh. *Matla' us Sa'dain* has been used mostly for the study of the ancestors of the Qutb Shahs of Golkonda and also for the ancestral background of the Safavids of Iran and the Mughals of India.

Safvat-u's Safā

This voluminous work, without a date of compilation, is based on the records and traditions preserved in the Safavid family. The author, Ibn Bazzaz Tavakkul bin Isma'il Ardabili, was a disciple of the Safavid household. The work mainly deals with the life of Shaikh Safiuddin Ishaq of Ardabil. It introduces the genealogical lineage of Shah Safiuddin upto 'Ali along with the mystic order to which he belonged. This work is hagiographic in nature. This is supposed to be a unique source on the dynastic origins and the religious career of the Safavids. Its abridged versions are also available in many institutions. One abridgement made by Abul Fath al Husaini is preserved at Salar Jung Museum and Library, Hyderabad.

Safvat-u's Safā had been made use of in the section on the ancestral background of the Safavids contained in Chap. 1 and 3.

Tārīkh-i 'Ālam-i Ārā-i 'Abbāsī

Iskandar Munshi was a court historian and a biographer of Shah 'Abbas I. He completed *Tārīkh-i 'Ālam-i Ārā-i 'Abbāsī* in 1025/1616. Iskandar Munshi was an eyewitness to most of the period covered in this work. He borrowed the early background of the dynasty from works like *Safvat-u's Safā*. He also gathered information from elderly scholars of his times who had memory of the early days of the Safavid regime.

Tārīkh-i 'Ālam-i Ārā-i 'Abbāsī opens with an introduction (*muqaddama*). The main work has been divided into two volumes containing several discourses (*maqālāt*). The first volume deals with the ancestors of Shah 'Abbas down to

Shah Muhammad known as Shah Khudabandah. The second volume is a detailed account of Shah 'Abbas I's reign. The description of events has been arranged in a chronological order, especially when the decisions and actions of Shah 'Abbas I are discussed. At the end of the description of some years, he has narrated and commented upon certain events under topical headings such as arrival of Elchis of various countries', 'clashes among nobles', etc. However, the details of such events do not mention specific dates. This renders it difficult to ascertain what part of the year such events took place. In any case, *Tārīkh-i 'Ālam-i Ārā-i 'Abbāsī* is a unique and rich source of Safavid political history up to the reign of Shah 'Abbas II.

Jāmi'-i-Mufīdī

The *Jāmi'-i-Mufīdī* of Muhammad Mufid Mustaufi Bafqi is a very useful Iranian source on Indo-Iranian relations. The author was born in Bafq where he received his early education in the year 1077/1666. He was appointed as the accountant of *Auqāf-i Yazd*. In 1081/1670, he travelled in various parts of Iranian and Arabian Iraq. In 1082/1671, he proceeded to India and reached Surat from where he went to Delhi and then to Golkonda. In 1086/1675, he went back to Delhi where he stayed for two years. In 1088/1677, he joined Prince Muhammad Akbar at Multan. Then he stayed at Lahore. In 1091/1680, he completed *Ausāf-ul-Amsār*.

The entire work comprises three ponderous volumes. The first covers the history of Iran from Alexander to Timur. The second deals with the Safavid dynasty from beginning to the reign of Shah Suleiman Safavi, and the third is a geographical account of Iran. This part is also known as *Mukhtasir-i-Mufīdī* or *Ausāf-ul-Amsār*, which is introduced separately below.

Ausāf-ul-Amsār

This is a historical geography of Safavid Iran with a complete gazetteer. In the preface to his work, Mustaufi has stated that in 1087/1676, while he was in Hyderabad in the company of nobles from various countries, he was surprised to know how little they knew about the geography of Safavid Iran. He, therefore, compiled *Ausāf-ul-Amsār* to enlighten contemporary elite about Iran.

Ausāf-ul-Amsār is based on such sources as *'Ajāib-ul-Buldān, Rauzat-us safā, Tuhfat-ul-Irāqain and Haft Iqlīm*, etc. He has furnished brief historical data and the geographical location of each place in terms of classical geography. Mustaufi has provided information on about 400 cities, 71 forts, 16 islands and 14 ports of Safavid Iran. He has given the names of provinces, districts, villages, etc., categorically in a tabulated form.

Ausāf-ul-Amsār is significant as it is a contemporary work of an eminent scholar who travelled widely. Although some of his sources like *'Ajāib-ul-Makhluqāt* are fictitious and Mustaufi is fond of including legends and anecdotes, *Ausāf-ul-Amsār* is nonetheless a valuable source, which can be used along with other contemporary sources. It has been utilized in the geographical profile of Iran in Chap. 1 as well as in the preparation of the map and note on Safavid Iran.

CORRESPONDENCE

The political correspondence of Safavid rulers is scattered in different Iranian, Mughal and Golkonda sources. All such important sources have been included in the bibliography. Yet there are a few systematic collections containing important letters, which may be introduced here:

Makātīb-i-Zamānah-i-Salātīn-i-Safaviyah

This is an extremely valuable collection of the correspondence of Safavid rulers from Shah Isma'il I to Shah Safi. The letters of each Safavid monarch have been edited in a separate chapter, and on occasion the replies addressed to monarchs have also been interpolated. The correspondence is international in character and includes letters to the rulers of the Ottoman Empire, the Uzbegs of Transoxiana, the Mughals of Hindustan and the Sultans of the Deccan. This book was compiled by 'Abdul Husain bin Adham during the reign of Shah Safi Safavi. It appears from editorial notes that it is based on some earlier work to which the editor of this collection added many more letters. He has also tried to arrange the letters in sequence and has supplied the dates in rubrics.

Makātīb-i-Zamānah-i-Salātīn-i-Safaviyah is identical to the *Nuskha-i-Jāmi'-i-Murāsalāt ulul Albāb* in the British Museum (MS, Add. 7688, also Or. 3482) of Abul Qasim Haidar Beg Iwaghli (Evoghlu). The contents of the two manuscripts are almost the same. The letters are generally in Persian but a few of those addressed to the Ottomans are in Turkish. The names of epistolarians have also been indicated. Most of the letters of the reign of Shah 'Abbas were drafted by I'timad u'ddaulah Mirza Hatim Beg (d.1019/1610).

The letters contained in *Makātīb-i-Zamānah-i-Salātīn-i-Safaviyah* and *Nuskha-i-Jāmi'-i-Murāsalāt ulul Albāb* form the basis of the diplomatic relations between Golkonda and Iran from the beginning up to the reign of Shah Safi. Letters addressed to some merchants like Haji Ibrahim and others contain information on Iran's commercial contacts with other countries.

Inshā'-i-Tāhir Wahīd

Muhammad Tahir Wahid Qazvini was a poet and an epistolarian. He was first a *munshi* under Mirza Taqiuddin Muhammad and then under Khalifah Sultan, the two successive prime ministers of Iran. In 1055/1645–6, Shah 'Abbas II appointed him court historian and epistolarian. In 110/1689–90, he became a minister. He died in 1120/1708–9. He wrote a history of the reign of Shah 'Abbas II entitled *Tārīkh-i-Shah 'Abbās Sānī* (MS 74 S.A.A.P. and MS 105, SJM & L). This is a useful political history of the reign of Shah 'Abbas II. However, more useful for the purpose of this study is his collection of letters addressed to the contemporary rulers of the Ottoman Empire, Transoxiana, Hindustan, Golkonda and Bijapur.

RELIGIOUS AND IDEOLOGICAL

Religious and ideological literature produced in Iran and imported to Golkonda was enormous. It was not possible to include a complete list of them even in the bibliography. The selected works of Muhammad Baqir Majlisi, Muhammad Taqi Majlisi, Mir Baqir Damad Mullah Sadru'ddin Shirazi, Qazi Nurullah Shustari indicated in the bibliography reached Golkonda. Apart from such contemporary sources there were the works of some earlier authorities like Nasiru'ddin Tusi and Sayyid Murtaza 'Alam ul Huda (d. 436/1044), whose ideas were furthered under the Safavids. A couple of such works are briefly introduced here:

Tabsirat-ul-'awām fī ma'rifat-i maqālat-ul-ānām

This was written much earlier by Sayyid Murtaza 'Alam ul Huda (d. 436/1044), a frequently cited authority in Golkonda. Its copy preserved in Salar Jung Museum and Library appears to have been prepared during the seventeenth century. This masterly work deals with various religious sects and schools of thoughts such as the Jews and Judaism, Christianity, worshippers of fire, *Falāsafah*, *Khawārij*, *Mu'tazilah*, *Murjiah*, believers in transmigration, Sufis, Imamites and others.

Dānish Nāmah-i Shāhī

The author, Muhammad Amin, was a great *mujtahid* of Iran and he was the founder of the *Akhbārī* school (Browne IV, 374). He had an opportunity to meet Shaikh Muhammad Ibn Khatun while the latter was in Iran as an envoy of the Qutb Shahs. Muhammad Amin sent the *Dānish Nāmah-i Shāhī* especially for Muhammad Qutb Shah through Shaikh Muhammad Ibn Khatun.

This is a very important work dealing with the various schools of scholastic philosophy discussed in Chap. 3. The author has also discussed the part played by Hellenistic thought on the development of these schools. He introduced his own Akhbari theory and discussed it in light of the various fundamentals of Islam. The author has cited previous authorities throughout his discussion. This work contains valuable information on the exchange of ideas between Golkonda and Iran.

MUGHAL SOURCES

POLITICAL HISTORY

The political and diplomatic relations of Golkonda and Iran were governed by their relations with the Mughals. It is not therefore possible to study their relations without looking into Mughal sources. Although Mughal sources are well known, some of the major sources have been briefly introduced here from the point of view of this study.

Bābur Nāmah

The monumental work of Babur provides ample information on how Babur established his sovereignty over Hindustan and how Indian potentates submitted their allegiance to him. The work also supplies information on Babur's relations with Shah Isma'il Safavi. The *Bābur Nāmah* has been used in Chap. 2 on diplomatic and political relations.

Tazkirat ul Waqi'āt

The author of this work, Jauhar Aftabchi, was Humayun's servant and was designated as ewer-bearer. He remained in Humayun's retinue for a long period. Although he does not seem to have been a scholar, he was an educated man who made keen observations in his memoirs. He was one of two people who accompanied Humayun on his flight to Iran and was perhaps closer to the emperor than any other person in his retinue. He recorded his memoirs of Humayun from 937/1530 up to the latter's death on 11th Rabi I 963/21 January 1556. Jauhar Aftabchi's *Tazkirat ul Waqi'āt* is a unique source with insights not just on Humayun but also on Indo-Iranian relations during his times. *Tazkirat ul Waqi'āt* is an important source of information for the discussion in Chap. 2.

Muntakhab-u'ttawārīkh

Mullah 'Abdul Qadir was born by about 949/1542 at Badayun and received his early education under Shaikh Mubarak Nagori. In 981/1573, he joined service in the court of Emperor Akbar. He was very close to Akbar and was held in great respect. He even led the prayers performed by the emperor. Mullah 'Abdul Qadir narrated events in the context of domestic and international policies of the Mughals.

Mullah 'Abdul Qadir completed this work in 1004/1595 and died the same year at Badayun. The second and the third volumes of *Muntakhab-u'ttawārīkh* are valuable sources for the sixteenth century, with important references to Indo-Iranian politics and court nobles. This work provides valuable background information and fills in many missing links on diplomatic episodes and events of Mughal history. It has, therefore, been used in Chaps. 2 and 3.

Akbar Nāmah

This is the work of Shaikh Abul Fazl Allami, who needs no introduction. He was born on 6th Muharram 958/1551 at Agra and was educated by his father Shaikh Mubarak Nagori, who was an eminent scholar. In the year 981/1573, he was appointed by Akbar as in-charge of *Dar-ul-Inshā'* (Chancellory). He ultimately rose to the position of *vazīr*.

Akbar Nāmah is a comprehensive history of the Mughals in three volumes. The first volume has been divided into two parts (*daftars*). Similarly, the second volume also has two parts, the second of which is a later contribution by Munshi Muhammad Salih, at the instance of Shah Jahan. The third volume is known as the *Ā'īn-i-Akbarī* and will be evaluated separately below. The first part of the first volume deals with the times of Timur until the death of Humayun. The second part of the first volume opens with the accession of Akbar and closes with his seventeenth regnal year. The first part of the second volume deals with the events from the eighteenth up to the forty-sixth regnal year of Akbar. He completed the work in 1010/1601. The second part of the second volume, contributed by Munshi Muhammad Salih, begins from the forty-sixth regnal year of Akbar and ends with his death in 1014/1605.

Abul Fazl was a scholar of high stature and intimately acquainted with the political affairs of Akbar's reign, in his official capacity in the *Dar-ul-Inshā* and as *vazīr*, and later as a political agent in the Deccan. Throughout his writings he is scrupulous to record all events with dates and maintains a chronological sequence. His consistent argument throughout his work is that Mughal Hindustan would never concede nor recognize the autonomy of regional potentates such as the Deccan sultanates. Abul Fazl has given an honest and vivid picture of Mughal military and diplomatic strategy in the Deccan. The work also gives an authoritative account of Akbar's relations with Iran. It has been used extensively in discussions on political and diplomatic relations.

Ā'īn-i-Akbarī

As introduced earlier under *Akbar Nāmah*, this work is the third volume of this work and offers a complete account of administration, culture, commerce and the nobility under Akbar. It was completed in the year 1010/1601. It has been used in Chaps. 2 and 4.

Tuzuk-i-Jahāngīrī

These famous memoirs of Jahangir entitled *Tuzuk-i-Jahāngīrī*, were recorded by the emperor himself from his accession until his seventeenth regnal year. From then onwards, the memoirs were recorded by Mu'tamad Khan who served as Jahangir's scribe. Mu'tamad Khan continued to write the events and read them out to Jahangir until the latter's death in 1037/1628. This work has also been referred to as *Tārīkh-i-Salīm Shāhī*, *Tārīkh-i-Jahāngīrī*, *Waqi'āt-i-Jahāngīrī*, *Kārnumah-i-Jahāngīrī*, *Maqālat-i-Jahāngīrī*. Jahangir himself assigned it the title of *Jahāngir Nāmah* but its most famous title is *Tuzuk-i-Jahāngīrī*.

The memoirs afford a graphic picture of the contemporary state of affairs together with Jahangir's sentimental responses to various internal and external events. No other work offers as vivid a picture as the one presented in *Tuzuk-i-Jahāngīr* of the trilateral relations between India, Iran and the Deccan. *Tuzuk* also contains specific statistics about gifts, tributes (*peshkash*) as well as some important documents on Indo-Iranian relations.

Iqbāl Nāmah

The above-mentioned Muhammad Sharif Mu'tamad Khan, scribe of *Tuzuk-i-Jahāngīrī*, also wrote an independent work called *Iqbāl Nāmah-i Jahāngīrī* in three volumes. The first covers the time from Timur to Humayun, the second covers the reign of Akbar and the third of Jahangir. The third volume runs parallel to *Tuzuk-i-Jahāngīrī* but is shorter. It is a valuable source as it provides some additional details that were perhaps discarded by Jahangir in his *Tuzuk*. This work has been used as a supplementary source in Chap. 2.

Bādshāh Nāmah

Muhammad Amin Qazvini migrated to India and joined the court of Shah Jahan during his fifth regnal year. Three years after he was appointed as the court historian, he wrote the *Bādshāh Nāmah*. It begins with an introduction describing the ancestry of Shah Jahan, starting from Amir Timur. The main content of the work covers the first ten years of Shah Jahan's reign supplemented by a *tazkirah* of court notables from his reign. This work is very useful in the study of Mughal relations with the Deccan sultanates, including Golkonda, between 1037/1627 and 1047/1637.

Latāif-ul-Akhbār

This work is also known as *Tārīkh-i-Qandahār*. The author Muhammad Badi' was a scholar of good calibre. He held the position of *diwān* under Zamana Beg Mahabat Khan.

The work mainly focuses on Dara Shikoh's expedition to Qandahar in the year 1063/1652. It is divided into three parts, the first of which supplies a valuable background on the Uzbeg occupation of Qandahar and the Mughal defence of it under Aurangzeb. The second part is Dara Shikoh's war diary from 10th Jamada II 1063 to 15th Zilqada 1063/28 April–27 September 1653, when he was on the expedition, and the third part deals with the return of Dara Shikoh. Qandahar was the bone of contention between Hindustan, Iran and the Uzbegs of Turan. Its contest had a bearing on Mughal expansion in the Deccan and thus on Golkonda-Iran relations. The work offers a clear insight and a unique perspective of this crucial issue.

Bādshāh Nāmah

Mullah 'Abdul Hamid Lahori was a student of Shaikh Abul Fazl and had received a good training in history. He wrote this valuable chronicle at the instance of Shah Jahan. It was simultaneously revised by Nawab Sa'adullah Khan Allami. The scheme of the work is as follows:

1. Volume I contains events of the first ten years from 1037/1627 to 1047/637 of Shah Jahan's reign.
2. Volume II contains events for the second decade 1047/1637 to 1057/1647 of Shah Jahan's reign.
3. Volume III contains events of the third decade 1057/1647 to 1067/1657 of Shah Jahan's reign.

'Abdul Hamid was too old and weak to complete the third volume of the series. Therefore, his student, Muhammad Waris, completed it at the instance of Shah Jahan. 'Abdul Hamid died in 1065/1654. The work has a complete chronology of Shah Jahan's reign and includes a number of sections on Mughal-Golkonda relations. It gives a detailed account of the events leading up to the execution of Deed of Submission.

'Amal-i-Sālih

Muhammad Salih Kamboh was the son of Munshi Inayatullah, the author of the renowned work *Bahār-i Dānish* and was himself a well-known scholar. This work is a complete chronicle of Shah Jahan's reign and was finished in the year 1070/1659. It also includes a *tazkirah* of nobles, scholars, physicians, and poets who were attached to the court of Shah Jahan. The author has recorded many political and diplomatic episodes. *'Amal-i-Sālih* is a work parallel to the *Bādshāh Nāmah* of Lahori and helps in authenticating facts from it.

Appendix II
Note on the Map of Golkonda and Iran

THE TERRITORIAL EXTENT of Golkonda underwent many geopolitical changes during the course of the Qutb Shahs' 140-year rule. Its largest expanse, shown in the map accompanying this book, was reached during the reign of 'Abdullah Qutb Shah. The boundaries of the kingdom, even during his reign, varied marginally under the pressure of the Mughals in the north and under Mir Jumla Mir Muhammad Sa'id in the south. The boundaries in the present map have been indicated according to the greatest extent of the sultanate.

The source material on the geopolitics of Golkonda is rather scattered and the best way to appreciate its territories may be through a statement of income and expenditure from the reign of Abu'l Hasan Qutb Shah, which confirms the division of the sultanate into thirty-seven *sarkārs*. Each *sarkār* is further subdivided into *parganas* as tabulated below:

Sarkārs and parganas in the Golkonda sultanate

Number	Sarkārs	Number of parganas
1.	Muhammadnagar (Golkonda)	22
2.	Medak	16
3.	Kaulas	5
4.	Melangur	3
5.	Elgandal	21
6.	Warangal	16
7.	Khammamet	11
8.	Devaraconda	13
9.	Pangal	5
10.	Mustafanagar (Kondaipally)	24
11.	Bhongir	11
12.	Nalgonda (Akrakara)	6
13.	Koilconda	13
14.	Ghanpura	8
15.	Murtazanagar (Guntur)	39
16.	Masulipatam	8
17.	Nizampatam	–
18.	Eluru	12
19.	Rajahmundry	24
20.	Sicacole	115
21.	Kanat (Rent)	–

The names of the remaining fifteen out of sixteen *sarkārs* as given in this income and expenditure document are listed:

Sarkārs of the Golkonda sultanate

1.	Siddhot	8
2.	Gandikota	15
3.	Gutti	12
4.	Gurramconda	12
5.	Kambam	18
6.	Vellore	8
7.	Tirupatur	10
8.	Udayagiri	6
9.	Chandragirl	10
10.	Chingleput	3
11.	Sarwapally	12
12.	Kanjivaram	15
13.	Trinomalai	11
14.	Gingi	8
15.	Vandewas	31

The above territories were the achievements of the period of 'Abdullah Qutb Shah and continued for sometime during the reign of his successor, Abu'l Hasan Qutb Shah.[1] The same administrative divisions were maintained by Aurangzeb and his successors.[2] The main changes in those divisions were made by the English East India Company after 1800.[3] The other *sarkārs* held by the Nizam were reorganized as districts after *zillabandī* took affect in 1865.[4] The survey maps of Major F.S. Scott, prepared in 1854, provide the extent of *sarkārs* in the Nizam's dominion as well as the district maps of the ceded *sarkārs*. This helps in reconstructing these *sarkārs* with the help of contemporary lists of *parganas* and villages prepared from the times of Aurangzeb to Mir Nizam'Ali Khan and the various treaties (*tahnāmajat*) of Nizam 'Ali Khan with the British government.

Entries

The entries of the names of *sarkārs* and *parganas* are based on Golkonda's statement of income and expenditure from the reign of Abul Hasan (1672–1687), Qutb Shahi chronicles such as *Tārīkh-i-Qutb Shāhī* and *Hadīqat-us-Salātīn* as well as *Dihbadih* of Aurangzeb's administration, *Savānih-i-Dakkan* of Mir Nizam'Ali Khan's period (1761–1803) and other manuscripts and documents. The names of places smaller than *parganas* have been entered exclusively from contemporary sources. Entries regarding ports can be found in the works of various European travellers.[5] There are a total of 238 entries in the map.

Boundaries

Despite obtaining the above divisions of *sarkārs*, a few loose ends remain on the boundaries of the Golkonda Sultanate. In the north-east of the sultanate the last *sarkār* is Sicacole, which according to contemporary sources had 115 *parganas*.[6] The northern *parganas* of Sicacole have been listed neither by the Qutb Shahi sources nor by the Mughals. Contemporary Qutb Shahi chroniclers broadly refer to the hilly regions of Kaling (which stretched up to Mahanadi in the north).[7] The northern boundaries on the eastern side have been worked out with the River Rishikuliga, Kalinga Ghat down to Parlakimidi, which may then be connected with F. Scott's border of Sicacole and Rajahmundry. The other *sarkārs* were Khammamett, Warangal, Melangur, Elgandal and Kaulas in the south of River Godavari.

In the west (from north to south) Scott's borders of the *sarkārs* of Kaulas, Koilconda, Ghanpura, Pangal determine definite territories. Below Pangal, the entire area of *taraf-i-karnātak*, comprising sixteen *sarkārs*, is not in its original form as the British made changes during the district organization of the Madras Presidency. Scott's maps of those parts gives us the south-western border of Golkonda but the north-western border from Kaulas to Pangal is less clear. From a detailed examination of the *pargana* lists of the *sarkārs*[8] of Bijapur Sultanate, it may be observed that even after the district organization of the *sarkārs*, the south-western borders of Golkonda did not change by more than 15 to 20 per cent, except immediately in the south of the River Krishna. At that point the 'Adil Shahi *sarkār* of Adhoni projected eastwards between the Qutb Shahi *sarkārs* of Pangal and Guttiand, the border between the two *sarkārs*, was somewhat unstable.

In the south too, the actual territories and boundaries changed time and again. If however, the Qutb Shahi statement of income and expenditure is taken as the basis, at least the sixteen *sarkārs* located down to Gingi and Trinomalaican be included in the sultanate, although the degree of Qutb Shahi suzerainty and control over these parts is debatable. The eastern border of Golkonda was most natural and ran along the east coast along the Bay of Bengal from Kalinga Ghat and Pondy in the north to Gingi in the south.

NOTES

1. A statement of Income and Expenditure, probably recorded by a Mughal intelligencer during the reign of Abu'l Hasan Qutb Shah, contains all the above details. *Zafrah*, pp. 173, 175; also *Dihbadih*, fols. 248(a) to 252(b); also see, Sherwani (Q), p. 655.
2. *Dihbadih*, Ibid., *Savanih*, fols. 67(b) to 90(b).
3. For the details of the districts ceded by Mir Nizam'Ali Khan to the British government, see Hollingbery, *A History of Mir Nizam Alee Khaun*, London, 1805.
4. Chiragh 'Ali, *Hyderabad under Sir Salar Jung*, vol. II, pp. 164–5, 177, 179, 182.
5. See bibliography for accounts of European travellers used in this study. Also see Sherwani (Q), p. 492.
6. See Sicacole in the statement of Income and Expenditure cited above; *Dihbadih*, fol. 250(a); *Savanih*, fol. 80(b).
7. *Hadīqat*, pp. 94, 144, 227, 242; Talqani, Letter no. 54. For the definition of Kaling, see Rao, *Kalingadesha Charitramu*.
8. For the lists of *sarkārs* and *parganas* of Bijapur see *Dihbadih* and *Savanih*, fol. 81.

Note on the Map of Safavid Iran

LONG BEFORE AND throughout this study's period, the physical borders of Safavid Iran shifted according to political conditions. Though Iran had distinct physical features, politically it was constituted by the migration of groups farther a field, who captured and lost political power in many stages.

During the reign of the last Ilkhanid ruler, Abu Sa'id Bahadur (716/1316–736/1335) the Iranian Empire stretched between 27°E to 73°E longitude and 23°N to 43.5°N latitude covering Antalya, Anqara and Sinop in the west. These limits stretched from Sinop to Tarabzon, Georgia, Gorganj to Peshawar (running below the Oxus) in the north, from Peshawar to Qandabil down to the Oman Sea running along the western bank of the river Sindh in the east, and from Antalya to Tarsus, Malatiya, Raqa to Basra, running south-west of the Euphrates and the coastal line of Persian Gulf and Oman Sea in the south.[1] Upon the death of Abu Sa'id Bahadur in 736/1335, the empire split into a number of principalities governed by local dynasties such as the Jalayirs, the Al-i-Muzaffar, the Sarabdars and the Al-i-Kurt.[2]

Those main divisions were subdivided into various dependencies like that of Chaupanis in the Jalayiri, the small Atabegs of Lur in the Muzaffarid dominions. In addition to the above, there were many families like Bawandis, Sadat-i-Marashi, Kiyas and Ishqvand families of petty principalities who ruled over Mazandaran, Rustamdad, Lahijan, Gilan, etc.[3] The successors of Abu Sa'id could not maintain and control their territories. Nevertheless the Jalayirid dynasty held its sway over western Iran stretching into Asia Minor beyond Dayar-i-Bakr. It was the Jalayiri province in which the Qara Quyunlu Turkman flourished with their centre at Arjish or Lake Van.

Lake Van

It may be worthwhile here to present a profile of Lake Van where the Qara Quyunlus, the ancestors of Qutb Shahs, first rose to power in fifteenth century Iran. Lake Van, which is located deep in the Western Zagros, is a huge water reservoir located between 42°E to 44°E longitudes and 41°N to 42°N latitudes. Immediately around Lake Van there is a strip of tableland with an altitude of 1,000 to 2,000 metres which is encircled further by a Zagros range with an altitude of 2,000 to 3,000 metres with two peaks in the north and south of Lake Van with an elevation of over 4,000 metres and a few passes in the south-west. Two large rivers pour into Lake Van from the eastern highlands. Very few cities developed in this valley. Van is located on the eastern side of the lake whereas Akhlat is in the west and Vastan in the south.

In historical sources, Lake Van has been referred to by various names. On the maps of Median kingdom, Seleucid domains, Parthian and Sassanian empires it has been indicated as Lake Thospitis or Darya-i-Nayiri. In the Tahiri, Saffari, Samanid, Ziyarid, Buyid, Ghaznavid dominions as well as in the Seljuq, Khwarazm Shahi and Ilkhanid empires it has been referred to as Arjish. The same name continued during the times of the Muzaffarids, the Timurids and the Safavids.[4] Hamdullah Mustaufi refers to it as Buhaira-i-Arjish (or the Sea of Arjish).[5] Nihavandi calls it Buhaira-i-Batlis (or the Sea of Batlis).[6] Muhammad Mufid Mustaufi shows Arjish in the Azarbaijan province of the Safavid Iran.[7] Arjish or Lake Van is now in modern Turkey, clearly separated from modern Iran by at least one longitude.

Safavid Iran

A map of Safavid Iran during the reign of Shah 'Abbas I has been given in the *Historical Atlas of Iran* in Plate No. 21. This bilingual map, drawn to a scale of 1 = 75,00,000 kms. has about 189 entries including the names of a few ports and islands. The names of large provincial divisions such as Iraq-i-Arab and Iraq-i-Ajam are are not given and the names of only 18 districts have been demarcated with bold entries.

This historical map of Iran has been reconstructed based on clues in *Ausāf-ul-Amsār* by Muhammad Mufid Mustaufi, *Kitābul Masālikwal Mamālik* by Ibn Khurdad Bih and *Nuzhat-ul-Qulūb* by Hamdullah Mustaufi and other contemporary Persian chroniclers. Based on these sources, the following provincial and district organization of Iran during Shah 'Abbas I's reign may be ascertained:

Provincial and district divisions during the reign of Shah 'Abbas I

Main divisions	*Subdivisions*
1. Iraq-i-Arab	1. Jazira
	2. Baghdad
	3. Khuzestan
	4. Lorestan
	5. Kordestan
2. Iraq-i-Ajam	1. Fars
	2. Isfahan
	3. Larestan
3. Azarbaijan	1. Daghistan
	2. Gurgistan
	3. Sherwan
	4. Talish
	5. QaraBagh
	6. Arran
	7. Irvan
	8. Kharput

(Contd.)

(*Contd.*)

Main divisions	Subdivisions
4. Taberistan (Mazandran)	1. Gilan
	2. Rustamdar
	3. Damavand
	4. Damghan
	5. Gorgan (Jurjan)
5. Khorasan	1. Abivard
	2. Gharjistan
	3. Badghis
	4. Ghor
	5. Isfarain
	6. Qohistan (Kuhistan)
6 Seistan	1. Seistan
	2. Hudian
	3. Qandahar
7. Makran	1. Makran
	2. Kich
8. Kirman	1. Kirman
	2. Jiroft
	3. Goasheer
	4. Sirjan
	5. Bafq

The above classification of main divisions and subdivisions is based on many sources that sometimes contradict each other, especially when it comes to a group of sub-divisions.[8] Similarly the names of Safavid ports have chiefly been derived from *Ausāf-ul-Āmsār*, which can also be identified and located with the help of Wilson's *The Persian Gulf* and its map.

Regarding the frontiers of Safavid Iran, particularly the eastern and western ones, it is not possible to show the borders for the reign of any single ruler, as these shifted quite rapidly. The boundaries demarcated in Plate No.21 of *Historical Atlas of Iran* have been adopted here. These boundaries suggest that the largest extent of Safavid Iran was reached during the reign of Shah 'Abbas I. The present map provides 300 entries indicating provincial and district organization, major cities, rivers and all ports.[9]

NOTES

1. Iran Atlas, Pl. 17.
2. The Jalayirs (the descendants of Ilkhanids) held western Iran between River Arax in the north and the Euphrates in the south stretching to Rey in the east and up to Roha and Raqqa in the west. The Al-i-Muzaffar governed southern Iran below Hamadan and Seistanin in the north, and the entire coast of Iran from the Persian Gulf and the Oman

Sea between the River Karun in the west and River Sindh in the east. The Sarabdars ruled over a tract covering western Khorasan and Seistan.

Al-i-Kurt reigned over north-eastern Iran from Nishabur in the west to Peshawar in the east; Tarmez in the north to Qandabil in the south.

3. *H.S.* III, II gives a graphic picture of the sway of these dynasties and the conduct of principalities; Sykes II, pp. 115–117; also see Iran Atlas, Pl. 18.

4. *Ausāf*, p. 115; Iran Atlas, Pls. 4 to 21.

5. Hamdullah Mustaufi, *Nuzhat ul-Qulūb*, p. 241.

6. 'Abdul Baqi Nihavandi, *Ma'āsir-i-Rahīmī I, II.*

7. *Ausāf*, p. 115.

8. The tabulation is mainly based on *Ausāf* combined with Fisher, 'Physical Geography' in *C.H.I.*

9. *Ausāf.* fol. 240 provides an exhaustive list of Safavid ports.

Appendix III
List of Selected Documents
used in this Study

كتابتى كه سلطان عبدك قطب شاه بنوابكبتى ستانى نوشته بود و چون واقعه محرر
روى بموده بود بنظر نواب اشرف درآمد

اى ذروه معارج نامى مكان نوله نوسده باردهان اسنان تو محامو مبادره قالاعقاد نعوى
ما في طوبت صورت برد تحفه وعالى كروبان ملا على استقبال آن زبد و هديه سانى
دلعات سوارق آن ديعالمو عالميان بريو افشاند دنيا زدركه ما ايمان جاه وفنا باركه فلك
اسياه اعلمجهريت كبوان دفعت كرد و دن حتت سناره حتم مكند رسور مريد دن علم انجار
سلاطين معم بالدين المبين واعضاد خواقين للمه بازارى الزرين مهر بهرسلت و جبانان
ما در دحنان ايمان خلافت وكشور سانى سلطان سلاطين لافاق برهان خوافين لعفارش
واستحفاق مالك مامالك اقاليم سعديا لطول و العرض جالس سوريا جعلنا جطبفته لاز
حر جمشيد فرموشيروان داد دارى خورشيد راى مكند استعدا ناصر دبانتخ وطور
دافع علام بدست فرجام سلطن لشور مهمار كارخانه دولت و دن مسدى كريمه
و نصل لله مجاهدين على الفا عدين جذيجان عرضه عالمواسط اس ومان رمزه بى دم
مهربا رسلمان تدد دمبزا ما حيدر طلوا رخامضرؤلاد مقدس بزاد حرمت سيد
المرسلين نفاه آن خاندان عصمت نشان طبين و طاهرين همبون اعظم وخاقان اعدلكم
صاحب الجلاله والعظمه والسطوه واللباس كار بوا فضل سلاطين معدلت ووصف اساس
بدء ثنا جلابق بماء خداى ستاس ابو المطفر ابو المنفور السلطان شاه عنا جالداله
نعالى بنائت سلطنته چ الشهور والسنن و بورسوارق معايله چ السماوت والارمن
مكرد ان و بعرض لبلباى دلت باهر مرجانه يكه الحمده شكرجنلله كه دروز دوز دلانواب
نخ سين وانا دسرع عرزاز صفحات رابات لشور سانى واضح لا بجات ولوامع لاببذ
دلو بح موفبقات برانى ازدوحات جباكبرى وجبانان طاهره و هوبدا وعلى الانفال
عاكرنفريت ماربورى دائال بيزو الكزه اسيمال لدخيان ارداب بعى معدران دد ونا
اعلاى خاندان براورده بالنز جام آباد رمعا ملز اعلى نابكاره ود انسقام ادسبط
دمين برهم وبير ماسيد بالبد ابلبد ازدن مساط ن بخت برزمين لكنشت ازدن نولد
سراج ازآسمان اكاروا هالى روز كاروا عاظم والوا هوه بار على الدردام بوصولا ين
ثناردت مدت امات مرام شكرگزارى دلوازم سياوارى فيا موايام دارنده واجمع

ازدیاد مراتب جاه وجلال واستداد ایام دولت بیزوال آن بکویذه خالقی لایلو ه بهار ازد ركه احدیت

مسلت سیمایند و بزبان صدق بیان مینماید الكویا می ارند که زمان درزمان از سهربلند

بفتح دكرما بوفیروزرسد ولعم ما فعل تحفۀ خرج میفرموده دم   فرد فتح ونصرت دكرت

ابن از برهاكه دلۀ جزوست   كا ركۀ هنوز دردتربت   دوسان وباكینی وكبجهان جبى

اندبیی وا حتمدات اینایت هت دكه جا عید ساحت ملا هواخزا هی واعلاهی الجدیده ولله

ازجایم نسایم اخبار راین فتوحات متعاقدۀ مولۀ نصارت وسوبنی داده اندوسلیهذۀ

ارادت وحسن اعتقاد ایشان نیز بزبكلهای رنكین فتح نامحات هیوۀ زبث زنت بافذ نزلیۀ

ابن اخضاص مراتبال وافزان ساهات میبود وباشد   دوسار كاجاكنی محروم   بوكرباد جنان

نطرداری   نا ناما بامع اطلال مرسالۀ دجون بعدازدحت معفرت ایات شوكت انبسا

عبۀ مقربان و دركاۀ خاقانی قام بلك مبین باخی اكند الله تعالی ذی فوا ولبوجنامۀ كارزفو

عواطف ساهاد كه هیتتشا الجلال ابن سلملۀ علیۀ بوده است بامثتو روافواف الزوودوتوضع ما

النورۀ یعنی باد بود فرح ورو دبجانت للدعفرانماب انارالله برهاند فرستادۀ بودۀ بوقی

موابع واخلال اوضاع طرف دسالك كه تفصل آن ازبعنی از دین بعمرۀ مقدس رسیدۀ

خواهد بود باعت بعویق ونا خیردوابذ بوذن منار البهسد بوذ وتجاعت دربغت ایات

عزت وسكوت انتساب سلالۀ الكرمی محذ قلی بك جفصدد مرجوم شارالیكۀ نزوكالت

صوری ومعوی رابتد دربه یاب صداق الولد سرا بات دوانذ ملازمت سوسوبعاۀ

بوبامۀ دبجنت عزت دكاۀ شارالیمارت ایام عزت انتساب عادت محمۀ

سكان خیرایتجامن سروبت خاصجلحمور ركۀ ازمعتهدان قدیم انجانبد ه دربابه

نا سیتلی مراج د این حسنظی نام بمنارالبهست وانذرانذركاۀ مان جاۀ بموذبسد

كه جدۀ وفتۀ در ركاب طفرانساب بوده باشندرانا بنذین محلعی لوازم حدمت   قابار

واقدام نمایۀ نزصدد ازمراحم شاها نامانكۀ نظرعاطفۀ كه هیتما ازجانبان جاس سرمر

ربا لذهی و فزما نفرما نی نست بابن خانواده قدیم الاراد ه سیدولیبوده اتبرفراد

داشتۀ سنتبال ارادت وصدق عقیدت صغر وكبربۀ سلملۀ علیۀ قوی داشتۀ جون

النار كحللۀ میجوبا سالیات دبتودوتفاصیل یعنی حزالۀ وصوح کۀ عرص بطلوبت زنقشر

رعت باهان شارالیما مبهر وصوح سید اللهبایت خنما ربدعا اولی بمود   جهان

اهنا انبات جوان باد   بهارعتت ابن زخزان باد نتاد اباد ملك نامقدار ب كبذۀ فا

نابا فجهان باد   بسوحانتۀ عزمت روی لارد طفرها بذبش نصرت همجنان باد تجمارللۀ

الکرام علیک علیهم ترایف النجنۀ و السلام

1. Letter dated 1038/1629 from ʿAbdullah Qutb Shah to Shah ʿAbbas I, carried
   by Khairat Khan. *Makātīb (Z)* ff. 314(b)–315(b), OMLRI, Hyderabad, AP.

سه رقعه از جانب نواب شرف بیادشاه مذکور مصحوب امام قلی بیك بیادبعت
کربایلجیکری نزد قطب شاه رفته

تا نهسوار انجمن نوابت وسپارالبق فلك زیران وربط غراوزمان باشدهواربهب
خوتخزام دولت ارجمندا علیحضرت خاقانی ظلسجانی درمضاربانك وجابانی وادهم
نزکام سلطنت پماننداان فارس عرض صاحقرانی وجالس اورتك کورکانی دربیلان تها
وکنتوریسانی بکام مراد درجولان باددرحقیقت مراتب محبت وجلال بنا وراكم مذکورطر
مهرکزین است بنا برفضویعبارات واستعادات الوده بیان نامختربزبان بینابی شرح جزا
ازو اظهار مینها بدکفنکوخیت بیادم بلیجخاموشی کاآكرب کتایم زخنیازائمه وحكم
القلب بهدی الی لقلب دران آنزا رجوع بقلب سلم نموده مکتوفصبیالهام بلرمسکریداند
اجون بوستنه مکتوب خاطر خطین است که بدستور ابا واجداد عظام جنت مقام درتضفیه
ساهل وفاق وتشید مبانی اتفاق اهتمام رودبامشرت عذب محبت موروثی ومع صفا
العت قدیمی ازجانب ثاك مةوجهت بیكا نكی منرق بوده بامدشد مراسلات مودت عنوان
کلسان امال دوستان خرّم ودربان باشد درهوقت رفعت بناه لایقالخدسرامامقلی
بیك بیا ولمحبت برم سفارت نزد سلطت بناه عالجاه سلطان عبدالله قطبناه كاطرنفر
اخلاص قندبی ولخصاصموروثی بدربن ودمان دارد فرستاده سید بدبن دوکلم
محزان مواد ودار ومجدد مراسم اتخاذ کردبیدمرجواآنگر ارجانب عالی بزرهین سیبو،
سلوك بوده هینه باجارسلامتی ذات قدسی سرایر واظهار مکنونات ضرحورشبد
نایر مسرت بخنن خاطخت ذخایر باشد زیاده جه بصدیع دهد توسنایام
رام وشاهد ارزو بکام باد

2. Letter dated 1043/1634 from Shah Safi Safavi to 'Abdullah Qutb Shah,
carried by Imam Quli Beg *Yasāwal Makātib* (Z) f. 306(a),
OMLRI, Hyderabad, AP.

كتابت نواب اشرف سلطان عبدالله قطبشاه درجواب كتابت مشاراليه

معجوب كلا او   كه دربابِ شأن اقوام خود باقاضي ظهير شاه بود ۱۲

مكتوب پرعون سعادت اسلوب بحضرت سلطنت وجلالت دستگاه بناء عظمت وشوكت دستگاه
حشمت ومعدلت اجناه پادشاه والاجاه آفتاب كلاه نهربار عالمدار لشكرفر سپاه نفاوه دودمان سلطنت
وجهانباني عماده خاندان شوكت وكامرانى المختصّ بمزيد العواطف من عندالله جلاله السلطنت ولعظمة
والتكر ولابهدوالعدل والعزو للانسان سلطان عبدالله قطبشاه علي الله تعالي شانه ووصل الى غايه
مابتناه كرمبني بخاربخت مزاج شريف وشعر باستحكام سوادِ مصادقت ودوستى بود بنظر كيميا
انزد رامده خاطر ملكوت ناظرا اتباط ومنت كافى ست داد اشعار بكر دربابِ رود بحذرات
اقوام عالمقام ان زمينه سهر بسلطنت وكامرانى بملك بان بان باراده توجه بينت بنا الحرام اراده الله
تعالي شرفا وتعظيم مدينه مشرفه حضرت سيد المرسلين وروضات مقدسات حضرت ائمه معصومين
صلوات الله علیهم جمیعین نموده بودناد وارد انصوب باصوب شاه اراده طواف مشهد مقدس
معلی نموده باتفاق سادات وجناب بناء عزت دستگاه سنا مصفور مرتضى سيادت وفضيلت
دستگاه شريعت انتباء مرصع الدين محمد قاضی معسکر بسعادت مستعدا بنفر سلطنت
همايون مرجعت نموده مورد اعزاز واحترام كرده بد معنوان ان دودمان بخلافت مكا را
عجلت مات ایشان مامور فرموده ايم وهرگاه اراده سفر جرايز مكه معظم بنا بمقضي المرام
روادخواه بندشد خاطر شريف رنجا بایشان جمع بما بابد رنامه محبت طراز قلبسده بود
كه بتجه الساده سنا بظفر مرتضى رخدمت محذرات سلسله جلله بوده باند در دینو لا
بعرض سابد كپادشاه والاجاه مشاراليه را طلع ده اما مرخص فرموديم كه روانه حديث
شود طریقه زودداد اكه خاطر مهر آکین را متوجه مطالب مارب داشته باشد بالراهات
شعور حقایق حالات فرحله مال وطها رىكنونات ضمیر محمد ومرهم خلوص عقایت واتحاد بود
هرگوشه مى دردیمب بأصوب شتیاست علام نمايند كه توجه حصول ان موصوف كرد رزیاده
اطاب نوقت بام سلطنت وعظمت حشمت معدلت والجلال بماناد

3. Letter dated 1049/1639 from Shah Safi to 'Abdullah Qutb Shah,
Sayyid Muzaffar Murtaza. *Makātīb* (Z) f. 315(b), OMLRI, Hyderabad, AP.

هو کتابٌ مِنْ محمدٍ صلی اللهُ علیه

جواب این کتابت پادشاه مذکور در اصفهان سعی حکیم الملک فرستاده بود در باب طلب

حکیم کریا ی یزدی

حضرت درفیع منزلت سلطنت و جلالت پناه عطیۀ شوکت دستگاه ابهت و معدلت انتباه پادشاه
عالیجاه نامدار شهریار کامکار عدالت انار خلاصه دودمان سلطنت و بختیاری نقاوۀ خاندان
دولت و مملکت داری المخصوص بزیاده معنایت رب عند اسم معزالملطنت و جلالت و المؤید و العدل له
و النصفه و العزه و الاستان سلطان عبداله قطبشاه علی اسرعالی شانه و اوصله الی ما تمناه
رافنون دعوات مجتبا انار عطوفت انجام و صنوف عنایت موالفت طراز ملاطفت فرجام
را محض بوجه خاطر خطیر دریا نوال و فرط تعلق ضمیر منزه و رضا شمال باعتلا معارج سلطنت
و اقبال و ارتقا مدارج دولت و جلال سلف و مهذی داشته
سپهود را ی مخالصت اقضا مصادقت انها مبکرد املکه درسولا انا نرد و حکمت منا فضیلت
کمالات اکتساب نظاما احمال حکم الملک در موصول محابت ببلدکا جهان پناه اشتریونه
بشرف تقبیل بساط سعادت قرین و مجالست مجلس هبت ابین مشرف و مستعید شده مورد
عنایات بلاها ایات کشت و شرح کردم نامه مخالصت خاتمه در باب فرستاده افادت و حکمت
پناه فرید العصری حکیم کریا ی یزدی قلمیه بود براینه ضمیر کهیما تا نیز بر موضوع الملحمه
مشار الیه را یر مساعنه بخصوص فرموده روانه خواهیم فرمود طریقه مصادقت و ودادا آتانکه
خاطر ملکوت ناظر ما متوجه هر یوسطلت است حکم سوی اویرا توقیف نموده فرموده بر خواهند
دوهی که بتوجه باند سعالیه سعایت و مجاما علام ما ییده توجه نما ها معمولا نه موصول
کرد دریاده اطناب نتذا انا اسلطنت و جلالت و قال لایزا لــــــــــــــ بـــــــــاد

4. Letter dated 1056/1646 from Shah Safi to 'Abdullah Qutb Shah,
carried by *Hakīm-ul-Mulk* Nizamuddin Gilani. *Makātīb (Z)* f. 316(a),
OMLRI, Hyderabad, AP.

کرد و زیاده اطناب قند انا بر سلطنت وجلالت و اقبال لا یزا...

کتابت اشرف یا دشاه مزبور دریامخوا جم محمد ابراهیم تاجر مصوبتی مُتیتنی

حضرت والا درنت سلطنت وجلالت پناه شوکت ومعادلت و ملک انا رخادضند دود مان سلطنت وختیارکی

سلطان عالیقدر نامدار شهر یارکا مکا رعالت انار خادضند دود مان سلطنت وختیارکی

عادت سوربان خا ندان دولت و مملکت داری لمحسوس عزیزلعا ہر منت عظمت مغز لمللطنت خلَّةُ

والنسوه والعدالة والصفقة والعزوالاسان سلطان عبّد وقطفا علیه نقاء لہ و وصل

الی ما ابناه واشراف عون محت انغار عمو قت انجام وجلالم حنیات مولفنصر و رسلاطف

وحام ارحض و رغم عا مر حضر ریا اول و رط نعلق صم رہر جور شید مال یا ر بقای حدیم

سلطنت واقبال واعللای مدارج دولت واجلال ان صا عد صاعد جاہ وجلال البلغ وارسال

داشتنی سنوید ادعونا بنجیکم بتزصد حصول این نا مولات انہ علی لک لقدر برسه ہذا اً بہای

رای مخالصت انصا سبکرد انذکا اندکا لمجهد والمذکر من توفیقات نا نشا هی آبی مجاری حالات

وسو انح بمہمات نجا بی رومفی مقدعای لاجاب و هموار فتوحات کونا کون قرہ حالا ادیا

دولت روز افزو نه انشروع کلی از بہات اطراف حاصل است و مخالفان دین و دولتکو

ومحد ملکشت از مرح از بعضی نظر مراحمت نقو سلطنت اید بوند واقع نده ار ہیح کرہ ضی

واقع بت محمد الرم حا لدجون درینو لاسعادت انار عنہ الاعیان والنجا رخوا حمحیا رہم

ولدسرحور حاجی میر سلطان بمزی کا انجا رصا حبا عبار ما ملک ہو وسرات و سنتہ مسار

قدیم بدین د ودسان و لایت نشان دار رسم تجارت مولایت ہند رفت بوا سطہ انجام بعضی

بہام متدئ دهتلم بندسیۓ جمائی بی و ولایت کی مسکن د استبدعر یا صوبی ہراز نکشته برحب

ر سا ندکه بعضی طالبات حنوای ازسردم دانلاایت ارد کہ دهنگام عزیمت اینصوب درا بسال

ان اهال بوده اند وجون ہرحام اسنعہ ابوده و فصل علام ان بدلنحضرت نیا فند لہذا درینو

جهته وصد و حصول مطالبات خود رواند انقصوب کرد بادونا ہر شیفقت شاہان در بارہ اینصار

ان نا مندهایوده سکوست متنمجون عزآرسال یافت کرد دهنگام وصول وکلا و سنوار رامیاد و

اعنت او ما مور ساحت دوفعی نمایندکه مطالبات حسابی کذار ہرکی استمدیا نندیا د عایدیکشته

مقضی المرام مراجعت نمایک موجب از دیا د مواد و د ادخواہد بود طریقہ محت آنکھ خاطر

مہر آکین ما راسو جدہ کو بنه مطلب مقصد دانسته هوار بار سال المرا سلات مسم یر سوانح

حالات و اظہاریکنونات خاطر شریف محد وسرام خلوص و انحاد عقیدت بود و هر کوند

نتی کرد درنصوب باصوادث استد باشدنی علایب بجاب اعلام نمایندک بوجہ عصول ان جمول

کرد د زیاده اطناب قنت انا بر ایام سلطنت وجلالت و علامت واجلال ما ناد کما نتی لہ بعد

5. Letter dated 1056/1646 from Shah Safi Safavi to 'Abdullah Qutb Shah, carried by *Hakīm-ul-Mulk* Nizamuddin Gilani. *Makātīb (Z)* f. 316, OMLRI, Hyderabad, AP.

6. *Khirqah-i-'Ulamā* by Ibn Imad Ruzbihan Isfahani compiled in 1046/1635.
Ms. No. 4, Kashkol, SJM & L, Hyderabad, AP.

7. *Risālah-i-Miqdāriyah* by Mir Muhammad Mu'min Astarabadi, a treatise on weights and measures. Ms. No. 127, Tibb, SJM & L, Hyderabad, AP.

بجهت ... که از کوگمران علی ...

(Persian/Urdu manuscript text)

8. Mughal Intelligencer's Report of Hyderabad dated 2nd Muharram 1072/
18 August 1661, conveying the news that 'Abdullah Qutb Shah sent
barrels (*tabla*) of fruit to Muhammad Muqim through the Iranian envoy.
Roznamcha Waqāi' Hyderabad, No. 3, SAAP.

9. Mughal Intelligencer's Report of Hyderabad dated 6th Muharram 1072/
22 August 1661. It conveys information about the Iranian *elchi*
and Sayyid Muzaffar, as well as preparations for war at Bhongir Fort.
Roznamcha Waqāi` Hyderabad, No. 6, SAAP.

10. Mughal Intelligencer's Report of Hyderabad dated 11th Muharram 1072/ 27 August 1661. It conveys the news that Muhammad Muqim, the *vakīl* of the Shah of Iran, sent two persons Murtaza Quli and Allah Quli to Budagh Sultan, the Chief Iranian ambassador to the Mughal court. The envoy also requested the news reporters to issue orders to the couriers to arrange for their safe journey from post to post. *Roznamcha Waqāiʿ* Hyderabad, No. 11, SAAP.

11. Mughal Intelligencer's Report of Hyderabad dated 23rd Safar 1072/
8 October 1661, conveying the news that the Iranian *Elchi*, Muhammad Muqim,
sent a gift of Persian fruits to 'Abdullah Qutb Shah. 'Abdullah Qutb Shah
called for the Iranian *Elchi* and favored him with a robe of honor, etc.
Roznamcha Waqāi' Hyderabad, No. 26, SAAP.

12. Mughal Intelligencer's Report of Aurangabad dated 6th Sha'ban 1073/ 7 March 1663, conveying the news that a person named Haji Muhammad sent by the Shah of Iran had arrived at Aurangabad from Surat with six Iraqi horses. *Roznamcha Waqāï* Aurangabad, No. 15, SAAP.

و قایع بلدہ دجستہ نبناد اور لگا باد

سلطان حسینہ

یم و در

۲۲ ماہ ہ

اگمہ حاجی محمد کس محمد مقیم کہ پیش از این از جانب والی

ایران بہ کلکندہ رفتہ از بندر مبارک صورت باش ارس

اسپ عراقی آمدہ بود دروانہ کلکندہ کنت سہ

اللہ بعد از دو یہ روز دو عدد دنلو حسب بحکم میر صنعفر خان

کمی نبام مختار خان و ددویم نبام غیاث الدین خان آمدہ

روانہ گردید سہ

13. Mughal Intelligencer's Report of Aurangabad dated 22nd Sha'ban 1073/ 23 March 1663, conveying that Haji Muhammad, a servant of Muhammad Muqim, had reached Aurangabad on 6th Sha'ban/7 March and proceeded to Golkonda. *Roznamcha Waqāi`* Aurangabad, No. 17, SAAP.

14. Mughal Intelligencer's Report of Hyderabad dated 16th Ramzan 1072/
25 April 1662, conveying the news that Musa Muhildar who was a lease
holder of a diamond mine (*ghānī*) presented three thousand *huns* to
'Abdullah Qutb Shah. It also notes that 'Abdullah Qutb Shah employed
English gunners and rocketeers and posted them at the Medak fort.
Roznamcha Waqāi' Hyderabad, No. 40, SAAP.

Bibliography

PRIMARY SOURCES

1. Persian Manuscripts

'Abdul Husain bin Adham, *Makātīb-i-Zamānah-i-Salātīn-i-Safaviyah*, no. 1214, Tarikh, OMLRI.

'Abdullah bin Nuruddin, *Tarjumah-i-Hidāyat-ul-Mu'minīn wa Tuhfat-ur-Rāghibīn*, no. 16, Fiqh Imamiah, SJM & L.

'Abdullah Tabib, *Tibb-i-Farīdī*, no. 763, Library of Nizamiah Unani Medical College, Hyderabad.

'Abdu'r Razzaq, *Matla-us-Sa'dain*, MS. no. 202, 203, Tarikh, SAAP.

Abu'l Fath 'Ali Husaini, *Safavat-us-Safa* (revised), no. 110, Tasawwuf, SJM & L.

Ahmad Ardabili, *Hadīqat-us-Shī'ah*, no. 49, 'Aqaid-wa-Kalam, SJM & L.

'Alam ul huda, Sayyid Murtaza, *Tabsirat-ul-'Awām Fī Ma'rifat-i-Maqālāt-ul-Ānām*, no. 20, 'Aqaid, SJM & L.

'Ali b. Hasan A'zzawari, *Tarāwat-ul-Lata'if Tarjumah-i-Kitāb-ul-Tarā'if*, no. 96, 'Aqaid-wa-Kalam, SJM & L.

'Ali bin Taifur, *Hadā'iq-us-Salātīn fī Kalām-ul-Khawāqīn*, no. 213, Tarikh, SJM & L.

———, *Minhaj-un-Najāh*, no. 184, Ad'iyah, SJM & L.

———, *Risālah-i-Ma'sumiyah*, IVASB: 1115.

———, *Tarjumah-i-Makārim-ul-Akhlāq-i-Tabrasī*, no. 11, Tarikh, SJM & L.

———, *Tuhfah-i-Qutb Shāhī*, no. 1471 MS EBI, Bodleian Library, Oxford.

———, *Tuhfat-ul-Gharā'ib*, no. 16, Mawa'iz, SJM & L.

'Ali Quli, *Riyāz-us-Shu'arā*, no. 253, Tazkirah, SJM & L.

'Ali Quli bin Mirza 'Ali, *Manhaj-ur-Rishād (Dar Usūl-i-Dīn-Shī'ah)*, no. 124, 'Aqaid-wa-Kalam, SJM & L.

'Ali Quli Jadid-ul-Islam, *Saïf-ul-Mu'minīn fī Qitāl-ul Mashrikīn (Radd-i-Nasara wa Yuhūd)*, no. 91, 'Aqaid-wa-Kalam, SJM & L.

Amin, Muhammad bin Muhammad Sharif Astarabadi, *Dānish Nāmah-i-Shāhī*, no. 54, 'Aqaid, SJM & L.

Anonymous, *Āhwāl-i-Sultān 'Abdullah Qutb Shāh wa binā nihadan-i-āshurkhānah*, no. 2, Tarikh, SJM & L.

———, *Dastūr-ul-'Amal*, MS. no. 2037, S.ii, Bankipur.

———, *Dih ba Dih*, no. 372, SAAP.

———, *Farmānhā-i-Padshāhān-i-Hind-wa-Deccan*, no. 357, Adab Nasr, SJM & L.

Anonymous, _Fazā'il-i-A'immah-i-Asna 'Ashar 'Alayhim-us-salām_, no. 122, Manaqib, OMLRI.

———, _Farāmīn-i-Shāhān-i-Hind-wa-Deccan-wa-Ruq'at_, no. 357, Adab Nasr, SJM & L.

———, _Hadīs-i-Murtazavī_, no. 1271 Kalam, OMLRI.

———, _Jama'-i-Kāmil-i-Irān-wa Hindustān_, no. 10, Tarikh, SJM & L.

———, _Kashkol_, no. 16, Kashkol, SJM & L.

———, _Majmū'ah-i-Farāmīn-i-Shāh 'Abbās Safavī wa Shāhān-i-Hindustān_, no. 382, Tarikh, SJM & L.

———, _Majmū'ah-i-Qutb Shāhī_, no. 78, Mawa'iz, SJM & L.

———, _Makātīb-i-Sultān 'Abdullah Qutb Shāh Ba Nāmi-i-Dārā Shikoh wa digar Salātīn wa Umarā_, no. 295, Adab Nasr, SJM & L.

———, _Makātibāt-wa-Murāsilāt-i-Shāh Tahmasp Safavī-ba-khawand kār-i-Qaysar-i-Rūm_, no. 292, Adab Nasr, SJM & L.

———, _Makātibāt-i-Shāhān-i-Safavī wa Shāhān-i-Hind_, nos. 296, 297, Adab Nasr, SJM & L.

———, _Makhzan-i-Tibb-i-Qutb Shāhī_, no. 243, Tibb, IAU.

———, _Mujmal Āhwāl-i-Salātīn-i-Qutb Shāhiyah_, no. 279, Tarikh, SJM & L.

———, _Risālah Dar Akhlāq_, no. 22, 'Aruz, SJM & L.

———, _Riyāz-u't Tawārīkh (Hālāt-i-Shāhān-i-Safaviyah)_, no. 293, Tarikh, SJM & L.

———, _Sirāt-ul-Mustaqīm wa Dīn-i-Qawīm_, no. 97, 'Aqaid, SJM & L.

———, _Tārīkh-i-'Abbāsī_, no. 104, Tarikh, SJM & L.

———, _Tārīkh-i-Sultān Muhammad Qutb Shāh (Tārīkh-i-Qutb Shāhī)_, no. 23, Tarikh, S.A.A.P., no. 85, Tarikh, SJM & L.

———, _Tārīkh-i-Sultānī (Hālāt-i-Shāhān-i-Safaviah)_, no. 7, Tarikh, SJM & L.

———, _Tawārīkh-i-'Abbāsī_, no. 170, Tarikh, SJM & L.

———, _Tawārīkh-i-Isma'iliyah_, no. 167, Tarikh, SJM & L.

———, _Tazkirat-ul-Hukamā_, no. 744, Jadid, OMLRI.

———, _Tazkirah-i-Shāh Tahmasp_, no. 302, Sawanih, SJM & L.

———, _Tuhfah-i-Sulaymānī_, no. 1, Nasab Namah, SJM & L.

———, _Usūl-i-Khamsah-i-Imāmiyah_, no. 11, 'Aqaid, SJM & L.

———, _Zamīmah-i-Tārīkh-i-Qutb Shāhī_, no. 680, Tarikh, OMLRI.

Badakhshi, Zainuddin 'Ali, _Tuhfah-i-Shāhī 'Atīyah-i-Ilāhī_, no. 25, 'Aqaid, SJM & L.

Bahauddin Muhammad bin Hasan 'Ali Amoli, _Jami'-i-'Abbāsī_, No. 18, Fiqh Imamiah, SJM & L.

Burhan, Muhammad Husain Tabrizi, _Burhān-i-Qāti'_, nos. 8, 9, Lughat, SJM & L.

———, _Sharh-i-Jami' 'Abbāsī_, no. 202, Fiqh Imamiyah, OMLRI.

Damad, Mir Baqir, _Sirāt-ul-Mustaqīm_, no. 237, Falsafah, OMLRI.

Dara Shikoh, _Majma'-ul-Bahrayn_, no. 53, Tasawwuf, SJM & L.

Fathullah bin Shukrullah Kashani, _Khulāsat-ul-Munhij_, vols. I, II, III, nos. 11, 12, 15, Tafsir Imamiah, SJM & L.

Fazalullah, _Risāla fī Isbat-i-Wājib-ul-Wujūd_, no. 61, 'Aqaid-wa-Kalam, SJM & L.

Ghulam Fath, *Tazkirat-ul-Mazāhib-wa-Ma'rifat-ul-Mazāhib*, no. 29, 'Aqaid-wa-Kalam, SJM & L.

Gilani, Nizamuddin Hakim-ul-Mulk, *Shajar-i-Dānish*, no. 39, Majami, OMLRI.

———, *Majmu'ah-i-Hakīm-ul-Mulk*, no. 306, Tibb, OMLRI.

———, *Risālah-i-Gilānī*, no. 75, Tibb, SJM & L.

Hasan bin 'Abdur Razzaq, *Shama'-i-Yaqīn*, no. 1256, Kalam, OMLRI; no. 95 'Aqaid-wa-Kalam, SJM & L.

Hasan, grandson of Sultan Rumlu, *Muntakhab-ut-tawārīkh-i-Salātīn-i-Safaviyah*, no. 431, Tarikh, SJM & L.

Hazin, Shaikh 'Ali, *Tazkirat-ul-Ma'āsirīn*, no. 21, Tazkirah, SJM & L.

———, *Tārīkh-i-Irān*, no. 105, Tarikh, SAAP.

Husain al Husaini al Yazdi, *Nikāt-i-Dawām-i-Dūdmān-i-Qutb Shāhī*, no. 445, Tarikh, SJM & L.

Husain bin 'Abdul Haq Ardabili, *Sharh-i-Nahj-ul-Balāghah*, no. 60, Mawa'iz, SJM & L.

Ibn Imad Ruzbihan, *Khirqah-i-'Ulamā*, no. 4, Kashkol, SJM & L.

Ibn Khatun, *Kitāb al-Imāmah*, no. 10, Manaqib, SJM & L.

———, *Tarjumah-i-Qutb Shāhī (Sharh-i-Arba'īn)* no. 10, Hadis, SJM & L.; no. 953, Hadis, OMLRI.

———, *Tuhfah-i-Majlis-i-Bihisht ain*, no. 10, Manaqib, SJM & L.

Ibn Khurdad bih, *Kitāb-ul-Mumālik wal Masālik*, tr. in Persian: Muhammad bin 'Ali bin Hasan, no. 557, Geography, SAAP.

Ibrahim Astarabadi, *Tarjumah-i-Risālah-i-Husainiyah*, no. 31, 'Aqaid-wa-Kalam, SJM & L.

Ivaghli, Abu'l Qasim Haidar, *Nuskha-i-Jāmi'-i-Murāsalāt ulul Albāb*, Ms. Add 7688, also Or. 3482, British Museum

Khalil bin Al Ghazi 'Ali Qazwini, *Safi Sharh-i-Kāfi (Kitāb-ul-Du'ā wa Fazl-ul-Qūrān)*, no. 36, Hadis, SJM & L.

———, *Sharh-i-Kāfi Kūlaynī*, no. 464, Hadis, OMLRI.

Khurshah bin Qubad al Husaini, *Tārīkh-i-Elchī-i-Nizām Shāh*, no. 71, Tarikh, SJM & L.

Lahiji, Abdur Razzaq, *Gauhar-i-Mūrād*, no. 244, Falsafah, OMLRI.

Mahmud Bin 'Abdullah, *Khulāsah-i-'Abbāsī (Hālāt-i-Shāh 'Abbās Safawī)*, no. 237, Tarikh, SJM & L.

Majlisi, Muhammad Baqir, *'Ayn-ul-Hayāt*, no. 65, Mawa'iz, SJM & L.; no. 422, Mawa'iz, OMLRI.

———, *Hadīs-i-Imāmiyah*, no. 29, Ad'iyah, SJM & L.

———, *Haqq-ul-Yaqīn*, no. 51, 'Aqaid-wa-Kalam, SJM & L.

———, *Hulyat-ul-Mūttaqīn*, no. 19, Hadis, SJM & L.

———, *Isbāt-i-'Aqaid-i-Asna 'Ashahriah*, no. 4, 'Aqaid-wa-Kalam, SJM & L.

———, *Jila-ul-'Uyūn*, no. 16, Sayr, SJM & L.

———, *Risālah Dar Bāb-i-Sūbūt-i-Ghibat-wa-Zūhūr-i-Hazrat-i-Sāhib-uz-zamān*, no. 67, 'Aqaid-wa-Kalam, SJM & L.

———, *Risālah fī Ikhtiyārāt-us-sa'at wal Āyyām wal Tawārīkh*, no. 28, Hadis, SJM & L.

Majlisi, Muhammad Baqir, *Risālah-i-Fiqh*, no. 47, Fiqh Imamiah, SJM & L.

———, *Sharh mā lā yahzar ul-Faqih*, no. 826, Hadis, OMLRI.

———, *Tarjumah-i-Āhādīs (dar mūnqabat-i-Chahārdah Ma'sūmīn)*, no. 12, Manaqib, SJM & L.

———, *Tarjumah-i-Hadis-i-Tauhīd-i-Mufazzil bin 'Ūmar*, no. 5, Hadis, SJM & L.

———, *Tazkirat-ul-Āimmah*, no. 11, Manaqib, SJM & L.

———, *Ūsul-ul-Fūsūl-ul-Tauzih (Rad-i-Sufiyah)*, no. 12, 'Aqaid-wa-Kalam, SJM & L.

Majlisi, Muhammad Taqi, *Hadiqat-ul-Mūttaqīn fī Ma' rifat-Āhkāmu'ddin*, no. 33, Fiqh Imamiah (Usul), SJM & L.

———, *Lawāmi'-i-Sāhib Qirānī (Tarjumah-i-Rauzat-ul-Muttaqīn)*, no. 39, Hadis, SJM & L.

———, *Risālah-i-Sāhib Qirānī (Tarjumah-i-Rauzat-ul-Muttaqīn)*, no. 39, Hadis, SJM & L.

———, *Risālah-i-Falāh*, no. 27, Hadis, SJM & L.

Mir Muhammad Mu'min, *Risālah-i-Miqdāriyah*, no. 127, Tibb, SJM & L.

———, *Ikhtiyārāt-i-Qutb Shahī*, no. 13, Tibb, SJM & L.

Muhammad bin Ishaq, *Manhaj-ul-Fāzilīn (fī Isbāt-ul-Imāmat)*, no. 125, 'Aqaid-wa-Kalam, SJM & L.

Muhammad bin Mahmud Amoli, *Nafāyis-ul-Fūnūn fī 'Arāyis-ul-'Ūyun*, no. 2, Majma'-ul-'ulum, SJM & L.

Muhammad Jalulu'ddin Taba Taba, *Tauqi'at-i-Kisravī*, no. 75, Adab Nasr, SJM & L.

Muhammad Muqim, *Dar Tahqīq-i-Ma'ād wa Hashr-i-Ājsād*, no. 1792 MS EB, Bodleian, Oxford

Muhammad Saleh, *Tarjumah-i-'Uyūn-i-Ākhbār-ur-Rizā*, no. 8, Hadis, SJM & L.

Muhammad Shah Jami, *Tarjumah-i-Kūk Shāstar*, no. 208 Tibb, SJM & L.

Mu'in Al-Yazdi, *Tārīkh-i-Salātīn-i-Irān (Āl-i-Muzaffar-i-Fars)*, no. 83, Tarikh, SJM & L.

Mu'izuddin Muhammad, *Ānis-us-salihīn*, no. 21, Ad'iyah, SJM & L.

Mu'izuddin Ardastani, *Faūzu'najāt*, nos. 1305 to 1308 MS XIV, Bankipur; nos. 117 to 119 MS, Buhar Library.

Munim Khan Hamadani, *Sawānih-i-Dakkan*, no. 22, SAAP.

Mustaufi, Muhammad Mufid, *Ausāf-ul-Āmsār*, no. 999, Geography, SAAP.

Qasim Tabasi, *Inshā'-i-Qasim Tabasī*, no. 31, Adab Nasr, SJM & L.

Qazvini, Muhammad Amin, *Pādshah Nāmah*, no. 85, Tarikh, SAAP.

Raziuddin Muhammad, *Sahifat-ul-Mūttaqīn wa Minhāj-ul-Yaqīn dar Zikr-i-Imāmat*, no. 261, Sier, OMLRI.

Saib, Mirza Muhammad 'Ali Tabrizi, *Jang Nāmah-i-Shah 'Abbās Safavī*, no. 1136, Tarikh, SAAP.

Saifpur Fatimi (Tr.), *Gulzār-i-Adabiyāt-i-Irān dar 'Ahd-i-Salātīn-i-Safaviyah*, no. 248, Takirah, OMLRI.

Shafiq, Lachminarayan, *Gūl-i-Ra'nā*, no. 38, Tazkirah, SJM & L.

Shah Qazi Yazdi, *Sawami'-ul-Malakūt*, no. 130, Ad'iyah, SJM & L.

———, *Tarjumah-i-Fiqh-ur-Rizā*, no. 15, Fiqh, SJM & L.

———, *Tarjumah-i-Tafsīr-i-Āyāt-ul-Āhkām*, no. 4, Tafsir, SJM & L.

Shah Raju, Sayyid Raziuddin, *Zād-ul-Mawāhhidīn* comp. by Husain bin Hasan, no. 271, I.A.U.

Shamsuddin 'Ali, *Tarjumah-i-Tazkirat-ul-Kuhhālīn*, no. 49, Tibb, SJM & L.

Shamsuddin bin Nuruddin, *Zubdat-ul-Hikam*, no. 277, Tibb, SJM & L.

Sharif, Muhammad Ma'sum Isfahani, *Shams-ul-Ittisāb fī Tahqīq-i-Nasab-i-Sayyid-ul-Āqtāb*, no. 25, Tarajim Sufiah, SJM & L.

Tabrizi, 'Abdul 'Ali, *Inshā'*, no. 6600, Add., B.M.

Tahir Wahid, Mirza Muhammad, *Tārīkh-i-Shāh 'Abbās Sānī*, No. 105, Tarikh, SJM & L; no. 74, S.A.A.P.

———, *Munshā'at-i-Tāhir Wahīd*, no. 506, SAAP.

Tahmasp, Shah Safavi, *Sawād-i-Raqam-i-Shāh Tahmasp*, no. 175, Adab Nasr, SJM & L.

Talqani, 'Abdul 'Azim Talqani, *Munshā'at-i-Munshī-ul-Mulk 'Abdul Azim*, Personal collection of Nawab Inayat Jung, Hyderabad.

Talqani, Haji 'Abdul 'Ali, *Munshā'at-i-Dabīr-ul-Mulk Hajī 'Abdul 'Alī Tālqānī*, Personal collection of Nawab Inayat Jung, Hyderabad; also no. 15, Adab Nasr, SJM & L.

Taqiu'ddin Muhammad Amoli, *Mīzān-ut-tabā'i Qutb Shāhī*, no. 266, Tibb, SJM & L.

Va'iz Kashifi Kamaluddin Husain, *Ārrisālat-ul-Auliyah fīl Āhādis-un-Nabawiyah*, no. 16, Hadis, SJM & L.

Va'iz Kashifi Kamaluddin Husain, *Rauzat-us-shuhada*, no. 254, Tarikh, SJM & L.

Wajih, Asadullah, *Diwān-i-Wajih*, no. 511, Adab Nasr, SJM & L.

2. Arabic Manuscripts

Anonymous, *Majmū'ah-i-Rasā'il-i-Hukamā*, no. 371, Falsafah, OMLRI.

Kashi, Muhammad Muhsin, *Al Haqāyaq*, no. 392, Mawa'iz, OMLRI.

———, *Minhāj-un-Najah*, no. 1182, Kalam, OMLRI.

———, *Qurrat-ul-'Üyūn fī A'izz-ul-Fūnūn (Al Miqālāt Ba Maknūn ul-Kalimāt)*, no. 1230, Kalam, OMLRI.

SECONDARY SOURCES

BOOKS

Persian

'Abdu'r Rahman, Mirza, *Tārīkh-i-'Ulama-i-Khorāsān Mashhad*, 1341/1823.

'Abdu'r Razzaq, *Naqshah-i-Irān*, Tehran, n.d.

Abu'l Fazl, *Ā'īn-i-Akbarī*, Lucknow, 1882.

———, *Akbar Nāmah*, Calcutta, 1873–87.

Ahmad, K. Nizamuddin, *Tabaqāt-i-Akbarī*, 1927.

Ahqar, Girdhari Lal, *Tārīkh-i-Zafrah* ed. Qazi Talammuz Husain, Gorakhpur, 1927.

Ālī, Ni'mat Khan, *Wāqi'āt-i-Ni'mat Khān Ālī (Waqāi' Golcondā)*, Lucknow, 1928.

Ardabili, Ahmad, *Sharh-i-Irshād-ul-Azhān*, Iran, 1272/1856.

Aurangzeb 'Alamgir, *Ruq'āt-i-'Ālamgir*, ed. Najib Ashraf Naqvi Sayyid, Azamgarh, 1930.

Azad Ghulam 'Ali Bilgirami, *Khazānah-i-'Amirah*, Kanpur, 1340/1822.

———, *Mā'asir-ul-Kirām (Sarv-i-Azād)*, vol. II, Agra, 1910.

Badayuni, 'Abdul Qadir, *Muntakhab-ut Tawārīkh*, eds., Ahmad 'Ali and Lees, Bib. Ind. Calcutta, 1865–68.

Bahar, Muhammad Taqi, *Sabk-Shināsī*, 3 vols., Tehran, 1940–44.

Bayazid Biyat, *Tazkirah-i-Humāyūn wa Akbar*, ed. M. Hidayat Husayn Bib. Ind. Calcutta, 1941.

Bhandari Sujan Rai, *Khulāsat-ut-Tawārīkh*, ed. Zafar Hasan, Delhi, 1918.

Dawwani, Jalaluddin, *Akhlāq-i-Jalālī*, Lucknow, 1203/1789.

Fazl ullah Rashiduddin, *Jāmi' ut Tawārīkh*, ed. E. Blochet, London, 1911.

Firishtah Muhammad Qasim, *Gulshan-i-Ibrāhīmī (Tārīkh-i-Firishtah)*, Bombay, 1832.

Hasan, Aqa, *Ahsan-ut-Tawārīkh*, Balrampur, 1852.

Hasan, Zaki Muhammad, *Sanāi' Irān*, Tehran, 1320.

Ibn Bazzaz, Tawakkul bin Isma'il Ardabili, *Safwat-us-Safā*, Bombay, 1329/1911.

Iskandar Beg Munshi, *Tārīkh-i 'Ālam-i Ārā-i 'Abbāsī*, Tehran, 1314/1896.

Jahangir, *Tuzuk-i-Jahāngīrī*, Lucknow, n.d.

Juwayri 'Alauddin 'Ata Malik, *Tārīkh-i-Jahān Gushā*, Leiden & London, 1912/1916/1937.

Kashifi Husain Va'iz, *Akhlāq-i-Mūhsinī*, ed. Muhammad Qamaru'ddin, Kanpur, 1323.

Kazim, Mirza Muhammad, *'Alamgīr Nāmah*, Calcutta, 1865–73.

Khan, Khafi, *Muntakhab-ul-Lūbāb*, Calcutta, 1869.

Khan, Shah Nawaz, *Ma'āsir-ul-Umarā* ed. Abd ur Rahim, 3 vols., Calcutta, 1888.

Khawand Amir Ghiyas uddin, *Habīb-us-Siyār*, 3 vols., Bombay, 1857.

Lahori, 'Abdul Hamid, *Pādshāh Nāmah*, Calcutta, 1867–8.

Lutf 'Ali, *Ātishkadah-i-Azar*, Bombay, 1299/1882.

Majlisi Muhammad Baqir, *Hulyat-ul-Muttaqīn*, Lucknow, 1240/1825.

———, *Mir'at-ul-'Uqūl Sharh-i-Kāfi-i-Kulaynī*, 4 vols., Iran, 1322/1904.

———, *Miqyās-ul-Masābīh*, Iran, 1311/1894.

———, *Rabi'-us-sabi'*, Iran, 1312/1895.

———, *Risālah-i-Hudūd*, Lucknow, 1262/1846.

———, *Sharh Min La Yahzara-ul-Faqih*, 2 vols., Iran, 1331/1913, 1342/1923.

———, *Tārīkh-i-Jannat*, Lucknow, 1262/1846.

———, *Zād-ul-Mā'ad*, Lucknow, 1261/1845.

Malikzadah, *Nigār Nāmah-i-Munshi*, Lucknow, 1882.

Mir 'Alam, *Hadīqat-ul-'Ālam*, Hyderabad, 1310/1893.

Mir Khwand (Muhammad bin Khwand Shah), *Rauzat-us-Safā*, Bombay, 1271/1854 & 1274/1857, Iran.

Muhammad 'Ali, *Nujūm-us-sama'*, Lucknow, 1303/1886.

Mustaufi, Muhammad Mufid, *Jāmi'-i-Mufīdī*, ed. Iraj Afshar, Tehran, 1340/1921.
Raza 'Ali Khan, *Majma'-ul-Fusahā*, Tehran, 1878.
Razi, 'Aqil Khan, *Wāqi'āt-i-'Ālamgīrī*, ed. Zafar Hasan, Aligarh, 1946.
Safa Zabihullah, *Tārīkh-i-Adabīyāt Dar Irān*, vols. I & II, Tehran, 1338/1920, 1339/1921.
Salih, Kanbuh, Muhammad, *'Amal-i-Sālih*, Calcutta, 1912–39.
Sam Mirza, *Tuhfah-i-Sāmī*, ed. Iqbal Husain, Patna, 1934.
Saqi, Musta'id Khan, *Ma'āsir-i-'Ālamgīrī*, Calcutta, 1871.
Shafaq, Rizazadah, *Tārīkh-i-Adabīyāt-i-Irān*, Tehran, 1934.
Shah Raju, Sayyid Raziuddin, *Risālah-i-Sawāl wa Jawāb*, Hyderabad, 1973.
Shirazi Nizamuddin Ahmad, *Hadīqat-us-Salātīn*, Hyderabad, 1961.
Shustari, Qazi Nurullah, *Ahqāq-ul-Haq*, Iran, 1273/1857.
———, *Majālis-ul-Mu'minīn*, Tehran, 1268.
Taba Taba Sayyid 'Ali, *Burhān-i-Ma'āsir*, ed. Sayyid Hashmi Faridabadi, Hyderabad, 1936.
Tahir Nasrabadi, *Tazkirah-i-Tāhir*, Tehran, 1883.
Tahir Wahid, *Inshā'-i-Tāhir Wahīd*, Lucknow, 1873.
Tusi, Nasiruddin, *Akhlāq-i-Nāsirī*, Calcutta, 1269/1853.
Yazdi, Sharfuddin 'Ali, *Zafar Nāmah*, Calcutta, 1887–8.
Zubairi, Mirza Ibrahim, *Basātīn-u'salātīn*, Hyderabad, n.d.

Arabic

I'jaz Husayn, Sayyid, *Kashf-ul-hujab wal astār*, Hyderabad, 1330/1912.
Razi Al, Fakhr u'ddin Muhammad b. Umar, *Mafātīh ul-Ghayb*, 8 vols., Cairo, 1308/1891.
———, *Muhassal Afkār al Mutaqaddimīn wal Muta'ākhkhirīna-al-Falasifah wal-Mutakallimīn*, Cairo, 1323/1905.
Rida Husain, Muhammad, *Al-Kalām ālā Falāsifat al-Islām*, Lucknow, 1905.
Shahristani Al, Muhammad, *Al-Milal wa l-Nihal* (Book of Religious and Philosophical Sects), ed. W.Cureton, London, 1842.
Shirazi, Mulla Sadra, *Kitāb-ul-Mashā'ir Ma' Hawāshī*, Lucknow, 1327/1909.
Suyuti Al, Jalal u'ddin, *Tārīkh ul Khulafā*, Calcutta, 1857.

English

Abbé Carré, *Travels of Abbé Carré in India and the Near East, 1672 to 1674*, tr. Lady Fawcett, ed. C. Fawcett, London, 1947.
Abu'l Fazl, *Ā'īn-i-Akbarī*, tr. Jarret and Jadunath Sarkar, Calcutta, 1948/1949.
Aftabchi, Jauhar, *Tazkirat-ul Waqi'āt*, tr. Major Charles Stewart, London, 1832.
Agha-Oghlu, Mehmet, *Persian Book Binding of the Fifteenth Century*, Michigan, 1935.
Aiyangar, K., *Sources of Vijaynagar History*, Madras, 1909.
Alam, Muzaffar, *The Languages of Political Islam 1200–1800*, Chicago, 2004.
Albuquerque, Afonso de, *The Commentaries of the Great Afonso de Albuquerque*, London, 1883.

Appadorai, A., *Economic Conditions in South India (1000–1500 A.D.)*, 2 vols., Madras, 1936.

Arjomand, Sa'id, *The Shadow of God and the Hidden Imam: Religion, Political Organization and Societal Change in Shi'ite Iran from the Beginning to 1890*, Chicago, 1984.

Arnold, T.W., *Painting in Islam: A Study of the Place of Pictorial Art in Muslim Culture*, Oxford, 1928.

Athar Ali, M., *The Mughal Nobility under Aurangzeb*, Aligarh, 1966.

Aziz Ahmed, *Studies in Islamic Culture in the Indian Environment*, Oxford, 1964.

Babur, *Babur Nāmah*, tr. Beveridge, A.S., London, 1922.

Bailey, H.W., *Content of Indian and Iranian Studies*, Cambridge, 1938.

Banerjee, G.N., *Hellenism in Ancient India*, London, 1920.

Banerji, S.K., *Humayun Badshah*, vol. I, Oxford, 1938; vol. II, Lucknow, 1941.

Barbosa, Duarte, *The book of Duarte Barbosa: an account of the countries bordering on the Indian Ocean and their inhabitants*, 2 vols., London, 1918–21.

Bashford, Dean, *Handbook of Arms and Armour: European and Oriental*, New York, 1915.

Bausani, Alessandro, *Religion in Iran: From Zoroaster to Baha'ullah*, Bibliotheca Persica Press, 2000.

Bedyabinod, B.B., *Supplementary Catalogue of Coins in the Indian Museum*, vol. I, Calcutta, 1923.

Bendrey, V.C., *Qutb Shahis of Golconda in the Seventeenth Century*, Poona, 1934.

Beni Prasad, *History of Jahangir*, 3rd ed., Allahabad, 1940.

Bernier, F., *Travels in the Mughal Empire*, tr. Constable, London, 1826.

Bilgrami, S.A.A., *Landmarks of the Deccan*, Hyderabad, 1927.

Boer, Tjitze J. de, *History of Philosophy in Islam*, tr. Edward R. Jones, London, 1903.

Boswell, J.A.C., *Manual of the Nellore District*, Madras, 1873.

Browne, E.G., *Literary History of Persia*, 4 vols., Cambridge, 1928.

———, *Abridged Translation of the History of Tabaristan*, London, 1905.

———, *Arabian Medicine*, Cambridge, 1921.

Bowrey, T., *Geographical account of the countries round the Bay of Bengal*, Cambridge, 1905.

Chenchiah, P. and Bhujanga Rao M., *History of Telugu Literature*, Calcutta, Association Press, n.d.

Commissariat, M.S., *History of Gujarat 1573–1758* (2 vols.), Orient Longman, 1957.

Crone, Patricia and Hinds, Martin, *God's Caliph: Religious Authority in the First Centuries of Islam*, Cambridge, 1986.

Barbaro, Giosofat & Contarini, Ambrogio, *Travels to Tana and Persia*, tr. from Italian by William Thomas and Eugene Armand Roy, London, 1873.

Danvers, F.C., *The Portuguese in India*, 2 vols., London, 1894.

Davar, F.C., *Iran and India through the Ages*, Bombay, 1962.

Devare, T.N., *A Short History of Persian Literature*, Poona, 1961.

Dilley, A.U., *Oriental Rugs and Carpets*, London, 1931.

Elgood, C., *Medical History of Persia*, Cambridge, 1951.

Elliot, Walter, *Coins of Southern India*, London, 1886.

Faruki, M.Z., *Aurangzeb and his Times*, Bombay, 1935.

Fawcett, C., *English Factories in India (The Eastern Coast and Bengal) 1670–1684*, vol. II (new series), Oxford, 1936–55.

Fisher, W.B., *Middle East: A Physical, Social and Regional Geography*, London, 1950.

———, *The Cambridge History of Iran*, vol. I, Cambridge, 1968.

Floris, Peter, *His Voyage to the East Indies in the Globe (1611–1615)*, ed. W.H. Moreland, London, 1934.

Foster, W., *Early Travels in India (1583–1619)*, ed. W. Foster, London, 1927.

———, *England's Quest of Eastern Trade*, London, 1933.

———, *English Factories in India* (13 vols.), Oxford, 1906–27.

———, *John Jourdain's Journal of a Voyage to the East Indies 1608–17*, London, 1905.

———, *Letters received by the East India Company from its servants in the East, 1602–1617*, London, 1896–1902.

Fryer, J., *A New Account of East India and Persia, in Eight Letters: Being Nine Years Travels Begun 1672 and Finished 1681*, 3 vols., ed. William Crooke, London, 1909/1912/1915.

Fürer Haimendor, Christoph Von and Others, *Tribal Hyderabad (Four Reports)*, Hyderabad, 1945.

Ghulam Sarwar, *History of Shah Isma'il Safawi*, Aligarh, 1939.

Goonawardena, K.W., *Foundation of Dutch Power in Ceylon, 1638–1658*, Amsterdam, 1958.

Grey, Edward, *Travels of Pietro della Valle to India*, vols. 1, 2, London, 1891.

Haig, Thomas W., *Historic Landmarks of the Deccan*, Allahabad, 1819.

Hamiduddin Khan, *Ahkām-i-'Ālamgīrī*, tr. Jadunath Sarkar, Calcutta, 1926.

Hanway, J., *Historical Account of British Trade over the Caspian Sea*, 4 vols., London, 1753.

Head, B.V., *The Coinage of Lydia and Persia*, London, 1874.

Hitti, P.K., *History of the Arabs*, London, 1973.

Ibn Khurdad Bih, *Kitāb al Masālik wa al-Mamālik*, ed. Goeje de, M.J., Leiden, 1889.

Hodivala, S.H., *Historical Studies in Mughal Numismatics*, Calcutta, 1923.

India, Government of, *Archaeological Report (Southern Circle)*, 1918.

———, *Cuddapah District Gazetteer*, 3 vols., Madras, 1915/1930/1933.

———, *Gazetteer of Rajahmundry District*, Madras.

———, *Godavari District Gazetteer*, Madras, 1907.

———, *Krishna District Gazetteer*, Madras, 1915.

Habib, Irfan, *The Agrarian System of Mughal India (1556–1707)*, Bombay, 1963.

Jahangir, Nuru'ddin, *Tuzuk-i-Jahāngīrī*, 2 vols., tr. Rogers, A.; ed. Beveridge, H., London, 1909–14.

Joshi, P.M., *Studies in the Foreign Relations of India (H.K. Sherwani Felicitation Volume)*, Hyderabad, 1975.

Kendrink, A.F., *Guide to the Collection of Carpets: Victoria & Albert Museum*, London, 1920.

Lewisohn, Leonard and Morgan, David, *The Heritage of Sufism: Late Classical Persianate Sufism (1501–1750)*, vol. III, Oxford, 1999.

Lamm, C.J., *Glass from Iran in the National Museum*, Stockholm, 1935.

Lambton, A.K.S., *Landlord and Peasant in Persia*, London, 1953.

Love, D., *Vestiges of Old Madras*, London, 1913.

Mackenzie, G., *A Manual of the Krishna District*, Madras, 1883.

Malcolm, John, *History of Persia*, 2 vols., London, 1815.

Manucci, Niccolao, *Storia do Mogor*, 4 vols., tr. William Irwine, London, 1907.

Master, Streynsham, *Diaries of Streynsham Master 1675–80*, London, 1911.

Miles, S.B., *The Countries and Tribes of the Persian Gulf*, 2 vols., London, 1919.

Minorsky, V., *Tazkirat-al-Mulūk: A Manual of Safavi administration*, London, 1943.

Modi, J.J., *The Influence of Iran on Other Countries*, Bombay, 1954.

Mookerji, R.K., *History of Indian Shipping*, London, 1912.

Moreland, W.H., *From Akbar to Aurangzeb*, London, 1923.

———, *India at the Death of Akbar*, London, 1920.

———, *Relations of Golconda*, London, 1930.

Morris, H., *A descriptive and historical Account of the Godavery District*, London, 1879.

Muid Khan, M.A., *Arabian Poets of Golconda*, Bombay, 1963.

Musta id Khan, Muhammad Saqi, *Ma'āsir-i-'Ālamgīrī*, tr. and ed. Sir Jadunath Sarkar, Calcutta, 1947.

Mustaufi Hamdullah, *Nuzhat al Qulūb*, ed. Le Strange, Guy, London, 1937.

Newman, Andrew J., *Safavid Iran: Rebirth of an Empire*, London, 2006.

Pelsaert, *Jahangir's India*, tr. Geyl, P. and Moreland, W.H., Cambridge, 1925.

Penrose, B., *Sherleian Odyssey, Being a Record of the Travels and Adventures of three Famous Brothers*, Taunton (England), 1938.

Pope, A.U., *The Spirit of Persian Art*, 6 vols., London, 1933.

Poole, R.S., *Coins of the Shahs of Persia*, London, 1887.

Purchas, Samuel, *His Pilgrims*, Glasgow, 1905.

Qanungo, K., *Dara Shikoh*, Calcutta, 1921.

———, *Sher Shah*, Calcutta, 1921.

Radhey Shyam, *Kingdom of Ahmednagar*, Delhi, 1968.

Raghavan, V., *Sringara Manjari of Akbar Shah*, Hyderabad, 1951.

Raju, P.T., *Telugu Literature*, Bombay, 1944.

Rao, R. Narasimha, *Corporate Life in Medieval Andhra Desa*, Hyderabad, 1967.

Rao, Hanumantha, *Religion in Andhra (A Survey of Religious Development in Andhra from early times up to A.D. 1325)*, Tripurasundari, 1973.

Raychaudhuri, Tapan, *Jan Company in Coromondel*, The Hague, 1962.

Ray, Sukumar, *Humayun in Persia*, R.A.S.B. Monograph Series Vol. VI, Calcutta, 1948.

Riazul Islam, *Indo-Persian Relations, A study of the political and diplomatic Relations between the Mughal Empire and Iran*, Tehran, 1970.

Roe, T., *Embassy of Sir Thomas Roe*, 1615–19, ed. W. Foster, London, 1926.

Rosenthal, Franz, *The Classical Heritage in Islam*, University of California Press, 1975.

Row, B.S., *History of Vijayanagar: The Never to be Forgotten Empire*, Madras, 1905.

Saksena, B.S., *Tārīkh-i-Dilkusha*, tr. and ed. V.G. Khobrekar, Bombay, 1972.

Sansbury, E., *The Court Minutes of the East India Company, in India Office Records Calendared upto 1633 in Calendar of State Papers*, Colonial Series, East Indies, Oxford, 1909.

Sarkar, Jadunath, *History of Aurangzeb*, vols. I–V, Calcutta, 1924–28.

————, *Mughal Administration*, Calcutta, 1920.

————, *Shivaji and his times*, Calcutta, 1948.

Sarkar, Jagdishnarayan, *Life of Mir Jumla*, Calcutta, 1951.

Savory, Roger, *Iran under the Safavids*, Cambridge, 2007.

Saxena, B.P., *History of Shah Jahan of Dihli*, Allahabad, 1958.

Schuman, Frederick, L., *International Politics*, London, 1953.

Shakeb, M.Z.A., *Mughal Archives*, vol. 1, Hyderabad, 1976 (in press).

Sharif, M.M., *A History of Muslim Philosophy*, 2 vols., Germany, 1963–66.

Sharma, S.K., *Mughal Bibliography*, Bombay, Karnatak Publication, n.d.

Sharma, S.R., *Religious Policy of the Mughal Emperors*, Bombay, 1962.

Shastry, N., *Sources of Vijayanagar History*, Madras, 1946.

Sherwani, H.K., *Bahmanis of the Deccan: An Objective Study*, Hyderabad, 1953.

————, *Cultural Trends in Medieval India*, Bombay, 1968.

————, *History of the Qutb Shahi Dynasty*, Delhi, 1974.

Sherwani, H.K. and Joshi, P.M., *History of the Medieval Deccan 1295–1724*, 2 vols., Hyderabad, 1975.

Shukala, M.S., *History of Gem Industry in Ancient and Medieval India (Part I—South India)*, Varanasi, 1972.

Siddiqui, Abdul Majid, *History of Golcunda*, Hyderabad, 1956.

Siddiqui, M.Z., *Studies in Arabic and Persian Medical Literature*, Calcutta, 1959.

Smith, V.A., *Akbar The Great Mogul (1542–1605)*, Oxford, 1919.

Sousa, S., *The Portuguese Asia*, tr. J. Stevens, London, 1935.

Srinivasachari, C.S., *History of Gingee and Its Rulers*, Annamalainagar, 1943.

Sykes, P.M., *History of Afghanistan*, 2 vols., London, 1940.

————, *History of Persia* (2 vols.), London, 1930.

Taftazani, S., *Commentary on the Creed of Islam*, tr. Earl Edgar Elder, New York, 1950.

Tara Chand, *Influence of Islam on Indian Culture*, Allahabad, 1942.

Tavernier, J.B., *Tavernier's Travels in India*, tr. John Phillips Esquire, Calcutta, 1905.

Thevenot and Careri, *Indian Travels of Thevenot and Careri*, ed. Surendranath Sen, Delhi, 1949.

Toynbee, A.J., *Between Oxus and Jumna*, London, 1961.

Tripathi, R.P., *Rise and Fall of the Mughal Empire*, Allahabad, 1956.

Vasumati, E., *Telugu Literature in the Qutb Shahi Period*, Hyderabad, n.d.

Wali, Abdul, *Qutb Shahi Coins in the Andhra Pradesh Government Museum,* Hyderabad, 1961.

Wallis, H., *Persian Ceramic Art belonging to Mr. F. Du Cane Godman,* London, 1890.

Wheeler, J. Talboys, *Early Records of British India: A History of English Settlement in India,* London, 1878.

———, *European Travellers in India,* Calcutta, 1956.

———, *History of the English Settlements in India,* London, 1878.

Wilson, A.T., *A Bibliography of Persia,* Oxford, 1930.

———, *The Persian Gulf,* London, 1928.

Wilson, H.H., *A Glossary of Judicial and Revenue Terms,* London, 1855.

Woods, John E., *The Aqquyunlu: Clan, Confederation, Empire,* University of Utah Press, 1999.

Yule, H. and Burnell, A.C., *Hobson-Jobson: being a glossary of Anglo-Indian Colloquial words and phrases and of kindered terms: etymological, historical, geographical and discursive,* Oxford, 1886.

Yusuf Husayn Khan, *Farmans and Sanads of the Deccan Sultans,* Hyderabad, 1964.

———, *Selected Documents of Aurangzeb's Reign,* Hyderabad, 1958.

———, *Selected Documents of Shah Jahan's Reign,* Hyderabad, 1950.

———, *Selected Waqai of the Deccan (1660–71),* Hyderabad, 1953.

Zuhuri, A. Wahab, *Physician—Authors of Greco-Arab Medicine in India,* Institute of History of Medicine and Medical Research, Delhi, 1968.

Urdu

Ghani, M. Najmul, *Mazāhib al Islām,* Lucknow, 1924.

Ibn Nishati, *Phulban,* ed. Abdul Qadir Sarwari, Hyderabad, 1357/1947.

Malkapuri, Abdul Jabbar, *Mahbūb-al-Watan,* Hyderabad, 1328/1919.

———, *Mahbūb-i-Anjuman,* Hyderabad.

———, *Mahbūb-i-Zaman,* Hyderabad, 1332/1923.

———, *Mahbūb-i-Zilminan,* Hyderabad.

———, *Mahbūb-i-Nav wa Kuhan,* Hyderabad.

Qutb Shah, Muhammad Quli, *Kulliyāt-i-Muhammad Qulī Qutb Shāh,* ed. Zor, Muhiuddin Qadri, Hyderabad, 1940.

Sharma, Sri Ram, *Dakhnī Zubān ka 'Āghāz-wa-Irtiqā,* Hyderabad, 1969.

Shamsullah Qadri, *Imādiyah,* Hyderabad, n.d.

———, *Mu'arrikhīn-i-Hind,* Hyderabad, 1933.

Shibli Numani, *Ilm-al-Kalām,* Azamgarh, 1923.

Siddiqui, A.M., *Muqaddamah-i-Tārīkh-i-Dakkan,* Hyderabad, 1940.

Vajhi, Asadullah, *Sab Ras,* ed. Abdul Haq, Aurangabad, 1932.

———, *Qutb Mushtari,* ed. Abdul Haq, Delhi, 1939.

Yazdani, Ghulam, *Hindustan ke Āsār-i-Qadīmah,* Hyderabad, 1939.

Zor, Mohiu'ddin Qadri, *Hayāt-i-Mir Mu'min,* Hyderabad, 1957.

———, *Farkhundah bunyād,* Hyderabad, Hyderabad, 1952.

Telugu

Avadhi, V., *Andhra Vangmaya Charitra*, Hyderabad, 1964.
Rao, Rallabandi Subba, *Kalingadesha Charitramu*, Rajahmundry, 1932.

Dutch

Terpestra, H., *De Vestiging van de Nederlanders aan de Kust van Koromandel*, Groningen, 1911.
Valentijn, F., *Oud en Nieuw Oost Indien*, Amsterdam, 1724–26.
Van Dijk, L.C.D., *Zes Jaren vit net Leven Van Wemmer Van Berchem*, Amsterdam, 1858.

French

Martin, F., *Memoires de Francois Martin (1665–1696)*, ed. A. Martinean, Paris, 1931.

ARTICLES IN JOURNALS

English

Eaton, Richard M., 'The Court and the Dargah in the Seventeenth Century Deccan', *Indian Economic and Social History Review*, vol. 10, no. 1, 1973, pp. 50–63.
Hossein, Hidayat, 'Shah Tahir of the Deccan', *New Indian Antiquary*, vol. 2, Bombay, 1939.
Joshi, P.M., 'Adil Shahi Administration', *Proceedings of the Indian History Congress*, Lahore, 1940.
———, 'Historical Geography of the Deccan', *History of the Medieval Deccan*, ed. Sherwani & Joshi, vol. I, Hyderabad, 1973.
———, 'Johan Van Twist's Mission to Bijapur 1637', *Journal of Indian History*, vol. XXXIV, 11 August 1956.
———, 'Textile Industry and Trade in the Kingdom of Golkonda', 2, *Indian History Congress*, 1942.
Minorsky, V., 'The Middle East in Western Politics in the 13th, 15th and 16th Centuries', *Journal of the Royal Central Asian Society*, vol. XXVII, October 1940.
———, 'The Qara-Quyunlu and the Qutb Shahs' (Turkmanica, 10), *Bulletin of the School of Oriental and African Studies*, vol. XVII, pt. I, 1955.
Ranjanam, Lakshmi K., 'Language and Literature: Telugu', in *History of the Medieval Deccan*, ed. Sherwani & Joshi, vol. I, Hyderabad, 1973.
Savory, R., 'The principal offices of the Safavid State', *Bulletin of the School of Oriental and African Studies*, vol. XXIV, pt. I.
Shakeb, Ziauddin Ahmed, 'The Black Sheep tribe from Lake Van to Golconda', *Itihas*, vol. III, no. 2, Hyderabad, 1975, pp. 35–80.

Shakeb, Ziauddin Ahmed, 'Man's nature and destiny: What do the *mufassirīn* say?' *Religion and Society*, vol. XX, no. 3, Bangalore, 1973.

Siddiqui, A.M., 'Mir Fazlullah Inju', *Islamic Culture*, Hyderabad, XXII, 1948.

Telugu

Tomati Donappa, 'Muharram Gitikalu Bharati', Madras, 1941.

Urdu

Azhar 'Ali, Sayyid, Qārā Qūyūnlū Turkmān Ru'idād Idārā-i-Ma'rifat-al-Islāmiah', First Session, Lahore, 1933

Index